LADIES-IN-WAITING

Anne Somerset is the author of a number of best sellers including *Elizabeth I* and *Unnatural Murder*. She read history at King's College, London, and for two years worked as a research assistant for various historians including Hugh Thomas, Antonia Fraser and Nigel Fisher. She lives in London.

Also by Anne Somerset

Elizabeth I (Phoenix Press)
Unnatural Murder: Poison at the Court of James I
The Life and Times of William IV

LADIES-IN-WAITING

From the Tudors to the Present Day

Anne Somerset

CASTLE BOOKS

To Grandma

This edition published in 2004 by
CASTLE BOOKS ®
A division of Book Sales, Inc.
114 Northfield Avenue
Edison, NJ 08837

This book is reprinted by arrangement with
Orion Publishing Group Ltd.
Orion House, 5 Upper St. Martin's Lane, London WC2H 9EA

First published in Great Britain
by Weidenfeld & Nicolson in 1984
Paperback edition published in 2002 by Phoenix Press
a division of the Orion Publishing Group Ltd.

A CIP catalogue record for this book
is available from the British Library.

ISBN 0-7858-1830-8

Printed in the United States of America

Contents

LIST OF ILLUSTRATIONS   vii

AUTHOR'S NOTE   ix

INTRODUCTION   1

I   The Court of Henry VIII   12
    'Continuance in the King's Favour'

II The Court of Edward and Mary   47
    'A Flock of Noble Ladies'

III The Court of Elizabeth I   60
    'But One Mistress'

IV The Early Stuart Court   94
    'Notorious Impudent Prostituted Strumpets'

V   The Court of Charles II   131
    'Nothing Almost but Bawdry'

VI The Later Stuart Court   160
    'The Very Ladies Are Split Asunder'

VII The Early Hanoverian Court   199
    'So Uncommon a Seraglio'

VIII The Later Hanoverian Court   228
    'Laborious Watchfulness and Attendance'

IX The Court of Queen Victoria   267
    'Duty and Affection for Me'

X   The Court Today   297

NOTES   311

BIBLIOGRAPHY   322

INDEX   333

Illustrations

BETWEEN PAGES 118 AND 119

1 Anne Boleyn, by an unknown artist (National Portrait Gallery)
2 Jane Seymour, by Holbein (Kunsthistorisches Museum, Vienna)
3 Catherine Howard, drawing by Holbein (By Gracious Permission of Her Majesty the Queen)
4 Catherine Parr, by an unknown artist, *c.* 1545 (National Portrait Gallery)
5 A Procession of Queen Elizabeth I, attributed to Robert Peake the Elder, *c.* 1600 (By Courtesy of Simon Wingfield Digby Esq)
6 Elizabeth I receiving two Dutch emissaries, by an unknown artist (Staatl. Kunstsammlungen, Kassel)
7 Lady Catherine Grey, Countess of Hertford, and her son. English School, sixteenth century (His Grace the Duke of Northumberland. Photograph by kind permission of *Country Life*)
8 Lettice Knollys, attributed to George Gower, *c.* 1585 (The Marquess of Bath)
9 Ann Vasavour, attributed to John de Critz (The Marquess of Bath. Photograph: A.C. Cooper)
10 Mary Fitton, by an unknown artist (Francis FitzRoy Newdegate Esq. Photograph: Royal Academy of Arts)
11 Costume design by Inigo Jones for a dancer in Ben Jonson's *Masque of Blacknesse*, 1605 (Devonshire Collection, Chatsworth. Reproduced by permission of the Chatsworth Settlement Trustees)
12 Costume design by Inigo Jones for Samuel Daniel's *Tethys Festival*, 1610 (Devonshire Collection, Chatsworth. Reproduced by permission of the Chatsworth Settlement Trustees)
13 Arbella Stuart, by Marc Gheeraedts (The Mansell Collection)
14 Frances Howard, Countess of Somerset, attributed to W. Larkin, *c.* 1615 (National Portrait Gallery)
15 The Duke of Buckingham and his family, by an unknown artist, 1628 (By Gracious Permission of Her Majesty the Queen)
16 Queen Henrietta Maria, Lucy Countess of Carlisle and other ladies, detail from *Apollo and Diana* by Gerrit van Honthorst (By Gracious Permission of Her Majesty the Queen)
17 Barbara Villiers, Duchess of Cleveland, after Lely (National Portrait Gallery)

vii

18 Frances Stewart, Duchess of Richmond and Lennox, by Lely, c. 1662 (By Gracious Permission of Her Majesty the Queen)

19 Nell Gwynn, by Simon Verelst, c. 1670 (Private collection. Photograph: National Portrait Gallery)

20 Louise de Keroualle, Duchess of Portsmouth, by Pierre Mignard, 1682 (National Portrait Gallery)

21 Sarah Churchill, Duchess of Marlborough, after Kneller, c. 1700 (National Portrait Gallery)

22 A portrait believed to be of Abigail, Lady Masham, by an unknown artist, c. 1700 (National Portrait Gallery)

23 The Duchess of Somerset, after Lely, c. 1679 (National Portrait Gallery)

BETWEEN PAGES 214 AND 215

24 Queen Anne in the House of Lords, by Peter Tillemans (By Gracious Permission of Her Majesty the Queen)

25 Charlotte Clayton, Lady Sundon, engraved after an unknown original by Edward Harding (BBC Hulton Picture Library)

26 Henrietta Howard, Countess of Suffolk, attributed to Charles Jervas (National Portrait Gallery)

27 Augusta, Princess of Wales and members of her household and family, by Jean-Baptiste Vanloo (By Gracious Permission of Her Majesty the Queen)

28 Fanny Burney, by E.F.Burney (National Portrait Gallery)

29 The Prospect Before Us: Rowlandson cartoon, published 1788 (British Museum)

30 Frances, Countess of Jersey, after D.Gardiner (BBC Hulton Picture Library)

31 Charlotte, Lady Douglas, engraved by Widdlemist after a drawing by A.Buck (BBC Hulton Picture Library)

32 Countess Oldi, engraved by T.Wright after a sketch by A.Wivell, 1821 (BBC Hulton Picture Library)

33 Lady Flora Hastings, engraving dated 1840 (British Museum)

34 Baroness Lehzen, miniature by Koeplee (By Gracious Permission of Her Majesty the Queen)

35 Cartoon by Doyle on the Bedchamber Crisis, 1839 (British Library)

36 Jane, Marchioness of Ely, c. 1880 (By Gracious Permission of Her Majesty the Queen. Photograph: W.&D.Downey)

37 Lady Augusta Bruce, 1859 (By Gracious Permission of Her Majesty the Queen)

38 The Drawing Room of Queen Victoria – A Ceremony of Presentation, engraved by H.Melville after the original by J.Gilbert (The Mansell Collection)

39 Queen Elizabeth II with her maids of honour and Mistress of the Robes after her Coronation in 1953 (Times Newspapers Ltd.)

Author's Note

An attempt to cover more than four centuries of English history, albeit from the somewhat specialized point of view of court ladies, was an ambitious – at times I felt too ambitious – project, requiring research on a daunting array of periods and personalities. In trying to sort out the jumble of unrelated anecdotes and miscellaneous items of information I have singled out a few individuals for special attention, and when doing this I decided not to concentrate exclusively on those ladies who at one time or another held positions in the royal household but also to broaden my scope by including women such as Frances, Countess of Somerset, who was never officially a lady-in-waiting, but whose life was mainly spent at court and whose activities there might be of interest to the reader. Apart from this, I have tried to throw some light on the lifestyle of ladies-in-waiting throughout the ages, but I was hampered in my quest for background information by a comparative scarcity of sources. All too often in the past, memoirists and letter-writers did not think it worthwhile to record details of a court routine which they took for granted, and with which the majority of their friends were anyway familiar. Writers such as Fanny Burney, who consciously set out to chronicle the minutiae of life at court, were in a depressingly small minority, and as there is a corresponding dearth of official records on the subject, I have frequently been reduced to gleaning what knowledge I could from tantalisingly oblique references and casual remarks which intersperse the diaries and letters of other, less analytically-minded ladies-in-waiting, who had no eye on posterity when they committed their thoughts to paper. Nevertheless, I hope I have succeeded in giving the reader some idea of conditions that prevailed in past courts, and of the nature and extent of the duties undertaken by both past and present generations of ladies-in-waiting.

When quoting documents I have in many cases updated spelling and punctuation that would appear unusual to the general reader today. Throughout the book I have also taken the new year to begin on 1 January, despite the fact that for much of the period covered the new year was held to start on 25 March.

I wish to thank Her Majesty the Queen for gracious permission to reproduce material in the Royal Archives at Windsor, and the Buckingham Palace Press Office for their help in compiling the last chapter. I should also like to thank Rosemary, Lady Ravensdale, for permission to quote from the Panshanger Manuscripts, stored in the Hertford County Record Office, and the Earl of Pembroke, for permission to quote from manuscripts at Wilton House. Thanks are also due to Joyse Bevan, Miss Frances Dimond, Mr E.R.Hanbury, Lady Hylton, Miss Jane Langton, Mr James Lees-Milne, Sir Robin Mackworth-Young, the Hon. Jessica Mancroft, Mr Douglas Matthews, Sir Oliver Millar, Alison Penny, Mr Ed Victor and the Duke of Wellington. Transcripts of Crown-copyright records in the Public Record Office appear by permission of H.M.Stationery Office. I should also like to express my gratitude to the staff of the London Library, for their unfailing helpfulness at all times.

In particular I would like to thank Lady Antonia Fraser, who read a part of the book when it was still in its very early stages and gave me much encouragement, and Dame Veronica Wedgwood, who very kindly agreed to read the finished typescript. Alan Palmer also read the typescript and made many helpful suggestions.

Lastly I should like to thank the following for permission to quote from works still in copyright: A.D.Peters and Co. Ltd, for *The Diary of Samuel Pepys*, edited by Robert Latham and William Matthews; Hodder and Stoughton, for Dorothy Laird's *Queen Elizabeth the Queen Mother*; Hamish Hamilton, for Cecil Woodham-Smith's *Queen Victoria, her life and times*; John Murray, for Victor Mallet's *Life with Queen Victoria*; Methuen, London, for Lord Hervey's *Some Materials Towards the Reign of King George II*; the Oxford University Press for *The Diary of Sir David Hamilton*, edited by Philip Roberts; Macmillan and Co., New York, for *The Correspondence of George Prince of Wales*, edited by Arthur Aspinall; the Earl of Airlie, for *Thatched with Gold*; Macmillan, London and Basingstoke, for *The Greville Memoirs*, edited by Lytton Strachey and Roger Fulford.

Introduction

'I do very much agree with you that happiness is seldom found in a court,'[1] John, Duke of Marlborough remarked in 1709 to his wife Sarah, the premier lady of Queen Anne's court. It was a statement that few would have cared to contradict, for over the centuries it had become something of a truism that courts were centres of falsehood, peopled by shallow self-seekers who would stoop to the basest forms of flattery to attain advancement, ruthlessly discarding old friends in the process. That happiness should elude the occupants of such a place was perhaps not surprising; more curious, however, was the fact that those who had had a taste of life at court acknowledged it to be virtually impossible to attain contentment elsewhere.

With the development of the English monarchy, the court had evolved from being the legal, military and administrative kernel of the kingdom into an infinitely more complex establishment. For years, of course, it remained the nation's powerhouse, the place from which government was conducted, and by the sixteenth century all persons desirous of political advancement knew that they could achieve it only through a career at court or by outright rebellion – a risky alternative indeed. But it was also the cultural and social centre of the realm, which drew to it all those with pretensions to refinement, as well as those whose aspirations centred on such objectives as titles for their family or good marriages for their children. To renounce the court entailed the renunciation of all worldly ambitions, and involved besides foregoing the company of all but social inferiors, losing touch with developments in fashion and art and, more often than not, living in seclusion on a remote estate. It was not a decision to be taken lightly.

In time political power ceased to be concentrated exclusively in the court, but the monarchy remained stable and the court continued to exert a compelling attraction. For those who sought ennoblement the Sovereign was still the fount of honour, and association with the royal family anyway brought with it automatic prestige. Besides, long after such ideas had ceased to be realistic, the notion lingered that it was easier to succeed in politics and other fields if one had connections at court; quite simply, the lives of the English aristocracy had revolved around the court for so long that they could not conceive of a world where things were arranged differently. As late as 1838 a former lady-in-waiting of George IV's wife, Queen Caroline, could write:

> Courts are strange, mysterious places; those who pretend most to despise them seek to gain admittance within their precincts; those who obtain an entrance there generally lament their fate, and yet, somehow or other, cannot break their chains . . . Intrigues, jealousies, heart-burnings, lies, dissimulation thrive in [courts] as mushrooms in a hot-bed. Nevertheless, they are necessary evils, and they afford a great school both for the heart and head. It is utterly impossible, so long as the world exists, that similar societies should not exist also; and one may as well declaim against every other defect attendant upon human institutions, and endeavour to extirpate crime from the world as pretend to put down courts and their concomitant evils.[2]

Until the present century the court was one of the few British institutions where women had a role to play, and one moreover that was not purely ornamental. At a time when virtually every profession was an exclusively masculine preserve, the position of lady-in-waiting to the Queen was almost the only occupation that an upper-class Englishwoman could with propriety pursue. At the end of the eighteenth century Miss Mary Berry, an intellectual young friend of the writer Horace Walpole, made precisely this point when Walpole sneered at people who thought royal service a noble career. Severely she told him: 'Much as attendance on princes and places at court are laughed at and abused (by those who can't obtain them) so desirable do I think any sort or shadow of occupation for women that I should think any situation that did not require constant attendance a very agreeable thing.'[3]

But the appeal of royal service did not lie simply in the fact that it enabled women who led an otherwise shallow existence to claim, with some justification, that they were making a useful contribution to society, for there were other, less altruistic, reasons for seeking a career within the royal household. Any lady with a position at court could feel she had a finger on the pulse of power, even if, as in most cases, she could not determine the rate at which it beat. For centuries, influential personal contacts were of paramount importance to those who wished their affairs to prosper and anyone who regularly consorted with the royal family undeniably had the best contacts of all. A word in the ear of a King or Queen could make or mar a career, confound the schemes of enemies or assure the success of a business undertaking, and ladies in royal service were in a position to utter that word. Small wonder, then, that they were courted, flattered and even bribed by those less fortunately placed who wished them to act as intermediaries on their behalf, and nor is it surprising that so many well-born women, whose horizons generally did not extend beyond matters which concerned their own family and household, should ardently desire to be elevated to a position of such consequence.

Furthermore, though the majority of great ladies at court could exert no more than an indirect influence over events, in the case of a few individuals real power was within their grasp. In particular, court ladies enjoyed unique opportunities to establish themselves as royal mistresses, a position which, if cleverly exploited, could prove both lucrative and influential. Though they operated in what was essentially a man's world, at times their sex could be an advantage.

It was not always thus. The courts of the Norman kings of England were very male-orientated assemblies. 'The splendour of the King's court', we are told, 'appeared very much in the confluence of . . . the chief men of the realm'.[4] William the Conqueror's Queen, Matilda, spent only a short time in England and though she was reportedly accompanied by a 'stately cortege of nobles, knights and ladies' when she first crossed the Channel in April 1068, the status of these attendants and the nature of their duties remain obscure. In the household of Matilda of Scotland, Henry I's first wife, there were three ladies bearing the Saxon names Emma, Gunilda and Christina, described as 'three virgins of God, sacred damsels who had belonged to the chamber of Matilda, the good Queen Consort of Henry I', and who entered a convent on Matilda's death, though whether voluntarily or because no other employment could be found for them at court is unknown. The first of the Plantagenet kings, Henry II, was married to Eleanor of Aquitaine, a formidable character and great heiress who spent much of her time presiding over her own court at Poitiers in France, a sophisticated assembly where women were held in some esteem. On the English court, however, she failed to have a civilizing effect and as her husband kept her in prison for much of the latter part of his reign this perhaps was not surprising. Henry's court has been described as 'almost oriental in its complete seclusion of female influences'[5] and

3

there is little evidence to suggest that the courts of either of his sons were very different.

By the mid-thirteenth century, however, women had begun to attain a definable status at court. When Henry III's Queen, Eleanor of Provence, arrived in England in 1236 she was accompanied by 'Lady Willelma', who had looked after her as a child and would stay with her until 1258 when, 'wearied in the service and worn out by old age and sickness' she retired 'for her better quiet to dwell in the Abbey of Lacock'. Evidently royal service could prove something of a strain but at least Willelma was well rewarded for her trouble: in 1251, for example, she had been granted 'the land of Blanche Roigne, sometime of William son of Humphrey', and when she finally retired she was awarded a pension of £48 a year. As befitted one of her age and experience, Willelma was the most highly paid of the Queen's ladies, but her immediate subordinates, the Queen's damsels, were also well provided for. In 1238 Emma Biset, 'sometime damsel of the Queen', was granted £10 a year for life, and her sister Margaret, who evidently took over her place in the household, was in 1242 allocated the yearly sum of £11 2d, and though she died soon afterwards, for three years the same amount was paid to her executors 'to be bestowed on pious uses for her soul'. It seems that the Queen's concern for her servants' welfare extended even to the next world.[6]

As the century progressed, so the number of ladies at court swelled further. A recently published study of the court of Eleanor of Castile, Queen Consort of Edward I, shows that by 1290 the household of a Queen was already an important entity in its own right. There were two categories of ladies-in-waiting, the damsels and ladies of the Queen's Chamber, the former being young relatives of Eleanor, who had brought them to court and selected suitable husbands for them. They appear to have had no specific duties and it has been suggested 'that the Queen merely kept them with her so they might acquire the manners of courtly life', whereas the ladies of the Queen's Chamber had rather heavier responsibilities. One of them in particular, Margerie de Haustede, performed a variety of services for her mistress: the Queen's jewels were generally entrusted to her keeping and she also undertook miscellaneous tasks, such as acting on the Queen's behalf when the latter wished to purchase some ornaments from the Parisian merchant, John Le Romeyn. As a result she became a personage of some importance at court and prior to Christmas 1289 a special chamber was built for her at the Palace of Westminster so that she could celebrate the feast in comfort.[7]

Isabella of France, Queen Consort of Edward II, also maintained a sizeable household, which included four ladies and eight damsels of the Chamber, an increase from the days of Queen Eleanor, for whom four damsels had sufficed. The ladies were all related to great aristocratic families and though the damsels evidently came of less eminent stock, four of them were of sufficient social standing to have servants of their own, the cost of whose upkeep was partly borne by the Queen herself. In short, the household of the Queen had become both grander and more numerous but despite these developments women remained very much in the minority at the English court. An ordinance of Edward II specifically decreed 'that none of the King's meignée [household] of what condition so ever he be . . . keep his wife at court, nor elsewhere as a follower to the court; but only such women to be there which are in chief with the King'.[8] The Queen's ladies-in-waiting were there on sufferance rather than by right.

It was really only in the reign of Edward III that women came to form an integral part of the court. Described as 'the first setter of certainties among his domestical meyne upon a grounded rule', Edward consciously strove to create a magnificent court, a new Camelot that would provide a fitting setting for the King of England and the would-be King of France. He relied on the presence of large numbers of women to add colour and refinement to its gatherings, and in the household of his wife, Philippa of Hainault, there were more than thirty ladies who ranged in rank from his daughter, the Countess of Bedford, to relatively humble individuals, such as Elizabeth Chaundos and Philippa de Lisle, who were described simply as 'demoiselles'. These ladies provided the court with a solid female core but additional women were also summoned to court for the great feasts that were held at regular intervals throughout the year. When, for example, the Order of the Garter was founded in 1248 women were present *en masse* at the inaugural celebrations, for the Queen attended a great feast 'accompanied by three hundred ladies and damsels, all of high birth and richly dressed in similar robes'.[9]

After Queen Philippa's death the court continued to be orientated towards women, too much so, indeed, in the view of some critics. While his wife was still alive King Edward had taken as his mistress Alice Perrers, a damsel of the Queen's chamber who one chronicler claimed to be the daughter of a tiler in Essex, though it is more probable that she came from a landed family in Hertfordshire. There are some indications that Alice bore the King a son soon after the start of their liaison, but it was only after the death of Queen Philippa in

1369 that she really came into her own. As a widower Edward slid rapidly into senility, and he proved easy to manipulate, with the result that Alice's wealth and influence grew apace: in 1371 she was granted the Manor of Wendover, and two years later the King bestowed on her a proportion of the late Queen's jewels, supplementing this with an annuity of £100, which apparently was intended for the upkeep of their son. By November 1375 her wealth was such that she could afford to lend Walter Fitzwater £1,000, secured by a mortgage on the Castle of Egremont, but perhaps more remarkable was her alleged control of the judicial system, for when in 1374 the Abbot of St Albans became involved in a dispute about land ownership with her, he was advised to drop his case on the grounds that 'This Alice de Perrers had such power and eminence . . . that no one dared prosecute a claim against her.' In 1375 her unofficial status as first lady of the realm seemed to be confirmed when a tournament was held in her honour at Smithfield, over which Alice presided as 'Lady of the Sun', driving to the jousts in a magnificent chariot, arrayed in a cloak of gold tissue and a pearl-embroidered gown trimmed in ermine.[10]

Inevitably such ostentation aroused enmity. In 1376 the House of Commons refused to grant fresh supplies of money unless the King redressed their grievances and in particular they demanded the removal of Alice Perrers, claiming that she had annually obtained from the King sums of up to £3,000, and that she had interfered with the course of justice, intimidating judges who were considering cases that concerned her property by coming and sitting beside them on the bench. With Edward's reluctant consent Alice's goods were forfeited and she was obliged to swear on the crucifix that she would never return to the King's presence. That, however, was not the last of her. The following year, another Parliament was summoned, less hostile than the last, and it reversed the sentences against Alice. Her goods restored, she returned to court, her hold over the King as absolute as ever. But her triumph was short-lived: Edward only survived till June 1377 and, according to one report, Alice did not even stay to see him die, preferring to abscond from the Palace with the rings she had stripped from the old King's listless fingers. This time, however, her luck had run out. In December 1377 a new Parliament confirmed the sentence originally passed on her in 1376, and though on appeal it was once again revoked, Alice spent much of the remainder of her life plagued by lawsuits and beset by debts. The first of a long line of ladies-in-waiting who became royal mistresses, Alice's career was nevertheless a remarkable one, and if in the end it went into decline on the whole the prizes had outweighed the pitfalls.

Though the rapacity of Alice Perrers had been checked by the death of Edward III, women were no less prominent at the court of his grandson and successor, Richard II. Under his auspices fashions for both men and women became ever more outrageous, particularly after 1381 when court ladies took to wearing massive horned head-dresses like those which his wife, Anne of Bohemia, had brought with her from abroad, and which attracted much unfavourable comment from the monkish chroniclers of the day. Other unwelcome imports were the horde of Bohemian ladies and gentlemen who arrived in the Queen's train, greatly to the annoyance of the English who resented having to pay for their upkeep at court. Indignation mounted still further when Agnes de Launcreona, 'a tolerably handsome pleasant lady whom the Queen had brought with her from Bohemia', became involved in an affair with the Earl of Oxford, a favourite of the King, who determined to dissolve his marriage and take Agnes for his bride. Unfortunately his first wife was a granddaughter of Edward III, and his decision to cast her off greatly antagonized the English, who considered it an affront to the old King's name. Already unpopular enough because of the favour that had been shown him by the King, Oxford's treatment of his wife was said to be 'one of the principal causes of the hatred England bore him', and particularly enraged his wife's uncles, the Dukes of Gloucester and York.[11] In November 1387 Gloucester was among those who demanded that Oxford be tried for treason and though Richard responded by raising an army to defend his favourite, in December his forces were scattered and Oxford had to flee the country, dying in exile in 1392. By that time Richard had re-established his authority in England but the episode had demonstrated how scandal at court could jeopardize the stability of the entire kingdom.

In 1394 Queen Anne died and two years later Richard took as his bride Isabella of France, who was only seven years of age although, according to Froissart, 'Young as she was, she knew well how to act the Queen'. Certainly her arrival in England did nothing to check the extravagance of the court: in 1397 the King was presented with a parliamentary petition complaining of the high costs of the royal household, which were held to be partly caused by the presence at court of excessive numbers of women, who put the realm to unnecessary expense. Richard rejected the petition as an infringement on his rights but two years later even he became alarmed by the extravagance of Isabella's attendants, particularly when he learnt that her French governess, the Lady of Coucy, lived 'in greater state, all things considered, than does the Queen.'[12] Lady Coucy was accordingly dismissed, but by that time such action was irrelevant, for in the summer of 1399 the King's cousin, Henry of Lancaster, invaded England and in August Richard was deposed, imprisoned, and subsequently murdered.

For a period the court went into eclipse. As a usurper Henry IV could not afford to antagonize his subjects with reckless extravagance, and when in 1406 Parliament asked him to economize on annual household expenditure, he promised that in future he would see that it did not exceed £10,000, less than a third of what his predecessor had spent in a typical year. His son, Henry V, preferred to devote the nation's resources to war with France rather than to the creation of a splendid court, and when he died in 1462 he was succeeded by the infant Henry VI, during whose long minority the court was little more than 'an academy for the young nobility'. Even when Henry attained manhood he 'held no household' to speak of, and anyway his own tastes were simple: when at Christmas one year a certain great lord tried to enliven the festivities at court by arranging for a troupe of half-naked girls to dance before the King, Henry was shocked by such immodesty, 'turned his back upon them and went out to his chamber saying "Fy, Fy, for shame!"'[13] Too unworldly to control the various factions that competed for power within the kingdom, Henry was unable to prevent the nation sliding into civil war and with the consequent disintegration of royal authority the court effectively ceased to exist.

Only with the deposition of Henry and the accession, in 1461, of Edward IV, was the court re-established as the nation's focal point. Both policy and inclination led Edward to maintain a magnificent court: as an unashamed sensualist and inveterate womanizer he naturally made the most of the facilities that the court afforded for the pursuit of pleasure, but he knew too that the image of the monarchy had been tarnished by years of civil war and that a calculated display of ostentation and wealth would do much to restore its prestige. The banquets, balls and jousting contests that were held at court throughout his reign were no mere senseless round of gaiety, but deliberate exercises in propaganda, stage-managed for maximum effect and designed to draw attention to the prosperity and strength of the King.

A natural showman, Edward laid great emphasis on ceremonial and pageantry, and in this he had the wholehearted support of his wife, Elizabeth Woodville, a haughty individual who lost no opportunity to stand on her dignity, despite the fact that she herself was of common extraction. It is indeed possible that prior to her marriage to Edward she had served in the household of her predecessor as Queen Consort, Margaret of Anjou, but if so this circumstance made her no less exacting a mistress now that she stood in her stead. Her coronation in 1465 was a particularly lavish affair: throughout the service she was attended by thirteen duchesses and countesses wearing furcoats of red velvet and ermine, and fourteen baronesses in scarlet and miniver, and though on normal occasions her retinue was more modest, even her most everyday activities were enacted with a degree of pomp that astonished observers. In 1466 a German visitor to the court saw the Queen dine in public and was amazed by the solemnity with which the meal was conducted, describing it in the following terms:

> The Queen sat alone at a table in a costly golden chair. The Queen's mother and the King's sister had to stand below. And if the Queen talked with her mother or the King's sister, they had to kneel before the Queen until she drank water. Not until the first dish was set before her were they allowed to sit down. The ladies and maidens and all who served dishes to the Queen, even if they were powerful Earls, had nevertheless to kneel, as long as she was eating. The feast lasted for three hours . . . And all were silent, not a word was spoken.'[14]

To a foreigner the exaggerated deference accorded the Queen might seem perplexing but the English saw nothing odd in it. With the restoration of stability in the realm they were only too willing to demonstrate their allegiance to a monarchy that formed a solitary bulwark against chaos, and besides, humility towards their superiors had been instilled in them since youth. It was the current practice of noble parents to lodge their children with neighbouring aristocratic families, in whose households they were frequently called upon to perform the most menial tasks, and because of this early training they found it quite natural as adults to wait on the King and Queen in the guise of domestic servants.

By this time the structure of the Queen's household had become more elaborate. Effectively there were four grades of ladies-in-waiting, whose salaries ranged from £40 to 56s 8d a year, and though as yet they were not distinguished from one another by formal titles, the divisions within the household anticipated the arrangements of early Tudor times, when the various ranks of attendants were classified as: great ladies, ladies of the Privy Chamber, maids of honour and chamberers.[15] In Queen Elizabeth I's day the hierarchy became still more stratified, for by then the great ladies were officially designated ladies of the Bedchamber, and the household even temporarily acquired a fifth tier in the shape of the ladies of the Presence Chamber, who were the immediate subordinates of the ladies of the Privy Chamber. These curious names derived from developments that had occurred in the layout of the royal palaces themselves: in medieval times the monarch had had only one room set aside for private use, known as the Chamber, but in time this had been sub-divided until it comprised an entire suite, consisting of an outer, or Presence, Chamber where the monarch gave audiences, a Privy Chamber where the monarch generally sat during the day, and the Bedchamber itself. Each successive chamber was more difficult – and hence more desirable – for the average courtier to penetrate, and the innermost sanctum of all, the royal Bedchamber, was denied to all but a privileged few. Far from giving an accurate indication of the exact nature of their duties, the titles of the Queen's principal ladies-in-waiting simply reflected the ascending order of importance of the rooms from which they took their names.

In time the pattern shifted once again. By the end of the seventeenth century the ladies of the Presence and Privy Chambers no longer existed, superseded by the chamberers, who had originally been little more than chambermaids, but whose increasing importance now led them to be styled women of the Bedchamber. On the whole however, the terminology remained remarkably stable, and though over the centuries the duties of ladies-in-waiting have changed beyond recognition, their quaint titles still survive; to this day the Queen employs in her household both ladies and women of the Bedchamber.

The two years following the death, in 1483, of Edward IV, saw the undoing of his life's work, the deposition of his son, Edward V, and the overthrow of his brother, Richard III, by a rival contender for the throne. In many respects however, the new King, Henry VII, was the spiritual heir of Edward IV, and certainly he attached equal importance to the task of establishing his court as the undisputed cynosure of the realm. Though naturally prudent with money, he accepted that his court must serve as the physical embodiment of the monarch's power and prestige and as such was not a department in which stringent economies could be made. Banquets were regularly held on all the great feast days, and occasions such as the christenings and weddings of his children were always celebrated with truly regal splendour. As before, ceremonial was still all-pervasive, so much so, indeed, that it was impossible to see the King without being constantly reminded of his exalted status.

The same elaborate formality surrounded the person of his Queen, Elizabeth of York, a daughter of Edward IV and Elizabeth Woodville. At her coronation banquet, for example, two of the ladies of her household 'went under the table where they sat on either side the Queen's feet all the dinner time . . . [and] the Countess of Oxenford and the Countess of Rivers kneeled on either side the Queen, and at certain times held a kerchief before her Grace'. That particular feast was of course a very special occasion but even so mundane a chore as the making of the Queen's bed was transformed into a stately ritual by household regulations that specified that the operation must be carried out by the Queen's ladies and gentlewomen who were to observe a precise routine: first pulling the bed-curtains, then stripping the mattress and giving it a good shaking, and finally separately replacing the covers, taking great care to ensure that none were askew and that no wrinkles remained. Pomp and circumstance even surrounded the Queen in childbed, for when her time came she was ceremoniously escorted to the door of her Bedchamber. 'Then all the ladies and gentlewomen go in with her, and after that no man to come into the chamber where she shall be delivered, save women; and they to be all manner of officers as butlers, sewers [i.e. servers], carvers, cupbearers; and all manner of officers shall bring to them all manner of things, and the women officers for to receive it in the chamber.'[16] These elaborate arrangements could not prevent the Queen from dying in childbed in 1503, but at least Henry could console himself that she had done so in style.

In an age so highly susceptible to outward show, appearances were all-important and Henry was careful not to neglect this aspect of kingship. Nevertheless, he was not a man to enter into the pleasures of the court for their own sake, and the scale and splendour of his household arrangements had little to do with his personal inclination. In the case of his son it was otherwise: Henry VII kept great state simply because it behoved a king to do so; Henry VIII was glad of the excuse.

I

The Court of Henry VIII

'Continuance in the King's Favour'

On 23 April 1509 Henry VIII was proclaimed King of England amid nationwide rejoicing. His father had bequeathed him a realm united, secure and prosperous; these advantages were supplemented by the personal endowments of a magnificent physique, a kingly manner and a dynamic personality. This royal combination of dynastic power and individual magnetism assured the position of the new monarch's court as the undoubted focal point of the kingdom. Only the lack of a queen rendered the court incomplete, and Henry's fulfilment of his father's deathbed wish in taking as his wife Catherine of Aragon, the widowed Spanish bride of his deceased elder brother, swiftly remedied this deficiency. At twenty-three, Catherine was five years older than the King, and in the seven years following her bereavement had been neglected and humiliated by English and Spaniards alike, and harrowed by the uncertainty both of her status and her prospects of remarriage to her brother-in-law. Most observers agreed, however, that the experiences of her widowhood had not impaired her looks, and with the acquisition of a loving husband it seemed that Catherine's problems had been resolved for ever. Apparently secure, she swiftly settled to her role of presiding over her husband's court and organizing her own household, distinct from that of the King.

The Queen's principal ladies-in-waiting were drawn from the highest ranks of the English aristocracy, the majority being not only well-married but of ancient lineage themselves. Thus three descendants of Edward IV – the widowed Margaret Pole, and the Duke of Buckingham's sisters Elizabeth and Anne Stafford – headed a list which included the Countess of Oxford (daughter of Sir Richard Scrope and wife of the Lord Chamberlain), the Countess of Surrey (married to the Howard Lord Treasurer), and the Countess of Derby (originally a Hastings). Great ladies like these were in attendance on the Queen whenever there was a special occasion at court, such as a banquet, christening or a reception for a foreign ambassador, while their colleagues, the ladies of the Privy Chamber, kept the Queen company at other times, sitting with her in her Chamber and attending to her everyday requirements. Though not as grand as the great ladies, every one of them derived from eminent families such as the Howards, Bourchiers, Greys or Talbots and, with the exception of Lady Boleyn, wife of the comparatively humble Sir Thomas, they had all married into the baronage.[1] The Queen also employed a number of unmarried ladies-in-waiting, known as the maids of honour, and these too were well-born, being for the most part the daughters of noblemen who entered royal service in their teens. The court was meant to serve them both as finishing-school and marriage-market for it was hoped that they would acquire in the Queen's household polished manners of a sort that would attract eligible suitors; in consequence aristocratic parents who were anxious that their daughters should have a good start in life went to extraordinary lengths to secure them a position about the Queen.

Despite their high rank, the duties imposed on these early Tudor ladies-in-waiting were at times of a very menial nature. Thus, later in the reign, the Marchioness of Exeter, married to one of England's foremost peers, waited on Queen Jane Seymour at table, handing her the basin of water for her pre-prandial wash, while Anne Boleyn was attended at her coronation banquet by the Countesses of Oxford and Worcester who intermittently 'did hold a fine cloth before the Queen's face when she list to spit or do otherwise at her pleasure'.[2] Ostensibly demeaning though such tasks were, it was accounted a real honour to be called upon to perform them, and the prestige of those involved was automatically enhanced, for they were seen not as humble servitors but as privileged persons whose favour with the royal family was apparent at a glance.

Nor were the rewards of royal service confined to such abstract satisfactions for those with positions in the household were guaranteed access to the monarchical ear, of unique importance at a time when royal support was often vital for the successful outcome of legal suits, business schemes or petitions. Anne Basset, a maid of honour to Anne of Cleves, was constantly pestered by her mother, Lady Lisle, to intercede with the King in the interests of her family and friends, errands which the diffident Anne found onerous in the extreme. On one occasion she informed her mother bluntly that she lacked the courage to importune the King 'for my Lord's matter', and another time pleaded that her temporary absence from court prevented her from approaching Henry about the pardon of one John Harryse, promising, however, 'If I can get anyone to speak to the King for his pardon I will be sure to do so.' Before engineering her daughter's appointment, Lady Lisle had had to rely on much more indirect methods of gaining royal favour; on one occasion in 1536 she had only narrowly avoided disaster, for, hoping to ingratiate herself with Anne Boleyn by giving her a pet monkey as a present, she fortunately discovered just in time that Anne had a horror of the creatures.[3] Having a daughter placed at court was infinitely preferable to such speculative procedures.

On a more mundane level, employment at court did much to minimize the expenses of day-to-day living. Those ladies lacking husbands with apartments at court were given free accommodation and board, while elaborate arrangements were laid down for the housing and feeding of the maids of honour. Permitted one servant and one spaniel each, every maid was entitled to a hearty daily breakfast of a chine of beef, two loaves and a gallon of ale, with similarly generous provision for the remaining meals of the day. Furthermore, the monetary value of the allowances of firewood and candles allotted to the maids was reckoned to be worth more than £24 per year, and in addition to such prerequisites the maids were paid annual salaries which rose from £5 to £10 during the reign. On this they were expected to furnish themselves with an adequate wardrobe, which was not always an easy task as requirements relating to court dress could be alarmingly exacting, but fortunately their stipends were occasionally supplemented with gifts from the Queen. In 1511 and 1512 Catherine of Aragon gave her chamberers (untitled women who assisted the ladies of the Privy Chamber in their duties) Mabel Clifford and Margaret Pennington gowns of crimson velvet and russet satin respectively. On a rather grander level, Queen Jane Seymour gave jewelled girdles to her ladies of the Privy Chamber.[4]

In all, the advantages of employment in the Queen's service were considered such that some ladies undertook it virtually as a permanent career, the only one open to women of good birth apart from the roles of housekeeper or mother. There were professional ladies-in-waiting who transferred their services to each of Henry's six Queens with the flexibility of a modern civil servant. Anne Parr started her career as a maid of honour to Catherine of Aragon and progressed to being chief lady of the Privy Chamber under Henry's sixth Queen, her sister Catherine Parr, while the appointment of the matronly Mrs Stonor as official chaperone to all the unmarried girls in royal service (or 'Mother of the Maids', as she was officially styled) also spanned the whole reign.[5]

In addition to the English attendants who formed the majority of Catherine of Aragon's household there was a contingent of Spanish ladies who remained in her service on her marriage, but the Queen was careful not to permit the development of an Iberian enclave within her husband's court. Despite the entreaties of the Spanish ambassador, Caroz, she refused to take back into her employ 'so perilous a woman' as Francesca de Caceres, one of her former maids of honour who had deserted her in her days of widowhood to elope with a Genoese banker based in London. Catherine knew that Caroz's enthusiasm for Francesca's reinstatement derived from his wish to have a spy within the court to prime him with current gossip for his dispatches; in her view Francesca's unreliability, disloyalty and indiscretion all disqualified her for a post in her household. Those Spanish ladies who remained in the Queen's service, such as Inez de Venegas and Maria de Salinas, were notable not only for their loyalty during the bleak days before her remarriage but also for their willingness to adapt to an English way of life, a fact that Caroz indignantly noted. 'The few Spaniards who are still in her household prefer to be friends of the English and neglect their duties to the King of Spain' the ambassador informed his master with patriotic choler, and his opinion of their apostasy was doubtless confirmed when both Inez and Maria married into the English nobility.[6]

Unquestionably this policy of integration was wise, for under Catherine there was little of the jealousy between English and foreign attendants that was to characterize the households of many subsequent queens from abroad. Nevertheless, the allegiance of her Spanish ladies was reserved for herself, rather than for their adoptive country. Many years later, when the wronged and discarded Catherine lay dying at Kimbolton, Maria de Salinas would ride through the night to be with her mistress on her deathbed, in superb disregard of the fact that such a visit was technically illegal, as she had not obtained beforehand the permission of the appropriate authorities.

A seemingly interminable round of pageants, feasts and tournaments formed the principal occupations of the court at the beginning of Henry's reign, and soon after her marriage Catherine wrote somewhat breathlessly to her father, 'Our time is spent in continual festival'. The crowded court agenda included woodland picnics and rural expeditions, and regular tournaments were held in honour of the ladies, the King himself competing gallantly in the lists. The evenings were enlivened by stately displays of dancing and mime on a scale unknown since the 1501 celebrations for Catherine's marriage to Henry's elder brother, for the court masque, which had only recently been introduced from Italy, now became a fashionable form of entertainment. It was generally performed by courtiers and ladies in disguise, who first enacted a series of well-rehearsed dance steps and then invited various members of the audience to join them for a more impromptu session of dancing. As yet the masque was only at a very primitive stage of its development but the cost of the necessary costumes and scenery nevertheless constituted a sizeable item in the court accounts and to contemporaries the productions seemed the height of sophistication. The New Year revels staged at Greenwich in 1512 were considered particularly impressive: a mock castle, containing six ladies of the court, was erected in the hall and was then besieged by the King and five courtiers, whereupon the ladies, 'seeing them so lusty and courageous, were content to solace with them, and upon further communication, to yield the castle, and so they came down and danced a long space'.[7]

Spectacles of this sort became if anything more extravagant with the rise to power of Thomas Wolsey, whose palaces at York Place and Hampton Court provided the setting for such events as the sumptuous banquet in honour of the French ambassadors in the autumn of 1518, at which the King and his sister Mary joined some of the most beautiful ladies of the court in an elaborate dance. All the participants wore costumes of green satin overlaid with gold and the ladies had head-dresses 'made of braids of damask gold, with long hairs of white gold', much to the admiration of the ambassadors who 'heartily thanked the King that it pleased him to visit them with such disport.'[9] Not all entertainments at court could be on such a lavish scale as this, but on more informal occasions the King indulged his love of dressing up by visiting the apartments of the Queen disguised as Robin Hood, or some other character from folklore, and Catherine and her ladies always dutifully entered into the fun and reacted to these intrusions with a suitable combination of amazement and delight.

As Catherine grew older her enthusiasm for these ponderous frivolities waned. The age-gap between her and her husband, which had not seemed important at the time of their marriage, subsequently grew more noticeable, for Catherine did not mature well. Regular pregnancies, of which all but one ended either in miscarriage or the early death of the child, sapped her spirits and impaired her looks, and as the reign progressed she and the more sedate of her ladies tended to retire early from court festivities, leaving Henry to roister with his friends. When not preoccupied with the education of her only surviving child, the Princess Mary, who was born in 1516, Catherine spent much of her time closeted in her apartments with her ladies, while her piety, always strong, now tended to absorb her to the point of excess.

Henry was not similarly engrossed by the call of his devotions. He was not, however, an insatiable lecher; indeed, for rather more than fifteen years of marriage, Henry, compared with fellow monarchs such as Francis I, was a model of husbandly temperance. He did have intermittent affairs but he ensured that his early mistresses never achieved a position which seriously rivalled that of the Queen, and Catherine in her turn generally responded to her husband's infidelities with the philosophic resignation expected of royal spouses. Only occasionally was her equanimity ruffled, as in 1510, when an incident involving the two Stafford sisters in her household brought her into conflict with the King.

The younger of the pair, Anne, had recently married Sir George Hastings, but court gossip nevertheless suggested that the King entertained romantic ambitions in her direction. This worried the elder sister, Lady Fitzwater, a staid and respectable dame much beloved of the Queen, and she asked her brother, the Duke of Buckingham, to speak sternly to Lady Hastings on the subject. Unfortunately, while the Duke was delivering a fraternal lecture to Lady Hastings in her apartments, he was interrupted by the arrival of Sir William Compton, a favourite of the King who was evidently contemplating an assignation of his own with the lady. As a result Lady Hastings's husband decided to remove her altogether from the sphere of temptation and incarcerated her in a convent some sixty miles from London. Henry was furious at losing Lady Hastings in this way and retaliated by dismissing Lady Fitzwater from his wife's service, muttering angrily that he wished he could do the same to all those women 'such as go about the palace insidiously spying out every unwatched movement in order to tell the Queen'.[9] The incident resulted in a perceptible coolness between the King and Queen, but, on this occasion the trouble soon blew over and both Lady Fitzwater and

Lady Hastings were permitted to return to court, where the latter cheerfully resumed her affair with Compton, an adulterous relationship for which he was subsequently rebuked by Wolsey's ecclesiastical court.

Of more consequence was the King's affair with Elizabeth Blount, whose relation Lord Mountjoy had secured her a position as maid of honour to the Queen while she was little more than a child. By 1514 she was featuring prominently in court dances and entertainments and though it remains unclear exactly when the King became attracted to her, by the autumn of 1518 it was noted that he was 'in the chains of love with her' and that his interest was returned. Soon afterwards her condition obliged her to leave the court and in the late spring of 1519 she gave birth to a 'goodlie manne childe'.[10] Delighted by this testament to his virility, the King proudly acknowledged the child as his, but Elizabeth herself was discarded, and she did not return to court until her position had been made acceptable by her marriage, in 1522, to Gilbert Tailboys. Soon after that she was given belated recognition for her services, for the young couple were granted the royal manor of Rokeby, and this gift was supplemented the following year by a further series of endowments in Yorkshire. Thenceforth, however, Elizabeth faded into respectable obscurity, devoting herself to the upbringing of her six legitimate offspring and receiving nothing more from the King than an occasional New Year's gift.

Elizabeth's child by the King, Henry Fitzroy, was brought up at court and accorded every mark of royal favour, being created Duke of Richmond and Somerset in 1525 and allotted so splendid a household that Queen Catherine was moved to protest at the implicit insult to Princess Mary. Her resistance only had the effect of annoying the King, and he reacted by dismissing three of his wife's Spanish ladies-in-waiting whom he suspected of encouraging her in her temerity so that, in the sardonic words of the Venetian ambassador, 'The Queen was obliged to submit and have patience.'[11] Fitzroy continued to be cossetted by the King and Catherine had to content herself with the reflection that though her child was only a daughter, she was at least legitimate.

The King's next mistress, Mary Boleyn, was to fare even less well than had her predecessor. Believed to have been born in 1503, Mary was probably the eldest of the three children of Sir Thomas Boleyn, the grandson of a London merchant who had risen to become Lord Mayor and to marry into the Hastings family. Thomas's own marriage to Elizabeth Howard, a daughter of the Earl of Surrey, had been a further step up the social scale, and he had since represented the King on several diplomatic missions abroad. This enabled him to secure for his eldest daughter a place first at the Flemish court of Margaret of Austria and then in the household of Queen Claude of France, at which establishment she was later joined by her sister Anne. There Mary seems to have distinguished herself primarily by a reputation for looseness, for an Italian observer later reminisced that the French King had regarded her as 'una grandissima ribald et infame sopre tutte',[12] and her morals were indeed such that soon after her return to England and her marriage, in 1521, to William Carey, she became the mistress of Henry VIII.

She was to profit very little from the attachment. Her cuckolded husband remained a comparatively lowly gentleman of the Privy Chamber, not even being knighted in return for his complaisance, and Mary herself was swiftly abandoned by the King. At William Carey's death in 1528 Mary was left virtually destitute, and only the fact that the King was by then enamoured of her sister Anne prevented him from being completely indifferent to her fate. Clearly at the English court the position of *maîtresse en titre* to the King quite lacked the lustre with which that role was invested in France, with the ladies in question merely losing their reputation and gaining very little in return. It was a fact that did not escape Anne Boleyn, and when she in turn succeeded in captivating the King she determined to hold out for rather more.

Anne had returned from the French court in 1522, having absorbed so much of the elegance and refinement that was its trademark that a patriotic observer there paid her the ultimate compliment of remarking that he 'would never have taken her for an Englishwoman, but for a Frenchwoman born'.[13] On her return her father secured her a position in the Queen's household and she swiftly established herself as one of the leading luminaries of the court, being one of the eight ladies who performed in the masque that Cardinal Wolsey held for the King in March 1522. She also engaged in a flirtation (at the very least) with a married man, the poet Sir Thomas Wyatt, before attracting the attention of Sir Henry Percy, the heir of the Earl of Northumberland, who sought her hand in marriage. To Anne's distress, however, Cardinal Wolsey intervened and the engagement was abruptly terminated, possibly because the Cardinal was already aware that the King wanted Anne for himself. For, by the middle of

1526, Henry had become completely infatuated with Mistress Boleyn and could think of no one else: a passion whose repercussions would be felt through the centuries and which was only fuelled by Anne's refusal to become his mistress.

The appeal of the woman who thus ensnared the King seems to have depended less on outright beauty (for many observers considered her face, figure and complexion to be only mediocre, though all agreed she had 'very fine black eyes') than on a natural grace and femininity, qualities which enabled her to turn even her minor deformities to advantage. The ladies of the court soon took to copying the hanging sleeves affected by her to conceal the incipient sixth finger on her left hand and the embroidered chokers which hid the large protruding mole on her neck. Furthermore, although no intellectual, Anne had ample cunning and knew how to play the royal suitor who, like some vast salmon, was now hooked upon her line. At all events, her powers of attraction and management were such that by the spring of 1527 conscientious theological scruples had sufficed to convince Henry that his marriage to Catherine was invalid and that the Pope must be induced to sanction its annulment to pave the way for a union with Anne.

Although by no means averse to the displacement of Catherine, who had failed to provide the kingdom with a male heir, Wolsey would doubtless have preferred her to have beeen supplanted by another foreign princess who would have brought diplomatic advantages in her wake, rather than by an obscure lady of the court who disliked him. Nevertheless he floundered into action. Prevented from quietly settling the matter in his own ecclesiastical court by Catherine's resolute opposition to divorce, Wolsey sought to persuade the Pope to pronounce in Henry's favour, but his diplomatic efforts in that direction proved unproductive, as indeed did efforts to pressure Catherine into entering a nunnery. When the case finally opened before Cardinal Campeggio's legatine court at Blackfriars in May 1529 it was referred back to Rome without a verdict having been reached. Egged on by Anne, who hated the Cardinal for his earlier interference in her love life, Henry abandoned Wolsey to his enemies, but the men who replaced the Cardinal proved no more adept at breaking the deadlock that confronted the King in his matrimonial projects.

All this time Catherine continued to preside at court, while Anne remained nominally in her service, an arrangement that not unnaturally led to occasional friction. Anne was therefore delighted when on his disgrace Wolsey gave the King his London house, York Place, for it contained no apartments suitable for the Queen, and when Henry was in residence there Catherine had perforce to stay at another of the royal palaces. But Anne could not rid herself of Catherine for long. Mistress Boleyn might preen herself as guest of honour at a magnificent banquet that Henry gave in early December 1530 but by the end of the month the Queen was back at court officiating over that year's Christmas revels. By January 1531 Anne's exasperation was such that she was overheard wishing all Spaniards to the bottom of the sea, a sentiment that earned her a stinging rebuke from the lady to whom she voiced it.

It was not until 11 July 1531 that Henry could be brought to forsake his wife permanently, creeping out of Windsor at dawn without her knowledge, and then shunting her from one royal residence to another, accompanied by an ever-dwindling train of servants. But desertion did not amount to divorce: technically the King remained firmly wedded to Catherine. A possible solution to Henry's marital entanglements would only emerge with the rise in 1532 of the brilliant Thomas Cromwell, who offered to rid Henry of his wife by the simple expedient of rendering him independent of the papacy. For a time Henry hesitated to take so radical a step, but by the beginning of 1533 Anne was pregnant and action could not be further delayed. On 25 January she and the King were secretly married, and four months later their union was made watertight when, on 23 May 1533, Archbishop Cranmer formally pronounced Henry's marriage to Catherine null and void. He did so not with the authority of the See of Rome, but by virtue of the acts pioneered through Parliament by Cromwell, creating Henry Supreme Head of the Church in England, subject to no power, temporal or spiritual, on earth, and therefore independent of papal jurisdiction.

A religious and political revolution which thus victimized the Queen could not be achieved without demur, and feelings were to run especially high amongst a large section of the ladies of the court. 'If the matter were decided by women the King would lose the battle', the French ambassador commented at an early stage of the divorce suit,[14] and a majority remained unremittingly hostile to the proceedings. While hardly constituting so formidable a challenge to royal policy as the alienation of eminent men like More or Fisher, feminine disapproval of the divorce created considerable tension at court and involved women in those internal faction struggles that did much to undermine the stability of domestic politics during the remainder of the reign. They were enmeshed in the controversy not only by feelings of outraged sisterhood for the injured Queen Catherine but also by religious sentiment, for unlike politics and foreign policy, religion was not a sphere in which women were prepared passively to acquiesce in the arrangements of their menfolk. As such 'The King's Great Matter' was not an issue which they could view with the ladylike detachment expected of them, and though the risks involved in opposing royal policy inevitably meant that only a courageous minority were prepared overtly to demonstrate their sympathy for Catherine, the loyalty of most court ladies to their new mistress was perfunctory indeed. When Anne too forfeited the love of the King she would find she was very much alone.

There were of course chinks in this wall of devotion to Catherine. Even in 1527, when the question of divorce was first mooted, Wolsey had sought to persuade some of the ladies in the Queen's entourage to spy upon their mistress, hoping that he would thus uncover Catherine's plans for resisting the annulment. At least one lady left the court rather than submit to such pressure but others were not as scrupulous and, in her eagerness to profit from the King's proposed marriage to one of her clan, Agnes Howard, Dowager Duchess of Norfolk, was particularly notable for her callous desertion of the Queen. Disregarding any claims upon her loyalty that arose from her long years in Catherine's service, the Duchess cheerfully gave evidence to the Blackfriars court which indicated that Catherine's first marriage to Henry's brother Arthur had been consummated, an allegation that the Queen always steadfastly denied.[15] Thenceforth she was regularly an honoured guest at court banquets and at Anne's coronation in June 1533 she and Anne's mother, Lady Wiltshire, took precedence over all other ladies of the realm. Nevertheless, such wholehearted support for Anne from members of her own sex was rare. Other women of the court would be prepared to go to considerable lengths to demonstrate their affection for Queen Catherine and their contempt for her successor.

Even the Howards were not unanimously in favour of Anne's ambitions to displace Catherine, and Elizabeth, Duchess of Norfolk, the wife of Anne's uncle, the third Duke, was in particular to emerge as a champion of wronged womanhood. Imperious and refractory, the Duchess prided herself on her Stafford blood, and found the prospect of according precedence and respect to a chit of a niece whose great-grandfather had engaged in commerce singularly unpalatable. Furthermore, as the subsequent upheavals in her private life would demonstrate, the Duchess entertained the strongest views on matrimonial fidelity and considered that it should be impossible for a husband to discard his wife in favour of a youthful mistress.

Throughout much of 1530 the Duchess kept up Catherine's morale by supplying her with cheering scraps of confidential information that she had gleaned from her husband's conversation. Later that year Anne Boleyn tried to isolate Catherine by forbidding courtiers to visit her apartments, but the Duchess still contrived to maintain a lifeline with the Queen for in November 1530 she sent Catherine a gift of poultry with an orange containing a letter from the English ambassador in Rome secreted within it. 'This seems to open a way for the Queen to communicate more freely with her friends', the Spanish ambassador commented with satisfaction,[16] and three months later the same channel was employed when the Duchess conveyed to Catherine the encouraging news of the stalemate that prevailed in the negotiations for divorce.

In the meantime the Duchess was also outspokenly condemnatory of Anne's every action. When the latter commissioned a magnificent, if specious, pedigree which traced her ancestry back to Norman times, the Duchess had no hesitation in indicating her doubts about its authenticity, plain speaking of a sort that was hardly welcome to her imperious niece. By October 1531 Anne's fury at her aunt's sarcasms was already leading to speculation that the Duchess could not remain at court much longer and the following May Anne finally secured her expulsion. 'The Duchess of Norfolk has been dismissed from court', the Spanish ambassador informed his master, 'owing to her speaking too freely, and having declared in favour of the Queen much more openly than these people like her to do'. Temporary exile from the court nevertheless left the Duchess quite unchastened, and at Anne Boleyn's coronation in June 1533 she was conspicuous for her absence, a calculated snub which a hostile observer smugly attributed to 'the love she bore the previous Queen'.[17]

Only the increasing complication of her own marital affairs would prevent the Duchess from interfering in those of the King. For some years the Duke of Norfolk had been conducting a passionate affair with Elizabeth Holland, a young lady for whom he had procured a place in the entourage of Anne Boleyn, and by the spring of 1533 the Duchess considered that the situation had become intolerable. Asserting indignantly that Norfolk was 'so far in love with that quean that he neither regards God nor his honour,' she left court of her own accord and installed herself in her-husband's manor at Redbourne.[18]

The Duke retaliated by confiscating her jewels and awarding her only the most meagre of allowances, and as a result the Duchess spent her time at her country retreat penning increasingly wild and embittered letters to Cromwell demanding redress of her grievances, a preoccupation with her own misfortunes which prevented her from concerning herself with Catherine's welfare.

Despite the neutralization of the Duchess of Norfolk, Catherine and her daughter were left far from bereft of allies. Mary's governess was the venerable and pious Countess of Salisbury, a niece of Edward IV's who had been a friend of Catherine since her arrival in England. Since the annulment of her parents' marriage Mary was technically illegitimate, but the Countess refused to countenance any diminution in the status of her charge, and when ordered to render up to the authorities the Princess's jewels and plate she would not do so until she had received the express command of the King. Unfortunately these obstructionist tactics led Cromwell to suspect that the Princess' sustained hostility to her stepmother was encouraged by her servants, and accordingly her household was dispersed in December 1533. Anne Boleyn's aunt, Lady Shelton, replaced the Countess of Salisbury as governess.

At court meanwhile, Gertrude, Marchioness of Exeter, was employing her talents on behalf of Catherine. A daughter of Lord Mountjoy, she had early in the reign married Henry Courtenay, the grandson of Edward IV, whom Henry had created Marquis of Exeter in 1525. In September 1533 the couple apparently remained in high favour at court, for the Marchioness was honoured with the appointment of godmother to Anne Boleyn's newly-born daughter, the Princess Elizabeth. Nevertheless, as a devout papist and a long-established friend of Queen Catherine, the sympathies of the Marchioness lay elsewhere and in the same month she entered into cautious communication with Eustace Chapuys, the Spanish ambassador whose instructions were to work for the reinstatement at court of Catherine and Mary. It was from her that Chapuys learnt of the impending plans to reorganize the households of both Catherine and Mary.[19]

Disaffection was almost impossible to conceal at a court riddled with Thomas Cromwell's spies and though he remained ignorant of the Marchioness's dealings with Chapuys, the King's chief minister did not fail to perceive that her loyalty to the regime fell short of the total commitment that he expected. He determined that dissent from the Marchioness and other influential personages in the court should not go unheeded, believing that information that had emerged during the interrogation of the associates of Elizabeth Barton (a half-demented visionary known as the Nun of Kent, whose prophecies that the King would not long survive his marriage with Anne Boleyn had embroiled her with the authorities) could be utilized to entrap those whose allegiance he doubted. A list was compiled of persons alleged to have seen copies of the Nun's prophecies, and who might be presumed to have concealed from the authorities their knowledge of her treasonous tendencies. The Countess of Salisbury, and the Marchioness of Exeter were amongst those referred to in the document, and though the former had had no further connection with the Nun, suspicions deepened when it emerged that the Marchioness of Exeter had once had a private consultation with her. Their discussion had in fact related to a purely family matter, but the Marchioness had some difficulty in convincing those concerned of the innocence of her dealings. Seriously alarmed, she wrote an abject letter to Henry in November 1533, assuring him that she had attached no consequence to the babblings of the Nun and insisting that her folly derived from the fact that she was a woman, and therefore one 'whose fragility and brittleness is easily seduced and brought to abusion and light belief',[20] but though her submissiveness secured her the pardon of the King the incident served to highlight the dangers of crossing the royal will.

Nevertheless, the Marchioness of Exeter was only temporarily subdued for, as the King's attitude towards Catherine and Mary hardened, she renewed her links with Chapuys. In November 1535 she informed him that the King had burst out in council that he was no longer prepared to tolerate their obstinate defiance, and that at the next session of Parliament he would seek to rid himself of them. She entreated Chapuys to enlist the support of his master Charles V to prevent such an eventuality, an appeal for foreign intervention that was undoubtedly treasonable. Two days later she visited the ambassador in disguise and repeated her supplication.[21] Nor was she inactive elsewhere: at court she was one of the foremost members of the cabal who were working to bring about the downfall of Anne Boleyn.

Freed from the constant strains and uncertainty of the years before her marriage, Anne had initially presided over a gay and youthful court. 'As for pastime in the Queen's chamber, was never more,' Edward Baynton confided to Lord Rochford in a letter of June 1533, but for Anne at least, the atmosphere at court soon soured. Henry's obsessive infatuation with Anne did not long survive their wedding: in September 1533 Chapuys detected the first signs of a disenchantment that was ultimately to become complete. With evident pleasure he reported that Anne and Henry had had a violent quarrel about the King's attentions to a nameless young lady of the court, an argument which had concluded with Henry insultingly informing his wife 'that she must shut her eyes and endure as those who were better than herself had done'.[22]

The birth of Princess Elizabeth, on 10 September 1533, did little to heal the rift, for Henry had confidently awaited the arrival of a male heir and was not pleased to be presented instead with a second daughter. With the restoration of Anne's looks and figure, the King's love for her was temporarily reawakened, but her injudicious tantrums and frenzied insistence that Henry adopt harsher measures against Catherine and Mary did much to erode this renewed affection. The King endured her temperamental outbursts in the belief that she was once again pregnant, but her admission, in September 1534, that she had mistaken her condition made her behaviour seem all the more vexatious. He revenged himself by taking another mistress, whose identity remains a mystery, but she was known to be a supporter of the Princess Mary and was hence a particularly dangerous rival for Anne to have to contend with.[23]

Lacking the reserves of dignity which had sustained Catherine during her husband's infidelities, Anne reacted by seeking to have the young lady in question dismissed from the court, enlisting for the purpose the aid of her sister-in-law, the extraordinary Lady Rochford. The daughter of Henry Parker, a distinguished scholar and court official, she had married in 1526 Anne's brother George, who at the time was only a comparatively humble cupbearer to the King. As the King became increasingly besotted with Anne, George's advancement had been rapid, and in 1530 he was created Baron Rochford. His wife too had shared in the family's good fortune, for upon Anne's marriage she had been appointed a lady of the Privy Chamber. It was a post in which she would serve three of Henry's subsequent Queens, and which afforded ample scope for the exercise of her undoubted talent for intrigue.

For the moment she was happy to deploy this in the service of her sister-in-law, seeking to secure the dismissal from court of Anne's rival by provoking her to insult the Queen. The plot failed, for Henry saw through this transparent scheme, and he responded by ordering Lady Rochford herself to quit the court. Anne was left without support, while her rival continued secure in the King's favour, even having the effrontery to send a message of encouragement to Princess

Mary, assuring her 'that her tribulations will come to an end much sooner than expected'.[24]

Her hold over the King's capricious affections was however less absolute than she imagined, for by February 1535 she had been superseded by another maid of honour, the Queen's cousin, Madge Shelton.[25] While hardly gratifying to Anne, Henry's involvement with her close relative represented infinitely less of a threat, since Madge Shelton was not opposed to her every interest. Furthermore, she herself enjoyed occasional returns to the favour of the King, so much so that by the autumn of 1535 she could confidently pronounce that she was once again with child. The gloom that this development inspired amongst those members of the court inimical to Anne was nevertheless somewhat mitigated when Henry, rarely the most attentive of husbands during the pregnancies of his wives, was observed to be paying highly flattering attentions to another of Anne's maids of honour, the demure Jane Seymour.

In January 1536 Queen Catherine died at Kimbolton, and Henry and his wife were temporarily reunited by an unseemly joy at her demise, until the reflection that the King could now discard her without having to acknowledge that Catherine was still his wife seems to have sobered Anne. Then, on 29 January 1536, the very day of Catherine's burial, Anne miscarried of the male child whose survival would have guaranteed her own. Spurned by her husband (whose reaction to this misfortune was anything other than sympathetic) and depressed by the loss of her baby, Anne drew consolation from the compliments and gallantries addressed her by various gentlemen of the court, indulging in flirtatious talk of a kind extremely dangerous for one surrounded by so much hatred. For, by early 1536, the opposition to Anne within the court had crystallized into a coherent faction, of which Sir Nicholas Carew and the Exeters were leading members, with the Marchioness of Exeter providing the conspirators with a link to Chapuys, whom she kept informed of the group's activities in order that they might co-ordinate their respective intrigues against the Queen. All concerned were aware that they must act swiftly before Anne safeguarded her position by once again conceiving, and the role to be played by Jane Seymour was central to their plans for securing the downfall of the Queen.

Rarely can there have been so unlikely an instrument of nemesis as Jane Seymour, hardly the conventional *femme fatale*. Her modest placidity formed a striking contrast to Anne's elegance and volatility.

'She is of middle height,' Chapuys reported dispassionately 'and nobody thinks she has much beauty. Her complexion is so whitish that she may be called rather pale. She is a little over twenty-five.'[26] She combined with these somewhat negative endowments a degree of determination that enabled her to accept with equanimity the grim implications of bringing about the downfall of Anne Boleyn, and though her forbears had been content with their prosperous but obscure existence on their estates in Wiltshire, she clearly possessed her fair share of that ambition that would later precipitate her brothers Edward and Thomas into the highest echelons of politics.

Originally a maid of honour to Catherine of Aragon, she had smoothly transferred to the service of Anne, while yet retaining a devotion to the wronged Queen and her daughter which would provide her with the moral justification for the betrayal of her mistress. Nor did she lack a certain shrewdness: although the cynical Chapuys questioned 'Whether, being an Englishwoman, and having been so long at court, she would not hold it a sin to be still a maid', she was sufficiently astute to erect an impenetrable wall of virginal reserve in the face of Henry's advances, exhibitions of modesty which quite enraptured the King. When he sent her a letter accompanied by a purse full of sovereigns she respectfully kissed the missive but declined the gift, imploring Henry to consider her reputation as 'a well-born damsel' and suggesting that he should wait until 'such a time as God would be pleased to send her an advantageous marriage' before bestowing a similar offering upon her. Henry's love for her in consequence 'marvellously increased'. Throughout the courtship Jane was assiduously coached by those at court antagonistic to the Queen, who reminded her 'not in any wise to give in to the King's fancy unless he makes her his queen', a course of action upon which – so Chapuys reassured his master – 'this damsel is quite resolved'.[27]

She was furthermore instructed to poison the King's mind against his wife by telling him, in the presence of witnesses upon whom she could rely to confirm her assertion, 'How much his subjects abominate the marriage contracted with the concubine and that no one considers it legitimate.'[28] Faced with this combination of subtle sexual teasing and unremitting attack upon Anne, any vestiges of affection that the King might have nurtured for his wife were converted into the deepest loathing, rendering him capable of believing the most outrageous accusations against her. On 24 April 1536 he authorized a commission headed by Cromwell and Norfolk to investigate Anne's conduct. By sifting through the amorphous whisperings of court gossip, they succeeded in fabricating a coherent enough case to warrant the arrest and interrogation of Mark Smeaton, a palace musician who stated under torture that he had committed adultery with the Queen. On 1 May Henry Norris, a gentleman of the King's Privy Chamber hitherto in high favour with Henry, was arrested upon similar suspicions, and he was later joined in prison by Sir Thomas Weston, William Brereton and Anne's brother, Lord Rochford. On 2 May Anne herself was conveyed to the Tower.

Exactly what evidence the council proceeded upon at this stage remains obscure. Cromwell was later to maintain that 'The Queen's incontinent living was so rank and uncommon that the ladies of her Privy Chamber could not conceal it', and he claimed that the charges preferred had resulted from their denunciations. Lady Lisle was informed by her knowledgeable agent in London that 'The first accuser was Lady Worcester and Nan Cobham and one maid more; but the Lady Worcester was the first ground,'[29] a statement that would seem to corroborate Cromwell's version of events. Possibly the Countess of Worcester had long been an active member of the cabal that plotted to encompass Anne's destruction, and used her privileged position as lady of the Privy Chamber to report to them details of Anne's behaviour upon which an unfavourable construction might be placed. Alternatively, her accusations may not have been quite so spontaneous as Cromwell implied, and the miscarriage that she suffered coincident with Anne's arrest may perhaps have been caused by distress at having unwittingly incriminated her mistress.

Evidently however, the council's case against Anne, such as it was, derived also from another source, and from a person upon whose support the Queen might justifiably have counted. Jane Rochford, resentful at her exclusion from the affectionate relationship that prevailed between Anne and her brother, had turned against the Queen since the days when they had conspired together to procure the departure from court of Anne's rival. Possibly embittered by the way that she alone had been disgraced then, she was determined now to claw her way back to the favour of the King. 'More out of envy and jealousy than out of love towards the King', she deposed not only that Anne and Rochford had claimed that Henry was impotent and mocked his incapacity, but that the Queen and her brother were guilty of incest together. In return for this helpful testimony she would be rewarded with the restoration of her position as lady of the Privy Chamber in the household of Anne's successor.[30]

Clearly however, Cromwell hoped to secure rather more conclusive proof of misconduct from the accused herself. Anne was attended in the Tower by women upon whom Cromwell felt he could rely, including her aunt, Lady Boleyn, who had always retained a loyalty towards Catherine of Aragon; Mrs Stonor, the Mother of the Maids, who had presumably witnessed much of the 'pastime in the Queen's chamber' that had occurred over the past three years; and Mrs Cosyns. Their instructions were to relay to Sir William Kingston, Keeper of the Tower, details of their conversations with Anne, and, in evident hopes of provoking Anne into incriminating herself, they taunted her with accounts of Mark Smeaton's ill-treatment in prison.

While in captivity Anne always denied that she had committed improper deeds with any of the accused, but she did hysterically recall items of injudicious banter that she had recently exchanged with them, all of which were noted by her ladies and faithfully transmitted to Cromwell. The Queen recollected that she had once teased Norris that he was delaying his forthcoming marriage because he was in love with her; she added that at the time she had even suggested that if any harm came to his bride Norris would have liked to marry her, Anne, instead. Norris had been careful to give her no encouragement, but Anne's description of the incident was enough to seal his death warrant. The Queen also admitted that she had once had to reprove Smeaton for gazing at her in a lovestruck way, while it was her own account of a flirtatious interchange between herself and Weston that brought that young man under suspicion in the first place. In moments of lucidity Anne showed herself aware that she was surrounded by enemies – 'The King wist well what he did when he put two such about her as Lady Boleyn and Mistress Cosyns', she remarked bitterly on one occasion – but her distress at her predicament prevented her from curbing her tongue accordingly.[31] Once communicated to Cromwell by her ladies, her revelations, which in themselves proved little more than that she was guilty of foolish indiscretion, were collated and woven into a damning indictment.

On 15 May 1536 Anne and her brother were tried in the Tower and despite her able defence she was convicted and sentenced to be beheaded or burnt at the King's pleasure. Rochford too was found guilty, with Cromwell confounding any hopes of his acquittal by producing before the court his wife's letter asserting her knowledge of the 'accursed secret' of Anne's incest with him.[32] On 17 May he and the four other supposed lovers of the Queen were executed on Tower Hill, and Anne herself was beheaded two days later. She was adjudged guilty of adultery with five different men, over a period of three years, her first offence with Norris having allegedly been committed as early as the autumn of 1533. The very multiplicity of the charges underlines their implausibility: that Anne could have long concealed an affair with a single gentleman of the court is unlikely, but that she could have conducted so many liaisons during virtually the whole of her married life without previous discovery is inconceivable. Anne was the victim, not of 'Her frail and carnal lust' as her indictment claimed,[33] but of a deadly combination of court intrigue and royal disfavour.

The King, at least, suffered no misgivings at the fate of his wife, utterly convinced of her guilt and positive that his former infatuation with her had been the product of witchcraft. Even while Anne was still in the Tower, the court had embarked on a frenzied round of gaiety, with Henry giving feasts for the ladies and staying up till after midnight. Chapuys remarked that Henry's delight was comparable to that 'a man feels in getting rid of a thin old vicious hack in the hope of getting soon a fine horse to ride'[34] and the seal was put on the King's happiness when, on 30 May 1536, he wed Jane Seymour.

The victory, it would seem, had been complete to those opposed to Anne Boleyn and all she stood for. The Marchioness of Exeter was restored to a position of high favour at court, and Lady Rochford was reinstated as a lady of the Privy Chamber. Yet while jubilant at being rid of his wife, Henry had no intention of reversing the policies initiated in her name. Under Cromwell's auspices the subjection of the English Church to the royal supremacy inexorably proceeded and opposition to his plans was firmly crushed. Even Queen Jane was stingingly rebuked when she implored Henry to halt the dissolution of the monasteries, and she was unable to secure the return to court of his daughter Mary until the latter had acknowledged the royal supremacy, forsworn Rome and declared herself illegitimate. Those who had hoped that the downfall of Anne Boleyn would have more far-reaching effects were naturally disappointed, a fact that Cromwell duly noted, and in the case of many of these malcontents it was only a matter of time before their loyalty was found wanting and they too shared Anne's fate.

Apart from her one, singularly unencouraging, attempt to intervene in State affairs, Queen Jane herself seemed content to confine herself to breeding and supervising the orderly conduct of her household. In February 1537 it was announced, amid riotous celebrations, that she was pregnant, tidings which were received with interest across the Channel in Calais by Lady Lisle, wife of the Governor of the Garrison there and harassed mother of four daughters by her previous marriage to Sir John Basset. Having already entrusted them to the care of various French acquaintances in an effort to imbue them with the accomplishments esteemed necessary for young ladies of good breeding (among which literacy was apparently not included, for Anne Basset would later confess to her mother that she was capable of writing no more than her own name), she was now anxious to install two of them as maids of honour in the household of the Queen. Her agent in London, the indefatigable John Hussey, was therefore instructed to make approaches to those persons whose standing with the Queen ensured that their recommendations about household appointments were highly valued.

Accordingly, wine was dispatched to Lord Daubeney and Mr Surlyard, and a ring bestowed upon Mrs Margery Horsman, one of the Queen's gentlewomen, while Lady Lisle herself sought to mobilize in her daughters' interest the Countess of Salisbury and her old friend the Countess of Rutland, a principal lady-in-waiting to the Queen.[35] All was in vain: Jane's servants had been sworn in only three days after her marriage, and fond mothers strategically placed to agitate directly for the selection of their daughters had already secured all the available places. Stranded at her posting, Lady Lisle was left with the assurance that Lady Rutland would continue to plead on the Basset girls' behalf, but in May 1537 they were still languishing in France.

Despite the disadvantages of a campaign conducted by remote control, Lady Lisle did not give up, and she continued to send presents to all at court whom she thought capable of assisting her daughters. The delivery, in July 1537, of a consignment of quails to the Queen herself was to pay handsome dividends. As Jane savoured the delicacies she enquired after Lady Lisle and her family, whereupon her attendants at table, the Countesses of Rutland and Sussex, responded with paeons of praise for the two elder Basset girls. In consequence the Queen demanded that these paragons be dispatched from France for inspection, guaranteeing that she would employ one of them. Tutored by Hussey upon how to comport themselves in royal society and reminded of the dangers that lurked at court, Katherine and Anne Basset were duly paraded before the Queen, with the result that Anne was enrolled in her service, while Mistress Katherine had to content herself with a place in the entourage of the Countess of Rutland, who had already been rewarded for her efforts on the girls' behalf by being inundated with quails from Calais.[36]

Unfortunately Lady Lisle's troubles were by no means over: having installed her daughters at court she had to ensure that they were suitably equipped and that Anne was supplied with bedding and apparel 'as is written in Mrs Pole's book of reckoning'. Queen Jane was very particular about the appearance of her ladies and though she agreed that Anne might wear out her French wardrobe, she stipulated that she must obtain 'a bonnet and frontlet of velvet', headgear which the regretful Hussey considered infinitely less flattering than Anne's own French hood. The birth, on 12 October 1537, of a baby Prince engendered an alarming set of fresh requirements relating to court attire. An agitated Hussey wrote to Lady Lisle that Mistress Anne would need new gowns not only for Prince Edward's christening but also for the churching of the Queen *and* the approaching Christmas festivities, despairingly assuring her that he would endeavour to undertake the appropriate arrangements himself.[37]

In the event they proved unnecessary: twelve days after producing the desired heir to the throne, Jane Seymour lay dead, a misfortune attributed by Cromwell to 'the neglect of those about her who suffered her to take great cold and eat such things as her fantasy in sickness called for'[38] but which in all probability was due to the onset of puerperal fever. Anne Basset's final melancholy duty to Queen Jane was to bear the train at her funeral, and thus deprived of her official position she was able to remain at court only by entering the service of the Countess of Sussex.

The court was to remain without a queen for over two years, a circumstance that doubtless facilitated Cromwell's plans for the reorganization of the royal household for, in the interests of economy and efficiency, he provided for a considerable reduction in the number of any future Queen Consort's attendants. But rationalization at court was not to be confined to this upheaval in the Crown's domestic arrangements: the shock occasioned by the northern rebellions of 1536–7 had determined Cromwell that the court must be cleansed from within of all trace of political disaffection. A purge was initiated against the Exeter and Pole families, descendants of Edward IV and ardent believers in the old religion, whose disenchantment with Cromwell's policies marked them out for destruction.

The Pole clan was headed by the elderly and devout Countess of Salisbury, who since the death of Queen Jane had retired to her manor of Warblington, the only overt sign of her disapproval of the Government's recent religious enactments being her occasional dismissal of servants who favoured the new learning. She was, nevertheless, the mother of the exiled Reginald Pole, a renegade Catholic who had compounded the crime of writing a tract condemning the royal supremacy with his acceptance, in December 1536, of a cardinal's hat; in the eyes of the King her loyalty was thus automatically impugned. Then, in August 1538 the disloyal grumblings of her second son, Sir Geoffrey Pole, resulted in his arrest, and the confessions extracted from him in the Tower sufficed to convince the authorities of the existence of a treasonous network co-ordinated by the Poles and Exeters. In November 1538 the Marchioness of Exeter followed her husband to the Tower, while royal commissioners hurried down to Warblington, intent on establishing that the Countess was implicated in the plots of her sons. They had little success, for the indomitable old lady proved adept at parrying their questions. 'Although we then entreated her in both sorts, sometimes with douce and mild words, now roughly and asperly, by traitoring her and her sons to the nineth degree, yet would she nothing utter,' reported Cromwell's agents in some perplexity,[39] but nevertheless the Countess was taken into confinement.

Meanwhile, the Marchioness of Exeter was repeatedly interrogated, sometimes by Cromwell himself, who sought to dredge up accusations deriving from her association with the Nun of Kent and to establish her criminal involvement in the alleged conspiracies of the Pole family. These examinations, and the depositions of her servants, yielded little more concrete than that she had once been overheard complaining that the King had discarded his noble advisers,[40] but even such flimsy evidence was enough for Cromwell to extract from Parliament an act of attainder which sentenced the Marchioness to death.

Despite the absence of convincing proof the Countess of Salisbury was likewise convicted of treason and in May 1539 she too was sentenced to death. Although her eldest son and the Marquis of Exeter had already been executed, for a time she survived, but in 1541, before his departure on a northern tour, Henry VIII decreed that potential focal points for rebellion must be eliminated, even one who represented so negligible a threat as this dowager of nearly seventy years of age. In May 1541 she was instructed to prepare herself for death. Chapuys reported in a despatch: 'When informed of her sentence, she found it very strange, not knowing her crime, but she walked to the space in front of the Tower, where there was no scaffold but only a small block. She there commended her soul to

God, and desired those present to pray for the King, Queen, Prince and Princess. The ordinary executioner being absent, a blundering "garçonneau" was chosen, who hacked her head and shoulders to pieces.'[41]

Thus the saga of the White Rose came to its grisly denouement. The Marchioness of Exeter, infinitely more compromised in treasonous intrigue than the Countess of Salisbury, avoided the same fate because she was not of the blood royal. She would survive the vicissitudes of Henry's reign and emerge from the Tower to become a lady-in-waiting to his eldest daughter.

Deprived of official employment by the absence of a queen, many ladies were obliged to retire to their husbands' country estates, taking with them the majority of the unmarried girls at court. From their point of view it was an unsatisfactory state of affairs, which they hoped the King would soon remedy by taking another wife. Nor indeed was bachelordom a state especially palatable to Henry, who hankered after the pleasures of wifely companionship and also wished to safeguard the succession by begetting more heirs. Accordingly the King proved amenable when Cromwell suggested that he take as his bride one of the two Princesses from the independent Lutheran Duchy of Cleves and, after scrutinizing portraits of both sisters executed by Hans Holbein, Henry announced a preference for the Lady Anne.

As the marriage negotiations neared their conclusion, intense excitement was generated at court. 'I trust we shall have a mistress soon', Anne Basset wrote to her mother on 5 October 1539, and the signing of the nuptial contract on the following day signalled the start of an unseemly scramble for positions in the new Queen's household. Their high rank ensured that the Duchesses of Suffolk and Richmond, the Countesses of Sussex and Hertford, and the King's niece, Lady Margaret Douglas, were obvious choices as ladies-in-waiting, but competition was fierce for the other posts available. Even before Anne set foot in England, her ladies of the Privy Chamber had all been selected, with the Countess of Rutland and Ladies Rochford, Edgecumbe and Browne sharing the honours. Anne was also presented on arrival with an almost full complement of maids of honour, for Anne Basset had been reinstated, and she was joined by others, including two nieces of the Duke of Norfolk and a daughter of the King's old flame, Mary Carey. Lady Lisle's hopes that Katherine Basset might be appointed too were frustrated for, as one of the officials in charge of household organization pointed out to her, he had somehow to accommodate Anne's 'own ladies and gentlewomen that be tarried with, with two other chamberers that were with Queen Jane afore, and Mistress Fitzherbert, chief chamberer, with many other ladies', and vacancies were in consequence scarce.[42]

In fact, by the time that Anne arrived in England in late December 1539, she found that Englishwomen had monopolized preferment in her household to such an extent that it was difficult for her to provide for the fifteen or so countrywomen who had accompanied her from Cleves. Described by the French ambassador as 'even inferior in beauty to their mistress and . . . moreover dressed after a fashion so heavy and tasteless that it would make them appear frightful even if they were belles', this unprepossessing bunch were given little time to adapt to their new surroundings. Although Anne was permitted to retain the services of a few trusted compatriots such as her homely companion Mother Lowe, and the pair cryptically referred to in court accounts as 'Katherine and Gertrude, Dutchwomen', Cromwell was soon arranging for the rest of the 'strange maidens' to return to Cleves.[43]

Encouraged by their departure, Lady Lisle continued her machinations to secure employment for Katherine Basset. On the advice of the Countess of Rutland, and spurred on by Katherine herself, she made overtures to Mother Lowe in hopes that she would persuade the Queen to give Katherine a job, and Anne Basset was also pressed into action, receiving instructions from her mother to intercede with the King on her sister's behalf. Primed with maternal advice concerning 'continuance in the King's favour', Anne tactfully presented Henry with a pot of home-made jam before raising the subject of her sister's promotion; but the King, who was doubtless pestered on all sides by similar applications, merely replied that he would only appoint those such as were 'fair and meet for the room', attributes that he was evidently far from certain that Katherine Basset possessed. Nevertheless, Lady Lisle's persistence was ultimately rewarded, for soon afterwards Katherine was installed in Anne's household; but events ensured that it was a hollow victory, for before long Henry and his wife were to separate and Katherine was among those who had to leave the court to go with Anne to her new establishment at Richmond. Lady Lisle, at least, was past caring. In May 1540 her husband had been imprisoned on suspicion of treason, a misfortune that so unhinged his spouse that 'She fell distraught of mind and so continued many years after'.[44] Thenceforth the Basset girls were obliged to manage their affairs without the assistance of their battling matriarch.

Henry's marriage to Anne of Cleves had been a fiasco from the start. From the moment when, brushing protocol aside, he had burst romantically into the apartments where Anne sat awaiting the moment for their formal introduction, the King had not been able to control his disgust for his coarse-featured Flemish bride. Unable to extricate himself from his commitment, he was obliged to proceed with the ceremony, but the solemnization of the marriage did nothing to reconcile him to it. So profound was his antipathy that, although he lay with his wife with dutiful regularity, he proved unable to consummate the match.

Abhorred by her husband, Anne was obliged to rely for companionship on those ladies of the Privy Chamber who had been foisted upon her, and as her English improved their conversations became positively intimate. When, in answer to their questions, Anne insisted that she could not possibly be pregnant, Lady Edgecumbe impertinently enquired, 'How is it possible for Your Grace to know that and lie every night with the King?' Lady Rochford solved the conundrum: 'By our Lady, Madam, I think Your Grace is a maid still?' she suggested, and her suspicions were confirmed by Anne's ingenuous reply. 'Why,' she said, 'when he comes to bed, he kisses me and taketh me by the hand and biddeth me, "Good night Sweetheart", and in the morning kisses me and biddeth me "Farewell darling". Is not this enough?' 'Madam,' remarked Lady Rochford with feeling, 'there must be more than this or it will be long 'ere we have a Duke of York, which all this realm most desireth.'[45] Subsequently the ladies would relate details of this exchange to a thunderstruck audience of clerics, who were investigating the validity of the King's marriage, affording dramatic support for Henry's contention that it had never been consummated, the grounds on which his plea for divorce partly rested.

For, while Anne had whiled away the time with her attendants, Henry's attention had been elsewhere, and by April 1540 it was clear that he was seriously attracted to one of his wife's maids of honour, the diminutive and pert Catherine Howard. Thoroughly enamoured of this vivacious beauty, Henry's pliable conscience had once again come into operation. Pious doubts assailed him as to the legitimacy of his marriage, convincing him that Anne's previous betrothal to the Duke of Lorraine's son nullified his own union with her, and that his impotence was an indication of divine disapproval for a match unsanctified by law. Naturally such doubts were encouraged by Catherine's avaricious horde of Howard relatives. Convinced that a marriage between Henry and Catherine would result in a resurgence of their own wealth and power, they overlooked in their enthusiasm the frailty of the girl upon whom their hopes were founded.

Having lost her mother while still a child, Catherine had been brought up by her step-grandmother, the Dowager Duchess of Norfolk, at whose establishment in Horsham, Sussex, sundry Howard relations and dependents were deposited during their childhood. After a spell at the Duchess's London residence at Lambeth, she transferred to court, where the influence of her uncle, the Duke of Norfolk, secured her a place as maid of honour to Anne of Cleves. Probably in her late teens on her initiation to the court, Catherine was no innocent, having acquired considerable sexual experience during her adolescence in Horsham and Lambeth. The girls' dormitories there often formed the setting for romantic assignations with young gentlemen attached to the household, and midnight feasts in the maidens' chambers frequently terminated in communal love-play. After a flirtation with Henry Manox, a musician in the service of her grandmother, Catherine had enjoyed an affair with Francis Dereham, a sophisticated young buck who was wont to sport with her 'both in his doublet and hose between the sheets and in naked bed'.[46]

Such attachments faded into insignificance in the excitement of awaking the interest of the King himself. Her relationship with Henry was carefully orchestrated by Norfolk and his ally Stephen Gardiner, the reactionary Bishop of Winchester, who were confident that, as the architect of the Cleves marriage, their enemy Thomas Cromwell could not survive its collapse, and that they would supersede him as the King's chief advisers. Chaperoned by her uncle, Catherine was paraded before her besotted Sovereign at dinners hosted by Gardiner, and, thus tantalized, the King determined that all obstacles to their marriage must be removed.

In July 1540 Anne of Cleves was ordered to proceed to Richmond, whence a deputation was dispatched to acquaint her with the King's misgivings concerning their union. Pragmatic and obliging, Anne agreed that convocation should investigate the matter, and when they pronounced the marriage illegitimate she accepted their verdict, contenting herself with her establishment at Richmond and her position as leading lady of the realm save for Catherine herself and the Princesses of the blood. On 28 July 1540, the Howards enjoyed a double triumph, as the celebration of Henry's marriage to Catherine coincided with the execution of Thomas Cromwell on trumped-up charges of treason.

Deeply in love with his pretty young wife, Henry sought to pander to her every whim, embarking on a round of gaiety at court reminiscent of the early days of his reign, and lavishing dresses and jewels upon her. Nor was she the only one to benefit, for Catherine's relatives were determined to extract maximum advantage from the circumstance of having one of their number upon the throne. Although 'great ladies' such as the Duchess of Suffolk, the Countess of Sussex and Lady Margaret Douglas were retained as Catherine's principal ladies-in-waiting, Howards were quick to grab other prize appointments in her household. Apart from her cousin, the Duchess of Richmond, her attendants included her aunt Lady William Howard, her cousin Lady Denny, and her sisters, Lady Arundel and Lady Baynton. Lady Rochford, another Howard connection, retained her position as lady of the Privy Chamber.[47]

Her kinsmen, however, were not alone in their eagerness to profit from Catherine's sudden elevation. Even before her marriage she was besieged by importunate letters from those girlhood companions who knew the secret of her giddy youth at her grandmother's home. Joan Bulmer, a young lady who had connived with Catherine over her romance with Francis Dereham, assisting the semi-literate girl in the composition of her love-letters, was swift to approach her former friend, beseeching her 'To have in your remembrance the unfeigned love that my heart hath always borne towards you,' adding – with perhaps a touch of menace – 'I know the Queen of England will not forget her secretary'. Like Katherine Tylney, Margaret Morton and Alice Restwold (who had also been associates of Catherine during her Lambeth days), Joan was appointed chamberer to the Queen. Nevertheless, although Catherine was surrounded by her girlhood friends it was Lady Rochford who established herself as her favourite attendant, so much so indeed that the rest of the household became jealous.[48]

The King had not been able to sustain for long the hectic schedule he had undertaken for the sake of his wife and by March 1541 the ulcer on his leg was causing him intense pain, necessitating the cancellation of all court festivities and causing Catherine to pine for the gaiety of her early months of wedlock. By that summer he had however recovered sufficiently to decree that the court should embark upon a northern progress, and, accompanied by Catherine and a numerous retinue, he toured in state Lincoln, Pontefract and York. It was while the court was thus occupied that details of Catherine's past indiscretions were first exposed.

Mary Lassels had been one of the gentlewomen in the service of the Duchess of Norfolk who had shared Catherine's bedroom at Lambeth, but unlike the majority of her room-mates she had failed to secure a post in the new Queen's household. Chided by her brother John for her failure to exploit an excellent opportunity, she had retorted that she had no wish to be employed by someone 'light both in conditions and living'.[49] On being pressed, she had revealed particulars of Catherine's intimacies with both Manox and Dereham, and Lassels had promptly passed this information to those members of the council who had remained in the south.

On 2 November 1541, shortly after the King's return to Hampton Court, Archbishop Cranmer nervously handed him a note which summarized Lassels's revelations. Convinced that the charges were groundless, Henry authorized an investigation in expectation that his wife's name would be cleared, but under interrogation both Manox and Dereham confessed that the allegations were in substance true. Furthermore, in an effort to establish that his relations with Catherine had been entirely innocent since her marriage, Dereham asserted that Thomas Culpeper, a gentleman of the King's Privy Chamber, 'had succeeded him in the Queen's affections', a statement that ensured that the proceedings assumed an altogether grimmer complexion.[50]

Catherine was confined in Syon House and there admitted that she had had several clandestine meetings with Culpeper, in the course of which she had called him her 'little sweet fool' and presented him with a cap and ring, but she denied that Culpeper had ever touched more than her hand. Nevertheless, her frightened chamberers were examined not only about their knowledge of the Queen's pre-marital sexual escapades (and it soon emerged that not only had most of them been aware of what Catherine had been up to, but that Katherine Tylney had 'lien in the bed' with her and Dereham) but also about whether they had seen anything that might confirm that Catherine had committed adultery. Anxious not to be further implicated in the delinquencies of the Queen, they denied having witnessed any specific instances of misconduct after her marriage, but proved zealous in their efforts to furnish the examiners with circumstantial evidence suggestive of Catherine's guilt. Both Katherine Tylney and Margaret Morton deposed that the Queen had behaved most mysteriously throughout the recent progress, habitually bolting her chamber door and forbidding anyone save Lady Rochford to enter without an explicit summons. Katherine Tylney maintained that when permitted to accompany the Queen to her chamber at night she had been shut in an adjacent closet to prevent her from seeing whether the Queen had had any visitors, adding that on occasion the Queen had asked her to deliver such strange messages to Lady Rochford that 'she knew not how to utter them'. For her part, Margaret Morton recalled having seen Catherine exchange a glance with Culpeper at Hatfield, 'after such sort she thought there was love between them'.[51]

Despite its inconclusive nature, all such information was highly welcome to Thomas Wriothsley, the officer in charge of the investigation: 'My woman Tylney hath done us worthy service, and true as it appeareth', he wrote with satisfaction to a colleague, but he was hopeful that interrogation of another of the Queen's ladies would yield even more positive results. All those interviewed in connection with the affair were insistent that Lady Rochford had been the evil genius behind it. Margaret Morton testified that if the Queen had committed evil, she believed that Lady Rochford was 'The principal occasion of her folly', while Catherine herself was adamant that it had been Lady Rochford who initially persuaded her to grant Culpeper the private audiences in her chamber, 'affirming that he desired nothing else but to speak with her and that she durst swear upon a book he meant nothing but honesty'. Culpeper too cast Lady Rochford in the role of procuress, asserting that she had 'provoked him much to love the Queen', and her own attempts to extricate herself from involvement in the affair by insisting that she had slept through all of Catherine and Culpeper's meetings availed her little, particularly in the light of her somewhat contradictory admission that she believed Culpeper 'to have known the Queen carnally considering all things that she hath heard and seen between them'.[52]

Whether Jane Rochford had in fact engineered the assignations in the face of Catherine's protests may be doubted: Culpeper stated that at each stage of the summer progress it was the Queen who would 'at every house seek for the back stairs and back doors herself', in order that he could visit her unobserved, and her participation in the affair seems throughout to have been entirely voluntary. Clearly however, Lady Rochford made no effort to urge Catherine to resist the approaches of Culpeper, advice that might have been expected from one of her years and with her memories of the downfall of Anne Boleyn. 'All her life she had the name to esteem her honour little', the French ambassador observed of her, and her almost instinctive love of intrigue seems to have prevented her from thinking rationally about the consequences if the Queen's romance was discovered. When her exposure and arrest forced her to face reality, the shock indeed sent her temporarily mad, but the King, 'desiring her recovery that he may afterwards have her executed as an example', sent his own physicians to nurse her through this bout of mental illness.[53] By 13 February 1542 she had sufficiently recovered to follow her mistress to the block.

Whether Catherine had ever actually committed adultery with Culpeper was never definitively established but in an age where it was construed as treason merely to wish harm to the King, she and her paramours had done quite enough to merit death. The very fact that the Queen had employed Katherine Tylney as her chamberer, 'A woman who was privy to her naughty life before', was interpreted as 'proof of her will to return to her old abominable life',[54] and helped to secure the Queen's conviction on a capital charge.

With the exception of Anne Basset, for whom the King, 'in consideration of the calamity of her friends', volunteered to provide at court, most of the unmarried ladies in Catherine's household dispersed to the shelter of family or friends in the country. Others, however, were not so fortunate: many of Catherine's female relations who had occupied a prominent place in her household now found themselves accused of misprision of treason for having concealed their knowledge of Catherine's ill behaviour prior to her marriage. The Dowager Duchess of Norfolk failed to convince the authorities that she had been ignorant of Catherine's activities in her house and she and Catherine's aunts, Lady Bridgewater and Lady William Howard, were sentenced to perpetual imprisonment and forfeiture of their goods, as were Catherine's unfortunate companions from her Lambeth days, Katherine Tylney, Alice Restwold and Joan Bulmer. To all of them, however, Henry was to display unwonted clemency. All except the Dowager Duchess were pardoned and released in February 1542, and she too was liberated in May of that year.[55]

Shattered by his betrayal, the King was notably subdued in the months following Catherine's arrest. After the execution of the Queen Chapuys opined, 'Unless Parliament prays him to take another wife he will not be in a hurry to do so,' adding caustically, 'besides, there are few, if any, ladies at court who would aspire to such an honour.' Cynics believed the list of potential candidates for the royal hand to be further restricted by the new act whereby it was declared treasonous for any woman who married the King to delude him into esteeming her 'a pure and clean maid' if such was not the case.[56] As it happened however, when the King contemplated matrimony again the question of his future wife's virginity did not arise, as he chose for his bride the twice-widowed Catherine Parr, selecting her more as a companion and nurse than as a bedmate. As for her wishes in the matter, they were not consulted: once Henry had indicated his preference she had little choice but to accept it, and in July 1543 the King married for the sixth time.

The new Queen could hardly have been a greater contrast to her dizzy predecessor. Already in her thirties at the time of her marriage to Henry, she was well-educated and intellectual, with distinct Protestant sympathies. Many of the ladies she selected as her attendants were of a similar persuasion, and though Catherine was reputed to keep them 'very strictly' the religious tendencies of the new Queen's circle would prove almost as dangerous as the sexual adventuring of her predecessor.

Religious divisions within the court accounted for the increasing bitterness of its faction struggles towards the end of Henry's reign, and the sympathies of the Queen and her ladies would precipitate them into the midst of these struggles. Theological ferment had been an inevitable subsidiary product of the break with Rome and though for some years there had been confusion surrounding the exact doctrinal position of the new State Church, the passage in 1539 of the Act of Six Articles (a measure that enshrined firmly Catholic principles) apparently signalled that Henry had come down on the side of orthodoxy. Nevertheless, it was already too late for the traditionalists to impose religious uniformity for a new spirit of enquiry was abroad, and by the early 1540s Protestantism had permeated the most respectable levels of society, numbering among its supporters members of the court of both sexes.

The Catholic faction at court, headed by the Bishop of Winchester, Stephen Gardiner, was naturally aghast at this state of affairs, but, for a time at least, the King's marriage to Catherine Parr prevented them from taking any steps to check the growth of Protestantism within the court. Between 1543 and 1546 there were very few prosecutions under the Act of Six Articles, and Protestants on the council assumed an increasingly important role in the conduct of State affairs, developments deplored by Catholic observers and attributed to the influence of Catherine and her ladies. 'The King favours these stirrers of heresy . . .' Chapuys noted indignantly, 'because the Queen, instigated by the Duchess of Suffolk, the

Countess of Hertford and the Admiral's wife [Joan Dudley, Lady Lisle], shows herself infected.'[57]

The Protestant predilections of the Queen and her ladies were emphasized by the regular sessions which were held in her chambers for the purposes of theological discussion and prayer, and which were attended by the 'ladies or gentlewomen of her Privy Chamber or others that were disposed to hear'. The sermons which the Queen's chaplain preached to these gatherings 'oftimes touched such abuses as in the Church there were rife', while during Lent the ladies were sometimes treated to expositions on the gospels by the radical Bishop Latimer.[58]

These proceedings were highly offensive to the Catholic faction at court, and its leader was hardly mollified by the insulting treatment which he received from some of Catherine's ladies. One lady of the Privy Chamber, the Countess of Hertford, chose to name her spaniel 'Gardiner' and the Bishop was also mercilessly ridiculed by her colleague, Catherine Duchess of Suffolk, a young lady who was renowned for her biting wit. Aware that his position was too weak to exact revenge, Gardiner was obliged to bide his time, for while the Queen remained secure in Henry's favour she and her ladies could flaunt their Protestantism with impunity.

Nevertheless, with a husband of so uncertain a temper as the King, Catherine's position was not impregnable, and the watchful Gardiner waited for the opportune moment to strike against her. In mid-1546 he thought he saw his chance. When sitting with her husband Catherine was wont to pass the time in theological discussion with him, a recreation of which Henry was normally very fond. On occasion, however, Catherine irritated her husband with her argumentativeness, as happened once when Gardiner chanced to be present. When his wife left them Henry remarked testily to the Bishop that at times he found his wife too opinionated, and Gardiner was swift to capitalize on his ill humour. He assured the King that if any other of his subjects had entertained the religious views expressed by his wife they would have 'by law deserved death', assuring Henry that by thus nourishing heresy he was imperilling his own soul. Genuinely appalled, the King authorized proceedings to be taken against the Queen.

Nevertheless Gardiner determined not to strike until he had accumulated detailed evidence against not only the Queen but her ladies too, and he was sure that a rigorous examination of Anne Askew, a Lincolnshire gentlewoman already convicted of heresy, would provide him with what he needed. Anne was an ardent Protestant who had become a leading luminary of advanced religious circles soon after her arrival in London in 1544, and since she had two brothers in royal service it is probable that she was an occasional visitor at the Queen's devotional gatherings in her Chamber. Unfortunately her forthrightly expressed beliefs had attracted the attention of the authorities and in 1546 she had been formally charged with heresy. On 28 June she was sentenced to death by burning, but Gardiner was determined that before she went to the stake he would extract from her all she knew of heresy in court circles.

Accordingly, Gardiner had dispatched Lord Chancellor Wriothsley and his acolyte Sir Richard Rich to interrogate Anne in the Tower. They had hoped that she could provide them with information against such ladies as the Duchess of Suffolk, the Countesses of Hertford and Sussex, and Ladies Denny and Fitzwilliam, but Anne denied knowing of anything that could incriminate them, although she did admit that her maid had told her that Lady Hertford and Lady Denny had sent her small sums of money to sustain her while she awaited trial. Wriothsley and Rich were nevertheless convinced that Anne could tell them much more than this, and, in a bid to make her reveal all, they had the unfortunate woman racked, operating the mechanism with their own hands when the Lieutenant of the Tower declined to co-operate in this unprecedented application of torture to a gentlewoman.[59] Despite their brutality, Anne remained silent and her tormentors had reluctantly to accept that they would never gain from her the evidence that would enable them to mount a wholesale purge of the Queen's entourage.

Anne's steadfastness obliged Gardiner to change his tactics, but he remained determined to proceed against the Queen and three of her closest associates, namely, her sister Lady Herbert (who was Catherine's chief lady of the Privy Chamber), her cousin Lady Lane, and Princess Elizabeth's future governess, Lady Tyrwhit. The issue in July 1546 of a royal proclamation forbidding any person to possess translations of the Bible apparently gave Gardiner the weapon he needed. Convinced that copies of the proscribed work would be found in their apartments, he made arrangements to take Catherine and her three ladies-in-waiting into custody. Fortunately the Queen learnt of these plans in good time. Distraught at her danger, she nevertheless perceived that her only hope of survival lay in recapturing the favour of the King. Attended by Lady Herbert and Lady Lane, she therefore paid an evening visit to his chamber, and there declared herself ready to be guided by her husband in all matters of religion. 'Not so, by St Mary . . .,' the King returned sharply, 'you are to become a doctor, Kate, to instruct us (as we take it) and not to be instructed or directed by us.' Humbly Catherine beseeched him to believe that such was not the case and, lulled by this endearing display of wifely submissiveness, Henry relented. 'And is it even so sweetheart?' he cooed, '. . . then perfect friends we are now again as ever at any time heretofore.'[60]

The narrowness of her escape was demonstrated on the following day, when a stroll with her husband and her ladies was interrupted by the arrival of Wriothsley and a detachment of guards. Unaware of the King's volte-face, the Chancellor was bent on her arrest, but he was greeted by a volley of insults from his master that compelled him to effect a hasty retreat. 'Arrant knave, beast and fool', Henry boomed at the unfortunate official, and the Catholic party's dreams of ending the reign in triumph promptly evaporated. Nevertheless, thenceforth Catherine was careful not to maintain too militant a Protestant stance, making no attempt to secure a mitigation of Anne Askew's sentence, and ceasing her attempts to convert the King to her own opinions in religion.

Under Henry, however, survival itself could be accounted a measure of success, and in this respect Catherine Parr was to fare better than many of her contemporaries. On 28 January 1547, Henry's vast frame finally succumbed to the disease that had wracked him intermittently for years, leaving his nine-year-old son by Jane Seymour as King of England, and Catherine as one of the most eligible widows in the country. The last of the four women from the court whom Henry had invited to share his throne, Catherine had, like them, discovered that elevation to so lofty an eminence brought with it perils of its own. The Crown itself might be within the grasp of mere ladies-in-waiting, but crowned heads could roll, and though it was true that the ultimate prize was on offer, the stakes were correspondingly high.

The Court of Edward and Mary

'A Flock of Noble Ladies'

Despite the precautions of Henry VIII, who had envisaged that his council would act as a coherent body and provide England with strong leadership during the minority of his son, the interlude between the old King's death and the accession of Elizabeth was marked by the intensification of faction and court intrigue, rather than by the development of responsible government. From these struggles the women of the court could not remain detached and, as court affairs became increasingly venal and embittered, the unity of the Protestant sisterhood over which Catherine Parr had presided in the closing years of Henry's reign proved unable to withstand the pressures, both of politics and personalities, that confronted them in that of his successor.

Catherine herself remained a widow for an almost indecently short time. Less than four months after the death of her husband, she secretly wed Jane Seymour's dashing but unscrupulous brother Thomas, with whom she had indeed been contemplating marriage before Henry had intervened to select her as his bride, and whom she proved unable to resist any longer. Seymour's brother, the Duke of Somerset, was now Protector of the Realm, and when news of the marriage emerged, it only served to reinforce the conviction of his imperious wife (who, as the Countess of Hertford, had been one of Catherine's principal ladies-in-waiting in former times) that she ought to take precedence over every other lady of the court. 'Shall I now give place to her who, in her former estate was but Latimer's widow, and is now fain to cast herself on a younger brother?' the Duchess was reputed to have demanded,[1] and although a re-examination of the terms of Henry VIII's will confirmed Catherine's right to precedence, the question was only settled to the Duchess's satisfaction in September 1548, when the

Queen Dowager died from complications arising from the birth of her first child.

The Duchess of Somerset was not to enjoy her supremacy at court for very long. Her husband was soon eclipsed by the rise to power of John Dudley Earl of Warwick, and in October 1551 the Duke and his wife were conveyed to the Tower. Somerset was executed the following February and his widow remained in prison for the remainder of the reign. Nevertheless, the vagaries of power were to prove more than usually unpredictable during these years, and the Duke of Northumberland (as Warwick became) depended for his on the frail existence of Edward VI. When the King died, in July 1553, the failure of Northumberland's attempt to found a puppet dynasty by proclaiming as Queen Edward's second cousin, Lady Jane Grey, resulted in yet another turn of the wheel of fortune. With the collapse of the rebellion, Edward's half-sister and rightful heir Mary ascended the throne, and Northumberland was executed.

Towards the other ringleaders of the rebellion Mary was inclined to be merciful. Although Lady Jane Grey was kept in the Tower, her father, the Duke of Suffolk, was released, and it was only in February 1554, after he had abused the Queen's trust by becoming involved in Wyatt's rebellion, that both he and his daughter were beheaded. Even so, Mary showed herself anxious not to let the memory of his treachery linger, for Katherine and Mary Grey, the younger sisters of Lady Jane, were taken into her service and throughout her reign were treated at court with every consideration.

As Mary's Catholicism formed the very essence of her existence, so it pervaded the atmosphere of her court. Visually, this was indicated by a change in fashion, for whereas the ladies of Edward VI's Protestant court had favoured sombre colours and sober styles of dress, the Queen's ladies emulated their mistress's typically Catholic fondness for ornamentation and display by affecting richly coloured garments, lavishly embellished with gold embroidery.[2] Seven masses were sung daily in the Queen's chapel, sign of a Catholic revolution within the court that Mary hoped would ultimately prevail throughout her entire kingdom, and ardent Protestants such as the Dowager Duchess of Suffolk (formerly one of Catherine Parr's ladies-in-waiting) and Lady Knollys had to flee abroad with their husbands in order to escape persecution.

The Queen's principal ladies-in-waiting not only shared the religious convictions of their mistress, but many of them had also been in

Mary's service at a time when she herself was suffering for her beliefs. Susan Clarencieux had been among those dismissed when Mary's household had been dispersed in 1533, and three years later, when the Princess was again permitted her own establishment, she had shown herself particularly anxious for Susan Clarencieux's reinstatement, assuring Cromwell that she had at all times served her 'faithfully, painfully and diligently'. Since that time she had remained in Mary's establishment, and at the Queen's accession Susan Clarencieux was appointed chief lady of the Privy Chamber and lady almoness, which meant that she was in charge of the money that Mary set aside for charitable donations. Universally known as 'Mrs Clarencieux' because of her marriage to Thomas Tonge, a herald and Clarencieux King of Arms, she was rewarded for her constancy to Mary with the grant of several manors in Kent and Essex, and she soon established herself as a person of importance at the Marian court. Mary Finch, for years custodian of Mary's jewels and keeper of her accounts, was also appointed to the Queen's Privy Chamber, while Mary Brown, a maid 'whom for her virtue I love' (as Mary had told Cromwell as long ago as 1536),[3] now became the Queen's chamberer.

Jane Dormer was another lady who was rewarded for having stuck by Mary in her days of adversity by being given a position in the new Queen's household. Jane was the product of a staunchly Catholic family with a tradition of service to Mary, for her aunts had waited on the Princess during her youth, and had furthermore resisted the attempts of Henry VIII to lure them away by offering them positions in the households of Mary's stepmothers. Jane herself had entered Mary's service during the reign of Edward VI when, as she later recalled, 'The house of this Princess was the only harbour for honourable young gentlewomen given any way to piety and devotion ... And the greatest Lords in the Kingdom were suitors to her to receive their daughters in her service.' She had since established a lasting hold on Mary's affections and remained high in favour after her accession, 'so as seldom or never would the Queen permit her absence. She slept in her bedchamber; many times with her; she read together with her our lady's office; she committed to her charge her usual wearing jewels and what else was of esteem ... At table she eat the meat that Jane Dormer carved for her.'[4]

So devoted was the Queen to Jane that she dreaded the prospect of her marriage, which would preclude her constant attendance at court. She was wont to observe that 'Jane Dormer deserved a very good husband and ... that she knew not the man worthy of her',[5] and she

even discouraged Jane from accepting a proposal from Henry
Courtenay, the principal noble in the kingdom, despite the fact that
the Lord Chancellor was highly in favour of the match. Unlike her
sister however, Mary was not so selfish as to forbid altogether the
marriage of her favourite ladies. Towards the end of Mary's reign,
Jane fell in love with a Spanish envoy, the Duke of Feria, and the
Queen gave their union her blessing.

Mary's former servants were not the only ones who had claims on
her gratitude, for she had not forgotten the way that the Marchioness
of Exeter had stood by her mother at the time of her parents' divorce.
During the years that the Marchioness had been in prison, Mary had
sent her regular gifts, and now she was released from the Tower and
restored to royal favour. The Marchioness was made a lady of the
Privy Chamber, and at Mary's coronation she was one of the four
ladies who, dressed in crimson velvet, led the procession. For the first
few months of the reign, she was one of the Queen's most intimate
associates, even on occasion sleeping with Mary in her room.

Although Mary had had frequently to rely on her own resources
during her years of adversity, she had never developed great faith in
her own judgement, and there were some who feared that as Queen,
Mary would be too easily influenced by the advice of those who
surrounded her, including her ladies-in-waiting. The Spanish ambassador, Simon Renard, considered the Queen to be highly vulnerable
to such pressures, and was particularly concerned by the way that her
ladies frequently deterred Mary from acting with what he regarded as
statesmanlike severity towards known traitors. 'The Ladies about the
Queen's person are able to obtain from her more than she ought to
grant them', he grumbled to his master, after the Queen had been
persuaded by the Marchioness of Exeter to pardon and restore to
favour the Earl of Pembroke, heavily implicated in Northumberland's conspiracy. The Marquis of Northampton, another of
Northumberland's fellow-plotters, was likewise reprieved after the
Marchioness of Exeter, Mrs Clarencieux and his first wife (whom he
had illegally divorced during the previous reign) all sued for his
pardon. 'They have told the Queen, in order to move her to pity, that
he never ceases weeping,' Renard reported in disgust, and though the
Marquis's second marriage was subsequently declared invalid and he
was obliged to separate from his new wife, he suffered no worse fate.
In 1556 Mrs Clarencieux was again instrumental in securing the
release of Lord Bray, suspected of complicity in the Dudley conspiracy of that year, while Foxe even includes a story that after a lady

of the Privy Chamber had appealed to the Queen on behalf of the arrested Protestant minister, Edwin Sandys, she agreed that he had been 'sufficiently punished' and ordered his release.[6]

However much Renard may have deplored Mary's merciful disposition, the influence of her ladies in encouraging her to indulge it cannot be accounted truly harmful since, with the exception of Suffolk, those nobles pardoned thenceforth presented little threat to her, and even the ambassador was ultimately obliged to admit that the Queen's popularity had been much enhanced by her clemency.[7] The extent to which the Queen's ladies promoted the idea that Mary should marry Philip of Spain, eldest son of Charles V, was to be of more consequence, for arguably the true explanation for the failure of Mary's reign lies in her disastrous decision to press on with the Spanish marriage.

Few of the Queen's subjects doubted that she ought to take a husband, but since it was assumed that she would conduct herself towards her chosen spouse with becoming feminine subservience, their concern that she select a partner who held the interests of England at heart was very natural. Henry Courtenay, the son of the Marchioness of Exeter, who as a child had been dispatched to the Tower to share his mother's imprisonment, and had only been released on Mary's accession, appeared to fulfil this requirement; but despite his evident suitability the Queen seems never to have seriously contemplated marriage with this effete youth. Spanish in sympathies and of Spanish blood, Mary yearned to strengthen the link between her own country and that of her mother, often her only source of support during her beleaguered past, and if many of her councillors were aghast at the notion that Mary should marry Philip, the majority of the ladies in her household were all in favour of the project. When the Spanish ambassador started cautiously to broach the subject of matrimony, Mary told him coyly that 'the ladies that were about her talked of nothing else but marriage',[8] and doubtless Philip's name had often been mentioned in the course of these discussions.

Even before her marriage, Mary's uncertainty as to the extent to which she could trust her quarrelsome and unwieldy body of councillors led her to form the habit of having secret consultations with the Spanish ambassadors, requesting the advice of Charles V on various matters of policy. Abetted by Jane Russell and Frideswide Sturley, who were both ladies of the Privy Chamber, Susan Clarencieux connived with the Queen in arranging these assignations, which only accentuated Mary's dependence on Spain, and thus paved the way for the Spanish marriage. And indeed, as negotiations for the marriage became more serious, these three ladies were active in signifying their support for the venture. A secretary at Renard's embassy was even later to maintain that Susan Clarencieux had acted as the Queen's agent while the project was still in an embryonic stage, having 'several times conferred in the house of a London alderman' with Diego de Mendoza, a representative of Philip's, who was in England to sound out the possibilities of the English alliance.[9]

The degree of truth in these assertions remains obscure, but certainly after Renard formally proposed on 10 October 1553 that Mary should marry Philip ('that she might be relieved of the pains and travails which were rather men's work than of the profession of ladies'), Mrs Clarencieux and her two companions unanimously recommended that she accept. For a fortnight Mary agonized over her decision, but on 29 October she summoned the ambassador to an audience, at which Susan Clarencieux was also present. The three of them knelt before an altar erected in the Queen's apartments, reciting together the '*Veni creator spiritus*' and there, in the presence of the sacrament, Mary vowed to wed Philip. As the triumphant ambassador rose from his knees, the affectionate regard of Susan Clarencieux convinced him that Mary's commitment had her full approval.[10]

This was soon confirmed: in the ensuing weeks, Mary busied herself in reconciling the council to the prospect of her Spanish bridegroom, and her Lady Almoness left no one in any doubt as to her feelings on the subject. 'Mrs Clarencieux has made known her decree and supports our cause to the utmost', Renard reported gleefully in early November, and with the eventual successful conclusion of the marriage negotiations he was not unmindful of the debt which he owed his three allies in the Privy Chamber. 'Your Majesty understands that His Highness, on arriving here, will have to present a few rings and other trifles to the Queen's ladies, and more substantial tokens to the three chief ones, named Clarencieux, Sturley and Russell, who have always stood firm for the match and are the Queen's most intimate confidants', he wrote to Charles V in the spring of 1554, and accordingly, 'the Queen's chief ladies' featured prominently on the list of those who were given gifts when Philip arrived in England the following July.[11] Led by their well-meaning desire to promote the Queen's happiness, the ladies had unfortunately strengthened her resolve to follow her instincts in the matter of marriage, and as such they must bear a share of responsibility for the calamities that ensued.

The projected Spanish match met with the approval of several more of the leading ladies of the court, for the Duchess of Norfolk, the Countess of Arundel and Lady Rochester were all in favour of it, and as such the French ambassador gloomily informed his master that they were 'more to be feared than their husbands in these circumstances'. Not all, however, were of the same persuasion: the Marchioness of Exeter still nourished hopes that the Queen would marry her son, and she and Courtenay joined forces to try and prevent the negotiations with Spain from coming to fruition. They approached the Earl of Pembroke and solicited his support, and together they agreed 'to persuade Parliament to speak to the Queen . . . begging her not to wed a foreigner'. It was not long before the Queen had gained a shrewd idea of the Marchioness's intrigues and she was swift to indicate her displeasure. The Marchioness of Exeter was evicted from her lodgings in the Palace, adjacent to those of the Queen, and sent with her son to sleep at Pembroke's house.[12]

Somewhat unnerved, the Marchioness deemed it prudent to abandon these underhand procedures, and when her son next wished to have a conference with the French and Venetian ambassadors, she apprised the Queen of his intentions and sought her authorization. The Queen in reply merely snapped 'that he had gone often enough without leave, and that she hoped he would behave prudently in all respects and do nothing inconsistent with his duty'. After the Marchioness had felt the royal displeasure for some days, the Queen relented, and she was permitted to re-instal herself in her apartments at the Palace, but she never again attained the same degree of intimacy with her mistress, and was never again to share the royal Bedchamber.[13]

Then, in February 1554, her son was suspected of involvement in Wyatt's rebellion, and after a short spell in prison he was encouraged to leave England for the Continent. Broken at the departure of the only surviving member of her family, his mother retired from court. She sought to maintain contact with her son by writing to him regularly, urging him to 'fly sin and evil counsel and bad company', and beseeching him, for the sake of her 'motherly heart', to preserve his health with care. Courtenay repaid this maternal concern by being no more than an indifferent correspondent, and when he did communicate with his mother, it was generally to inform her that he had no news 'save that his purse waxed light'. By the summer of 1555, Courtenay was optimistic that the Queen would permit his return, and his mother showed herself pathetically eager for their reunion. 'If wishing might take place you should be there', she assured him tremulously, and although well aware that 'my years require rest', she promised that she would return to her post in the Privy Chamber 'if my waiting can do you good'. But though she was as good as her word, the Marchioness failed to convince her mistress of the wisdom of summoning Courtenay home. In 1556 he died of a fever at Padua, leaving his desolate old mother with 'as little worldy comfort as ever woman had'.[14]

The announcement of the Queen's impending marriage had been greeted with predictable dismay by a wide cross-section of her subjects, and the discontent was such that within weeks the capital was abounding with rumours of an imminent insurrection designed to prevent the match. The Queen's ladies so disturbed their mistress by repeating to her alarmist talk they had heard from some of the gentlemen of the court that she became ill with worry, but when, at the end of January 1554, these insubstantial murmurings materialized into the threat of genuine rebellion, the Queen demonstrated that though she lacked many of the Tudor characteristics, she had her fair share of the family courage. On hearing that a band of Kentish men were marching on London under the leadership of Thomas Wyatt, Mary responded by riding in state to the Guildhall, where she made a rousing appeal to the Londoners' loyalty and then retired to Whitehall to await events. By 3 February, Wyatt had reached Southwark, and the lords of the council awoke the Queen in the early hours of the morning to plead with her to flee London while there was still time but, doubtless to the regret of the more timorous of her gentlewomen, Mary responded that she was determined to 'tarry there to see the uttermost'.

From Southwark, Wyatt marched upriver in order to cross the Thames unopposed, and then approached the city from the west, and on 7 February Mary and her ladies awaited the outcome of the encounter between the rebels and her troops. Although many of her gentlewomen had previously shared perilous experiences with their mistress, including the days when she had faced Northumberland's treason, collectively their nerves now broke under the strain. When an armed detachment of gentlemen pensioners presented themselves at the Queen's Chamber door to stand guard, the reaction of her ladies was deplorably faint-hearted, and 'some lamenting, crying and wringing their hands said, "Alas there is some great mischief toward; we shall all be destroyed this night! What a sight is this to see the Queen's chamber full of armed men; the like was never seen or heard of."' Complete bedlam erupted at the receipt of an unfounded report that the Earl of Pembroke, Commander of the royal forces, had defected to the enemy: 'There should ye have seen running and crying of ladies and gentlewomen, shutting of doors and such a shrieking and noise as it was wonderful to hear', a bemused observer of this scene was later to recall,[15] but Mary herself remained calm. 'Fall to prayer – I warrant you we shall hear better news anon', she admonished those around her, and in the event her faith was to prove justified. Wyatt surrendered without undue bloodshed, and the usual vengeance was enacted on him and his followers; if an armed uprising aimed at preventing his arrival was hardly an encouraging augury for the prospective bridegroom, in practical terms the rebellion had achieved nothing.

Although overt resistance to the marriage had been crushed, in the ensuing months Renard became increasingly apprehensive that the approaching encounter between the English and Spanish courts would be marked by hostile clashes, and he felt that the risk of friction between the rival cultures would be appreciably enlarged if the Spaniards in Philip's suite were accompanied by their womenfolk. Charles v was in full agreement as to the inadvisability of including a female contingent in his son's entourage – 'I believe even soldiers would be more likely to get on well with the English', he told his son[16] – but nevertheless, several Spanish noblewomen were permitted to accompany their husbands when Philip embarked for England in June 1554. On 18 July they landed at Southampton, and from there Philip proceeded to Winchester for the first encounter with his bride who, at thirty-eight, was more than ten years his senior. Understandably enough, Mary had selected only the more ancient of her attendants to wait on her during her first meeting with her future husband, but only minutes after having been introduced to the Queen, Philip expressed somewhat ungallant curiosity to see the remainder of her household. They were duly summoned, and as the Prince kissed each of them in turn ('so as not to break the custom of the country, which is a good one'[17]), his courtiers surveyed the assembled flower of English womanhood with a critical eye.

Their verdict on this and subsequent occasions was on the whole unfavourable. 'Those I have seen in the Palace have not struck me as being handsome,' one Spaniard was to inform a correspondent at home, 'indeed, they are downright ugly.' The comparatively short skirts worn by English ladies seemed immodest to the Spaniards, prompting comments that 'they really look quite indelicate when they are seated', while the fact that many Englishwomen excelled at horsemanship appeared almost equally brazen to Spanish eyes. The language barrier was an additional complication, for the two nationalities had great difficulty in communicating with one another, and accordingly the Spanish gentlemen huffily decided that they would not give Mary's ladies any of the presents which they had brought with them from Spain until they had devised a way of making themselves understood. Dancing was likewise problematic, for the Spaniards were naturally unfamiliar with the traditional English dances, whose steps they anyway considered graceless, asserting that they consisted only of 'ambling or trotting'. 'They are not women for whom the Spaniards need put themselves out of the way in entertaining or spending money on them, which is a very good thing for the Spaniards,' one visitor was ultimately to decide, and he added that not one of his compatriots had fallen in love with any of the court ladies. In fact, the Duke of Feria was subsequently to claim Jane Dormer as his bride, while an anecdote even exists of an attempt by Philip to flirt with Magdalen Dacre, a particularly priggish maid of honour who firmly repulsed his advances,[18] but undoubtedly the majority of Spaniards were singularly unimpressed by their hostesses.

Furthermore, as Renard had feared, the Spanish ladies who had accompanied their husbands to England only aggravated the ill-feeling between the rival nationalities at court. The Queen herself had admittedly made a particular effort to extend a warm welcome to the Duchess of Alba, the wife of the principal nobleman in Philip's suite. Seeking to break down the barriers of protocol between them, she had commanded the Duchess to sit beside her at their first meeting, an honour that did not deter the Duchess from subsequently complaining that she had received such discourteous treatment from the rest of the English that she would not go to court again. Donna Hieronima de Navarra and Donna Francisca de Cordoba likewise declared that they would not wait upon the Queen 'as there is no one to speak to them at court, these English ladies being so badly behaved', while Donna Maria de Mendoza exacerbated the Spaniards' simmering resentment at the fact that all their duties were now performed by the English household assigned to Philip, by declaring that they had 'far better go and serve the Emperor [Charles v] in war' rather than loitering where they were 'quite vagabonds . . . and of no use to anyone'.[19]

By September 1554, relations between the two sets of courtiers had deteriorated to an alarmingly hostile level, and it took the announcement that the Queen was with child to defuse the situation. The Spaniards could reflect that their sufferings at the hands of the English had not been entirely futile, and at the series of banquets and masques that were held to celebrate the Queen's quickening it was noted that a new spirit of international harmony prevailed. At Easter 1555 the Queen retired to await her confinement at Hampton Court, where a 'flock of noble ladies' now congregated to witness the birth of a Catholic heir, but as the weeks went by and the delivery seemed as far off as ever, discordant whispers began to circulate about the true nature of the Queen's condition. By the end of May the French ambassador had received intelligence from a man intimate with the midwife in charge of the case that both she and one of her colleagues, an old lady who had been with the Queen for more than twenty years (possibly Susan Clarencieux), were of the opinion that Mary was not pregnant at all. They believed that no woman in an advanced stage of pregnancy could sit as Mary did, on the floor with her knees drawn towards her. 'To content her with words more than anything else', the midwife nevertheless regularly assured the Queen that the delayed delivery was due merely to a miscalculation of the original date of conception, a fiction that the Queen's ladies were still steadfastly maintaining as late as the following July.[20]

By August Hampton Court stank in consequence of its unexpectedly prolonged occupation by the royal household, and Mary was forced to the bitter admission that she had been deluding herself. Summoning to her Mistress Frideswide Sturley, who, alone of all her ladies, had refused to acknowledge that the Queen was pregnant, Mary told her sadly, 'I see they all be flatterers, and none true to me but thou.'[21] Later that month she faced the additional mortification of witnessing the departure for home of the husband she loved, for Philip had been kept in England solely by his expectations of an heir, and when the latter had failed to materialize there was nothing further to detain him. On 29 August 1555 Mary bid her husband farewell at Greenwich, and though at the time she successfully maintained a dignified public façade, one of her ladies was later to tell the Venetian ambassador that, once safely in the privacy of her own apartments, the Queen broke down and wept.

Abandoned by her husband, rendered increasingly unpopular by the policy of religious persecution, and surrounded on all sides by treachery and intrigue, the Queen succumbed to melancholia. In May

1556, after Philip had ignored several appeals for his return, the French ambassador reported that Mary had retired to her chamber, permitting only five of her ladies to see her, and that she passed her sleepless nights crying and writing letters imploring her husband to join her. An additional source of misery for the Queen was the knowledge that her failure to produce an heir had made it more than ever likely that her successor would be her half-sister Elizabeth, the sincerity of whose conversion to Catholicism she justifiably doubted, particularly since she noted that the Princess 'had not a single servant or maid of honour who was not a heretic'.[22]

Mary's isolation was scarcely alleviated by the arrival of Philip in March 1557. He came not as a loving husband, but to coerce his wife into supporting him in his war against France and the papacy, and Mary's submission to his wishes resulted in England losing Calais to the French in January 1558. Having accomplished his mission, Philip had left England the previous July, and if Mary had been in part consoled for his departure by the renewed belief that she was pregnant, her symptoms were nothing more than the early signs of the disease that was ultimately to kill her. By May 1558, the Queen was obliged to admit that her hopes had been illusory, and with dismal practicality her thoughts turned from childbirth to the contemplation of her own end.

Even throughout her final illness the Queen still retained her consideration for those in her service, sending Jane Dormer from Hampton Court to London in a litter on hearing that she was unwell, and lamenting that she would not live to see Jane's wedding to her Spanish aristocrat. She was still occasionally tormented by the thought of her failures as a ruler, which prompted her famous remark to Susan Clarencieux that 'When I am dead and opened you shall find Calais lying in my heart', but she was at least consoled by what she believed to be visions of a better world to come. As she lay dying, the Queen comforted her ladies by telling them 'What good dreams she had, seeing many little children like angels playing before . . . giving her more than earthly comfort.'[23]

Nevertheless, she could not as yet completely shrug off her wordly responsibilities. Before Mary finally died, in the early hours of 17 November 1558, she dispatched Jane Dormer to Elizabeth at Hatfield, bearing 'the rich and precious jewels that were in her custody', and three final requests to her sister. She begged her to look after her ladies, to pay her debts, and, above all, 'to uphold and continue the Catholic religion',[24] a commission which the poor

Queen no doubt realized that Elizabeth would not fulfil. She bequeathed to her sister a nation religiously and politically divided, reinforced only in its conviction of feminine unfitness to rule. It was a poisoned chalice, on the contents of which Elizabeth was to thrive.

The Court of Elizabeth I

'But One Mistress'

As Elizabeth I well understood, the court had somehow to encapsulate the majesty and mystique of the monarchy itself. In order to provide a setting worthy of a great Queen, its visual impact must be stunning, and the presence at court of large numbers of ladies-in-waiting was an indispensable element in the scenario. Nevertheless, these ladies were supposed to act as mere foils to the Queen, forming the decorative backdrop against which the imposing figure of the Sovereign herself stood out in sharp relief, and if the role of the ladies-in-waiting may be compared to that of a chorus line in a big-budget musical, Elizabeth was very much the star of the show. The merest hint that the attractions of her ladies in any way exceeded her own was enough to set the Queen aflame, and it was no doubt to guard against unfavourable comparisons that Elizabeth required her maids of honour to wear dresses of white and silver, insipid colours that were designed to make her own bejewelled ensembles appear to best effect. Even in her private life she did not wish to be outdone by her ladies, begrudging them the happiness they attained through their husbands and families, and she would have been well pleased if the majority of her attendants had rendered homage to her own virgin state by remaining celibate themselves. Unfortunately, by no means all of them were prepared thus to sublimate their individuality in order to magnify the cult of Gloriana, and though there was no lady at the Elizabethan court capable of eclipsing the remarkable woman at its centre, there were plenty who, contrary to the Queen's wishes, would make their own mark on it.

By the time that Elizabeth ascended the throne in 1558, the structure of the royal household had become more elaborate, so that within the court hierarchy, the ladies of the Privy Chamber were now sandwiched between their grander colleagues, the ladies of the Bedchamber, and a substratum of ladies of the Presence Chamber. These last had no specific duties, and were expected simply to be in attendance on the Queen when she wished to be seen at her most impressive, as when she received the visit of a foreign ambassador or a parliamentary delegation. On more informal occasions, the six unmarried maids of honour formed the Queen's train, accompanying her on her morning walks and going with her to church. They also regularly danced before their mistress, for whose benefit they did 'daily trip the measure in the council chamber'.[1]

When selecting her household at the beginning of the reign, Elizabeth, like Mary before her, rewarded those who had served her loyally in the difficult years before her accession. Her former governess and confidante, Kat Ashley, became chief gentlewoman of the Privy Chamber, and on her death in 1565 she was succeeded by Blanche Parry, another old servant of the Queen who had actually rocked her cradle in her infancy. The Queen was also acutely conscious of family connections, and liked to give her relatives positions in the household. Thus, at Elizabeth's accession, Lady Knollys, daughter of Anne Boleyn's sister Mary, became a lady of the Privy Chamber, while her nieces, Katherine and Philadelphia Carey, were appointed maids of honour. For those who had no such claims on the Queen's favour, obtaining a position at court was more difficult, and competition for the remaining places was fierce. When in 1597 it was rumoured that Lady Leighton was contemplating resigning her position in the Bedchamber, the excitement was intense, and certainly there was no shortage of contenders eager to take her place. 'Here is already a whole dozen of ladies that would succeed her . . .' Rowland White informed Sir Robert Sidney, 'But it is thought that either my Lady Hoby, my Lady Borow or my Lady Thomas Howard will have it.' In such fiercely-disputed contests, it did not do to trust to luck alone, and those who desired preferment at court had to devote all their energies to pursuit of this goal. In 1583 it required a sustained effort on the part of Arthur Throckmorton to secure his sister Bess a place about the Queen, and it was only after he had presented Elizabeth with a jewel worth £15, and enlisted the support of Ladies Heneage and Stafford, that he finally learnt that his tactics had paid off and that Bess was to be enrolled as a lady of the Privy Chamber.[2]

The routine of the court revolved around elaborate ceremonial, much of which involved the Queen's ladies-in-waiting. Elizabeth dined in public only on occasional feast days, but even when she ate alone, her ladies served her meals with the maximum formality. A foreign visitor at the English court noted the procedure with some astonishment, reporting that after the Queen's table had been laid in an outer chamber, one of her ladies appeared, and having 'prostrated herself three times in the most graceful manner, [she] approached the table and rubbed the plates with bread and salt with as much awe as if the Queen had been present'. Each dish was then sampled as a precaution against poisoning, and then 'a number of unmarried ladies appeared, who, with particular solemnity, lifted the meat off the table and conveyed it into the Queen's inner and more private chamber'.[3]

In return for performing such services, the ladies-in-waiting were given modest salaries: the maids of honour were paid £40 a year, while the ladies of the Privy Chamber seem to have done rather less well, for at the beginning of the reign one of their number received a stipend of just under £34. In addition, while they were at court, the ladies were maintained at royal expense, a commitment that the Crown found increasingly burdensome at a time of rising prices. Pilfering and cheating were almost impossible to control in so large an institution as the court, and like most departments there, the cost of feeding the Queen's gentlewomen far exceeded estimated expenditure. In 1576, for example, it was calculated that £495 would suffice to feed the ladies of the Privy Chamber, but the actual cost was nearly £680, and an investigation into the accounts for the ladies of the Bedchamber revealed a similar discrepancy.[4]

Doubtless, however, many of the Queen's ladies felt that their services were cheaply bought, for Elizabeth could be an exacting mistress, and a position at court was no sinecure. No lady in royal service could absent herself from court without the Queen's permission, which was often very difficult to obtain, for Elizabeth had a possessive nature and did not like to be parted from her favourite associates. In 1575, the Earl of Leicester reported that Lady Cobham wished to visit her husband at his country home 'to rest her weary bones awhile, if she could get leave', but he evidently considered it most unlikely that she would succeed in persuading the Queen to let her go. Besides being time-consuming, attendance on the Queen could be nerve-racking in the extreme, for Elizabeth's moods were subject to the vagaries of affairs of State, and at times of political crisis her temper could be alarmingly erratic. When in 1575 the Queen was distracted by worries relating to the war in the Netherlands, she even beat 'one or two of her ladies-in-waiting', and though at other times she generally confined herself to purely verbal assaults on her ladies, her sarcastic tongue and withering wit still combined to render her an object of terror to her apprehensive attendants. Throughout the late 1590s, the prolonged strain of receiving incessant bad news from her commanders in Ireland made her particularly disagreeable, and her irritable criticism of even the minor shortcomings of her maids of honour frequently reduced them to tears, making them 'cry and bewail in piteous sort'.[5] Though at times the most kindly and gracious of mistresses, under pressure the Queen could be transformed into the worst sort of domestic tyrant.

As Elizabeth's ladies were expected to serve their mistress regardless of whether she was in sickness or in health, attendance on the Queen could entail a genuine risk to their well-being. In 1562, there was an epidemic of smallpox at court, and in October the Queen herself succumbed. 'The Duchess of Suffolk had it first, the Countess of Bedford died of it, and divers ladies of forty and forty-five have died. This disease is best acquainted by duchesses, marchionesses and countesses, so it is no marvel that at last the Queen should have it,' the English ambassador in Paris reasoned on hearing of the news. The Queen was to emerge from the attack comparatively unscathed, but Lady Mary Sidney, who contracted the disease not (as the ambassador would doubtless have assumed) by virtue of her rank, but because she fulfilled her duties as a lady of the Bedchamber and nursed the Queen through the illness, was to fare less well, and never fully recovered her health. She was left horribly disfigured, and her husband, Sir Henry Sidney, who had been absent when she had been struck down, was appalled at the alteration which the ravages of the disease had effected in her looks. 'I left her a full fair lady, in mine eye at least the fairest,' he was later to recall, 'and when I returned I found her as foul a lady as the smallpox could make her; which she did take by continual attendance of Her Majesty's most precious person, sick of the same disease.' Thenceforth Lady Mary lived largely withdrawn from society, but upon her occasional returns to court she was to discover that no great premium was attached to her self-sacrifice: when she paid a visit to Hampton Court in the autumn of 1578, she found that, despite the fact that as a semi-invalid she could rarely leave her bed, she and her husband had been only allotted one room in which to sleep and live, which was also expected to serve as Sir Henry's office for the conduct of State affairs. Attempts to secure rather more extensive accommodation proved unsuccessful.[6]

If Lady Mary was a rather more deserving case than most, she was by no means alone in having to endure cramped and uncomfortable quarters while at court. At Windsor, the apartments of the maids of honour were so primitive that they were obliged to ask 'to have their chamber ceiled, and the partition that is of boards there to be made higher, for that the servants look over', while the accommodation provided for the Queen's ladies when the court was entertained at country houses during its summer progresses could be of an even more makeshift nature. In 1574, the Queen was scheduled to visit the Arch-bishop of Canterbury at Croydon Palace, but when her Usher of the Black Rod was sent ahead to make the necessary preparations, he was appalled to discover what limited space was available. 'For my Lady Carewe there is no place with a chimney for her,' he reported to court in some trepidation, concluding that there was no alternative 'but that she must lay abroad by Mistress Parry and the Privy Chamber'. Lord Treasurer Burghley's house at Theobald's was particularly dreaded by courtiers who liked their creature comforts, and there all the gentlewomen of the Privy Chamber were obliged to sleep with their servants 'in a garret, two rooms', while only one of the rooms allotted to the ladies of the Bedchamber had a fireplace in it.[7]

Nor were conditions at court merely uncomfortable; generally they were squalid as well. Even when not on progress, the royal household was never sedentary for long, for in an age of virtually non-existent sanitation, a palace could only be occupied for a few weeks before it became so smelly as to be almost uninhabitable, and then the court had to move to another of the royal residences while their last resting place was given a good airing. A contemporary of the Queen's godson, Sir John Harington, encouraged him to persist in his attempts to design a water closet, as he felt it would be of particular use to the Queen 'in her Palace of Greenwich and other stately houses that are oft annoyed with such savours as where many mouths are fed can hardly be avoided'.[8] Habitual exposure to these disagreeable odours must have somewhat blunted the Elizabethans' sensitivity about such matters, but they cannot have been inured to them altogether.

Life at court was neither very luxurious nor very refined, and it was the allure of the Queen herself, rather than the comfortable existence of those that surrounded her, that invested it with its glamour. The majority of those who had access to the court regarded the favour of the Queen as completely central to their existence, and their devotion to her transcended considerations of mere expediency, and was founded on a genuine reverence for her person. Those who forfeited her goodwill were filled with a profound sense of personal depriva-tion, in which practical concern for the future was often a purely secondary consideration. 'Who, wanting the Prince's favour, may count himself to live in any realm?' Lord John Grey demanded when his niece Katherine fell into disgrace, and few of his contemporaries would have found such sentiments extravagant. When another of his nieces, Lady Mary Grey, incurred the Queen's displeasure, she was to express herself even more poignantly than her uncle. 'The Prince's favour is not so soon gotten again,' she lamented, 'and I assure you to be without it is such a grief to any true subject as no torment can be greater, as I most woeful wretch, have too well tried, desiring rather death than to be any longer without so great a jewel as Her Majesty's favour should be to me'.[9] Language such as this cannot be dismissed as mere hyperbole, and though it is difficult for us nowadays to fathom the emotional intensity of the link that bound Elizabeth's subjects to their Sovereign, it is only in this context that one can understand why they found it so hard to resist the siren-song of her court.

The extent of the influence wielded in the court by Elizabeth's ladies remains debatable, and certainly at the time some people were inclined to dismiss it as negligible. Sir Walter Ralegh, for example, maintained that 'like witches they could do hurt but could do no good', but nevertheless it was understood by the majority of courtiers that if a lady-in-waiting could be persuaded to drop a judicious word on their behalf to the Queen, it could oil the wheels of patronage around which society revolved, and open up the path to preferment. The Countess of Warwick, a lady of the Bedchamber high in the Queen's favour, was endlessly pestered by relatives and friends to extract from Elizabeth concessions in their interest, and she did her best to satisfy them. In response, for instance, to the appeals of Rowland White, agent to her nephew Sir Robert Sidney, she repeatedly begged the Queen to recall Sir Robert from his post as Governor of Flushing so that he could transact important business in England; and she promised too that she would do her best to persuade Elizabeth to create her nephew a peer.[10]

Rowland Vaughn, a relative of Blanche Parry's, subsequently reminisced how 'in little lay matters' the Countess of Warwick, Lady Scudamore and Blanche herself 'would steal opportunity to serve some friends turns', but in fact the influence of the Queen's ladies could extend into questions of ecclesiastical preferment as well. The Queen was no supporter of the Puritan element within the Anglican Church, but several of her ladies were known to be their partisans:

Lady Knollys, the Queen's first cousin, who had become a lady of her Privy Chamber on her accession, had followed her husband into exile during the Marian persecution, as had Lady Stafford, 'a great lady of honour about the Queen', while the Countess of Warwick was also believed to favour the reformers. Elizabeth did not share their sympathies, but the chronic shortage of able clergymen meant that she could not be too fussy about Church appointments, and in the circumstances she was occasionally inclined to listen to the recommendations of her ladies in such matters. In July 1582, a Dr Mathew wrote to the Countess of Warwick asking her to assist him to obtain the Deanery of Durham by making 'favourable speeches' on his behalf to the Queen, and he was suitably grateful for her intervention when he was subsequently appointed. In 1569 the Archbishop of Canterbury, Matthew Parker, was trying to obtain a prebend for the Master of Benet College, and he wrote to Lady Stafford requesting that she 'speak some good word' on the subject to the Queen: although it remains unclear whether any consequent appeal from Lady Stafford had a successful outcome, the fact that the highest dignitary in the Church should approach one of the Queen's ladies-in-waiting for assistance of this kind indicates how widespread the assumption was that they were important people, and well worth cultivating.[11]

Those who wished to approach the Queen personally, rather than to use her ladies as intermediaries, still found it worthwhile to sound them out beforehand to discover whether Elizabeth was in an amenable mood, and even so seasoned a favourite as the Earl of Leicester welcomed the assistance of his 'best friend in the Privy Chamber', Blanche Parry, who encouraged him in his courtship of the Queen by informing him of propitious moments at which to press his suit. Less privileged courtiers, who did not enjoy right of access to the Queen, were grateful merely for the opportunity of having an interview with her, and frequently their best hopes of obtaining one lay in persuading a lady-in-waiting to ask Elizabeth to grant them an audience. Mary Radcliffe, a kindly spinster who spent all her adult life in royal service, graduating from maid of honour to lady of the Privy Chamber, frequently obliged courtiers with favours of this sort, and in November 1593 Anthony Standen informed Anthony Bacon that since she had promised 'to procure him private speech with Her Majesty', he was spending all his time hovering in the public gallery at court, waiting for the summons.[12]

In return for such good deeds, the ladies could expect some token

of recognition from grateful courtiers. After Mary Radcliffe had performed a kind office for the young Earl of Rutland, he was told by a
more experienced courtier that she was 'worthy to be presented with
something', and when the Queen was finally moved to grant Sir
Robert Sidney leave from his post at Flushing, Rowland White told
his master that the Countess of Warwick was 'among those who look
for thanks and it is due'. Nor were such offerings undeserved: Elizabeth disliked excessive 'importunity and expostulation', and could be
very irritable when pestered with unwelcome applications, and by no
means all of her ladies-in-waiting considered it worth their while to
jeopardize their relationship with their mistress by exerting themselves on behalf of others. In February 1598, Rowland White
grumbled to Sir Robert Sidney that though another of his aunts, the
Countess of Huntingdon, was 'with Her Majesty twice a day very
private', she was failing to use the opportunity to put in a good word
for her family and friends.[13]

Undoubtedly, therefore, the ladies deserved some reward for their
efforts, but the situation was nevertheless open to abuse, and as
always, the line between courtesy and corruption could be alarmingly
slender. A Government official was later to recall that there were
some at court who capitalized on their favour with Elizabeth by
demanding payment from petitioners whose interests they served,
'taking bribes for such suits as [the Queen] bestowed freely'; and
such immoral trafficking was by no means confined to men alone. In
1599, Rowland White reported that a courtier wished the Queen to
sell him Clarendon Park, and had offered '1,000 crowns to a lady to
move it', while Edward Wootton pressed £1,000 on a lady of the
court in hopes that she would encourage the Earl of Essex in his
efforts to obtain him a peerage.[14]

There was however no guarantee that such irregular payments
would prove to be sound investments, for though the Queen took into
account the arguments of her ladies when distributing patronage and
granting rewards, the final decision in these matters was very much
her own. She was particularly implacable about granting new titles,
believing that an extensive creation of peers could only debase the
nobility as a whole, and when making official appointments she paid
little attention to the advice of outsiders, preferring to rely on her
own judgement. In 1572 George Carew was appalled to find that the
Queen had appointed him ambassador to France, but although he
made 'great labours to the contrary by her ladies of the Privy Chamber', Sir Thomas Smith laconically informed Sir Francis Walsingham

in Paris that he might confidently await his arrival. In March 1597, Lady Scudamore presented Elizabeth with a letter from Sir Robert Sidney, soliciting for the position of Warden of the Cinque Ports, but the Queen's only response was to read it through derisively, 'with no other comment than two or three "pughs!"' and the place was subsequently conferred on Lord Cobham.[15]

If the influence of the Queen's ladies on the disposal of patronage was limited, it was virtually non-existent in matters that encroached on the welfare of the State, concerns which Elizabeth regarded as completely beyond her ladies' sphere. In September 1599 Elizabeth placed under house arrest her one-time favourite, the Earl of Essex, after the latter had relinquished his command of the army in Ireland and returned to England without her permission, and she remained quite unmoved by appeals from the ladies of the court (with whom Essex was something of a darling) that she relent. The Queen's cousin, Lady Scrope, a lady of the Bedchamber who had been in royal service since her youth, braved Elizabeth's wrath by donning mourning weeds for the outcast and pleading in the young man's favour, saying 'much that few would venture to say but herself', but Essex's position in no way improved. The Earl's sister, the dark-eyed beauty Penelope, Lady Rich, was anxious to obtain permission to visit her brother, and attempted to mollify the Queen by showering her with costly gifts but, as Rowland White reported to Robert Sidney, 'Her letters are read, her presents received, but no leave granted'.[16]

When Lady Rich abandoned this soft-sell for a rather more forceful approach, she soon found herself in trouble, for Elizabeth reacted fiercely when she wrote a letter begging her to grant the Earl an audience, as only from the Queen would he receive a fairer hearing than he could 'expect of partial judges, or those combined enemies that labour on false grounds to build his ruin'. The implication that Essex's downfall had come about through the intrigues of his rivals at court rather than through his own folly infuriated the Queen, and she was all the more offended when printed copies of the letter were circulated round the capital. Lady Rich was summoned before the council 'to answer and interpret her riddles' and soundly rebuked, and in June 1600, when Essex was called before a panel of judges to be censured for his conduct, Francis Bacon referred to his sister's letter as 'insolent, saucy, malapert . . . an aggravation of the offence'.[17] Lady Rich would have done well to remember that the Queen was determined to have at court 'but one mistress and no master', and that any lady who sought to tamper with the royal prerogative did so at her peril.

While the Queen did not discuss affairs of State with her waiting women, she relied on her discussions with them to keep her abreast of events within the court, permitting her to display a familiarity with the movements of her courtiers which they at times found most disconcerting. On the whole, of course, her ladies' chatter consisted of little more than idle gossip, but occasionally Elizabeth gleaned from it items of real interest. In the summer of 1569, it was the babbling of her ladies that first alerted Elizabeth to the fact that the Earl of Leicester was encouraging the Duke of Norfolk to marry the captive Queen of Scots, and it was this that enabled her to confront Leicester and extract from him the particulars of a potentially dangerous intrigue.

It was not only the Queen, however, who found her ladies a useful source of information. As they were so regularly in the company of their mistress, and were frequently in attendance when she held audiences in the Presence Chamber, they were in some respects closer to the centre of affairs than many of the gentlemen of the court, and at least one foreign diplomat was convinced that, if exploited with care, the Queen's ladies could prove to be a valuable source of intelligence. Baron Breumer, representative in England of the Austrian Archduke Charles, went so far as to commission François Borth, a young man 'on very friendly terms with all the ladies of the Bedchamber', to report to him anything of interest that he gathered in his conversations with them.[18] Too implicit a reliance on hearsay emanating from the Bedchamber nevertheless had its dangers, for on one occasion the Queen took advantage of the situation to feed the envoy false information. In 1559 she was being wooed in proxy by the Habsburg Archduke Charles, the candidate for her hand favoured by both the Spanish and Imperial courts, and while Elizabeth was loth to accept him as a husband, she was anxious that he remain in pursuit. She realized however that his interest would only be sustained if he believed himself to have a good chance of winning her and so, to bolster the morale of the Archduke's agents in England, she determined to employ Lady Mary Sidney as her unofficial emissary.

At first sight Lady Mary might seem a somewhat curious choice of decoy. She was the sister of Lord Robert Dudley (later the Earl of Leicester), who, at this early stage of the reign, had so far overcome the handicap of being a married man as to establish himself as a principal favourite of the Queen. If Elizabeth took a husband, it would almost inevitably have had an adverse effect upon Dudley's position at court, and hence Lady Mary might have considered the

Habsburg match to be against the interests of her family. In fact, however, like the majority of loyal subjects at the time, Lady Mary regarded it as both necessary and desirable that the Queen acquired herself a consort, and proved only too willing to promote the Archduke's cause. She was therefore delighted when, in early September 1559, the Queen summoned her and asked her to give private assurances to the Imperial and Spanish ambassadors, to the effect that if they pressed their suit in earnest, they would have every hope of success. Lady Mary hastened to carry out her mission, telling the diplomats that they must persevere even if initially the Queen seemed unreceptive to their proposals, 'as it is the custom of ladies here not to give their consent in such matters until they are teased into it', and in her enthusiasm, she even exceeded her instructions by admitting that she had approached them not upon her own initiative, but at the specific behest of the Queen. Joyously the Spanish ambassador noted that his master would have to reward Lady Mary well, 'Better than he does me',[19] while his colleague lost no time in broaching the subject of marriage with Elizabeth. To his surprise, however, she responded only tepidly, and in the ensuing weeks she resolutely declined to commit herself.

Anxious to clarify the position, on 13 November the Spanish ambassador told Elizabeth bluntly that he had only persisted with the Archduke's suit because 'some of the principal persons of the court had assured him that she would marry him'. Imperturbably, the Queen replied that although his informants had no doubt acted with the best intentions, these communications had been made without her permission. On learning of this bland disclaimer, Lady Mary was justifiably resentful, realizing that she had been duped into making assurances which her mistress had no intention of fulfilling. Excitably she told the ambassadors, 'That if perchance the Queen should bring up this subject, she would speak to her in plain English . . . That she was prepared to remind her royal Majesty of all that she had been commanded to tell us,' but it is highly unlikely that Elizabeth was ever so unguarded as to refer to the incident in Lady Mary's presence, and the latter would have known better than to initiate a discussion of the matter herself.[20]

The Queen's conviction that her marriage was not an issue in which lesser mortals should meddle made it indeed a topic not to be embarked upon lightly. Admittedly, in August 1559, the Queen's old governess, Kat Ashley, had thrown herself at her Sovereign's feet and passionately implored her to take a husband, claiming that this alone

could stop the malicious gossip that had been prompted by Elizabeth's evident affection for the married Lord Robert Dudley, and the
Queen had reacted remarkably mildly. While insisting that there was
no impropriety in her relationship with Dudley, she had acknowledged 'That these were the outpourings of a good heart and true
fidelity', and although she had ignored Mrs Ashley's advice to marry,
the outburst had reminded her of the vulnerability of one in her
position to any sort of scandal.[21] No doubt she recalled Mistress
Ashley's words in September 1560, when Dudley's wife Amy was
found dead in mysterious circumstances, and it helped her to accept
that although he was now free, it would be unthinkable for her to
marry a man whom some people believed to be responsible for his first
wife's untimely end. Kat Ashley, however, occupied a unique place in
the Queen's affections, having brought her up since childhood and
shared her tribulations under Edward and Mary, and as such she
could risk speaking to her former charge a good deal more plainly
than any other lady of the court. After her death in 1565, none of
them would be able to venture such frank opinions with impunity,
even when Elizabeth abandoned her normal practice and consulted
them as to the advisability of marrying.

Despite the onset of middle age, the Queen continued to regard her
availability as one of her main diplomatic assets, and with the
opening of the 1570s she acquired a new suitor in the person of the
King of France's younger brother, Henry, Duke of Anjou, a staunchly
Catholic bisexual nearly half her age. Elizabeth was nevertheless assured by her ambassadors that he was a personable young man, and
since an alliance with France was too valuable to be wantonly thrown
away, negotiations had reached a serious stage by February 1571. As
always, however, the prospect of commitment made the Queen
uneasy, and she sought reassurance by unburdening herself to Ladies
Cobham and Clinton, two of her ladies of the Bedchamber 'in whom',
as she claimed, 'she trusted more than all others'. Telling them that
she knew that objections had been voiced to her marriage with Anjou
on the grounds of the difference in their ages, she asked for their
candid assessment of the chances of it succeeding. Lady Clinton knew
better than to take her mistress literally: warmly endorsing the marriage project, she 'strongly praised' the qualities of Monsieur, and
asserted that his lack of maturity was of no consequence, but Lady
Cobham was less tactful. She opined that in general the happiest
marriages were those in which each party was roughly the same age,
'but that here there was a great inequality'. She was soundly snubbed

for her pains. The Queen interposed irritably (and inaccurately) that 'There are but ten years between us',[22] and although the negotiations for a marriage to Anjou were abandoned early in the following year, it was his religious fervour rather than his age which presented the main stumbling block to their successful conclusion. Elizabeth was so far from taking to heart Lady Cobham's unpalatable advice that she willingly accepted the suggestion of Anjou's mother, Catherine de Medici, that he be replaced as a suitor by his still more youthful brother, the Duke of Alençon, who would be altogether more accommodating in the matter of religion. Even on the rare occasions when the Queen affected to take her ladies into her confidence on the question of her marriage, she expected them to reinforce her own line of thinking rather than to express an original viewpoint.

Alençon was to remain an aspirant to the Queen's hand for over a decade, and after some years the pace of an initially perfunctory courtship perceptibly quickened and brought him impressively close to his goal. Having initially wooed Elizabeth from afar, in August 1579 the Duke paid a brief visit to England so that he could press his suit in person, and the Queen was so captivated that she would have almost certainly accepted him had it not been for the lack of enthusiasm of her council for the project. It did not take long, however, for her natural caution to reassert itself, and after a few months it seemed that, while still fully aware of the importance of maintaining the friendship of the French, she no longer truly desired to cement the alliance by encumbering herself with a consort.

It was therefore all the more astonishing that when Alençon visited England for a second time in the autumn of 1581, on 24 November the Queen crowned his visit by announcing to a thunderstruck group of attendants that she intended to marry him. On this occasion, so the chronicler tells us, the intervention of her ladies was decisive. When she retired to bed, 'they lamented and bewailed and did so terrify and vex her mind that she spent the night in doubts and cares without sleep', and the following morning she sent for Alençon to tell him that she had been forced to reconsider and that, for the moment at least, marriage was impossible.[23] Yet one may justifiably doubt whether it was really the hysterical wailings of her waiting women that persuaded the Queen to alter course: the obvious reluctance of her council to endorse the Alençon match two years earlier had already convinced her that the majority of her subjects would prefer her to die single than see her wedded to a French Prince, and in the ensuing interval her own ardour for her youthful suitor had cooled. More plausibly, she had accepted Alençon in the knowledge that she could count on vociferous opposition from her entourage, which would enable her to claim that though she was still eager to marry him, pressure of public opinion had forced her to defer her plans. By the end of 1581, her apparent interest in Alençon was nothing more than a diplomatic exercise designed to sustain the alliance with France, but by this latest manoeuvre the Queen succeeded in convincing the French that it was otherwise. Only when Elizabeth chose were her ladies permitted to involve themselves in her marital affairs, and then she invariably ensured that it was upon her own terms and operating to her own advantage.

If the Queen declined to solve the question of who should succeed her by marrying and bearing children, she had no wish to see any possible claimant to the throne complicate the problem by doing exactly that themselves. As she well knew, any heir-apparent formed a natural focus for rebellion, particularly if their claim had been strengthened by a judicious marriage, and hence it was understood that all those who stood in the line of succession could only marry if they obtained beforehand the express sanction of the Queen. There was no one to whom this should have been more clear than the Queen's first cousin, Margaret, Countess of Lennox. The daughter, by her second marriage, of Henry VIII's elder sister, Queen Margaret of Scotland, the Countess was eighteen years older than Elizabeth, and during her youth at the Henrician court she had twice been arrested after having embarked upon unauthorized love affairs. In July 1544 she had married, with the King's approval, the Earl of Lennox, but though this had removed her from the sphere of romantic temptation it had also furnished her with two sons, whose claims to the throne she would subsequently do all in her power to further, and it was this that was to bring her into conflict with Queen Elizabeth.

On her accession Elizabeth had appeared to be on fairly good terms with her cousin, but she had soon discovered that the Countess of Lennox was intriguing with various Scottish nobles in hopes of bringing about a marriage between the widowed Mary Queen of Scots and her son, Henry Lord Darnley. Mary was not only a rich prize in herself, but also another of Elizabeth's potential successors and by this dynastic marriage Darnley's claim to the English throne would be merged with hers and (so Lady Lennox reasoned) reinforced. Elizabeth, however, had no intention of letting the marriage take place. In November 1561 the Countess of Lennox was placed under house arrest and her husband was imprisoned in the Tower, and though no charges could be proved against either of them, they were kept under restraint for over a year. Once released however, they quickly re-established themselves in royal favour, and in July 1563 it was noted that the Lennoxes were 'continual courtiers and much made of'.[24]

Nevertheless, her narrow escape had failed to make the Countess any more prudent: her ambitions on behalf of her son, although perforce in temporary hibernation, were to be resurrected at the first opportunity. In the autumn of 1564 Sir James Melville arrived in England on an embassy from Scotland, having received secret instructions to confer privately with Lady Lennox about the possibility of a marriage between Darnley and the Scottish Queen. The Countess naturally promised to do all in her power to further the project, and when Mary then formally requested of Elizabeth that Darnley should be permitted to visit her in Scotland, his mother apparently succeeded in persuading the Queen that no harm would ensue from the meeting, for in February 1565 Darnley was allowed to leave for the North. To Elizabeth's fury, however, Mary promptly fell madly in love with her guest, and by June 1565 it was clear that she and Darnley were set on marriage. Enraged at being duped, Elizabeth retaliated by sending Lady Lennox to the Tower, and there she remained for the next eighteen months. During that time the Countess could at least console herself that she had sacrificed herself for the sake of her son, but in early February 1567, this premise was cruelly shattered when news arrived that Darnley had been murdered, possibly with the connivance of his wife. Elizabeth showed compassion by freeing her prisoner immediately, but Lady Lennox was left with the reflection that years of sustained scheming to exalt the destiny of herself and her son had wrought nothing but tragedy for them both. Once again Elizabeth had triumphed, if in an unforeseen way.

Even so grim a lesson could not induce the Countess of Lennox to forbear from indulging in one final intrigue, with consequences that one of her experience might have been expected to foresee. In October 1574 Lady Lennox interrupted a journey to Yorkshire to stay at Rufford, the Huntingdonshire house of her old friend the Countess of Shrewsbury. There, as the two matrons had doubtless planned all along, Lady Lennox's son fell in love with the Countess of Shrewsbury's daughter, and their mothers wasted no time in exploiting this favourable development. Lady Lennox, whose finances were by no means as impressive as her lineage, was allured by the rich dowry that Elizabeth Cavendish would bring to her son, while the Countess of

Shrewsbury (better known as Bess of Hardwick) was gambling on a rather higher prize.

Already thrice-widowed, the Countess of Shrewsbury had risen from comparatively obscure origins to become, in her own right, one of the richest women in England, and marriage and re-marriage had been the instrument whereby she had consolidated her fortune. Having emerged from her second marriage as a considerable landowner in Derbyshire, she had been the principal benefactress of her third husband's will (much to the fury of all his other relations) and before accepting the proposal of the wealthy and pedigreed Earl of Shrewsbury she had demanded that he allied her prospective step-children with two of her offspring by a previous marriage, thereby forging a compact and affluent family unit. Pecuniary considerations were not, however, uppermost in prompting her to bestow another of her daughters on the impoverished Lord Charles Stuart, for it was rather the glittering prospect that he, or his child, might one day inherit the throne that inspired her.

The young couple were rushed to the altar almost indecently soon after their first meeting, with neither Countess running the risk of enabling the Queen to forbid a match so mutually advantageous by bothering to inform her of it beforehand. Predictably, however, Elizabeth was transfixed with rage when she learnt of this summary disposal of her near relative, and on 17 November 1574 all protagonists in the affair were summoned to London to explain themselves. Clearly unwilling to reach her destination, Lady Lennox travelled southward slowly, insisting all the while that the union had been the outcome of nothing more sinister than young love. 'Touching the marriage,' she wrote to the Earl of Leicester, 'other dealing or longer practice was there none, but the sudden affection of my son,'[25] but the Queen was not impressed. Having ordered the Earl of Huntingdon to mount an investigation into the circumstances of the marriage, she dispatched Lady Lennox to the Tower on 27 December, and there she remained until the Queen's anger had subsided some months later.

After her release the Countess was prone to bewail her ill-fortune for having so often been in trouble on account of mere 'love matters',[26] but her self-pity had little justification, for she had more reason than anyone else at the Elizabethan court to know that love and marriage, power and politics, were too interdependent to be satisfactorily disentangled. As for the Countess of Shrewsbury, her husband (whom she had not even deigned to apprise of the transaction in advance) assured the Queen that his wife had already made innumerable unsuccessful attempts to procure a suitable husband for her daughter and had simply taken advantage of this unexpected opportunity, 'without having therein any other intent or respect than with reverend duty towards Your Majesty she ought',[27] but it is highly unlikely that she had acted with the total lack of premeditation that her husband suggested. The full extent of her aspirations was exposed by her behaviour towards Arbella Stuart, the only child that her daughter managed to produce before Lord Charles's early death. After her flight to England in 1568 Mary Queen of Scots spent some time in the custody of the Earl of Shrewsbury, and on one occasion the Countess of Shrewsbury allegedly informed Mary that Arbella's right to the throne was superior to her own. After the question had been settled by Mary's execution, she commanded the child's cousins to curtsey whenever they met Arbella, and she subsequently had the temerity to appeal to Elizabeth to grant Arbella a substantial allowance, so that she could be maintained 'as is fit for her calling'. Although she succeeded in extracting only £200 a year from that quarter, her obvious belief that Arbella was the Queen's natural successor makes it clear that when she had arranged the marriage with Charles Stuart, she had not been motivated, as she had claimed, by a natural maternal desire for the happiness of her daughter, but had nursed explicit hopes of being the grandmother of England's future monarch.

Another of the Queen's potential successors was Lady Katherine Grey, who, like the youthful Countess of Lennox, was to be the victim of romantic notions essentially blameless, but fatal in one of her time, place and rank. The second of the unfortunate Grey girls, and a descendant of Henry VIII's sister Mary, Lady Katherine was a second cousin of the Queen. The grim lesson of her sister's execution seems to have made little impression on her, for it was while Queen Mary was still alive that Katherine fell in love with the Earl of Hertford, eldest son of the late Protector Somerset, a particularly unfortunate choice in view of the fact that the Queen could hardly fail to object to a marriage between a sister of Lady Jane Grey and a first cousin of Edward VI. With the accession of Elizabeth, the young couple's chances of happiness deteriorated still further, for in Lady Katherine's case, the habitual distrust with which the new Queen regarded any potential successor seems to have been sharpened by personal dislike, and the odds of her consenting to this potent combination of Grey and Seymour blood were slender indeed.

Nevertheless, in March 1559 Katherine and Hertford informed

their parents of their love for one another, and it was agreed that Katherine's mother, the Duchess of Suffolk, would go to court to try and persuade the Queen to agree to their marriage. Unfortunately, the Duchess's ill health made it impossible for her to perform this errand immediately, and in the ensuing interval Katherine's behaviour was hardly calculated to increase the probability of it succeeding. 'Angry and offended' at the Queen's obvious distaste for her, she took to confiding in the Spanish ambassador, complaining that Elizabeth had humiliated her by demoting her from her former place in the Privy Chamber to a mere lady of the Presence Chamber, and grumbling of the Queen's obvious reluctance to designate her her heiress. Friendly conversations such as these led the Spaniards to reflect that should Elizabeth die, they would infinitely prefer to see Lady Katherine as her successor than the probable alternative, the francophile Mary Queen of Scots, and they wondered whether Lady Katherine could not be 'enticed away' to Spain where they could set her up as their own pet claimant to the English throne. It was not long before the Queen learnt of these plans through her agents in Spain, with the result that she came to regard her cousin as even more of an inconvenience than before.[28]

She was hardly mollified when Katherine's temper snapped under the strain of waiting for her future to be resolved, provoking her to utter 'very arrogant and unseemly words in the hearing of the Queen and others standing by'.[29] In these circumstances it is unlikely that Elizabeth would ever have been induced to consent to Katherine and Hertford's marriage, but in November 1559 the situation worsened still further when the Duchess of Suffolk died without ever having approached the Queen on their behalf. Lacking the nerve to broach the subject with Elizabeth himself, Hertford told Katherine's step-father that he would 'meddle no further in the matter' but in fact he and Katherine continued to steal secret meetings together, an expedient infinitely more risky than the direct confrontation with the Queen that he had shunned.

In both Hampton Court and Whitehall the setting for these assignations was generally the dressing closet allocated to Hertford's sister, Lady Jane Seymour, a determined young maid of honour who was an eager accessory to the intrigue. It was during one such encounter at Whitehall, shortly before Christmas 1560, that the pair sealed their fate by agreeing to marry secretly, vaguely trusting that the Queen would countenance their union retrospectively when eventually she learnt of it. A few days later, Katherine pleaded tooth-ache to avoid going with the Queen on a hunting expedition, and after the court's departure she made her way to Hertford's house at Canon Row, Westminster, accompanied by Lady Jane Seymour. There the lovers were married by an unknown priest engaged by Lady Jane for a fee of £10. He disappeared immediately after the ceremony, leaving Lady Jane alone with the newly-weds and she, 'perceiving them ready to go to bed', tactfully withdrew. After the hasty consummation of the marriage, Lady Katherine dressed and she and Lady Jane made their way back to Whitehall, where their absence had gone unremarked. In the months that followed Katherine and her husband, abetted as ever by his sister, snatched at every opportunity of having 'company' together, with the result that in March 1561 Katherine informed Hertford that she believed herself to be pregnant. An already grim situation was radically altered for the worse by the death, later that month, of Lady Jane, and the subsequent enforced departure of Hertford on a diplomatic mission abroad, leaving Katherine to face alone the crisis that clearly could not be long deferred.[30]

By July her condition made further concealment impossible and since her letters to Hertford pleading for his return had gone astray, she was forced to take the initiative herself. While the court was on summer progress in Suffolk, Lord Robert Dudley was astonished to awake one night to find Katherine kneeling at his bedside sobbing out her story, pleading with him to break the news to Elizabeth as gently as possible. Having done her best to enlist Dudley on her side, the girl's only other resource lay in seeking out the sleeping Lady St Loe, a lady of the Bedchamber to whose child Katherine had once stood godmother. Though at that time still married to her third husband she was, in fact, none other than the future Countess of Shrewsbury, whose own hard-headed attitude to matrimony made her peculiarly unfitted to assist one who had risked all for love. Unsurprisingly, her only response to Katherine's tale of woe was to disassociate herself from her completely, and the wretched mother-to-be was left to brave the Queen's fury bereft of friends.

It turned out to be fearsome. When the story emerged, Lady Katherine was instantly consigned to the Tower and Hertford was summoned home for questioning. Nurtured in conspiracy herself, the Queen now scented it here, convinced that the marriage had originated from some deep design and that it could not have been accomplished without the connivance of 'sundry personages'. 'The Queen thinks, and others with her, that some greater drift was in this, but I can find none such', the Queen's principal secretary, William Cecil, noted in some perplexity,[31] and even the most stringent examinations of Lady St Loe failed to reveal that she had any foreknowledge of the affair or that a larger number of people were involved. Hertford, on his return, exactly corroborated Katherine's account, and under Cecil's direction the inquiry now took a different turn. On their own admission, the only witness of Katherine and Hertford's marriage was dead, the officiating priest had disappeared, and Katherine had mislaid the only document in existence which could confirm her story, a paper recording details of property settled on by her by her husband. There was, therefore, no proof that the marriage had ever taken place at all, and without positive evidence to the contrary, the council saw no reason to accept that it had. Pronouncing the marriage a fiction held a double attraction for Elizabeth: the child that Katherine was bearing would automatically be bastardized (and could hence have no claim upon the throne) and its wretched mother could be prosecuted for her immorality, thus enabling the Queen to rid herself permanently of a troublesome relation.

With her fate still undecided Katherine produced on 24 September 1561 a healthy son, but motherhood was no recommendation for mercy in the eyes of Elizabeth, for on 12 May 1562 a commission headed by the Archbishop of Canterbury declared that the couple had had 'undue and unlawful carnal copulation' and recommended perpetual imprisonment for them both. Katherine and her husband remained in the Tower, initially in quite mild conditions, for a sympathetic jailer permitted them access to one another, but when this resulted in February 1563 in the birth of another son, Elizabeth's fury surpassed even her original displeasure. The Court of Star Chamber ruled that Hertford had compounded the crime of having 'deflowered a virgin of the blood royal in the Queen's house' by having 'ravished her the second time', and fined him £15,000, and thenceforth he and Katherine were never to meet again.[32] Although an outbreak of plague in the city necessitated their removal from the Tower in August 1563, they were by no means forgiven, and any remaining hope of their ultimate redemption was finally crushed when John Hales, a fanatical Protestant who dreaded the accession of the Catholic Mary Queen of Scots, produced a pamphlet asserting the validity of Katherine's marriage and implying that her son was the rightful heir to the throne.

For a time Katherine was committed to the custody of her uncle, Lord John Grey, a kindly man whose attempts at consolation only drew from her the lament, 'Alas, uncle, what a life is this to me, thus to live in the Queen's displeasure; but for my lord and my children, I would to God I were buried.' Elizabeth remained immovable in the face both of his remonstrances for mercy and of letters from Katherine, acknowledging 'the greatness of my fault'. After the death of Lord John his niece was shunted from one country house to another, her misery contributing to the steady deterioration in her health. On 22 January 1568 she died. Elizabeth affected becoming sorrow at the news, but as the Spanish ambassador caustically noted, 'It is not believed that she feels it as she was afraid of her.'[33]

The story of the youngest Grey daughter, who remained at court as a maid of honour after Katherine's disgrace, seems almost a grotesque parody of her sister's, for as a despised and hunch-backed dwarf Lady Mary lacked the physical attributes that fitted Katherine for her role as a tragic heroine in a romance. Neglected and unloved since birth, she may have supposed herself of too little consequence for her marriage to create much trouble, imagining that the Queen would acquiesce in her choice if presented with a *fait accompli*. As a result, when she acquired an admirer in the unlikely shape of Thomas Keyes, a widowed middle-aged giant who was the sergeant porter at Whitehall, she consented to become his wife.

One night in early August 1565 she stole from her rooms in Whitehall to Keyes's lodgings over the water-gate, and there the couple clandestinely married, having nevertheless taken the precaution of arranging that there were several witnesses to the ceremony. While this ensured that the marriage could not be subsequently invalidated, it also made it virtually impossible to preserve secrecy for very long, and within a fortnight the news had leaked out, creating all the more sensation since the unfortunate disparity in size between the lovers only seemed to emphasize the evident unsuitability of the match. 'Here is an unhappy chance and monstrous,' William Cecil groaned to Sir Thomas Smith on 21 August, 'The sergeant porter, being the biggest gentleman in the court, hath married secretly the Lady Mary Grey, least of all the court.' Ominously, however, he added, 'The offence is very great' and the Queen, at least, was not disposed to see the comic aspects of the matter.[34] However personally insignificant Lady Mary may have been, there was still a possibility that she would one day wear the crown, and hence she could not plight her troth with the insouciance of a common milkmaid. Unlike her sister, whose claim to the throne had seemingly been enhanced by marriage, Lady Mary's had been weakened as a result of her ridiculous misalliance, but both girls had affronted the Queen equally by circumscribing her freedom of action in the question of who should succeed her.

While unable to deny the fact of the marriage, the Queen was determined to contain its evil consequences by ensuring that no children resulted from it. Keyes was dispatched to the Fleet prison and confined there under the most arduous conditions, and though in 1571 he was transferred to the more salubrious Sandgate Castle, his health was already so broken that he died in September of the following year, news 'which Lady Mary taketh very grievously' when she heard of it. Though treated more leniently than her husband, on the discovery of the offence she had been bundled off to Chequers in the custody of Sir Richard Hawtrey, and had since been billeted upon a variety of guardians, none of whom had been at all pleased to have the responsibility of her care and upkeep imposed upon them. In 1573 she was eventually permitted to live without supervision, but although by January 1578 she and the Queen were on sufficiently good terms to be exchanging gifts in the New Year celebrations, Elizabeth cannot have long mourned the passing of the last of the Grey girls when Lady Mary died later that year.

If some have condemned the Queen's punishment of her cousins' marriages as unnecessarily vindictive, from the constitutional point of view her logic was impeccable; but her intense fury whenever any of her ladies made unauthorized marriages can less easily be explained. Few women in Elizabethan times regarded the single state as anything other than uncongenial, and the fact that a career at court carried with it excellent opportunities of making the acquaintance of the most eligible bachelors of the day constituted one of its main attractions in the eyes of many unmarried young ladies. But since marriage and its attendant distractions might well prevent any lady in royal service discharging her obligations to the satisfaction of her mistress, the Queen's consent had to be obtained beforehand, a step that was considerably more than a mere formality. Elizabeth blandly maintained that she had 'always furthered (in good sort) any honest and honourable purposes of marriage or preferment to any of hers when without scandal or infamy they have been orderly broke to her', but few people at court would have supported this statement. Her attitude towards marriage was known to be so unreasonable that even though she frequently feigned kindly interest in the future of her ladies, and enquired of them whether they hoped to find husbands, 'the wise ones did well conceal their liking thereto', as an answer in the affirmative always put the Queen in a rage,[35] and there is little doubt that at heart she would have preferred it if many more of her ladies had followed the examples of Blanche Parry and Mary Radcliffe and remained single like herself.

Having suppressed her own romantic tendencies through self-discipline, the Queen had no inclination to indulge them in others, and if she received an application for a marriage between partners of unequal social status she rejected it without hesitation. In such circumstances the only way a young couple could reach the altar at all was by eloping, a course that guaranteed their disgrace. In July 1583, the Earl of Essex's sister, Lady Dorothy Devereux, absconded with the comparatively lowly Thomas Perrot, marrying him at a secret ceremony with 'two men guarding the church door with swords and daggers under their cloaks',[36] a misdemeanour that so infuriated the Queen that even four years later she flew into a rage when she learnt that Dorothy would be among the guests who would welcome her when she visited the Countess of Warwick's house, North Hall. Sir Thomas Shirley, an impecunious knight who ran off with the maid of honour Frances Vasavour in the summer of 1591, paid even more dearly for his gallantry, which earned him a nine-month spell in Marshalsea prison.

The penalties for young love could therefore be dire, but to the majority of her contemporaries the Queen's displeasure would not have seemed misplaced. To them, marriage was too serious a business to be dependent on the arbitrary affections of two individuals; it was rather the social standing and financial situation of each party that decided the question of who should marry whom. The parents of many young girls in service at court could not be there in person to monitor their conduct, and they welcomed Elizabeth's unwillingness to permit their daughters to marry indiscriminately, but they did resent it when the Queen was awkward about letting her ladies-in-waiting marry eligible young men simply because she was reluctant to lose their services. In 1594 for example the Countess of Rutland was anxious to find a good husband for her daughter Lady Bridget Manners, but as Bridget was one of the Queen's favourite maids of honour, she knew that Elizabeth would be loth to part with her. Bridget's servant Mary Harding suggested that the girl feigned measles and withdraw into quarantine, as Elizabeth would be more likely to let her marry once she had become accustomed to her absence, but the Countess of Rutland was anxious that the Queen would still withhold her consent and therefore she arranged a marriage for

Bridget without consulting Elizabeth at all.[37] When the Queen found out she was so angry that she imprisoned Bridget's new husband for three months, but though she was technically justified in this, she might perhaps have reflected that Bridget and her mother had been driven to subterfuge only by her known reluctance to permit her ladies to make even perfectly respectable marriages, an unreasonable attitude that invited deception.

Even when Elizabeth did give her ladies permission to marry, her consent was often only wrung from her after the most alarming outbursts. When Mary Shelton approached the Queen in January 1576, seeking permission to marry James Scudamore, her infuriated mistress 'dealt liberal both with blows and evil words', breaking her maid of honour's finger in the process, and although she was subsequently so remorseful that she not only assented to the marriage but promoted the new Lady Scudamore to a position in the Privy Chamber, all at court shudderingly agreed that 'No one ever bought a husband more dearly'. At other times the Queen succeeded in keeping her temper, but nevertheless gave her blessing with very ill grace, as in 1585, when Frances Howard reported to Lord Hertford that the Queen did not grant her request for permission to become his second wife until she had made a spirited attempt to deter her, using 'many persuasions . . . against marriage . . . and how little you would care for me'.[38]

The arguments that the Queen put forward on this occasion indicate that her opposition to her ladies marrying stemmed from rather more than mere jealousy that they should attain contentment of a sort that she would never know. Although she occasionally lamented her spinsterhood, simultaneously she entertained an altogether contradictory conviction that matrimony was an undesirable condition for women, a view not altogether surprising when one recalls that her father had executed her mother and stepmother, and the marriage of her sister had been a fiasco. It may well have been her early experience that instilled in her that instinctive aversion to the married state that amounted almost to a neurosis, and perhaps it helps to explain what provoked her to such unmeasured anger when her ladies inconsiderately submitted themselves to what the Queen saw as the subjection of the nuptial bond.

Ideally, indeed, the Queen would have liked it if both sexes at her court had voluntarily eschewed matrimony for her sake, her preference for bachelor courtiers being so marked that in 1602 observers at once deduced from Lord Clanricard's rejection of an advantageous match with a wealthy widow that 'he more regards courtly hopes than present profit'.[39] Elizabeth was only too ready to accept protestations from the single gentlemen of her court that their adoration of her prevented them from marrying, and her disillusionment when they subsequently recruited wives from amongst the ladies of her court was in consequence very real. To her it therefore seemed the ultimate betrayal when the Earl of Leicester, to whom she herself had so nearly surrendered, abandoned her to marry another woman.

Aware that the Queen regarded him as her exclusive property, Leicester had remained a widower even after his own chances of marrying her had become increasingly remote, satisfying himself instead with discreet affairs with several court ladies. Amongst his enemies indeed, the Earl had the reputation of being an insatiable lecher, and one particularly scurrilous contemporary work asserted that he was wont 'to seek pasture among the waiting gentlewomen of her Majesty's great chamber', offering them as much as £300 a night to gratify his lust. The story may be discounted, not least because Leicester was clearly capable of attracting women without the necessity of stooping to financial inducements. In May 1573, for example, Gilbert Talbot informed his father, 'There are two sisters in ye court who are very far in love with him, my Lady Sheffield and my Lady Frances Howard. They, of like striving who shall win him better, are at great war together, and the Queen thinketh not well of them, and not the better of him.'[40]

Leicester had in fact been having an affair with Lady Douglas Sheffield, 'a lady of great beauties', for several years, having allegedly first seduced her as early as 1568. According to a relative of her husband's, he had met her while the court was staying at Belvoir Castle and 'being much taken with her perfections', had made advances, with the satisfactory result that he shortly enjoyed 'the unlawful fruition of her bed and body'. Her husband had apparently learnt of her adultery when a compromising letter from the Earl came into his possession, but he had died before he could take any action, as a result, his family assumed, of being poisoned by the Earl. Leicester continued his relationship with the widow, but he nevertheless refrained from irrevocably committing himself to her. An undated letter from Leicester to an anonymous woman (almost certainly Lady Douglas Sheffield) is still in existence, and in this he explained his reluctance to marry again. From the beginning of their relationship, he wrote, he had told her that marriage was out of the question, as it would entail him forfeiting 'that favour' which he would 'rather never have wife than lose', and he suggested that she accept one of the many offers of marriage she was receiving from other gentlemen at court.[41]

Lady Douglas did not accept the advice. At the end of 1573, she became pregnant by the Earl, and although at the time there were rumours that Leicester had in consequence finally agreed to marry her, the truth of them was never established, and he clearly continued to regard himself as a free man even after the birth of Lady Sheffield's son in August 1574. It would take Lettice Knollys, a woman of infinitely stronger character than the lightweight Lady Douglas, to make Leicester prepared to risk jeopardizing his position with the Queen by remarrying.

Lettice (or Laetitia) Knollys was the granddaughter of Mary Boleyn and hence Elizabeth's first cousin once removed. Red-haired like the Queen, and accounted by the Spanish ambassador 'one of the best-looking ladies of the court', she had a self-assurance which men found magnetic and women supercilious. At the beginning of the reign she had been a maid of honour to Elizabeth, with whom she was then something of a favourite, but she had soon left royal service to marry Walter Devereux. As early as 1565, she and Leicester had had a brief flirtation together, which he ended after a tempestuous scene with the Queen in which she upbraided him for disloyalty. He did not, however, entirely forget the alluring redhead, and when he had tired of his relationship with Lady Sheffield, his thoughts turned to her once again. Created Earl of Essex in 1572, Lettice's husband had volunteered the following year to raise an army to subjugate the Irish, and it was soon whispered at court that his prolonged absence on campaign there was not unwelcome to Leicester, who 'loved the Earl's nearest relative better than he loved the Earl himself'. By December 1575 gossip surrounding the relations between Leicester and the Countess of Essex had reached such proportions that it was rumoured that she had borne him two children,[42] and when Essex died suddenly of dysentery in September 1576, Leicester's enemies believed he had poisoned him. By now Lady Sheffield had been altogether discarded in favour of Lettice, and on 21 September 1578, the triumph of the latter was completed when, at a private ceremony at his house in Wanstead, Leicester took his already pregnant mistress as his wife.

For nearly a year however, Leicester contrived to keep the secret of his marriage from the Queen, keeping his wife out of Elizabeth's way by 'carrying her up and down the country'. But his luck could not hold out for ever: in August 1579, the French ambassador, Simier, saw fit to apprise the Queen of the facts, revealing to her that one of the few men in whom she had always placed implicit trust was not only faithless but also deceitful. In her initial fury she wanted to send Leicester to the Tower, and although she was with difficulty dissuaded, she was still determined that Leicester and his wife should suffer for their treachery. In November 1579, Lady Douglas Sheffield, finally convinced that she had lost Leicester for ever, married Sir Edward Stafford, but the Queen now recalled the earlier rumours of her secret wedding to Leicester. If she could establish that they had any foundation, she could insist that the Earl honour his previous commitment to a woman he no longer loved, or be sent to 'rot in the Tower', while Lettice would be branded an adulteress. Accordingly, the unfortunate Lady Stafford underwent the most searching interrogation at the hands of her husband, Lord Sussex and the Queen herself, but it could elicit from her no more than a tearful insistence that 'she had trusted the said Earl too much to have anything to shew to constrain him to marry her', and Elizabeth was obliged to abandon that line of action.[43]

Married or single, Leicester was too important to her life to be excluded from it for ever, and gradually he succeeded in rebuilding his relationship with the Queen, almost on the same terms as before. His Countess, however, could not draw on the same reserves of tenderness, and Elizabeth was never really to forgive the woman whom she had once regarded as a friend, and who had rewarded her by so slyly stealing the man she had denied herself for the good of her people. Such was the Queen's bitterness, indeed, that for the remainder of the Earl's lifetime, Lettice was denied the court.

Nevertheless, Lettice was quite capable of making her presence felt from afar. Nothing that Elizabeth could do could alter the fact that she was Countess of Leicester, and to the Queen's fury Lettice openly exulted in her status. When journeying to town, or to her husband's estates, she travelled in great style, her horde of outriders and attendants attracting attention which, in the opinion of Elizabeth, one in semi-official disgrace ought more properly to have shunned. In September 1585 Sir Francis Walsingham noted that the Queen had recently been somewhat cold to the Earl of Leicester, which he sorrowfully attributed to the 'great offence taken at the conveying down of his lady',[44] but however much it might annoy Elizabeth, ultimately she was powerless to enforce that the wilful Countess's travel arrangements should be more discreet.

Nevertheless, when it seemed that the Countess of Leicester's love of display could have unfortunate repercussions on English foreign policy, the Queen was swift to pounce. In December 1585, Elizabeth had reluctantly dispatched Leicester to Holland to assist the Dutch rebels in their struggle against their Spanish overlords, but as she was unwilling to aggravate relations with Spain more than was absolutely necessary, she had instructed the Earl to maintain the lowest of profiles while abroad. He had disobeyed her by accepting an inflated title from the rebels, and the Queen's ire at this affront was enormously magnified when she heard reports that the Countess was preparing to join her husband abroad, accompanied by 'such a train of ladies and gentlemen, and such coaches, litters, and side-saddles as her Majesty had none such'. In a paroxysm of rage, Elizabeth declared that 'she would have no more courts under her obeisance than her own', and Lady Leicester's plans to set herself up as premier lady of the Netherlands were perforce abandoned.[45]

With Leicester's sudden death in September 1588, the main source of contention between Elizabeth and Lettice was removed from the scene, but the Queen's antagonism towards her cousin was not to be buried with the Earl. He had died more than £50,000 in debt, of which £25,000 was owed to the Crown, and the Queen remorselessly insisted that his goods were auctioned to meet these liabilities, a procedure which stopped short of actually beggaring his widow, but which showed scant regard for her sensibilities. Far from being overwhelmed by these misfortunes, within a year of Leicester's death Lettice had found herself a new husband in the person of Sir Christopher Blount, but since even the meteoric rise at court of her son, Robert, Earl of Essex, could not induce the Queen to mellow perceptibly towards her, she and Sir Christopher lived together in rural exile for nearly a decade. If the Queen alluded to her banished cousin at all, it was generally in unfavourable terms, as when she remarked balefully of Essex's wayward nature that 'He held it from his mother's side.'[46]

Nevertheless, by the autumn of 1597, Lettice could see no reason for her continued estrangement from the Queen, and she begged her son to make Elizabeth 'hearken to terms of pacification', and permit her to come to court. In this mission the Earl apparently succeeded, and accordingly in February 1598 his excited mother came up from the provinces, but by that time the Queen had experienced a change of heart. Every time the eager Lettice was brought to the Privy Galleries for presentation, Elizabeth 'found some occasion not to come', and at

the last moment she backed out of a dinner engagement with Lady
Chandos because she knew that Lettice would be present. Finally
however, she relented: 'My Lady Leicester was at court,' Rowland
White joyously reported to Sir Robert Sidney on 2 March, 'Kissed
the Queen's hand, and her breast, and did embrace her and the
Queen kissed her', but the reunion was to be short-lived. Within days, Elizabeth was expressing herself on the subject of Lettice
with 'some wonted unkind words', and she denied the Countess
permission to revisit her before her return to the country.[47]

They were never to meet again. Lettice was anxious to come to
court to plead for her son when the Earl of Essex was disgraced in
September 1599, but the Queen refused to receive her, unmoved
even by the presentation of a 'most curious fine gown' worth more
than £100.[48] In February 1601, distraught at his lasting fall from
favour, Essex broke into rebellion, and the Queen's final melancholy
triumph over the wife and mother of the two greatest favourites
of her reign was marked, after the collapse of the enterprise, by
the execution not only of the Earl but also of his follower, Sir
Christopher Blount.

Bess Throckmorton was another lady at the Elizabethan court
who incurred the wrath of the Queen by marrying a royal favourite.
Although less traumatic for Elizabeth than the discovery of Leicester's union with Lettice, Bess's marriage to Sir Walter Ralegh
technically constituted the greater offence, for as a lady of the Privy
Chamber she had sworn to serve the Queen, and her deliberate
duplicity was a gross violation of that oath. Furthermore, it can only
have added to Elizabeth's vexation that the dazzling genius whose
wit and charm had captivated her for over a decade should have
been snatched from her by a fatherless, dowerless girl with no great
pretension to beauty.

The exact facts relating to the marriage remain obscure, and we
do not know if the following racy anecdote from John Aubrey's pen
refers to Ralegh's courtship of Bess Throckmorton. According to
Aubrey, Sir Walter

> loved a wench well: and one time getting up one of the maids of honour
> aginst a tree in a wood ('twas his first lady) who seemed at first boarding
> to be something fearful of her honour, and modest, she cried, 'Sweet Sir
> Walter, what do you me ask? Will you undo me? Nay sweet Sir Walter!
> Sweet Sir Walter!' At last, as the danger and pleasure at the same time
> grew higher, she cried in the ecstasy 'Swisser Swatter! Swisser Swatter!'
> She proved with child . . .[49]

Although it is possible that the Raleghs were married as early as February 1591, a recent authority suggests that January 1592 is a more likely date,[50] and since by that time Bess was already far gone with child, seduction had certainly preceded marriage – though whether in the colourful circumstances alluded to above we can only conjecture. Incredibly, however, she stayed in the Queen's service until the last stages of her pregnancy, only removing to her brother's house at Mile End in February 1592, where on 29 March she was delivered of a son. Although Bess's absence from court had inevitably caused tongues to wag, Ralegh still declined to acknowledge the marriage, and at the end of April Bess put her child out to nurse and returned to her position in the Privy Chamber as though nothing had happened, a piece of effrontery for which Elizabeth subsequently never forgave her. When the Queen finally learnt the truth in May she kept the offenders in suspense for some time, but in July 1592 Ralegh was committed to the Tower and joined there by his wife early in the following month.

Bess bore her imprisonment with fortitude, concerned that her husband's prospects should not be further affected by her behaviour. 'It is not this imprisonment, if I bought it with my life, that should make me think it long if it should do harm to speak of my delivery,' she wrote from the Tower, a stoical attitude that was fortunate in view of the fact that although Sir Walter was released after five weeks to undertake some business for the Queen, his wife remained in custody till 22 December. Once freed, however, she anticipated that the Queen would eventually welcome her back at court, but she deluded herself, for although Elizabeth made her peace with Sir Walter in an interview of June 1597, she did not consider that Lady Ralegh had done enough to atone for her sins. Even at the end of the reign an enemy of Ralegh and his wife could gloatingly report that although 'much hath been offered on all sides to bring her into the Privy Chamber of her old place', Lady Ralegh remained firmly excluded from 'that restitution in court which flattery had led her to expect'.[51] Despite the fact that Bess had served her faithfully for seven years, Elizabeth remembered only that she had betrayed her in the end, and saw no reason to overlook her perfidy.

Marriage was clearly fraught with difficulties for those at the Elizabethan court, but indulgence in extra-marital sex could be equally risky. In July 1571 the marriage of the handsome and rakish Earl of Oxford to Anne Cecil, daughter of Lord Burghley, had provoked 'great weeping, wailing and sorrowful cheer' amongst the ladies of the court he had spurned, but they need not have worried, for henceforth they were not to be denied his attentions. Anne Vasavour, a maid of honour who had already acquired a reputation for promiscuity, was among those thus favoured and as a result, in March 1581 she was brought to bed at court of a son fathered by the Earl. 'The gentlewoman the self same day she was delivered was conveyed out of the house and committed to the Tower',[52] and after an attempt at flight, Oxford was apprehended, imprisoned for a short while and denied the court for two years.

Anne's Knyvet relatives nevertheless considered his punishment inadequate, and in the ensuing four years they sought to avenge her honour by waging intermittent gang warfare with Oxford and his supporters. Both Oxford and Thomas Knyvet were wounded in the course of this vendetta, which was also responsible for the deaths of four of their followers, and although his father-in-law pleaded to the Queen that the Earl had in consequence suffered twice for his crime, once at her command, and once at the hands of 'the drab's' family, she could hardly be expected to sympathize, having difficulty enough in preserving the balance between rival groups of courtiers without having the issue complicated by the sexual escapades of her maids of honour. As for Anne herself, the evident belief of the Knyvets that she was an innocent party in the affair was apparently misplaced, for although she married some years after the incident, she subsequently left her husband to become the mistress of Sir Henry Lee. She bore him an illegitimate child and after his death remarried, only to be convicted of bigamy and fined £200. It was perhaps hardly surprising that her court career had ended in the way it did.

Mary Fitton was another maid of honour who was ruined when she strayed from the path of virtue. When Mary had first come to court, aged about seventeen, her father had asked his old friend Sir William Knollys to keep a protective eye on her, and with quixotic fervour Sir William had promised to 'defend the innocent lamb from the wolfish cruelty and fox-like subtlety of the tame beasts of this place'. His own feelings for Mary had nevertheless soon progressed beyond the merely paternal, but since he was already encumbered with a perfectly healthy wife of his own, he had no hope of gratifying this passion until, as he put it, 'the old tree be cut down'. Unfortunately, Mary was not disposed to wait until this day, and fearful that 'while the grass is growing the horse may starve', she looked for rather more immediate romantic sustenance by striking up an affair with Lord Pembroke's son, William Herbert.[53]

To facilitate assignations with her lover out of court, Mary would 'put off her head tire and tuck up her clothes and take a large white cloak and march as though she had been a man', and as a result of these precautions Elizabeth remained for a time in ignorance of the affair. Nevertheless, by February 1601, Mary's swelling belly made exposure inevitable, and though under examination her lover (who had become Earl of Pembroke on the death of his father earlier in the year) acknowledged paternity, he 'utterly renounceth all marriage'.[54]

Mary was confined to Lady Hawkins's house, there to be delivered of a stillborn son, and the Earl was sent for a spell in the Fleet prison, where he busied himself writing moralistic verses censuring Mary for her conduct:

> Then this advice, fair creature, take from me,
> Let none pluck fruit unless he plucks the tree,
> For if with one, with thousands thou'lt turn whore,
> Break ice in one place and it cracks the more.

Mary was confident that after his release, Pembroke would make her his Countess, but her father, expecting 'no good from him that in all this time hath not shewed any kindness', bore her back to the country, where she subsequently came near to fulfilling Pembroke's strictures, incurring 'such shame as never had Cheshire woman' by having an illegitimate son by Sir William Polewhele. Sir William Knollys was ultimately to take a Howard as his second bride, while the Earl of Pembroke reserved himself for the Earl of Shrewsbury's wealthy but deformed daughter, for whose fortune, in the opinion of a contemporary, 'He paid much too dear ... by taking her person into the bargain.'[55]

However much the Queen might wish to maintain moral standards in her court, it was an uphill struggle while the Earl of Essex was in his heyday. In the spring of 1590 Essex had secretly married Sir Philip Sidney's widow but though the Queen was fiercely resentful when she learnt the news, her anger subsided comparatively quickly, and within a few months Lady Essex was permitted to come to court. Having countenanced his marriage, the Queen was therefore all the more annoyed when Essex neglected his wife to chase several of her maids of honour, but though she made her feelings very clear, she proved unable to restrain either the Earl or his lady-loves.

Having allegedly seduced and made pregnant Elizabeth Southwell, Essex had started a flirtation with Lord Chandos's daughter, Elizabeth Brydges, with the result that in April 1597 'The Queen used the fair Mistress Brydges with words and blows of anger', and expelled her from court for three days. Lady Mary Howard was the next to fall for the Earl, and the Queen was particularly incensed by the way that her maid of honour flaunted herself in front of him in a varied array of sumptuous costumes, clearly wishing 'more to win the Earl than her mistress' goodwill'. According to Sir John Harington, Elizabeth was on one occasion so outraged by an especially lavish outfit of Lady Mary's, that the following day she filched it from the girl's closet and donned it herself. Since Lady Mary was rather more petite than her mistress, the effect was somewhat bizarre, but the Queen imperiously informed the girl that if the dress 'become not me as being too short, I am minded it shall never become thee as being too fine', and proceeded to confiscate it altogether. Lady Mary responded to this treatment by going on strike, refusing to bring the Queen her cloak for her morning walk, or to carry her cup of grace at meals, but the pleas of her friends, alarmed by the enraged Elizabeth's vows to tolerate no longer 'such ungracious flouting wenches' induced her to reconsider and to shun both her rich clothing and the company of the Earl.[56]

The Queen's anger at the antics of the Earl and his playfellows was more than just the envious spite of an elderly and embittered virgin. As she well knew, the reputation of her court reflected on her own, and her severe treatment of moral relapses seems the more justified in view of the fact that the debauched behaviour of so many at the court of King James was subsequently to contribute to a decline in respect for the monarchy itself. Besides this, the wasteful feud that had resulted from the Earl of Oxford's seduction of Anne Vasavour demonstrated the threat that unbridled sexual licence posed to law and order within the court, at a time when most men went armed and violence was never far from the surface. If, in the opinion of Sir John Harington, there was at court 'no love but that of the lusty God of Gallantry', the Queen had good reason for her determination that this deity should not be permitted to rampage over-freely.[57]

Despite Elizabeth's vigilance, morals at court seemed to be slipping throughout the 1590s, and as the century drew to its close the Queen came to be regarded as a figure belonging more rightly to the past than to the future in respects other than just her refusal to countenance permissiveness of any sort. As she aged, her courtiers and ladies began to glance surreptitiously across the border, anxious to establish themselves with King James, the man most likely to succeed her. As one of Elizabeth's first biographers recorded, 'They adored [James] as the rising sun, and neglected her as being now ready to set.' As early as 1589, the Earl of Essex's sister, Penelope Rich, had been sending letters to the Scottish court, signed with the pseudonym 'Rialta', and in them the Queen was referred to by the codename of 'Venus', while Essex featured as 'the weary knight' who, 'accounting it a thrall that he now lives in', was eagerly anticipating change. The Countesses of Cumberland and Warwick took advantage of this correspondence to send 'commendations . . . in humbleness' to King James,[58] and with the advent of the seventeenth century, the practice became more widespread.

In the melancholy knowledge that half her court was preparing for the time when she would no longer be there, the Queen clung grimly on to a life which had ceased to hold much joy for her. At the beginning of the seventeenth century, old ladies, 'among whom there is come a kind of mortality', were dying like flies,[59] and in early 1603 the death of the Countess of Nottingham, the Queen's much loved first cousin who had been in royal service since the opening of the reign, saddened Elizabeth's last weeks and emphasized again that her own end could not be long delayed. Sure enough, at the end of February she entered on her final illness.

One of her last acts was to order that her body was not to be embalmed, but when she died, on 24 March 1603, her wish was overruled, possibly in deference to the sensibilities of her ladies, who were to perform one final duty for their mistress. As the majority of her court scurried northwards to welcome their new Sovereign, six of the Queen's principal ladies remained behind to watch over her body as it lay in state for five weeks at Whitehall awaiting burial. One night, 'To the terror and astonishment of all that were present,' the coffin broke open with a deafening crack. This, however, was no resurrection from the dead, for it turned out that the embalmer had bungled his job and the Queen's putrefying corpse had in consequence swelled. Consoling themselves 'that if she had not been opened, the breath of her body would have been much worse',[60] the shaken ladies resumed their vigil. Right to the end, Elizabeth had retained her capacity to intimidate and surprise her ladies, but nothing could alter the fact that she had finally gone for ever.

The Early Stuart Court

'Notorious Impudent Prostituted Strumpets'

On the night of 26 March 1603, King James VI of Scotland was aroused from his bed to be told by Sir Robert Carey that he was now King of England. James wasted no time in claiming his inheritance, setting off for the South on 5 April, but for the moment he left behind him his three children and his wife, Anne. At the time of his accession to the English throne, James had been wed to this Danish Princess for nearly fourteen years, and though their life together was scarcely the stuff of which romance is made, it could not be accounted an outright failure. Fundamentally good-natured, but shallow and petulant when crossed, Anne had neither the looks nor the brains to wean James away from emotional dependence on his own sex, but the couple were reasonably fond of one another and had at least already managed to spawn two sons and a daughter; an achievement which, it was hoped, would make fears that a disputed succession and civil war would follow the death of the Sovereign a thing of the past. Now she was once again pregnant and hence in no condition to travel, but James was anxious that she should be introduced to their new subjects as soon as possible and even while still far from London he was making arrangements for the reception of his wife and his two elder children, instructing the council to 'send some of the ladies of all degrees who were about the Queen as soon as the funerals be past . . . to meet her as far as they can at her entry into the realm or soon after, for that we hold needful of her honour'.[1]

There were however some ladies at court whose curiosity about their new mistress was too intense to permit them patiently to await her arrival in England. In a bid to pre-empt the official reception committee assembled by the council at Berwick, a bevy of noblewomen, which included the Countess of Bedford and Ladies

Hatton, Harington, Hastings and Cecil, streamed north of the border to make the Queen's acquaintance, hoping that their pioneering spirit would earn them the prize positions in her household. Sensibly, however, Anne refrained from making any premature commitments in the matter of household appointments, although she was sufficiently taken with Lucy, Countess of Bedford – a young wife who had already established a reputation for herself as 'a fine dancing dame' at the court of Queen Elizabeth – to appoint her to her Bedchamber. In the years to come the Countess was to be an influential figure at the Jacobean court, not only as a patron of playwrights and poets and a connoisseur of art but also because she 'was so great a woman with the Queen as everybody much respected her', whose friendship ambitious careerists and anxious petitioners found it worthwhile to cultivate.[2]

Having miscarried of the baby she was expecting, Anne departed southwards at the end of May, accompanied by her two elder children. She travelled towards Windsor in easy stages, encountering *en route* an ever-growing number of ambitious ladies desirous of preferment. They were relieved to learn that Anne had permitted only two Scottish ladies to accompany her, but even though the wives of the Scottish nobility had thus been rendered *hors de combat*, the infighting amongst the English ladies at court for a place in the Queen's household was quite acrimonious enough, as Lord Worcester described in a letter to a friend in which he sought to amplify the various and confusing gradations of the 'feminine commonwealth'. He wrote:

> You must know we have ladies of divers degrees of favour, some for the private chamber, some for the drawing-chamber, some for the bedchamber, and some whose appointments have no certain station, and of these only are lady Arbella and my wife. My Lady Bedford holdeth fast to the bedchamber; Lady Hertford fain would but her husband hath called her home. Lady Derby (the younger), Lady Suffolk, Lady Rich, Lady Nottingham, Lady Susan de Vere, Lady Walsingham (and of late) the lady Southwell for the drawing-chamber; all the rest for the private chamber ... but the plotting and malice among these ladies is so great, that I think envy hath tied an invisible snake about their necks, to sting each other to death ...[3]

With the accession of the Stuarts, positions in the Queen's establishment tended to become more specialized, acquiring imposing titles which give us a clearer idea of the exact nature of the duties involved.

In the reign of Elizabeth the most important woman in her household was the first lady of the Bedchamber, but by the outbreak of the Civil War the first lady was rather more grandly referred to as the Mistress of the Robes. Her duties included looking after the jewels which the Queen selected for her daily use and accounting for them to the jewel house; arranging for the payment of tradesmen who had supplied the Queen with items and materials for her wardrobe and, when occasion demanded, making arrangements for the provision of linen for the Queen's lying-in. Jane Drummond, one of the two Scottish ladies the Queen had brought with her from the North, became Anne's first lady of the Bedchamber in 1603, retaining the position until September 1617 when an argument with the Queen about her husband's status at court led to her returning to Scotland in a huff 'being nothing so gracious as heretofore'. Lady Grey of Ruthin, Lady St John and Lady Walsingham were all in hot competition to succeed her but eventually Lady Grey carried the day and held the post until the Queen's death in 1619.[4]

Another quaintly named post in the Queen's household was the Mistress of the Sweet Coffers, who supervised the chests scented with musk and sweet herbs in which was stored the Queen's linen, kept scrupulously clean by the Laundress of the Body, responsible for the scrubbing of the Queen's underwear, rather than the royal person, as the name might seem to imply. Far more important than these, however, was the Groom of the Stool, who in subsequent centuries came to be known as the Groom of the Stole before the office disappeared altogether. In the section of the *Book of the Court* dealing with the workings of the royal household W. J. Thoms asserts that the stole referred to was 'a narrow vest . . . lined with crimson sarcenet', apparently under the impression that the Groom of the Stole was a sort of ceremonial dresser to the Queen, but in fact her duties were of a much more practical nature. The 'stool' of the original title was the close stool, for even the divine right of kings could not free the Stuarts from the necessity of performing the most human functions and as such someone had to be responsible for the provision of chamber pots and the disposal of their contents. That the Groom of the Stool fulfilled these requirements is shown by the fact that when the French wife of Charles I arrived in England in 1625 her French attendants translated the title as '*la dame de la chaise percée*' noting in some surprise that in England the position was considered to be 'a mark of great distinction'.[5] Lady of the Lavatory would indeed have been a more appropriate, if less sonorous, appellation for the incumbent of an office that entailed these duties, and for which, astonishingly, the grandest women in England would ardently compete for the remainder of the century.

The universal eagerness for employment at the early Stuart court is perhaps the more understandable in view of the fact that the pecuniary benefits of royal service had never been greater. Of these benefits the official salary paid to ladies in the Queen's household was by no means the most considerable. In 1630 the maids of honour were paid only £10 annually (although their wages had risen to £20 by the eve of the Civil War) while the Mistress of the Robes received £300 and the Mistress of the Sweet Coffers was paid the mysterious sum of £26 13s 4d. Of far more importance was the fact that those in the household were entitled to free board and lodging at court which enabled the more privileged to feed not only themselves but also their servants and family at royal expense. The amount of food provided daily for specified members of the household was determined according to the relative importance of their position within it. Thus the Groom of the Stool was allotted a 'diet' of seven dishes twice a day, while the Queen's chamberers had to make do with four. The value of such perquisites could be sizeable: Sir Robert Carey's wife was Mistress of the Sweet Coffers and a lady of the Privy Chamber to Queen Anne, but the Queen's death in 1619 resulted in the dissolution of her household and as Sir Robert later recalled, his wife was thenceforth obliged 'to keep house and family which was out of our way £1,000 a year that we saved before'.[6]

The housing and feeding of royal servants was a traditional, if unwelcome, drain on the resources of the Crown, but James's and Anne's habitual generosity to those in their favour was to place impositions on the exchequer of a sort quite unknown in Queen Elizabeth's day. With the onset of old age, indeed, Elizabeth's inborn sense of thrift had tended to degenerate into outright miserliness, and many loyal servants of the Queen had died without having received suitable recognition for their labours. James, however, was to redress the balance rather too far. In 1605, for example, he authorized a grant of £2,000 to Jane Drummond, first lady of the Bedchamber to his wife, 'as free gifts for her services to the Queen', and Audrey, Lady Walsingham received the same amount in 1616, in addition to the yearly pension of £200 that she had already been granted in 1604. In 1611 Katherine Bridges, Mother of the Maids, was given £100 while in March 1617 the Countess of Nottingham was allocated an annuity of £600 out of the customs revenue.[7]

Apart from this the Queen could always be relied upon to give substantial wedding presents to any of her ladies who married. Even Jane Mewtas, a Bedchamber woman comparatively low in the hierarchy of the Queen's household, received 'a jewel of gold set with diamonds' worth £60 upon her marriage to Sir William Cornwallis; and when Jane Drummond married Lord Roxburgh in 1613 the Queen excelled herself. Although she had been full of good resolutions when she heard of the engagement, insisting that since her first lady of the Bedchamber was 'rich enough . . . as well in wealth as in virtue and favour', she would spend no more than £500 on providing the marriage bed and staging a celebratory masque, she had ended up by laying out more than £3,000 on the festivities.[8]

Such excessive liberality placed a severe strain on the royal revenues, but although there was intermittent talk of inaugurating economic reforms at court nothing effectual was ever done. Nevertheless cash-flow problems occasionally obliged the King and Queen to reward their followers in rather more subtle ways than the mere disbursement of large sums of money, enriching them by bestowing on them privileges only indirectly financed by the Crown. The King, for example, had the power to grant monopolies, and at the request of the Queen, he could confer upon one of her ladies the sole right of producing or exploiting a product or commodity. Thus in July 1616 it was decreed that only the Countess of Bedford was permitted to coin farthings in England, thereby inflicting serious losses on the firm that had previously been engaged in minting them. Rather more unusual, and, one imagines, considerably less profitable, was the privilege exclusively accorded the Queen's favourite maid of honour, Mary Middlemore, of searching for treasure amongst the ruins of Glastonbury Abbey.[9]

Profits from sales taxes and customs impositions on specified items could also provide favoured denizens of the court with a lucrative source of income if the King could be prevailed upon to part with them. Once again, the Countess of Bedford succeeded in capitalizing on her intimacy with the royal family by securing a licence in November 1619 to exact a toll of 2d on every chaldron of sea coal purchased in England. Other ladies would supplement their official salaries by gaining permission to collect and keep fines levied on offenders by the law courts; Audrey, Lady Walsingham made quite a speciality of thus raising revenue, earning a comfortable livelihood out of repeated grants enabling her to pocket the fines of several wealthy recusants.[10]

Under James, too, titles, so jealously guarded and rarely bestowed by Queen Elizabeth, became another article of merchandise in which the experienced courtier might profitably traffic. Recipients of titles were expected to pay generously for the honour and if he felt so inclined James could instruct a fledgling peer to transfer this remittance to the individual of his, James's, choice, as in 1622 when it was rumoured that the King had offered 'the making of a baron' to the Duchess of Lennox as a wedding present. Even if the King did not wish to forego his share in the transaction, it was understood that if he ennobled someone at the instigation of an influential person at court the recipient of the title was expected to reward not only the King but also the individual who had interceded in his favour. Those who omitted to observe such formalities had little hope of gaining a peerage: in 1605, for example, cynics assumed that although William Cavendish was pestering his niece Arbella Stuart to extol his merits to the King, he would not be made a baron, as his failure to give her 'anything that might move her to spend her breath for him' had made her a less than articulate champion of his cause.[11]

Large as they were, the fringe benefits of employment in the royal service were not necessarily sufficient to support the exorbitant life-style expected of a courtier. 'Being a time of peace', Bishop Goodman ruefully admitted, 'we fell to luxury and riot', and the efforts of the less well-to-do members of the court to maintain the extravagant standards set by their more prosperous counterparts often drove them to the brink of insolvency. Despite, for instance, the King's notable generosity to Lucy, Countess of Bedford, her debts were such that by 1620 she found herself obliged to sell her estate at Birley on the Hill in Rutland to the Duke of Buckingham. Ostentatious display was the order of the day, and John Chamberlain, a contemporary letter-writer, reported that at the performance of the *Masque of Beauty* in 1608 one lady was wearing jewels valued at over £100,000 (a particularly flamboyant exhibition in view of the fact that pickpockets always wrought havoc upon the audience's possessions on such occasions); while at the 1613 wedding of James's only daughter, Lady Wotton paraded herself in a gown 'that cost £50 a yard the embroidery', and Lord Montacute 'bestowed £1,500 in apparel for his two daughters', despite the fact that as a Catholic he had already been mulcted of large sums in recusancy fines. Such profligacy shocked the more frugal of King James's subjects, who shared John Chamberlain's sombre view that 'this extreme cost and riches make us all poor', and who were understandably resentful that even so everyday a transaction as the purchase of a sack of coal could not be conducted without some great lady of the court taking her percentage. Increasingly, courtiers and their wives came to be seen as a parasitic breed whose exotic lifestyle was underwritten by the honest toil of ordinary citizens.[12]

If improvidence was a common failing at the Jacobean court, so too was drunkenness, possibly because James himself was a heavy drinker with an especial penchant for sweet wines. But it was not only the gentlemen of the court who tended to over-indulge, for Sir John Harington, accustomed to the more temperate habits of Elizabethan days noted reprovingly, 'The ladies abandon their sobriety and are seen to roll about in intoxication', and in 1606 a masque presented in honour of the visit of the King of Denmark and which had as its theme the story of Solomon and the Queen of Sheba deteriorated into total farce because the principal performers were so completely incapacitated. According to Harington,

> The Lady who did play the Queen's part did carry most precious gifts to both their Majesties; but, forgetting the steps arising to the canopy overset her caskets into his Danish Majesty's lap, and fell at his feet . . . Now did appear in rich dress, Hope, Faith and Charity: Hope did assay to speak, but wine rendered her endeavours so feeble that she withdrew and hoped the King would excuse her brevity; Faith was then all alone . . . and left the court in a staggering condition. Charity came to the King's feet, and seemed to cover the multitude of sins her sisters had committed; in some sort she made obeisance and brought gifts . . . She then returned to Hope and Faith, who were both sick and spewing in the lower hall.[13]

The court of Queen Elizabeth, 'at once gay, decent and superb' seemed very far remote from this bacchanalia.

The moral fibre of the court seemed indeed to have disintegrated completely now that the Virgin Queen was no longer there to enforce standards. Lady Anne Clifford, a formidably virtuous northern heiress who was a regular visitor to the court, noted in her diary 'how all the ladies of the court had gotten such ill names that it was grown a scandalous place'. In part this was due simply to the fact that a younger and more free generation was now in the ascendant, for as Anne of Denmark was only twenty-seven when she arrived in England, it was hardly surprising that she preferred the company of the more youthful ladies of the court to that of the graver matrons who had surrounded Queen Elizabeth. The more censorious nevertheless felt that the new Queen selected her attendants with scant regard for the proprieties. Lady Anne Clifford primly recorded that the Queen 'shewed no favour to the elderly ladies, but to Lady Rich and such like company'[14], her evident disapproval deriving from the fact that, as all society well knew, Lady Rich had long been living in adultery with Lord Mountjoy and that at least three of her seven children were fathered by him.

Penelope Rich was by no means the only lady at the Jacobean court – described by the Puritan Lucy Hutchinson as 'a nursery of lust and intemperance' – whose private life could not have borne close scrutiny. Katherine Howard, Countess of Suffolk, a great beauty who lost her looks only in late middle age after an attack of smallpox, was the mistress of Sir Robert Cecil, although she had to share his embraces with Lady Walsingham and Lady Derby who were also known to be his 'great favourites'. The Countess of Suffolk's daughters were to carry on the tradition established by their mother, for the eldest, Lady Wallingford, produced two sons who were almost certainly not fathered by her husband, while her younger sisters, the Countesses of Essex and Salisbury, were believed to be the mistresses of Viscount Rochester and the Duke of Buckingham respectively.[15]

Although the moral frailty of their women seems to have been something of a Howard family failing, their sinfulness at this period was perhaps exceptional but certainly not unique. When Lettice, Lady Lake died in 1619, it was discovered that she left behind her an illegitimate daughter of uncertain paternity, although her husband, Sir Arthur, could hardly complain in view of the fact that it was believed that for some time he had been conducting an incestuous relationship with his sister Lady Roos. As for the unmarried ladies of the court, their reputation was such that when the Queen announced that she intended to celebrate Jane Drummond's wedding by staging 'a masque of maids', doubts were entertained as to whether she would be able to unearth a quorum of performers within her court. Some indeed believed that the actual performances of the masques themselves were nothing more than 'incentives to lust', and that the courtiers invited citizens' wives to the shows 'on purpose to defile them in such sort'; certainly while most of the court were engaged in watching the New Year's masque of 1605, one lady was discovered in the most compromising of positions, 'being surprised at her business at the top of the Terrace' that adjoined the Banqueting House at Whitehall.[16]

It is of course impossible to quantify precisely whether there was a greater degree of immorality at the Jacobean than the Elizabethan court, but certainly the general verdict of contemporaries seems to have been that sexual licence was both more widespread and more winked at in the reign of James I than in that of his strait-laced predecessor.

Although the King was comparatively relaxed in his attitude about incidentals such as manners and morals, in matters which related to the security of the State he was as vigilant as even Elizabeth could have wished, as his unfortunate cousin, Arbella Stuart, found out to her cost. For the majority of courtiers and their ladies, marriage was to be an infinitely less complicated business than in the days of the old Queen. At times the King seemed to take an almost sentimental pleasure in smoothing the path of young love, attending the wedding of Sir Frederick Cornwallis to a Bedchamber woman of the Queen despite the fact that his mother had not consented to the match, and promising that in addition to settling £3,000 on the young couple, he would reconcile the mother to the union.[17] But despite his habitual leniency in such cases, the King's reaction to the unauthorized marriage of a near relation who might one day be set up as a rival claimant to the throne was to be altogether different, and the accident of being born of royal blood was to prove as calamitous to Arbella Stuart as it had to the fated trio of Grey sisters.

Lady Arbella Stuart was the product of that marriage between Lord Charles Stuart and Elizabeth Cavendish that had so enraged Queen Elizabeth, and she was hence James's first cousin. Twenty-eight at the time of James's accession to the English throne, she had hitherto lived a pathetically retired existence, for Elizabeth had preferred that Arbella spent most of her time in the country under the redoubtable eye of her grandmother, the Countess of Shrewsbury. At different times several names, including that of her cousin James, had been put forward as suitable bridegrooms for Arbella, but nothing had ever come of the suggestions, and after more than a decade of sequestration from court Arbella had turned into a neurotic spinster, desperate to escape the irksome supervision of the old Countess. In December 1602 she contrived to send a message to the Earl of Hertford suggesting that she marry his grandson, Edward Seymour, but Hertford's youthful experiences following his own marriage to Katherine Grey made him loth to embark on a similar escapade in old age, and he promptly informed the council. Interrogated by a council official at her grandmother's home, Hardwick Hall, Arbella now implied that she had another lover 'great with her Majesty', whose identity she would only disclose if summoned to London, but further questioning revealed that this mysterious admirer was a mere figment of her imagination. A final desperate attempt to escape from the confines of Hardwick with her disreputable uncle, Charles Cavendish, completely miscarried, and Arbella was obliged to remain with her grandmother until the death of Queen Elizabeth.

With the accession of James, however, it seemed that Arbella's prospects had brightened. 'Desirous to free our cousin . . . from that unpleasant life which she hath led in the home of her grandmother, with whose severity and age, being a young lady [she] could hardly agree', the King summoned her to court and treated her with every mark of favour. In August 1603 the Venetian ambassador reported that Arbella was being treated as a Princess of the blood, taking precedence of all other ladies at court and bearing the Queen's train when she went to chapel. In his opinion however there was not 'wanting a certain mystery in the situation', and in view of her un-stable behaviour in the final years of Queen Elizabeth, when her fanta-sizing, hysteria and inconsistency left the council representative who examined her with the impression that she had 'vapours on her brain' it was perhaps too much to hope that Arbella would be content to settle indefinitely into dignified spinsterhood, accepting forever the unfulfilling role of honorary maiden aunt to the court.[18]

For a time, admittedly, all went well. She remained completely aloof from a wild plot of Lord Cobham's to put her on the throne, which was crushed without incident to herself. In October 1604 the Earl of Shrewsbury learnt from a correspondent that 'My lady Arbella spends her time in lecture, reading, hearing of service and preaching and visiting all the Princesses. She will not hear of mar-riage.' But even while leading this apparently tranquil existence, she was beset by money worries, for although by 1605 she enjoyed an income of about £3,000 per annum, as a kinswoman to the King she was expected to keep a certain amount of state, dressing richly and employing numerous servants. Furthermore, although she had found her isolated life in the country distasteful, she now found it difficult to adapt to the social whirl of the court, dominated as it was by frivolity and malice. In her letters to her relatives she complained of being forced to enter into the endless round of children's games in which the Queen delighted and of 'this everlasting hunting'.[19]

After a few years of these questionable delights, she became decidedly restless. By January 1610 Arbella was apparently contem-plating buying a country house and withdrawing from court, but her plans were still unresolved when, for reasons that have never been satisfactorily explained, she was called before the council. However, the council's suspicions, such as they were, were evidently soon allayed, for the King handled her graciously and told her – so it was said – that should she wish to marry she 'could make her choice of any subject within this kingdom' with his approval.[20]

Encouraged by such talk, William Seymour, the younger brother of that Edward Seymour to whom Arbella had indirectly proposed in 1602, determined to make a bid for her hand. Although more than ten years her junior, William was under the impression that Arbella was a lady 'of great means' and felt that marriage with a wealthy relative of the King's might improve the condition of an impoverished second son with few prospects. Arbella proved not unreceptive to his addresses, but the council took alarm on hearing of the association, and less than a month had elapsed since Arbella's previous appearance before them when they intervened again. Whatever he may have said on an earlier occasion, the King had no intention of permitting his cousin to marry into a family whose own links with the throne were far from distant, and he was anxious to discover how far the courtship had progressed. He was reassured by Seymour's insistence that although he and Arbella had hoped to marry, they would never have proceeded without his sanction, and when the young man promised to forswear thenceforward all hope of bringing his fiancée to the altar, James, not by nature a vindictive man, decided to take a lenient view of the matter. Arbella resumed her life at court, matrimony apparently as remote a possibility as ever.

Unfortunately she proved unwilling to eschew what she realized would probably be her last opportunity of wedlock. She succeeded in convincing Seymour that he could not break off the engagement without compromising her honour, for she believed that in the eyes of God they were already husband and wife and therefore she 'could never have matched with any other man, but to have lived all the days of my life as an harlot'. The subsequent events give those familiar with the history of the Grey girls a depressing sense of *déjà vu*. On 22 June 1610 Seymour secretly married Arbella at four o'clock in the morning in her chamber at Greenwich, a development of which the council was aware in little more than a fortnight. Within two days both of them were in custody, Arbella being confined to Sir Thomas Parry's house at Lambeth. From there, apparently unaware of the gravity of the situation, Arbella wrote to Jane Drummond asking her to mobilize the Queen on her behalf, but Anne, though well enough disposed towards the prisoner, could elicit from her husband no more than the gruff observation that Arbella 'had eaten of the forbidden tree'.[21] Only when James entrusted her to the care of the Bishop of Durham, in whose northern diocese he hoped she could not involve herself in any mischief, did Arbella finally realize the true extent of her predicament.

In March 1611 Arbella began her journey north in a state of hysteria, but her party had only reached Barnet when her enfeebled condition gave rise to such concern that their progress came to a halt. Grudgingly James agreed that she might stay there a few weeks to recover her strength, a temporary respite which Arbella was to employ in making contact with Seymour and arranging for their flight. On 3 June 1611, only shortly before she was scheduled to resume her course, Arbella slipped out of the house where she was billeted, disguised as a man, and having reached a nearby inn where her manservant was waiting with horses, she made for London. It had been pre-arranged that William Seymour should almost simultaneously effect an escape from his apartments in the Tower – not apparently a very difficult task for one not kept in particularly close confinement – and meet her at Blackwall, from whence they could row down river and take ship to France. Unfortunately Seymour was delayed and to Arbella's distress she was obliged to set sail without him on the morning of 4 June. By this time the authorities had been alerted and since Arbella ordered the captain of her ship to linger in the Channel in hopes that Seymour would catch them up, a government pinnace sent in her pursuit was able to overtake and recapture her. Ironically, although it had been Seymour's safety that had concerned her most, he reached the Continent unhindered some hours later.

Back in England again, Arbella was unceremoniously dispatched to the Tower, for her defiance had brought out the ruthless streak in the King. As one who had supplanted his mother on the Scottish throne at the age of only thirteen months, James was only too aware of the threat that close relatives could pose to ruling monarchs, and in view of the fact that it soon emerged that Arbella's Catholic aunt, the Countess of Shrewsbury, had provided her with the money necessary for her escape it was perhaps not unreasonable for him to assume that her flight would have been the prelude to her converting to Catholicism and becoming the tool of intriguers at foreign courts. Although Arbella was never formally tried (and indeed technically had committed no offence), hers was to be a life sentence. Forgotten by the majority of the court, she mouldered in the Tower, losing all will to live once she realized that the King would never relent. Refusing nourishment and medication, she sank into a decline, and on 25 September 1615, at the age of forty, she died.

Over questions such as the treatment of Arbella Stuart, Anne of Denmark had no control. James kept her happy by showing her innumerable small kindnesses, frequently granting her suits and 'preferring many upon her recommendations' but ministers were relieved to note that 'she carrieth no sway in matters of state' and such influence as she did have was further undermined by her natural indolence. 'I have not forgotten to put the Queen in mind of her promise to you, but in that as in all other matters she is slow in performance,' the Countess of Bedford wrote crossly to her old friend Jane, Lady Cornwallis, in 1617, but she added firmly, 'I will not be so in soliciting her until you have your desire', and clearly the Queen's ladies were quite capable of ensuring that she did not neglect their interests. Left to herself, Anne preferred to immerse herself in frivolity rather than in the cold realities of courtly politics, and at her separate establishment at Somerset House, which the King, 'ever best when furthest from the Queen' had bestowed upon her, she and her attendants girlishly immersed themselves in parlour games, her ladies being 'persuaded by the princely example . . . to play the child again'. Such infantile amusements held little appeal for the King, but he could at least respond when Anne's taste for childish pleasures was refined and elaborated on a grand scale to result in the presentation of the spectacular court masques of the period, in which the Queen and her ladies frequently appeared, and of which James, 'being not a little delighted with such fluent elegancies as made the night more gorgeous than the day', was an avid spectator.[22]

The Jacobean masque was a magnificent amalgam of poetry, spectacle and dance. Under Elizabeth, the masque had featured on the agenda of courtly entertainments, but expenses were kept to a minimum by concentrating on costumes rather than scenery, and there is no record that the Queen herself ever performed in the productions, apart from occasionally joining in the dancing between the masquers and the audience at the end of the evening. Anne however revelled in being the central focus of the theatrical extravaganzas of her day, performing against settings on which more imagination and money had been lavished than ever before in England. Arrayed in exotic creations, the Queen and her ladies executed the dance routines which formed a major part of the entertainment, leaving the delivery of the script to professional actors. Those not invited to participate could at least see the show, to which all the court, plus numerous citizens and their wives, were admitted. Public interest was indeed such that space in the auditorium became at something of a premium, prompting James to issue a proclamation in 1613 denying access to the Banqueting House (where the masques were staged) to ladies wearing farthingales, as 'this impertinent garment took up all the room in the court'.[23]

On 8 January 1604 the Queen, assisted by eleven of her ladies, appeared in a masque written by the poet Samuel Daniel, recommended to her by the Countess of Bedford, but though we have it on the author's authority that 'by the impartial opinion of all beholders ... it was not inferior to the best that ever was presented in Christendom', it was in fact the *Masque of Blackness*, written by Ben Jonson and designed by Inigo Jones and performed in January 1605, that was to create the infinitely greater sensation. The Queen had first heard Jonson's work when he was commissioned by Lord Spencer to write the entertainment staged in her honour when she stayed at Althorp on her way down from Scotland. Now his poetic talents were to be merged with the artistic genius of Inigo Jones, responsible for the fabulous costumes, scenery and special effects that so impressed contemporaries; a dynamic collaboration that was ultimately to be disrupted by their quarrel over whether it was the spectacle or the poetry that contributed more to the essence of the masque as an art form, but which resulted while it lasted in some of the most grandiose productions ever to be presented by amateurs in the history of the English stage.

The *Masque of Blackness* was not, admittedly, universally well-received. The background for the opening scene, lyrically described by Ben Jonson as an artificial sea 'which was seen to shoot forth as if it flowed to the land, raised with waves which seemed to move', was witheringly dismissed by the diplomat Dudley Carleton as consisting of 'all fish and no water' and he added that the costumes of the Queen and her ladies were 'rich, but too light and courtesan-like for such great ones'. The innovation of blacking-up the faces of the performers instead of disguising them as usual with masks or vizards met with his open contempt: 'You cannot imagine a more ugly sight than a troop of lean cheeked moors', he bluntly informed his correspondent. Jones's royal patrons were nevertheless sufficiently pleased with his devices to reappoint him as Jonson's collaborator in the New Year masque of 1606, *Hymenaei*, in which the Queen did not dance. He took no part in the production of the *Masque of Beauty*, presented by Anne and sixteen court ladies on 14 January 1608, but early in the following year he was responsible for the design of Jonson's *Masque of Queens*, whose setting was the House of Fame, 'a glorious and magnificent building', supported by golden pillars and adorned with statues of ancient poets and heroes, on top of which the Queen and her ladies danced. In 1609 he surpassed himself with the settings for the *Tethys Festival* in which the Queen and her ladies were represented as the nymphs of the various rivers of England against an appropriately aquatic background of dripping caves and spouting water, their costumes draped with shells and 'festoons of maritime weeds'.[24]

Such spectacles were costly affairs. The *Masque of Blackness* cost £2,000, the *Masque of Queens* over £3,000, while the Queen's silkman's bills for just the gold and silver braid used in the *Tethys Festival* came to £1,984 8s 2d. By late 1610 the depleted exchequer restricted expenditure on such a scale. In December it was noted that although the Queen was planning to present two masques over the New Year Festivities she was spending no more than £600 on them.[25] Her enthusiasm for these lavish amateur dramatics was anyway by then on the wane and in February 1611 she was to make her last stage appearance in Ben Jonson's *Love Freed from Ignorance and Folly*. Thenceforth it was her eldest son Prince Henry and, after his death in 1613, his younger brother Charles, who were to represent the royal family in the court masques, and with the Queen no longer actively involved the all-female entertainments of her heyday became something of a rarity, as would-be lady masquers now found that they were usually expected to bear the costs of the production themselves.

One may conjecture that this was a development that did not greatly sadden King James, who doubtless had always derived more pleasure from displays of dancing by the gentlemen of the court than from the elegant contrivances of the Queen and her ladies. Noting that his master soon tired of the company of his wife, Bishop Goodman remarked in his memoirs that 'The King himself was a very chaste man and there was little in the Queen to make him uxorious', but whether James was as chaste as the unworldly old cleric assumed is open to question. Although no one could accuse him of promiscuity with the opposite sex, he had throughout his life been emotionally and physically attracted to good-looking young men, and it is not unreasonable to presume his relationships with some of them were actively sexual. There was therefore scant hope that a lady of the court could better herself by establishing herself as *maîtresse en titre* to the monarch although, if one may believe contemporary scandal, the Countess of Suffolk sought to make the best of a bad job by selecting 'choice young men, whom she daily curled and perfumed their breaths' in hopes that having secured the King's affections they would duly reward their patroness.[26]

Furthermore, if an affair with the King was beyond the horizon of the court ladies of his day, it was not necessarily impossible to have one with the current favourite, which in some people's eyes amounted to the next best thing. In December 1611 the Earl of Suffolk (husband of the King's alleged procuress) informed a friend that James had found a new favourite, one Robert Carr, 'a straight-limbed, well-favoured, strong-shouldered and smooth-faced' young Scot, who already exerted a stranglehold over much of the business of the court. 'The King doth much covet his presence; the ladies too are not behindhand in their admiration', sneered the Earl, adding mockingly that although there were some men who would react fiercely 'were Carr to leer on their wives', there were others who permitted their spouses to receive his attentions, 'Yea, and like it well too that they should be . . . noticed' by so influential a person.[27] Suffolk would have done well to have bitten back his contempt: his own aristocratic disdain for this Scottish upstart evaporated quickly enough when his daughter Frances, Countess of Essex fell in love with Carr and wished to marry him, a connection which, as the Earl was well aware, could prove of considerable value to the Howards.

There was only one problem. In 1606, at the age of thirteen, Frances had been married to the Earl of Essex, the charmless fourteen-year-old son of Queen Elizabeth's executed favourite. On account of their youth the couple had not lived together after their marriage, Essex undertaking a four-year visit to the Continent to complete his education, while Frances assumed her place at court. A beautiful young girl let loose in society with little affection for an absent husband is certain to be exposed to temptation, and it was perhaps not surprising that Frances, nurtured in the belief that marriage was an institution more closely concerned with the amassing of wealth and power than with emotional commitment, would be quick to succumb. According to contemporary gossip Frances lost her virginity when she seduced James's eldest son, Prince Henry, but their relationship came to an end when Frances started an affair with Robert Carr.

Essex's return from the Continent only confirmed that he and his wife were completely unsuited to one another. Despite repeated attempts on his part, the marriage was never consummated, a circumstance which, in view of Frances's love for Carr, afforded her considerable relief. Besotted with the handsome favourite, she determined that their affair should have no other outcome than marriage, and it was relentless pursuit of this goal that was to drive her into criminality and bring her to the brink of execution.

To ensure that her marriage remained unconsummated, she enlisted the aid of her old friend and confidante, Mrs Anne Turner. This pert young widow, a companion to Frances when the latter was a child, had established herself on the fringes of the court by introducing to England a fashionable coloured starch which dyed ruffs and cuffs bright yellow, and it was allegedly at her house in Hammersmith that Frances and Carr (created Viscount Rochester in 1611) had their adulterous encounters. She counselled recourse to Dr Forman, a physician whose blend of quackery and sorcery had made him popular with courtiers who wanted assistance in the conduct of their love affairs. Forman supplied the Countess with love philtres with which to ply Rochester and with potions designed to incapacitate her husband, and whether in consequence of these measures, or in the natural course of events, Essex remained unable to fulfil his marital duties, while Rochester became more enamoured than ever. Desirous to marry her, he approached the King, who surprisingly enough seems to have felt little jealousy when his favourites acquired wives for themselves, and the latter enthusiastically agreed that an ecclesiastical commission should be appointed to decide whether Frances's marriage with Essex was still binding.

So far things had gone well for Frances but as she well knew, there was one man capable of obstructing her plans. Sir Thomas Overbury was an arrogant and outspoken courtier who until recently had been Rochester's best friend and adviser. Initially he had not objected to Rochester's pursuit of Frances, even assisting him in the composition of his love-letters, but when he discovered that the Viscount was contemplating marriage with a woman whom Overbury evidently considered little better than a whore, and whose family he detested, he made his disapproval very evident. Returning to his chamber late one night after an assignation with the Countess, Rochester found Sir Thomas waiting for him. 'Will you never leave the company of that base woman?'[28] he demanded offensively, and an angry exchange ensued, which only succeeded in alienating Rochester from his former friend and which earned Overbury the implacable enmity of Lady Essex.

The couple realized however that Sir Thomas could be a dangerous foe. In order to obtain a divorce that enabled her to remarry, Frances had to claim that she had never known any man carnally, but as Overbury was presumably familiar with the details of their affair, he was in a position to dispute this and the lovers had no doubt that he would not hesitate to put his knowledge to good use. To neutralize Overbury, Rochester persuaded the King to appoint him ambassador to Russia, and when Sir Thomas declined the mission, his refusal was artfully represented to the King as a calculated insult. Thus inflamed, James ordered him to the Tower in April 1613. Once there, Overbury's health steadily declined and on 15 September 1613, after days of appalling torment, he died, his passing mourned by only a few members of his immediate family.

Meanwhile, an ecclesiastical commission headed by the Archbishop of Canterbury, George Abbott, had convened in June 1613 to consider Frances's nullity suit. The case filled Abbott with misgiving, partly because he was evidently acquainted with court gossip concerning the nature of Frances's relationship with Rochester, and partly because Overbury had apparently succeeded in giving him some intimation of the true state of affairs prior to his arrest in April. Although her husband agreed that he had never had intercourse with his wife, the commission would not accept that Frances was a virgin until she had undergone a gynaecological examination at the hands of a committee of matrons composed of two midwives and three noblewomen who, understandably enough, 'came unwillingly to it'. To the amazement of everybody they pronounced Frances 'a virgin uncorrupted', a verdict which, it was suggested, had been reached only because the Howards had taken advantage of the concession permitting the lady to be veiled during the proceedings and substituted for Frances her cousin Mistress Fines – of whom one courtier did not scruple to note that though she was 'at that time too young to be other than *virgo intacta* . . . within two years after, had the old ladies made their inspection, the orifice would not have appeared so small to have delivered such a verdict as they did'. The real explanation was probably less sensational, for as the Bishop of London pointed out to his colleagues, the ladies who had conducted the examination 'knew not well what to make of it . . . they had no skill, nor knew what was the truth; but what they said was upon the verdict of the midwives which were but two, and I knew not how tampered with'.[29]

Despite these reservations, on 25 September the commission decided, by a majority of seven to five, that the marriage of the Earl and Countess of Essex should be dissolved. Frances did not remain a divorcee for long, for on 30 December she and her lover (whom James had thoughtfully created Earl of Somerset in order that she might suffer no diminution in rank upon remarrying) were wed, Frances defiantly reaffirming her maiden status by wearing her hair unbound, 'pendant almost to her feet', in the manner of a virgin bride. The King and Queen both graced the nuptials and in the ensuing months the couple were the toast of the court, Frances having apparently become 'the King's favourite as well as her husband'.[30] By late 1614, however, Somerset was troubled by the rise in royal favour of George Villiers, an exquisitely featured young man to whose charms James seemed highly susceptible. Unwisely, he sought to reassert his hold over the King by subjecting him to torrents of abuse, exasperating James, who would have liked both old and new favourite to have lived in peaceful co-existence, and weakening his own position still further. His immoderate behaviour rendered him vulnerable to attack – and he was a man with many enemies. In the autumn of 1615 Secretary of State Ralph Winwood uncovered information suggesting that Sir Thomas Overbury had been poisoned in the Tower and that the Earl or Countess of Somerset was responsible for his death. He hastened to reveal this to the King, who, genuinely appalled, declared he would do nothing to shield the perpetrators of this crime from justice. On 17 October 1615 Lord and Lady Somerset were separately put under restraint. Two days later the first of their alleged confederates went on trial.

Among these was Mrs Anne Turner, the obliging widow from Hammersmith who, it was claimed, had acted as an intermediary between the Countess of Somerset and James Franklin, the apothecary who had supplied the various poisons intended for Overbury. Richard Weston, a former servant of Mrs Turner who had been the gaoler of Sir Thomas Overbury, had already been convicted of his murder, following his admission that Mrs Turner and the Countess had arranged to supply him with certain substances to administer to his prisoner. There was hence little doubt that the jury would find Mrs Turner an accessory to the crime, but her trial was prolonged and enlivened by the prosecution producing a wealth of sordid and irrelevant evidence designed to blacken her character. Details of the earlier dealings of the Countess and herself with Dr Forman (whose own death had prevented him from having anything to do with Overbury's murder) were paraded before the court, and the exhibits plundered from Forman's surgery included a lead statuette of a copulating couple and a list detailing 'what ladies loved what lords in the court' which, to the annoyance of all spectators, the Lord Chief Justice did not allow to be read out. After the jury had brought in the expected verdict against her, Sir Edward Coke informed the weeping woman that she was 'a whore, a bawd, a sorcerer, a witch, a papist, a felon, the daughter of the devil Forman' and sentence of death was pronounced on her forthwith. A week later she was taken to Tyburn for public execution and 'many men and women of fashion came in coaches to see her die'.[31]

Protected by her rank, Frances herself was to have a much easier time. Her trial had been delayed because she was pregnant when arrested, but having given birth to a daughter on 9 December, she was interviewed early in the following year and admitted that tarts and jellies which she had had sent to Overbury in the Tower had contained poison. She insisted, however, that her husband had had no knowledge of her doings, and indeed the evidence of his complicity in the plot was far from overwhelming. On 24 May 1616 a panel of peers presided over her trial in Westminster Hall which was packed with 'more ladies and other great personages than ever . . . were seen' at any previous hearing for murder.[32]

The case was conducted with every regard for the sensibilities of the accused, for the King had specifically instructed that 'no odious or uncivil speeches' should be used against the lady. Dressed all in black, save for a ruff and cuffs of cobweb lawn, her sober demeanour wrung the hearts of most spectators, although John Chamberlain considered her bearing 'more curious and confident than was fit for a lady in such distress'. Holding her fan before her face during the reading of the indictment, she pleaded guilty in a low voice. The Attorney General now rose to praise her for her frankness, suggesting to the assembled peers that Lady Somerset could not 'but be a spectacle of much commiseration if you consider either her sex – a woman – or her parentage – honourable',[33] and though the Lord Chancellor proceeded apologetically to pronounce sentence of death upon her, his proviso that in view of the 'humility and grief' with which she had confessed her crime, the Lords would mediate for the King's mercy for her, left few present under the delusion that the penalty would be enacted.

The following day her husband was tried, and despite his staunch defence he too was found guilty and condemned to death. Neither sentence was ever carried out. Frances was reprieved in July 1616, greatly to the annoyance of the common people, who felt that this proved that there was one law for the rich and another for the poor. The Overbury murder case, described by one contemporary as 'the gross production of a then foul state and court, wherein pride, revenge and luxury abounded',[34] had outraged the nation, and by failing to punish the principal culprits the King drew upon himself a share of that odium which would otherwise have devolved exclusively upon them.

In January 1622, Frances and her husband were released from the Tower and permitted to retire to the seclusion of the country. For ten years they lived unhappily together, for their love for one another had not survived the disclosures of the murder trials. In 1632 Frances died, aged only forty, from a loathsome disease which Arthur Wilson gloatingly described in a history of his own times dedicated to her first husband: 'That part of her body which had been the receptacle of most of her sin grown rotten . . . the ligaments falling, it fell down.'[35] It would have been better for her to have been executed.

Curiously enough, Frances was not the only member of the Howard family who brought ruin on her husband. Her father, Thomas Howard, Earl of Suffolk, had been Lord Treasurer since 1614, but in the summer of 1618 the King was made privy to the widely known fact that it was impossible to conclude any business with the treasury unless a large sum had previously been paid to the Earl's wife, Katherine, Countess of Suffolk. On 19 July 1618 Suffolk resigned and the following November he and his wife were brought to trial in the Court of Star Chamber, accused of 'extortion, oppression, bribery, false dealing, embezzlement of the King's jewels etc.'. The Earl was 'more pitied than condemned, the Countess more condemned than pitied', for it was felt that Suffolk had merely passively acquiesced in the dishonest arrangements of his wife. Several of the Countess's letters – described by the prosecution as 'impious in style and odious in matter' – were aired in court, proving her guilt beyond doubt. At the trial's conclusion the Attorney General asserted that 'her subtleties . . . had made my Lord's house a snare for the subject'[36] and the Suffolks were fined £30,000 and imprisoned during the King's pleasure. As so often, however, the King extended mercy towards those who least deserved it. Their fine was remitted to only £7,000 and they were released after ten days' imprisonment.

The discomfiture of the Howards was completed by the ousting of Lord Wallingford, who had married the Suffolks' eldest daughter

Elizabeth, from the lucrative post of Master of the Court of Wards. His wife angered the King by circulating at court a rhyming 'lewd libel' against George Villiers. In January 1619 James accepted Wallingford's resignation, telling him that 'he was loth to remove him, but only he had one fault common to him, with divers others of his friends and fellows ... that he was altogether guided and overruled by an arch-wife'.[37] At least, however, it could never be said that the Suffolks' youngest daughter, Katherine, Countess of Salisbury, had ruined her husband's career by setting herself in opposition to the favourite; on the contrary, it was said that she had taken him for her lover.

The rout of these meddling females delighted many gentlemen at court. In early 1619 it was noted approvingly that 'The King is in a great vein of taking down high-handed women',[38] but in fact those who had fallen into disgrace were to be swiftly replaced, for the rise of George Villiers (created Earl of Buckingham in 1617) had resulted in the court being overrun by his female relatives, of whom his mother, the masterful Lady Compton, was the most notable. She had been born Mary Beaumont and though of gentle blood she had been so poor in her youth that she had been obliged to enter the service of a wealthy relative in the capacity of waiting gentlewoman. While thus employed, her looks had attracted the attention of George Villiers, a Leicestershire squire who subsequently took her as his second wife, and Buckingham was the second of the three surviving sons of this marriage. Since Sir George Villiers's death, she had twice remarried, but her present husband, Sir George Compton, was a drunkard whom she held in complete contempt and for whom she would do nothing even at the height of her good fortune.

As Buckingham rose, so his mother pushed herself to the forefront of the court, and by 1616 she was already 'intermeddling in affairs' to an extent that Buckingham warned her 'is not so well taken'. Basically, however, he was devoted to her, and as the King had come to view all of Buckingham's relations through the lens of love, Lady Compton could get away with assertive behaviour that would have been tolerated in no other lady of the court. That she was not to be trifled with was demonstrated when James banned Lady Hatton from court for having uttered 'braving and uncivil words to the Lady Compton and vouching the Queen her author', and on 1 July 1618 she received even more striking proof of the King's regard for her when, six months after making Buckingham a marquis, he created his mother Countess of Buckingham in her own right, an arrangement that left her husband languishing as a humble knight.[39]

The death of the Queen, on 2 March 1619, made her position if anything more secure, for with Anne gone, James depended increasingly on Buckingham and his relatives to surround him with the cosy family atmosphere which in his declining years he had come to appreciate. Thus, as a disgruntled courtier sourly remarked, it came about that the King 'that naturally in former times hated women, had his lodgings replenished with them'.[40]

Buckingham's control over the dispensation of patronage steadily tightened, and being a dutiful son, he was naturally inclined to prefer those who had recommended themselves to his mother. In consequence, men of ambition fawned upon her in hopes that she would support their aspirations, and she was besieged by petitioners entreating her to draw Buckingham's attention to their problems, as in 1623, when Sir John Mitchell asked her to move him 'to procure a hearing of his cause by the Lord Chief Justice . . . and end his miseries in Chancery'. According to Arthur Wilson, indeed, 'Her hand was in all transactions, both in Church and State, and she must needs know the disposition of all things, when she had the feeling of every man's pulse, for most addresses were made to her first and conveyed by her to her son, for he looked after his pleasure more than his profit.'[41]

This in fact was something of an exaggeration, for although Buckingham took note of many of his mother's suggestions, he was both too ambitious and too energetic to have permitted his mother to have monopolized his affairs in this way. It was also too readily assumed that all appointments at court were controlled by mother and son, whereas James was careful to retain his independence in such matters. In July 1621, for example, the Venetian ambassador deduced that the Countess's chaplain, John Williams, had been appointed Lord Keeper at the instigation of Buckingham and his mother, but in fact the King had previously rejected two of Buckingham's nominees for the post and Williams was very much his own choice. Although Lord Carew, Secretary Naunton and the Earl of Arundel all assiduously danced attendance on her in hopes that she would arrange for one of them to succeed the disgraced Earl of Suffolk as Lord Treasurer, Henry Montagu was appointed in December 1620, whereupon it was simply assumed that the Countess had procured him the job in return for a bribe of £20,000. Such a sum had indeed changed hands upon Montagu's promotion but it was the King rather than the Countess who had received it as a loan.[42] Powerful as the Countess was, belief in her omnipotence was in part a myth that fed upon itself.

The Spanish ambassador, Gondomar, had long been wont to quip that England was ripe for conversion to Catholicism, 'for there are more prayers and oblations offered here to the mother than to the son', and this jest acquired a sinister significance in the eyes of God-fearing Englishmen when after some months of wavering in her faith, the Countess finally 'relapsed into popery' in September 1622. She was in consequence denied the court for a while, but her exile was far too short for the liking of many who were fearful 'that the Duke would be ring-streaked with spots of Popery by resorting to his mother's trough'.[43] As it happened, they need not have worried, for Buckingham was to remain a staunch Anglican, pursuing in the years to come an aggressively Protestant foreign policy against both the major Catholic powers on the Continent.

It was as a matchmaker that the Countess of Buckingham truly ruled supreme. It was not enough for her that Buckingham himself should wed the great heiress, Lady Katherine Manners; his mother also insisted that her eldest son, John, should marry Sir Edward Coke's wealthy daughter Frances, despite the fact that the girl herself had no wish to be joined to this pathetic simpleton and had only consented to the match after her father had tied her to the bedpost and whipped her. The Countess's two remaining offspring were already accounted for and so nothing further could be done for them in the marriage stakes (although Sir William Feilding, married to Buckingham's sister Susan, was raised to the peerage as Lord Denbigh) but the Countess's children were not the only ones on whom her matchmaking talents were focused. She had a horde of poor relations 'so numerous as were sufficient to have peopled any plantation', and as one who had herself been raised from comparative poverty by an advantageous marriage, she was determined that they should share her present good fortune. Contemporaries were moved to grudging admiration by her conscientious remembrance of these dependents, but nevertheless the brazen way in which confirmed bachelors and elderly misogynists sought to further their own careers by scrambling to the altar on the arm of some needy member of the Countess's kindred aroused comment even in an age where marriage was acknowledged to be a practical rather than a romantic concern. The homosexual Sir Anthony Ashley 'was snatched up for a kinswoman'; Sir Christopher Perkins, a septuagenarian 'woman hater that never meant to marry' broke a self-imposed vow of celibacy to wed the Countess's sister in order to secure for himself the position of Master of Requests; and the brilliant and ambitious Lionel Cranfield found that his career at court unaccountably ground to a halt when he expressed reluctance to marry the Countess's relative, Anne Brett, a young lady who had 'little money but good friends', and only resumed when he bowed to pressure and took her for his wife.[44]

Created a Duke in 1623, Buckingham would remain in the ascendant even after James's death on 27 March 1625, for after an initial period of antagonism Prince Charles succumbed to his charm, and by the time that he ascended the throne Buckingham was already established as his best friend and adviser. This was the more remarkable because Charles, cultured, sober and reserved to the point of prudery, was in most respects a complete contrast to his father. Upon his accession, the lax ways of the court perceptibly tightened as a series of regulations, designed both to promote decency and restraint and to emphasize the King's exalted status by keeping him remote from the vulgar gaze, were put into effect. By early April 1625 the Countess of Bedford reported that the new King had 'already changed the whole face of the court very near to the same form it had in Queen Elizabeth's time, suffering none but the council and his [gentlemen of the] Bedchamber to come further than the Privy Chamber where he continually abides.'[45] Nevertheless this new order was not to prevail for long, for in June 1625 it was disrupted by the arrival of Henrietta Maria, the fifteen-year-old French Princess to whom Charles had been betrothed the previous December, and to whom he had been married at a proxy ceremony in Paris on 8 May.

Although ushered over the Channel by a deputation of Villiers ladies who had crossed to meet her at Boulogne, the new Queen brought in her wake a numerous retinue including a swarm of French noblewomen who, according to the terms of the marriage treaty, were for the time being to monopolize positions in her household. The English greeted the foreigners without enthusiasm: 'the Queen's train, poor pitiful women, not worth looking after' one onlooker commented scornfully, and it was only a matter of time before more serious complaints had arisen. The King for some reason had taken an almost instantaneous aversion to Madame St Georges, the daughter of Henrietta Maria's former governess and now her principal attendant. Soon after their arrival the King refused to permit Madame St Georges to travel in the same coach as himself and the Queen, claiming that there were English 'women of better quality to fill her room', and as even the French ambassador admitted, Henrietta, wilful, proud and determined not to be imposed upon by strangers, showed her resentment at this snub rather too plainly. A disagreeable

1 Anne Boleyn, by an unknown artist

2 Jane Seymour, by Holbein·

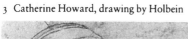

3 Catherine Howard, drawing by Holbein

4 Catherine Parr, by an unknown artist, c. 1545

5 *A Procession of Queen Elizabeth I*, attributed to Robert Peake, *c.* 1600. A maid of honour, dressed in silver, is standing on the right.

6 Elizabeth I receiving two Dutch emissaries in the Privy Chamber, by an unknown artist. Several ladies-in-waiting are in attendance during the audience.

Four ladies whose marriages or love affairs angered Elizabeth I
7 Lady Catherine Grey, Countess of Hertford and Edward, her son. English school, sixteenth century
8 Lettice Knollys, portrait attributed to George Gower, *c.* 1585
9 Ann Vasavour, portrait attributed to John de Critz
10 Mary Fritton, by an unknown artist

11 Costume design by Inigo Jones for Ben Jonson's *Masque of Blacknesse*, performed by Anne of Denmark and her ladies, 1605. One member of the audience considered the costumes to be 'rich, but too light and courtesan-like for such great ones'.

12 Costume design by Inigo Jones for Samuel Daniel's *Tethys Festival*, a masque performed by Anne of Denmark and her ladies in June 1610

13 Arbella Stuart, by Marc Gheeraedts

14 Frances Howard, Countess of
Somerset, attributed to W. Larkin

15 The Duke of Buckingham and his family, by an unknown artist, 1628. The Duke's sister, Lady Denbigh (far left), his wife (holding his hand) and his mother were all ladies-in-waiting to Queen Henrietta Maria.

16 Queen Henrietta Maria, Lucy, Countess of Carlisle and other ladies; detail from *Apollo and Diana* by Gerrit van Honthorst

17 Barbara Villiers, Countess of Castlemaine
and Duchess of Cleveland, after Lely

18 Frances Stewart, Duchess of Richmond
and Lennox, by Lely, c. 1662

19 One of the last ladies of the Privy
Chamber: Nell Gwynne, by Simon Verelst,
c. 1670

20 Louise de Keroualle, Duchess of
Portsmouth, by Pierre Mignard, 1682

21 Sarah Churchill, Duchess of Marlborough, after Kneller, *c.* 1700. At her waist hangs the gold key of the Bedchamber, the insignia of the Mistress of the Robes, which was probably added to the picture after Queen Anne's accession.

22 A portrait believed to be of Abigail, Lady Masham, by an unknown artist, *c.* 1700

23 The Duchess of Somerset, after Lely, *c.* 1679

scene ensued and the ill feeling lingered because thenceforward the King took the precaution of always travelling with his wife in a coach which he said was too small to fit in Madame St Georges although, as Henrietta Maria sulkily observed, it proved capacious enough to accommodate Buckingham's niece, the Marchioness of Hamilton.[46]

The King was the more intransigent because he did not wish to seem weak to Buckingham, who was naturally concerned that if the Queen succeeded in asserting herself over her husband his own influence would decline, and therefore advocated firm treatment of her. He suggested that Henrietta would prove more pliable if his mother, wife and sister were installed in positions in her household and in July 1625 the Queen's brother, Louis XIII, was approached with requests that the marriage treaty might be modified to that effect. As befitted a man who had just expelled his Spanish wife's native attendants from his country, Louis was initially amenable, but he was deterred by the representations of his advisers that such concessions were inconsistent with the honour of France. At the end of August he rejected the proposal and Buckingham was obliged to bide his time.[47]

Disagreements continued to multiply between the French and their reluctant hosts. When Charles sent Henrietta a copy of the regulations drawn up for the benefit of his mother's servants, the Queen petulantly observed that she trusted Charles would 'give her leave to order her house as she list herself'. To the King's annoyance she failed to learn English, preferring to sit chattering in her own tongue with her French attendants. Religion, as ever, proved a fruitful source of discord, for though the marriage treaty had expressly provided that the Catholic Queen and her household should have freedom of worship in England, they aroused hostility by displays of piety which bordered on exhibitionism. On Holy Thursday 1626 the Queen and her ladies publicly processed from Somerset House to the chapel at St James, an exploit which rumour quickly magnified into a report that they had filed barefoot to Tyburn so that the Queen could kiss the gallows where so many Catholic martyrs had suffered. While flaunting their devotion to their own church, they made evident their contempt for all forms of Protestant ceremonial. In February 1626 Henrietta excused herself on grounds of conscience from being crowned with the King according to the rites of the English church, but having given way in the face of what he imagined to be sincere religious sentiment, the King was irritated when he emerged from the service to see Henrietta watching the proceedings from an overlooking window, 'her ladies frisking and dancing in the room' behind her. Some months earlier, Protestant feathers had been ruffled by an incident which occurred while the court was staying at Tichfield in Hampshire on a hunting expedition. A Protestant service in progress in the hall had been rudely interrupted when Henrietta and a crowd of French attendants emitting 'the loud cries usual in chasing hares', had streamed into the room with a pack of little hunting dogs.[48]

As the score of grievances accumulated, the King became ever more exasperated, but though he told Buckingham as early as November 1625 that he was contemplating sending the 'Monsieurs' packing, the potentially serious consequences of breaking the marriage treaty deterred him for a while. Never one to assess both sides of a situation, Charles believed that the French were deliberately engendering bad blood between his wife and himself by encouraging her to behave tiresomely, without considering that her youth, her homesickness and even his own shortcomings as the husband of an inexperienced girl might also account for her waywardness. Even his initially unsatisfactory sexual relations with his wife he ascribed to the malign influence of her attendants, delegating Buckingham to approach Madame St Georges with the request that she persuade her mistress to be more forthcoming in the bedroom. Sensibly remarking that some reserve was to be expected in a young girl who had had a very sheltered upbringing, she loftily informed him that she never meddled in 'ces affaires là'.[49]

By the summer of 1626, the King had resolved no longer to suffer those that he deemed to be the 'cause and fomentors' of Henrietta's ill conduct. On 25 July 1626 he announced to the Queen that she must accept four English ladies of the Bedchamber, imposing on her not only Buckingham's wife, but also his sister, Lady Denbigh, his niece, the Marchioness of Hamilton, and even the woman believed to be his mistress, the Countess of Carlisle. The Queen protested that though she had no objection to the Duchess of Buckingham (who, she said pointedly, was at least virtuous) she loathed the Countess of Carlisle, but her husband peremptorily informed her that she was in no position to entertain such aversions and she was obliged to submit. That night her French attendants 'as presaging what would befall them', denied the new ladies of the Bedchamber access to the Queen, but their defiance was to do them no good. Marching into Henrietta's apartments the following day, the King found a scene of great merriment, with several of her servants 'unreverently dancing and curveting in her presence', but the festive mood was soon dispelled when Charles led his wife away and locked her in his rooms, leaving Lord

Conway to inform her thunderstruck suite that they should go to Somerset House to await the King's pleasure.[50]

Having a fairly shrewd idea of what the King's pleasure would be, the French made a terrible scene: 'The women howled and lamented as if going to execution, but all in vain' for, despite their protests, the Yeomen of the Guard forcibly evicted them all from the Palace precincts. Hearing the tumult from her prison and guessing its cause, Henrietta Maria became hysterical, breaking the panes of the window with her hand and shouting to her compatriots in the courtyard below, until Charles finally dragged her away. That afternoon he informed the French that having 'occasioned many jars and discontents between the Queen and him' they must leave at once, and though at first they 'contumaciously refused to go'; claiming that the English owed them large sums in arrears of pay, they submitted after some days of haggling had extracted from Charles more than £8,000 in cash and some jewellery for the ladies. 'Sullen and dogged' the French embarked in early August from Dover, where a hostile crowd had gathered to speed them on their way.[51]

No one was surprised when Charles, to counter possible French objections that Henrietta's faith would be endangered by the expulsion of her countrywomen, appointed Buckingham's Catholic mother and mother-in-law as additional ladies of the Bedchamber, leaving the Queen with a household comprised entirely of women who, in one way or another, were intimately connected with the man whom she probably hated more than anyone else in the world. Her situation was, however, less grim than it seemed, for having imposed his will upon his wife, the King would treat her with greater consideration than before, and her new attendants were not without compassion for their forlorn little mistress. When Charles had given the French their marching orders, Lady Denbigh had successfully appealed to Buckingham to persuade the King to permit his wife to retain at least her nurse and one other French lady so that she was not completely severed from all contact with home. 'Brother,' she had told him, 'if you did but see and hear her it would grieve your heart to the soul', and it was this kindly gesture that was to lay the foundations of what was ultimately to become a firm friendship between the Queen and herself. In September the Tuscan ambassador reported 'The Queen is treated with the most tender solicitude. She is surrounded with ladies of the highest rank, as if to show the French ambassador that she is both better served and with more deference than she was by her French attendants', and by the following month he could announce that Henrietta, initially sulky and morose after the replacement of her suite, was now 'very happy and cheerful'.[52]

French resentment of their treatment was nevertheless to have serious consequences. In September 1626 the Maréchal de Bassompierre was dispatched from France with instructions to remind the English of their treaty obligations. In November an agreement was signed providing for the restoration of forty-six members of the Queen's former household, but Louis XIII subsequently repudiated it, claiming that the concessions by the English were inadequate. Relations between the two countries had anyway seriously deteriorated over the last months and this final insult was to bring them to breaking point. By mid 1627 England and France were at war, but though England was to fare disastrously in the hostilities, Charles could at least console himself that when peace was finally concluded in April 1629, he was not obliged by its terms to accept back a single one of his wife's French servants.

As Henrietta became more settled in England her attitude towards her new household changed from acceptance to affection. On 23 August 1628, the Duke of Buckingham was assassinated and the King, distraught with grief, was nevertheless touched to note that his wife took especial pains to comfort 'the many distressed ladies in the court upon this accident'.[53] Lady Denbigh, by now established as Mistress of the Robes, was confirmed in her place, and her daughters, the Marchioness of Hamilton and Lady Elizabeth Feilding, remained in their respective positions as ladies of the Bedchamber and of the Privy Chamber.

Yet, fond as the Queen had become of the Villiers, her commitment to them was not total, for to their annoyance she had reversed her original opinion of Lucy, Countess of Carlisle and had come to regard her with all the fascinated admiration that a naïve young woman can have for a sophisticated companion some years her senior. The daughter of the Earl of Northumberland, Lucy Percy had caused a sensation in 1617 when, at the age of eighteen, she had defied her father to marry James, Lord Hay, a Scot of undistinguished origin with whom King James had been briefly infatuated and of whom he remained sufficiently fond to create him Earl of Carlisle in 1622. Acknowledged as the reigning beauty of her day, his wife had a sharp intellect which, had she been a man, might have taken her far, but which, in the circumstances, she could put to no better use than wit and intrigue. Her sex appeal was such that half the gentlemen of the court were enamoured of her, although possibly none of them loved her with the intensity with which she loved herself.

The majority of her admirers sighed for her in vain: Thomas, Lord Cromwell confided to a friend that he could not stop thinking of her 'and my wife gets something by such thoughts nightly wherein I commit I doubt not adultery', while the poet Sir John Suckling had to content himself with mentally undressing her while she took her daily walk in the garden of Hampton Court, admitting that as he watched her,

> I was undoing all she wore
> And had she walked but one turn more
> Eve in her first state had not been
> So naked or so plainly seen.

Evidently, however, the Duke of Buckingham went further than the realms of fantasy in his relations with her. In 1619 it was noted that her husband had been sent abroad, ostensibly on a diplomatic mission, but in reality so that the Duke might more easily conduct a love affair with a 'close connection' of the absentee. Buckingham's mother, wife and sister, on the other hand, loathed the Countess of Carlisle, 'Not only for the Duke's intimacy with her, but also that she hath the Queen's heart above them' and they were not alone, for despite (or perhaps because of) her seductiveness, there were many men at court who distrusted her, and feared that she might have a bad influence on the Queen. 'She has already brought her to paint and in time will lead her into more debaucheries', one observer noted darkly, but Henrietta herself seemed to have no doubts about her friend, having become so devoted to her that when the Countess went down with smallpox in the summer of 1628 it was only with difficulty that the Queen could be kept from her side.[54]

At the beginning of 1630, however, the Countess was nearly unseated by the scheming of her enemies. Rivalry over who should succeed the dead Duke of Buckingham as Lord Admiral had lately thickened the court's atmosphere of jealousy and intrigue. Lord Holland desired the position for himself, while the Earl of Carlisle was anxious that either Lord Dorset or Lord Pembroke should be appointed, so that he in turn might inherit the court offices which they held at present. In January 1630 the Venetian ambassador reported that matters were 'going in favour of Carlisle because the Countess, his wife, has for some time enjoyed the special favour of the Queen', but to counter this Lord Holland asked the French ambassador to use his influence on his behalf with Henrietta. The ambassador, angered by the way that Lady Carlisle had frequently made him the butt of her humour, informed the Queen that the Countess 'abused her favour and bore herself with little respect in her actions, going so far as to make sport of her', and Henrietta was evidently too familiar with her friend's talent for mockery to disbelieve that it could have been turned against her. Hurt and resentful, she dismissed her from court. The Countess's foes were jubilant, but as it turned out, not for long, for within the month Charles had persuaded his wife to accept her back at court. Although some of the warmth had gone out of their friendship for ever, by November 1631 Lady Carlisle had so re-established herself in the Queen's favour that she was invited to stand godmother to her second child Mary, a forgiving gesture which Henrietta would come to regret.[55]

Buckingham's death had drawn the King and Queen closer together emotionally and as Henrietta had matured, she had also come to share her husband's moral outlook, valuing order and decorum and determining that the court should be a showcase for the domestic virtues exemplified in their marriage. The high standards of conduct expected from all those in royal service were outlined in a series of regulations similar to those issued on Charles's accession, in which the maids of honour, presumably accounted the most vulnerable morally, were singled out for particular attention. They were forbidden 'to suffer any other but such as are fit to bear them company' to sit with them as they awaited the Queen's pleasure in the Presence Chamber, or to leave the court without the permission of the Queen, the Lord Chamberlain or his deputy. Needless to say, they were also reminded that 'when they shall be retired into their chamber they shall admit of no man to come there'. Inevitably, there were occasional transgressions: Henry Jermyn, for example, was expelled from court after he impregnated the Queen's maid of honour Eleanor Villiers and refused to marry her, but on the whole the moral tone of the court improved. Even the wife of a parliamentarian colonel subsequently acknowledged that 'the nobility and courtiers who did not quite abandon their debaucheries had yet that reverence to the King to retire into corners to practise them'.[56]

The admirable, if unrealistic, aspirations of the King and Queen were reflected in the court masques of the period, which took for their subject-matter such high-minded themes as the excellence of Kingship as a state of government, or the quest for a love based on spiritual affinity rather than the lusts of the body. The Queen and her ladies regularly appeared in the productions and instead of relying on professional actors to address the audience they themselves took speaking parts, making clear the extent to which the Queen identified with the message embodied in the text. Yet though the sentiments expressed were commendable enough, the Queen's delivery of them caused consternation, for the English were unaccustomed to seeing women, let alone royal women, declaim on stage, and like all novelties, it met with a mixed reception. When the Queen made her dramatic début in England with her appearance of February 1626 in Racan's French pastoral play *Artenice*, the Tuscan ambassador hailed it as a triumph, 'Not only in the decoration and changes of scenery but also in the acting and recitation of the ladies, the Queen surpassing all others', but there were murmurs at court of impropriety, and one courtier darkly informed a relative 'I hear not much honour of the Queen's masque, for if they were not all, some were in men's apparel'.[57]

The country's growing band of Puritans found the Queen's involvement in courtly theatricals even more reprehensible, for to them the stage reeked of sin, and royal patronage of it only confirmed the impression, which Charles and Henrietta had tried so hard to eradicate, that the court was a nest of vice. William Prynne, a Puritan barrister from London, voiced his feelings on the subject in his book *Histrio-Mastix*, a weighty tome which unfortunately for him was published in the autumn of 1632, when the Queen and her ladies were rehearsing their parts in the *Shepherd's Paradise*, another pastoral play which Walter Montagu had written specially for her. In his book Prynne described female actors as 'all notorious impudent prostituted strumpets', and when this passage, among others, was drawn to the attention of King Charles, he interpreted it as a direct slur on the reputation of his wife.[58] Accordingly Prynne was sentenced to lose both ears in the pillory, a savage and almost unprecedented punishment upon a professional man which raised great ill-feeling against Charles. It was ironic that the plays and masques of the Caroline court, which were intended to be praiseworthy celebrations of virtue and elegance, should only contribute to the widening rift between the King and a growing number of his subjects.

Discontent with the court was also fuelled by the continued economic exploitation of the population as a whole by the tiny minority who surrounded the King and Queen. Monopolies had been theoretically outlawed in 1624 but Charles had made use of a legal loophole to revive them, and, as before, the ladies of the court were among the few who benefited. In 1635, for example, Buckingham's sister, Lady Denbigh, was granted a patent for the production of a new strain of hops, estimated to be worth more than £1,000 a year, and the Duchess of Lennox was awarded a monopoly over the transportation of white and undressed cloths.[59]

Inevitably, such privileges were unpopular with those who did not enjoy them, and particular fury was aroused when in 1631 Charles accorded a company of Gentlemen Soapboilers, who claimed to have invented a new manufacturing process, exclusive control over the distribution of all soap in England. Laundresses throughout the country complained that the new soap blistered their hands, and the outcry was such that in December 1633 a committee was held in the Guildhall to adjudicate on the matter. In what can be considered as the seventeenth-century prototype of the modern washing-powder commercial, two laundresses 'indifferently chosen' were set to work scrubbing garments using the rival soaps. After two days the committee, fortified by assurances from eighty ladies of note that their maids agreed that the new soap harmed neither their hands nor the linen, pronounced it superior. Little faith was attached to the verdict however, for it was suspected 'that most of those ladies that have subscribed have all of them their linen washed with Castile soap', and that they had pretended otherwise only because they had a vested interest in the continuance of the system of monopolies. Certainly the Queen's laundress, Mrs Sanderson, confided to her mistress that although the Gentlemen Soapboilers had induced her to endorse their product, she never used anything other than traditional soap for her work. Black market sales of the old soap continued to flourish and the controversy only subsided in 1637 when its manufacturers were granted official permission to go into business again.[60]

As the 1630s progressed the court, already regarded as an economic burden on the nation, acquired in addition the damaging reputation of being religiously unsound, for under the influence of the Queen, Catholicism had become fashionable, particularly among the ladies of the court. During Henrietta Maria's early years in England, the King, aware of the strength of anti-popish feeling, had carefully guarded against Catholic infiltration at court, forbidding any English lady to accompany the Queen to mass and confining Lady Falkland, wife of the Lord Deputy of Ireland, to her mother's house when she converted in 1626. Nevertheless, as the Queen acquired more influence over her husband, the climate of the court became more accommodating to those of her faith, the rule against accompanying her to chapel was relaxed and, as the consequences of embracing Rome became less daunting, so the number of proselytes increased. With the arrival, in June 1636, of Father George Con, a Scottish Catholic accredited as official papal agent at Henrietta Maria's court, the pace of conversions appreciably accelerated.

His business with the Queen naturally brought the urbane and charming Con into the circle of her ladies and their friends, and having established himself in their confidence he could proceed to tackle them on religious matters. His success as an apostle was notable: 'Our great women fall away everyday', an Anglican clergyman lamented, and many Protestants feared that these conversions were merely the preliminary stage of an offensive designed to reclaim the whole of England for the Pope. Con was assisted in his work by the Catholic Countess of Arundel, a zealous exponent of her faith, and Mrs Endymion Porter, whose husband was a Groom of the Bedchamber to the King. Mrs Porter induced her mother and sister-in-law to change religion, and only failed to notch up her cousin the Marchioness of Hamilton as a gain on the Catholic scoreboard because the Marquis denied Catholics access to his wife as she lay on her deathbed, thus ensuring that her conversion was never acknowledged.[61]

Undaunted, Mrs Porter turned her attentions on her sister, Lady Newport, whose Protestantism crumbled before her onslaught, and by the autumn of 1637 Lady Newport was receiving instruction from Con. The Archbishop of Canterbury was outraged by what was the latest in a long series of defections and he demanded that the King take steps to prevent a repetition of the incident. There was talk of renewing the ban on any English lady attending mass with the Queen, but she pleaded with her husband to be less severe, and the anti-Catholic proclamation issued on 20 December 1637 was in consequence a very feeble document whose complete ineffectiveness was demonstrated only five days later when Henrietta mustered all the recent converts, including Lady Newport, for midnight mass in her chapel.

The exodus of Protestants continued, discrediting not only the Church of England but also the court and hence the Government itself. Puritans were convinced that the publicly acknowledged conversions were only the tip of the iceberg and that many of the gentlemen of the court maintained a superficial allegiance to their church only for the sake of their careers. In fact, many of the ladies who renounced Protestantism had done so in the face of stern resistance from their husbands: Lord Newport had been infuriated when his wife abjured her faith, and Sir William Balfour was so enraged to find his spouse at worship in the Queen's chapel that he ordered her out and then administered the attendant priest a sound thrashing with his cane. The Puritans, however, were convinced that Catholics had succeeded in infiltrating society, an attitude which could be said to be comparable to the mentality of the McCarthy era; they were therefore not reassured by isolated instances of husbandly wrath.

There was speculation that the Countess of Carlisle might be among the Romish recruits, but as Con himself wryly observed, 'The poor lady had no religion but her complexion', and her interests in these years centred on more worldly matters. Fascinated by the aura of power but unable to achieve it in her own right, she habitually attached herself to men of influence in hopes that some of their authority would brush off upon her, and it was thus not surprising that in the mid-1630s she allied with Thomas, Lord Wentworth, who, as the King's Lord Deputy in Ireland and the principal executor of royal policy, was very much the man of the moment. Wentworth was delighted when he returned from Ireland on a brief visit in July 1636 to be accorded the most gracious of receptions by the recently-widowed Countess. On the practical level, he hoped that Lady Carlisle would use her influence to promote him in the Queen's favour, for, as he told the Archbishop of Canterbury, 'I find her Ladyship very considerable, for she is often in place and is extremely well skilled how to speak with advantage and spirit for those friends she professeth unto',[62] but his gratification at her overtures was doubtless enhanced by the consideration that though she was nearing her forties, the Countess remained an attractive woman. Indeed they behaved so flirtatiously, even exchanging full-length Van Dyck portraits of one another, that rumours soon arose that they were lovers.

In November 1640, a catastrophic economic and military situation compelled Charles to summon a Parliament, whose first act was to arrest Wentworth (now Earl of Strafford) as the man they held responsible for their grievances of the last decade. The King was powerless to intervene, although the Queen and a party of wild young cronies talked of raising an army to rescue Strafford in the Tower and then seize power in a military coup. This came to nothing and in March 1641 Strafford was brought to trial on charges of high treason. The Queen and her ladies (including the Countess of Carlisle) attended the hearings, sitting in a specially prepared box 'like so many Sempronias, taking notes at the trial all day and discoursing it at night'.[63] All in vain, however, for Parliament sentenced Strafford to death by an act of attainder to which the King, after agonies of indecision, assented on 10 May. Two days later his minister was beheaded on Tower Hill.

The death of Strafford had the curious effect of propelling the Countess of Carlisle into the camp of his executioners, in the apparent belief that as the King and Queen had abandoned the Earl to his enemies, they no longer merited her loyalty. Sex may also have played a part in her apostasy, for it was subsequently insinuated that she had become the mistress of John Pym, the parliamentary leader. Exactly when she established contacts with his party, or how much information she gave them, is obscure, but certainly Pym always displayed an almost uncanny knowledge of royal deliberations and plans, and it is not unreasonable to assume he derived much of it from Lady Carlisle. Furthermore, as an intimate of Strafford's and friend of the Queen, she had been 'admitted to all the consultations which were for his preservation and privy to all the resentments had been in his behalf and so could not but remember many sharp statements uttered in that time', which, when relayed to Pym, could be used by him to whip up antagonism to the King.[64]

For some months, however, she played the role of double agent, retaining her position at court and evidently convincing the King and Queen that she used her contacts with their opponents to spy on their behalf. But as civil war drew nearer, even the Countess of Carlisle could not dart from side to side with such feather-light insouciance, and in January 1642 she finally cast herself off from the court. By then the King had decided that only by a show of force could he reassert himself over his opponents, and on 4 January he went to the House of Commons intending to arrest his five principal opponents there. Before he left Whitehall he told the Queen that he would have made his move within the hour and when that time elapsed Henrietta, ever impetuous, turned to Lady Carlisle and enjoined her to rejoice, for Charles was now 'master of his kingdom'. In fact her husband had been delayed on his way to Parliament, which enabled Lady Carlisle to send word of his approach to the five members and by the time that Charles reached the chamber, his birds had flown.[65]

With civil war looming, Henrietta Maria, accompanied by Lady Denbigh and the Duchess of Lennox, left for Holland in February 1642, ostensibly to settle her daughter in the home of her new Dutch husband, but really to raise money on Charles's behalf. By the time that they returned a year later, the conflict had already been in progress for over six months. In place of their former gilded existence, she and her attendants now had to cope with the exigencies of wartime, enduring bombardment from enemy guns on one occasion and living for some months with the royalist troops in the north before reaching the King's headquarters at Oxford in July 1643. There, for a time, the lifestyle of the court was recreated, with performances of pastoral plays, displays of dancing and the conduct of love affairs commanding as much attention as ever they had at Whitehall. Inevitably, however, reality soon impinged on these charades. In April 1644 the King deemed it wise to send his now pregnant wife to the West Country and in July the advance of parliamentary troops obliged her to take ship for France, even though she had not recovered from the birth of a daughter only a month earlier.

There, she was joined by Lady Denbigh, now a war widow, and as her French relatives received her kindly, she presided initially over a fairly sizeable establishment within the French court. But, as her niece Mademoiselle de Montpensier recorded, this did not last for long, for although the Queen at first appeared 'with the splendour of a royal equipage . . . all vanished . . . little by little and at last nothing could be more mean than her train and appearance'. As royalist fortunes dwindled, disillusion and penury became the lot of the emigrés, and with the execution of the King, the establishment of the Protectorate and the final defeat of royalist forces at Worcester, it seemed that the cause of the English monarchy had been extinguished for ever. During the long years of exile it would have needed the foresight of a seer to believe that in 1660, following the Restoration of her eldest son, Henrietta would be re-established in Somerset House surrounded by a full complement of ladies-in-waiting and living on an income of £60,000 a year.

V

The Court of Charles II

'Nothing Almost but Bawdry'

On 13 May 1662 the Infanta of Portugal, Catherine of Braganza, landed at Portsmouth, the intended bride of King Charles II of Great Britain, who two years earlier had been invited by his people to return from exile and reclaim the crown that had been his in name only since the execution of his father in 1649. During his years abroad his prospects had been so poor that he had been unable to find a European princess whose parents were willing to let her marry this bankrupt pretender to the English throne, and he had had to make do with a succession of mistresses, said to have numbered seventeen in all. With the unexpected reversal of his fortunes, however, he became a highly eligible *parti* on whom any continental royal family would have been happy to bestow a daughter, and by securing the hand of Catherine of Braganza Charles won one of the biggest prizes of all in the European marriage-market, for though small and ill-proportioned with sticking-out teeth, she brought with her a massive dowry, financed by the wealth of the Portuguese colonial empire.

The King's younger brother, James, Duke of York, had done rather less well for himself. He too had had to spend the Interregnum abroad and while on the Continent he had become irrevocably committed to Anne Hyde, daughter of Edward Hyde, who was Charles's principal political adviser while in exile. In 1653 Anne had been appointed a maid of honour to James's sister Mary, wife of the Dutch Prince of Orange, and James had first met her in 1656 when she had accompanied her mistress on a visit to the widowed Queen Henrietta Maria in Paris. Although somewhat dumpy and plain Anne was well-educated and witty, and made such a lasting impression on James that on 24 November 1659 he became secretly contracted in marriage to her, having seen her only rarely in the intervening years. By the time that Anne accompanied her family back to England on the Restoration she was already carrying James's child, and at first the Duke stood loyally by her. To make her position more secure he remarried her in another secret ceremony on 3 September 1660 and informed the King that if he was not permitted to acknowledge Anne as his wife he would 'immediately leave the kingdom and spend his life in foreign parts'.[1]

Confused reports of these events soon seeped out and were received on the whole with dismay: the Earl of Sandwich, in conversation with the diarist Samuel Pepys, proudly recalled an unattractive maxim of his father's, 'that he that doth get a wench with child and marries her afterward it is as if a man should shit in his hat and then clap it upon his head'; while the reaction of Anne's father (who on Charles's return to England had been appointed Chancellor) was even more extreme. He had had no inkling of Anne's involvement with the Duke of York, but he now realized that his enemies would claim that he had engineered the match out of personal ambition, and he seriously proposed that his daughter should be promptly removed to the Tower to await execution. James's sister and mother were also outraged by his lamentable *mésalliance*, for the Princess of Orange declared that she could never accept as a sister-in-law 'a woman who had stood as a servant behind her chair' and by early October both she and her mother had hurried over to England from the Continent intent on preventing 'so great a stain and dishonour to the Crown'.[2]

Faced with such overwhelming opposition, James himself had begun to waver, partly no doubt because heavy pregnancy had not enhanced Anne's looks, which anyway compared unfavourably to those of many of the beauties who now thronged the Restoration court. At this stage five of his friends obligingly volunteered the information that he was not the only putative father of Anne's expected baby and furnished him with the most explicit details of their own supposed intimacies with her. Harry Killigrew, for example, described how 'he had found the critical minute in a certain closet built over the water, for a purpose very different from that of giving ease to the pains of love' and which indeed he claimed had been the location for many of Anne's romantic assignations. When Sir Charles Berkeley, another of Anne's alleged paramours, offered to marry her to preserve the Duke 'from taking to wife a woman so wholly unworthy of him',[3] it seemed to James that he could without embarrassment rid himself of Anne, whom he now denied having ever married.

The King, however, was not prepared to connive at this caddish conspiracy. On 22 October 1660 Anne had given birth to a short-lived son, insisting throughout her labour that the Duke of York was not only the child's father but also her lawful husband, and though Charles was hardly overjoyed by his brother's foolhardy disposal of himself, he believed that Anne's claims were valid and that her marriage could not be overturned. Having decided to make the best of a bad job, he tersely informed his brother that 'He must drink as he had brewed and live with her whom he had made his wife', and the subsequent admission of Berkeley and his associates that their accusations had been baseless meant that Anne's future was assured. James himself had been suffering pangs of conscience about his behaviour to Anne and appeared relieved when on 21 December 1660 his marriage was to her finally 'publicly owned'. Three days later the Princess of Orange died of smallpox expressing regret for the harsh things she had said of her former maid of honour, and though Henrietta Maria seemed irreconcilable to the match, proclaiming that 'whenever that woman should be brought into Whitehall by one door she would go out of it by another door and never come into it again', even she relented after a time, consenting to receive Anne in her presence on 1 January 1661 and doing it with such style that it appeared 'as if she has always liked . . . from the beginning' the prospect of a commoner as her daughter-in-law.[4]

Anne had hardly made the most dignified of entrances into the ranks of royalty but once established as James's wife she compensated by becoming very much the Duchess, and she soon attracted criticism for being more regal than the royal family. Having had to struggle so hard to gain acceptance it was perhaps understandable that Anne was determined to make the most of her victory; nevertheless her pretension made her unpopular and when Charles announced in May 1661 that he was to marry the Infanta of Portugal there was satisfaction that instead of choosing for his bride some homegrown impostor who would act as if she had been born a princess, his Queen was to be the genuine article.

The announcement that the King had selected a wife was popular for another reason: to many people one of the most welcome aspects of the Restoration had been the renewed prospects of lucrative employment at court, and even though a foreign queen would bring with her a train of native attendants she would still require an English household, and thus extend the range of job opportunities for place-hunters. That there were many contenders for every place at court was not surprising, for throughout the reign the terms of employment for those in royal service remained extremely generous. On Charles's accession the royal household had been established on lines virtually identical to that of his father, with all court officials entitled to meals at the King's expense, but the old system had always been a ruinous drain on the Crown's finances and now proved too costly to maintain for very long. In August 1663 it was announced that henceforth there would be no more 'public diets' for the majority of royal servants, who would be compensated with board wages. Predictably the reforms were received with 'great murmuring, considering his Majesty's vast revenue and plenty of the nation', but retrenchment in this area had been long overdue and though the courtiers plainly thought otherwise, the King's economic situation was not such that he could afford to pamper them with the hospitality of a bygone age.[5]

Even those still fed by the royal kitchens had to accept reductions in their diet, the maids of honour's rations at both dinner and supper being cut to a mere seven dishes, which one contemporary observer considered so scandalously inadequate that he declared himself 'unwilling to name the number' when writing to inform a friend of these developments. In fact, as the menu for a typical midday meal at the maid of honour's table featured roast beef, roast mutton, roast goose or chicken, boiled mutton, rabbit, steak pie and tart, not to mention beer, Gascon wine and four different sorts of bread, they were probably still eating more than was good for them,[6] and certainly the chubby features which stare out from Sir Peter Lely's portraits of seventeenth-century court beauties are not suggestive of deprivation.

In addition to their meals, which cost the Crown an average of £700 a year, the maids received annual pensions of £200 and they could also count on a substantial cash payment when they left royal service. In 1670 for example, Simona Cary, maid of honour to the Queen since her arrival in England, was paid off with an award of £2,000 'as royal bounty for her service and attendance' and a year earlier her colleague Catherine Boynton had done even better when she had scooped a payment of £4,000 which made up her dowry for her marriage to Colonel Richard Talbot. Admittedly the Crown was not the most dependable of paymasters, for at times of cash shortage financial obligations to the maids of honour tended to be overlooked. In 1671, Margaret Blagge, a pious maid of honour who found the lewd atmosphere of the court so uncongenial that she quit it after seven years in royal service, found that such high principles could prove expensive: four years later she was still waiting for her golden hand-shake, and in 1675 she was obliged to return to the court briefly in hopes that her reappearance would jog the memories of those in charge of the royal purse-strings.[7] Clearly payment of these redundancy bonuses could be somewhat erratic, but they were at least worth waiting for.

For those no longer entitled to meals at court, royal service still held many attractions. The Mistress of the Robes and Groom of the Stool (positions which were henceforth combined) was indemnified for her loss of diet with board wages of £547 per annum while the women of the Bedchamber, also known as chamberers or dressers, received annual board wages of £60 in addition to stipends, graduated according to seniority, of between £200 and £150. The women of the Bedchamber were principally concerned with the practical tasks of helping the Queen to dress herself and arrange her hair, while their aristocratic counterparts, the ladies of the Bedchamber, attended the Queen in public, waiting on her during meals and accompanying her on walks and when she went to chapel. They too still enjoyed tangible advantages on account of their jobs, quite apart from the prestige that surrounded the position. Although no longer automatically entitled to lodgings in Whitehall they could still count on perquisites such as 'bouge of court': allowances of bread, beer and wine, plus enough candles and wood to provide them with light and heat throughout the year.[8]

At the time of the King's marriage, economic reform still lay in the future and royal service hence seemed all the more desirable. It was understandable, therefore, that prior to Catherine's arrival Charles should be inundated with appeals from importunate ladies anxious to secure positions in her establishment. Many of them were the wives, widows or daughters of needy Cavaliers who had undergone consider-able privation in the Civil War and were now hoping for restitution. 'Having by undaunted courage and constancy of mind promoted His Majesty's interest in the darkest time of its eclipse', Dame Frances Baker now expressed the hope that she would be compensated with the post of dresser to the Queen, as did Anne Gery, who pointed out that 'her father and kindred lost considerable estates in the late King's service, whereby she is reduced to indigence'. Both of these piteous appeals were unsuccessful, as indeed was that of the eccentric Dame Martha Jackson who claimed that during the war she had 'suffered much for the service of horse and foot soldiers and was once shot in the thigh', misfortunes which appeared to have permanently unhinged her, for now she demanded the wholly imaginary posts 'of gentlewoman of the horse and Lady of the Crupper to the Queen; also to be Countess of Pall Mall, Viscountess Piccadilly and Baroness of the Mews'.[9] Very early in his reign Charles had discovered that it was impossible to satisfy all the expectations entertained of his return; the Queen was to bring with her a sizeable Portuguese suite and in consequence initially required only four English dressers, and as the vacancies had been swiftly filled, disappointment was inevitable for the majority of applicants.

Although there was already a full quota of women of the Bedchamber and maids of honour weeks before the Queen's arrival, there hung an air of mystery over the appointment of the ladies of the Bedchamber. In April 1662 the Countess of Suffolk was designated 'Groomess of the Stool, first lady of the Bedchamber and Mistress of the Robes and Keeper of the Privy Purse', but there was no official announcement concerning the selection of her immediate subordinates. The reason for this secrecy lay in the King's resolve to appoint his current mistress, Barbara Palmer, Countess of Castlemaine as a lady of the Queen's Bedchamber.

Barbara had been born a Villiers, and in her the King had found someone equally if not more libidinous than himself. When she had become Charles's mistress in the spring of 1660 she was not yet twenty but she had already graduated from being (according to one childhood acquaintance) 'a little lecherous girl . . . [who] used to rub her thing with her fingers or against the end of forms' to become the mistress of Philip Earl of Chesterfield, an affair which had continued even after her marriage in 1659 to a Buckinghamshire gentleman named Roger Palmer. Chesterfield had nevertheless been swiftly forgotten when she made the acquaintance of Charles, possibly after having been sent in early 1660 as an emissary to the exiled court in Breda on behalf of a group of royalist conspirators.[10] Blatantly sensual with magnificent looks, Barbara was dazzlingly attractive, but her imperious and acquisitive nature ensured that she had the temperament, as well as the appearance, of a prima donna. Initially however, this only enhanced her appeal and helped smooth her path to the King's bed, which, by the time that Charles returned home to claim his inheritance, had already been established as very much her own territory.

The Lord Treasurer and Chancellor Hyde were frankly disapproving of the attachment and they determined to prevent the lady from profiting from it by refusing to seal any document which bore her name. But stern looks from elderly statesmen did little to deter the King, and anyway the rest of the court seems to have found it quite natural that a mature and attractive bachelor should regard a beautiful mistress as one of the necessities of life. In February 1661, almost exactly nine months after the Restoration, Barbara gave birth to a daughter whose paternity was variously ascribed to Chesterfield, Charles or even (though not very often) to Palmer himself. At the end of the year her husband was created Earl of Castlemaine with the proviso that the title would be passed on to 'the heirs of his body gotten on Barbara Palmer his now wife' – 'the reason whereof', Samuel Pepys noted in his diary, 'everybody knows'.[11] By then Barbara was already pregnant with her second child and this time nobody doubted that the father was the King.

As the Queen's arrival drew nearer Barbara showed no inclination to melt into the background. Rumours that she was to be appointed to the Bedchamber soon reached the ears of outraged court ladies, who suspected that the King would not find it easy to forswear Barbara and deemed it insufferable that he should inflict her presence on the Queen. The Duchess of Richmond (whose tongue was possibly the sharper because of her jealousy at the appointment of Barbara's aunt, the Countess of Suffolk, as Mistress of the Robes) went so far as to compare Lady Castlemaine to Jane Shore, the mistress of Edward IV, whose body had been flung on a dunghill, and to tell her that she hoped that she came to the same end. Barbara was undaunted. Arrogant, unscrupulous and devoid of compunction, she considered the very audacity of the proposal that she should wait on the Queen enhanced its appeal. It was only with difficulty that she was dissuaded from arranging to have her lying-in for the baby due in May at Hampton Court, where the King and Queen were to spend their honeymoon; it was therefore hardly likely that she would consent to give up an illustrious position at court for the sake of the Queen's sensibilities.[12] As for the King, the fact that he refrained from publishing a list of his wife's Bedchamber ladies shows that he recognized the need to proceed cautiously, but he remained resolute that Barbara should serve his wife in an official capacity.

Such was the situation when Catherine of Braganza landed in England. On 21 May 1662 she and Charles were married in Portsmouth and six days later the royal party set out for Hampton Court. Catherine was accompanied by a sizeable Portuguese entourage and, as usual in the case of foreign households imported by new Queens, the English were highly critical of the ladies in the party. 'For the most part old, ugly and proud' was the withering verdict of Chancellor Hyde (by now created Earl of Clarendon), while the Portuguese contingent of maids of honour were dismissed as 'six frights', although at least it was conceded that Catherine herself was the best-looking of the bunch. The appearance of these ill-favoured creatures was not improved by their obstinate refusal to follow Catherine's example and adopt English fashions, preferring to cling to their outmoded and cumbersome farthingales – wiry structures worn under voluminous skirts – which came to be known as 'guard infantas'.[13] They complained bitterly of English meat (too fatty) and English water ('so much poison') and caused difficulties by refusing to sleep in any bed which had previously been sullied by the presence of a man. They were also offended by their hosts' habit of urinating in public, grumbling 'that they cannot stir abroad without seeing in every corner great beastly English pricks battering against every wall'. Not all of them could claim to be immaculate however, as only a month after the Queen's arrival a new-born baby 'conceived to be the child of a Portugal woman' was found abandoned at Hampton Court. The King directed that she should be cared for and baptized Lisbona and the identity of the mother remained a mystery.[14]

But if the Queen's Portuguese attendants were universally unpopular, at least Charles professed himself delighted with Catherine herself, declaring that he would 'outdo all that pretend to be good husbands'. Unfortunately the King did not define a good husband as one who abjured the company of a former mistress and even in these early weeks of marriage, when his behaviour to Catherine was impeccable and she fell completely under his spell, there was an underlying tension, for the unresolved question of the Countess of Castlemaine's appointment to the Queen's Bedchamber posed a continual threat to the tranquillity of the court. In June Lord Cornbury informed a friend that there was still 'not one lady of the Bedchamber named, beside my Lady Suffolk', and he added ominously 'there are twenty little intrigues and factions stirring but with these I do not meddle ... only thus much I will tell you, that there are great endeavours used to make you know who a lady of the Bedchamber, but it is hoped by many they will not take effect ... I will not say more for fear of burning my fingers.'[15]

Meanwhile in early June Barbara had given birth to a son at her husband's London house. Shortly afterwards she and Castlemaine separated, after she had finally exhausted his patience by insisting that the child should be brought up in the Anglican faith, rather than as a

Catholic like himself. After a violent row Barbara flounced off to her uncle's house in Richmond, conveniently close to Hampton Court and the King. To him she could represent herself as a forsaken woman for whose ruin he was morally responsible and Charles proved eager to make gentlemanly amends. He reckoned, however, without the Queen, whose confessor had apprised her of the existence and identity of the royal mistress, and who had resolved never to receive her in her presence. The result was that when Charles submitted to her a list of ladies of the Bedchamber which included Lady Castlemaine's name, she indignantly scored out the offending entry. Grimly, the King adopted different tactics.

The unsuspecting Queen was holding a reception when without warning Charles presented the Countess of Castlemaine to her. Failing at first to recognize her Catherine received her graciously, but when she realized who she was the shock was such that it brought on a violent nosebleed and she fainted. Charles was not prepared to tolerate what he interpreted as defiance. That night he and his wife had their first argument: Catherine was evidently unimpressed by Charles's assurances that he had not touched his mistress since her arrival, greeting his renewed demands that she accept Lady Castlemaine as her servant with 'a torrent of rage'.[16] Determined to make his wife submit, Charles enlisted the aid of the unfortunate Chancellor Clarendon, to whom the very name of Lady Castlemaine was anathema, but who would, he knew, try to calm Catherine in the name of duty.

Initially Clarendon himself had remonstrated against the Countess of Castlemaine's appointment, pleading that Charles was expecting his wife to consent to that 'which flesh and blood could not comply with', but he was brought to heel by a letter of unmistakable menace from the King. 'Whosoever I find to be my Lady Castlemaine's enemy in this matter', he informed the Chancellor, 'I do promise upon my word to be his enemy as long as I live.'[17] In consequence, Clarendon had resigned himself to becoming the reluctant champion of the Countess, but unfortunately three separate lectures to the Queen on the subject of wifely compliance failed to elicit anything more from her than tears, recriminations and threats to return to Portugal. Clarendon retreated in perplexity and the King drew the conclusion that his wife had all the wilfulness of the Countess of Castlemaine, but none of the beauty or power to fascinate. In the circumstances it was not surprising that the Countess was able to capitalize on the estrangement between

Catherine and her husband and re-establish herself in the King's affections.

Like his father before him Charles suspected that his wife's recalcitrance was incited by her foreign household, and encouraged by Lady Castlemaine he resolved to dismiss them forthwith. Catherine was naturally appalled, piteously imploring that 'she might not be left wholly in the hands of strangers' but although Charles relented so far as to permit her to retain her aged nurse, the Countess of Penalva, and 'some few inferior servants', the majority of her compatriots were unceremoniously deported, without receiving the customary parting gifts and 'not very pleased with the court which they did not find so liberal as they had expected'.[18]

Homesick and lonely, Catherine found herself rejected by her husband and ignored by the court, miserably aware that there prevailed in that assembly 'an universal mirth in all company but hers'. Those English ladies who had been delegated to look after her displayed the true instincts of the courtier in their dealings with her, 'shewing more respect and more diligence to the person of the lady than towards their own mistress who they found could do them less good'. Such a situation was too intolerable for Catherine, stubborn and courageous though she was, to endure indefinitely, and by the time that the court returned to Whitehall in August 1662 she was on the verge of surrender. Having hitherto treated Lady Castlemaine with freezing reserve she swallowed her pride 'and on a sudden let herself fall first to conversation and then to familiarity' with her rival.[19] Thenceforth her policy was to accept with dignity what she was powerless to prevent.

By mid-October Samuel Pepys had heard that 'The Queen do know how the King orders things and how he carries himself to my Lady Castlemaine and others as well as anybody; but though she hath spirit enough, yet seeing she doth no good by taking notice of it, for the present she forbears it in policy.' Although Barbara was still officially not a member of the royal household Clarendon reported that 'everybody takes her to be of the Bedchamber for she is always there'. Catherine had told him 'that the King promised her on condition she would use her as she doth others that she should never live in court', but by April 1663 the King had broken his side of the bargain, for Lady Castlemaine was installed in lodgings above the Holbein Gate in Whitehall. On 1 June her triumph was sealed when a warrant was issued admitting her and four others as ladies of the Bedchamber to the Queen.[20]

Had Lady Castlemaine been capable of exercising restraint the situation might have been less painful for Catherine but it was in Barbara's nature to exult at the Queen's discomfiture. When Charles had been pressuring his wife to agree to the Countess's appointment he had been full of airy assurances that 'the lady would behave herself with all possible duty and humility unto her which if she should fail to do she should never see the King's face again', but in fact Barbara comported herself so disrespectfully towards her mistress that in later years the Queen described her behaviour as nothing short of cruel. Only once did she go too far, even for the King. One day in conversation with her ladies the Queen voiced her concern that her husband, who supped nightly with the Countess of Castlemaine, was endangering his health by keeping such late hours. Barbara promptly retorted that she and the King *never* stayed up late, unaware that Charles had entered the room and overheard her. Whispering in her ear that 'she was a bold impertinent woman' he dismissed her from court, but the Queen was not rid of her for long. Within days she was back at court as before, and she and Charles 'all friends again'.[21]

Although the King treated Barbara's lapses from good taste leniently enough, he was determined to ensure that her fellow ladies-in-waiting accorded her the respect that she denied the Queen. When Charles discovered that Lady Gerard, a French-born lady of the Bedchamber who was devoted to her mistress, had been speaking ill of Lady Castlemaine and 'not sparing the King himself', he temporarily dismissed her from his wife's service. Towards the end of the reign a similar incident occurred when another of Charles's mistresses, the Duchesss of Portsmouth, 'went crying to the King' to complain that Phyllis Temple, maid of honour to the Queen, had been maligning her and he instructed his wife to withhold the next quarter of Miss Temple's salary.[22] Clearly Charles expected discretion from his wife's ladies-in-waiting, unless of course it was with him that they committed the indiscretion.

Once the Queen had resigned herself to her husband's infidelities, she proved herself the most accommodating of wives. She was never a nonentity, however. After some months in England she endeared herself to the court by abandoning her original solemnity and becoming much more friendly and outgoing, and her looks also improved to such an extent that Samuel Pepys, in his own opinion a connoisseur of beauty who normally reserved his praise for Lady Castlemaine, or her younger rival, Frances Stuart, could spend a night in the absence of his wife 'sporting in my fancy with the Queen'. Furthermore, although normally a model of wifely tolerance, on at least one occasion Catherine could not resist administering a sound snub to her rival. Entering the Queen's bedroom late one morning and finding her still in the hands of her chamberer, Barbara had condescendingly remarked that she wondered Catherine had the patience to spend such a long time at her toilette. 'Oh I have so much reason to use patience that I can very well bear with it', came the acid return, and for once even Barbara would have had to concede that her mistress had come out best from the exchange.[23]

Patience the Queen certainly required in abundance for the Countess of Castlemaine was by no means the only lady of the court with whom the King was to become romantically involved. As early as 1663 fifteen-year-old Frances Stuart, 'the prettiest girl in the world and the most fitted to adorn a court', had attracted his interest. She had grown up in France during the Interregnum and had originally been a maid of honour to Charles's sister Henriette Anne, married to the younger brother of the French King Louis XIV. In 1662 however she had crossed to England to become one of Queen Catherine's maids of honour and her looks had quickly established her as 'the only blazing star' at court, and one furthermore which the King hoped would soon be twinkling in his firmament. But although no intellectual – according to Count Grammont, an irrepressible Frenchman who spent some time in England, 'It was hardly possible for a woman to have less wit or more beauty' – she proved more than the King's match when it came to fending off his advances. She was happy enough to accept his adulation, permitting him to retire into corners with her at court balls and stand 'kissing her to the observation of all the world', but she refused to let him 'do anything more than is safe to her'. Her resistance only inflamed the King the more, and when Catherine became dangerously ill in the autumn of 1663 there were many who believed that if she died Charles would marry Frances, for although he showed genuine distress at his wife's condition, he found time throughout her illness to continue his assiduous attentions to Mistress Stuart.[24]

In the event Catherine recovered and Frances was left only with the unpalatable options of becoming the King's whore or rejecting him altogether. For a surprisingly long time she contrived to do neither, giving Charles enough encouragement to sustain his interest but denying him the final favour. Frances in fact was not so insipid as she seemed, for beneath her frivolous exterior she concealed an unshakeable determination to preserve herself for marriage, but her problem was that for years she had allowed the King to think that ultimately she would become his property, and now no man dared brave his wrath by seeking her hand. It seemed that Frances had manoeuvred herself into an emotional impasse when rescue came in the shape of the Duke of Richmond, a bibulous but honourable nobleman who successfully proposed to her. Desperate not to lose Frances, the King withheld his permission for the match on the grounds that the Duke was in financial difficulties, whereupon in April 1667 the couple eloped. Charles was genuinely aggrieved, resolving never to permit Frances to come to court again, but his animosity evaporated the following year when she contracted smallpox and was in danger of losing her looks. Frances and her husband were once again admitted to court and in July 1668 she was appointed a lady of the Queen's Bedchamber. The gossips claimed that after Frances had married the King found her rather more approachable but it seems probable that they maligned her, and that in fact Charles's relationship with her, married or single, never went beyond the stage of flirtation.

For the Queen her husband's infatuation with her beautiful maid of honour had no doubt been an irksome interlude, for she was for ever coming across the couple embracing in the Palace and she became quite hesitant about entering her own apartments for fear of finding them together. After Frances's marriage Catherine nevertheless completely forgave her and she subsequently became one of the Queen's most devoted servants; and indeed, she had always represented more of a threat to Barbara than to Catherine. Initially Barbara had reacted to the King's pursuit of Frances with contemptuous indulgence, evidently incapable of believing that his affection for someone so inconsequential could be anything other than transitory. At a time when it was perfectly normal for women to share the same bed she would regularly invite Frances to sleep with her, taunting the King with the fact that what was unattainable for him was readily available to her. By 1663 Barbara herself was already having affairs with several other courtiers and so she was not displeased that the King was too distracted to take note of her peccadilloes, but when he showed no signs of modifying his passion she took alarm. Fortunately for her, although Frances's virtuous rejection of Charles's suit made him pursue her all the more ardently, it left him physically dependent on Lady Castlemaine, with the result that by the time that Frances finally married her Duke in 1667

Barbara had produced three more children which the King – albeit somewhat hesitantly – had acknowledged as his own. Emotionally, however, he was growing apart from Barbara throughout these years, and although the hideous scenes and tantrums which she periodically subjected him to in an effort to reassert her will over him had the temporary effect of bringing him back to her side, ultimately they only accelerated the process of estrangement.

Even physically, she could no longer dominate him as she had done before, for apart from his futile chase of Frances the King also indulged in casual affairs with various other ladies of the court. These included Lady Falmouth, a widowed lady of the Queen's Bedchamber whose name was later to be romantically linked with the Duke of York, and Jane Roberts, a clergyman's daughter who subsequently became the mistress of the Earl of Rochester, and then died repenting her impious way of life. Winifred Wells, a maid of honour to the Queen who was blessed with 'the carriage of a goddess and the physiognomy of a dreamy sheep' was another of the King's intermittent bedmates, for being 'of a loyal family and her father having faithfully served Charles I, she thought it her duty not to revolt against Charles II.'[25]

By the end of the first decade of his reign the King was also dipping into a lower sphere of society for his sexual pleasures. During the Interregnum all theatres had been closed but soon after the Restoration two dramatic companies had been established under royal patronage, and for the first time in the history of the English stage the terms of the patent governing the Theatre Royal authorized the employment of professional actresses, thereby spawning an exciting new breed of *demi-mondaines* who proved eager recruits to the King's bed.

In the previous reign ladies of the court had played at being actresses; now the position was reversed, for the Lord Chamberlain's *Establishment Books of the Household* for the period include lists of 'His Majesty's women comedians' who were among the troupe that regularly performed before the court in the Hall Theatre at Whitehall. As the court audience grew accustomed to professional standards of acting they grew correspondingly less appreciative of the sort of amateur theatricals that had been popular before: when the Duke of Monmouth and various court ladies appeared in a production of Dryden's *Indian Emperor* in January 1668 Pepys heard 'that not any woman but the Duchess of Monmouth and Mrs Cornwallis did anything like, but like fools and sticks'. Nor was the tradition of staging regular masques at court seriously revived after the Civil War, for though in 1671 a 'grand ballet' was performed by ladies of the court and in 1675 the masque *Calisto* was written in honour of the Duke of York's two young daughters, such events were exceptional and though the term 'masque' was still in common use, more often than not it was now applied to a masquerade, or fancy dress ball, rather than referring to the formal spectacles of yesteryear.[26]

The King himself was a keen theatre-goer but his interest in the stage was more than academic. It had quickly become fashionable among men-about-town to take an actress for a mistress and the King soon did likewise. Having first 'spoiled' and then discarded Elizabeth Weaver, he had an affair with her colleague Moll Davis, to whom he gave a ring worth £700 and a house in Suffolk Street, and his relationship with her continued even after her more famous rival Nell Gwynn became his mistress in 1667. Nell, an irrepressible cockney whose comic genius had made her one of the Theatre Royal's most popular actresses, endeared herself to the King by her rough wit and lack of pretension, and by the end of 1671 she had presented him with two sons and was installed in a house in Pall Mall. According to the contemporary historian Bishop Burnet, the King 'never treated her with the decencies of a mistress but rather with the lewdness of a prostitute' but although never ennobled like her principal rivals, she was at least made a lady of the Queen's Privy Chamber, for in a document of 1684 she is described as such. The position was of course purely honorary and entailed no duties; nevertheless the title must have had an agreeably prestigious ring to one who, upon her own admission, had been 'brought up in a bawdy house to fill strong waters to the guests'.[27]

Although the King's relationship with Nell Gwynn survived until his death she was never more than a sideline to him. By 1670 Barbara's relationship with Charles was in decline and when he bestowed on her the title of Duchess of Cleveland in July of that year 'in consideration of her noble descent, her father's death in the service of the Crown and by reason of her own personal virtues' it was in the nature of a parting gift. But it was not Nelly, 'the indiscreetest and wildest creature that ever was in a court', who was to succeed her as *maîtresse en titre* (or 'miss of state' as one contemporary anglicized it) but the altogether more refined Louise de Keroualle, a Frenchwoman who became Charles's mistress in the autumn of 1671.[28]

Louise came from an aristocratic but impoverished Breton family and had started her career at the French court as a maid of honour to

Charles's sister, Henriette Anne, Duchess of Orleans. She had accompanied her mistress across the Channel when she visited England in May 1670 and had immediately excited Charles's admiration, but the Duchess, who was well aware of her brother's proclivities, had insisted upon taking her with her when she returned home. Soon afterwards however, Henriette Anne died, not without suspicion of poison, and the French, anxious to maintain recently established friendly relations with England, had suggested that the now unemployed Louise should be dispatched to the English court to console Charles. Accordingly she was installed as a maid of honour to Charles's long-suffering Queen, although it was immediately apparent that the King wished her to undertake duties of a rather different nature. To the despair of the French ambassador she declined to co-operate for a year, but in October 1671 she was finally seduced at a house-party of the Earl and Countess of Arlington's. Nine months later she produced a son and in August 1673, having been naturalized as an English subject, she was created Duchess of Portsmouth and made a lady of the Queen's Bedchamber and was thus able, in the exultant words of the French ambassador 'to rank as high as any of the older mistresses who were Duchesses'. Henceforth, although at times in apparent danger of being superseded by one of the many society beauties eager for her place, her hold over the King's affections proved enduring, so that on his deathbed Charles could declare, 'I have always loved her, and I die loving her.'[29] The majority of his subjects felt otherwise, for although it was acknowledged that Louise was 'wondrous handsome' she represented their twin bugbears of France and Catholicism; she had besides a maddening habit of standing on her dignity – which prompted Nell Gwynn to enquire why, if she was so well born, she had stooped to prostitution. Although elegant, cultivated and intensely feminine, as a character Louise lacked human warmth.

From the Queen's point of view Louise, with her finely honed awareness of life's decencies, was a preferable rival to Barbara, but it was typical of Louise that she interpreted Catherine's civility towards her as proof of a genuine fondness on the Queen's part. In fact Catherine had a natural reluctance to be in Louise's company more than was absolutely necessary, and she accepted her as a lady of the Bedchamber only on the tacit understanding that Louise was never in attendance on her. When on one occasion Louise ignored this arrangement and came to wait on Catherine at table, 'which was not usual', the Queen was visibly upset.[30]

146

Catherine could at least draw perverse consolation from the fact that her brother-in-law treated his wife much as the King treated her. 'Having quieted his conscience by the declaration of his marriage', the Duke of York 'thought that he was entitled . . . to give way to a little inconstancy', and while the increasingly corpulent Duchess consoled herself for his infidelity by indulging to the full in the pleasures of the dining table, her husband acquired a well-deserved reputation as 'the most unguarded ogler of his time'. Although less discriminating than the King, James was equally amorous and cut swathes through the assorted ladies of his wife's household. If the object of his fancy was not already in royal service he used the offer of a position in Anne's household as an inducement to coax the lady into bed, although several gentlemen of the court considered this inadequate compensation for being cuckolded by the Duke. Both the Earl of Chesterfield and Lord Roberts whisked their wives back to their country homes in order to keep them out of York's clutches, and when the Earl of Southesk discovered that York was having an affair with his wife he even claimed that he had deliberately contracted venereal disease in hopes of passing it on to the Duke, although when solemnly challenged to confirm the story, he denied it was true.[31]

Had it been otherwise the disease would have reached near epidemic proportions at court, for James went on to have an affair with Goditha Price, a maid of honour to the Duchess, and discarded her in favour of Lady Denham, the young wife of an elderly poet, who responded to the bait of a guaranteed place as lady of the Bedchamber to James's wife. She proved an exacting mistress, however, for unlike her predecessors she refused 'to go up and down the Privy Stairs but will be owned publicly', evidently considering that the position of *maîtresse en titre* to the heir presumptive was one that merited official recognition. James obliged by abandoning all semblance of discretion, seeking Lady Denham out at court balls to exchange lovers' confidences in view of all the world. In the past the Duchess of York had borne her husband's infidelities with composure but naturally such flagrant behaviour distressed her, and she was known to be resisting the appointment of his mistress as one of her ladies of the Bedchamber when Lady Denham's death, in January 1667, solved the problem in an unforeseen way. At once it was whispered that she had been poisoned, either by her husband or by the Duchess herself, and though a subsequent autopsy failed to produce a shred of supporting evidence, the general un-pleasantness which had surrounded the affair prompted the Duke to declare that he would 'never have another public mistress again'.[32]

Unfortunately the temptations of the flesh remained as alluring as ever for the Duke and he soon found a successor to Lady Denham in the shape of Arabella Churchill, a maid of honour to the Duchess and sister of the future Duke of Marlborough. At a time when plumpness was in vogue, Arabella's tall and skinny figure was not admired and no one could understand why the Duke was attracted to her until she was thrown from her horse before the court, revealing such excellent legs that the onlookers 'could hardly believe that limbs of such exquisite beauty should belong to Miss Churchill's face'. Such was their appeal for the Duke that in August 1670 Arabella was obliged to retire to Moulins in France to give birth to James Fitzjames, who was to be the eldest of four illegitimate children by her lover.

On 31 March 1671 the Duchess of York died, probably from cancer of the breast, and James was once again a bachelor, but he proved surprisingly eager to fetter himself with new marital ties. When the King learnt that James had promised marriage to Lady Bellasyse, a vivacious but not very pretty young widow, he felt obliged to intervene, telling his brother 'that it was too much that he had played the fool once; that it was not to be done a second time and at such an age'.[33] James was instructed to search among the European Princesses for his bride and the disappointed Lady Bellasyse had to be contented with the promise of a peerage in her own right and an assurance that when James eventually made a suitable choice she would be one of the new Duchess's ladies of the Bedchamber.

It might in fact have been more politic to have permitted James to wed a Protestant commoner, for his marriage in 1673 to the Italian Mary Beatrice d'Este was very unpopular because she was a Catholic, and the revelation, earlier in the year, that James himself was a convert had already intensified anti-popish feeling in England. Having braved a storm of protest to marry this beautiful fifteen-year-old one might have thought that James would have settled for the pleasures of monogamy, but though he professed himself delighted with his new wife he soon revived his connection with Arabella Churchill, with the result that less than a year after the marriage she produced another little Fitzjames. The relationship eventually came to an end and in 1677 Arabella married Colonel Charles Godfrey and settled down to family life with him, leaving James to embark the following year on an affair with Catherine Sedley, yet another of his wife's maids of honour who, at twenty-one, had already acquired a reputation as being 'none of the most virtuous'. She made up for her lack of looks with a forthright and pithy wit which she disloyally claimed that

James was too dull to appreciate, but which must have held some appeal for him as his relationship with her was to continue into the next reign.

Highly-sexed though York unquestionably was, there was little danger that his mistresses would acquire political influence. While Anne Hyde was still alive Pepys was informed that 'the Duke of York in all things but his codpiece is led by his wife' and Anne was too self-assertive to permit any of her husband's trollops to encroach upon what power she enjoyed. To York, the idea of political pillow talk was anyway highly distasteful, and even before the death of Lady Denham his ardour for her had begun to cool because 'she troubles him with matters of State'.[34] The King, however, was widely regarded as being more susceptible to political pressure from his womenfolk, and to many people it seemed that he was the slave not only of passion, but of his mistresses as well.

In consequence developments in Charles's love life were scrutinized with an interest that might nowadays be reserved for the outcome of a Cabinet reshuffle or a by-election, and in particular the French ambassador, Colbert de Croissy, took great pains to keep Louis XIV informed about 'those little affairs on which so much often hinges'. Convinced that a francophile mistress could persuade the King to enter into closer relations with France, the ambassador set out to make himself as agreeable as possible to all the ladies in whom Charles had any interest. In April 1667 he was authorized to make 'a handsome present' to the Countess of Castlemaine, his superior in Paris reflecting that 'Ladies are fond of such keepsakes . . . and a nice little present can in any case do no harm', and he followed this up with regular gifts to all of those ladies whom he considered 'the chief personages' at the English court. To his surprise the bribes failed to bring in the expected dividends. In Lady Castlemaine's case, she was happy enough to accept these endowments from the French but considered herself under no obligation to the donors; but in any case Charles was not dominated by his lady friends to the extent that the French imagined. By 1669 the ambassador was thoroughly disillusioned: 'I have given away all that I brought from France, not excepting the skirts and frocks made up for my wife, and I have not money enough to go on at this rate', he wrote irritably in February, and he declared that he no longer considered it worthwhile to satisfy 'the greed of the women here for rich keepsakes'. In future he suggested gifts to Barbara should be restricted to 'such trifling tokens as a pair of French gloves, ribands, a Parisien undress gown, or some little object of finery.'[35]

The arrival of Louise had naturally put fresh heart into the French ambassador, although he was appalled by her initial refusal to let Charles into her bed, and made it plain that in his opinion it was her duty to lie back and think of France. In this he had a somewhat unlikely ally in the shape of Charles's Secretary of State, the Earl of Arlington, who had come to the conclusion that the King's mistresses 'could whenever they pleased, render ill services to statesmen and defeat their plans' and who was therefore relieved that Charles now favoured the sort of woman with whom he felt he could come to terms. Louise, he observed urbanely to the French ambassador, 'was no termagant or scold, and when the King was with her persons of breeding could, without loss of dignity go to her rooms and pay him and her their court'. He was supported by his wife, a Dutchwoman who was subsequently to become Mistress of the Robes, but whose friendship with the Queen did not prevent her from trying to be on the best of terms with the King's mistresses. On her husband's instructions she pointed out to Louise that in view of her impoverished condition her only alternatives were 'either to yield unreservedly to the King or to retire to a French convent' and it was significant that it was at the Arlingtons' house that Louise finally succumbed. But the Arlingtons failed to reap the expected rewards from Louise's capitulation, for she was too self-centred to consider that she owed her success to anyone else and saw no reason to divide its fruits. By 1673 the Earl was lamenting to the French ambassador that Louise had 'as soon forgotten the obligations he conferred on her as any of the good dinners she had eaten'.[36]

Arlington took revenge by inviting to England a rival to Louise, in the shape of Hortense Mancini, Duchess of Mazarin. Brought up in France, in 1668 she had separated from her eccentric husband to embark upon a life of wild romance with lovers of both sexes and every class. She arrived in England in the summer of 1675, 'befeathered and bewigged', preceded by her reputation as a beauty and sexual adventuress, a combination guaranteed to appeal to the King. Sure enough, in July 1676 the French ambassador learnt 'that Madame Mazarin is extremely well-satisfied with the conversation she has had with the King of England', which was a euphemistic way of saying that Hortense had become Charles's lover. However it soon emerged that Hortense was too unreliable to work at the serious business of being a royal mistress, annoying Charles by taking another paramour, and thereby ensuring that Louise, who had been in temporary despair over Hortense's new found favour, regained her ascendancy with the King. But even had Hortense remained Charles's favourite mistress, she would never have meddled a great deal in affairs of State as she was completely apolitical, and though the Arlingtons continued to hover around her 'in hopes of exploiting her influence', by the spring of 1677 the French ambassador had concluded that 'the King of England is a gallant enough man to profit by their designs and yet mock at them'.[37]

The truth was that though it was widely believed that the royal mistresses were all powerful, Charles was much too strong a character to be subjected to a petticoat tyranny. Should his mistresses' wishes in matters of patronage coincide with his own, he was happy to oblige them, but he would not be pressured into policies which he considered contrary to his interests. Nevertheless, the misconception remained that he was their bondman, and all too often the King's activities were attributed to the influence of his mistresses when in reality he was acting on his own initiative. In 1667 for example, Lord Chancellor Clarendon was dismissed from office and forced to flee to the Continent, and his fall from power was ascribed to the 'buffoons and ladies of pleasure' who surrounded the King, and notably to the influence of Lady Castlemaine. Yet Barbara had been an enemy of Clarendon's for years, all to no avail until the King himself became disenchanted with Clarendon's officious manner and uncongenial policies and decided to be rid of him. Barbara of course throve on the delusion that she was omnipotent, graciously accepting bribes which she did little to repay. Thus in 1672 Sir Robert Howard paid her £10,000 in hopes that she would persuade Charles to grant him and his friends the exclusive right to collect taxes in England, but in the event the King decided that his own commissioners should retain the concession. Despite that, Barbara hung on to her money.[38]

The notion that under Louise's tutelage Charles became a puppet of France also owes more to the vivid imagination of his contemporaries than to realistic assessment of the facts. The French, who had hailed Louise's installation as royal mistress as a diplomatic *coup* of the first importance, were soon to find that her self-interest outweighed her patriotism. Successive French ambassadors had regular meetings with her in her apartments in hopes that she would strive to bring Charles round to their way of thinking, but it was a two-way process, for Charles too found her a useful intermediary and relied on her to put his viewpoint to the French. For example, according to the terms of the secret treaty of Dover, which Charles signed with France in 1670, he was supposed to declare himself a Catholic at the first convenient moment, and after three years the French were becoming impatient at his continued failure to do so; nevertheless, far from pressuring Charles to make the announcement, Louise insisted to the French that he was right to delay. Sometimes, indeed, the French found her lack of concern for their interests hard to swallow, and when she refused to support the candidacy of the Duchess of Guise, whom the French had hoped would become the second wife of the Duke of York, Colbert de Croissy was so vexed that he declared 'I own I find her on all occasions so ill-disposed for the service of the King [of France] . . . that I really think that she deserves no favour of His Majesty.'[39]

Yet although the King's mistresses were hardly the potentates of popular imagination, they were at least well-paid. Charles was a generous man, and the more avaricious of his concubines had little difficulty in exploiting him financially. Even in the early days of the reign, when Clarendon had blocked payments to Barbara, Charles had bypassed him by endowing her with lands in Ireland, over which the Chancellor had no control. Once Clarendon had been ousted, Charles was able to put her finances on a more official footing. In 1672, as Duchess of Cleveland, she was granted a pension of £6,000 from the excise revenues, supplemented the following year by an annual grant of £5,500 from the wine leases, the gift of Nonsuch Palace and property in the Duchy of Cornwall, with a grant of £5,500 thrown in as a bonus. The Duchess of Portsmouth was no less prosperous: in October 1676 her pension of £10,000 was increased by £8,600, and was further augmented in 1681 by an annual grant of £1,000 which was drawn, inappropriately enough, from the profits on taxes paid by the clergy. All this was in addition to valuable gifts of jewellery from both Charles and Louis XIV and intermittent grants from the Treasury for sums which ranged between £11,000 and nearly £23,000. Even Nell Gwynn, though less well-salaried than her aristocratic counterparts, received an annual pension of £4,000, the 'grant of the logwood' (the traditional tax on all wood exported out of England) which she farmed out for £500, all supplemented by *ex officio* payments from the Secret Service funds.[40]

At the highest end of the scale, therefore, the wages of sin could be very substantial and even those with whom the King had only casual affairs did not do too badly. For example, Winifred Wells, the maid of honour with the physiognomy of a dreamy sheep, received the unromantic but practical gift of the profits arising from the sale of timber from three of Charles's coppices in the New Forest. On her marriage, in 1673, to a Mr Wyndham, she was appointed one of the Queen's dressers and awarded £2,150, although admittedly that was no more than most girls who had been maids of honour for several years could expect to be given when they found themselves husbands. According to Count Grammont, the reason why the King did not reward her better was that he found her too easy a conquest to take seriously, and he added that Charles was also put off by 'certain other facilities still less pleasing' described by Buckingham, in an indelicate verse which punned upon her name, as 'the horrible depth of this well'.[41]

Whatever her failings, Miss Wells fared very much better than many of her contemporaries, for the merry and free Restoration court had its share of tragedies. With the King and the Duke of York hardly setting the best of examples it was not surprising that immorality was rife, but at a time when the sexual pressures on unmarried girls at court could never have been greater the penalties for those who were caught overstepping the bounds of propriety remained dire. For the maids of honour, unwanted pregnancies were an occupational hazard, which if no longer resulting in automatic imprisonment in the Tower almost inevitably brought ruin on the mother-to-be. The King's physician, Alexander Fraser, was reputed to be very popular with the ladies of the court because of his skill 'in helping slip their calves when there is occasion' but he was not infallible and in many cases it was the career of the unmarried mother, rather than her pregnancy, which was terminated. Few had such fairytale endings to their stories as Miss Warmestre, a maid of honour to the Queen who spurned the suit of an obscure country gentleman in the belief that her glamorous lover, Lord Taaffe, was planning to marry her. Unfortunately, when she was brought to bed with Taaffe's child he promptly disowned her, ungallantly wondering 'why she should father it upon him than any other'. The wretched girl retired to the country, her future in shreds, and was only saved by the unexpected reappearance of her former admirer, whose proposal she was now grateful to accept.[42]

She was lucky, however, for not many of her contemporaries who found themselves in similar circumstances could hope to salvage happy marriages from the shipwreck of their virtue. In 1678, for example, Miss Trevor, accounted 'the prettiest of the Duchess's maids of honour', had to make a hasty exit from court for 'had she stayed much longer she had been delivered at St James', and though she claimed that Thomas Thynne had pledged marriage to her he denied that they had come to any such understanding and refused to be browbeaten into owning her, even when her father challenged him to a duel. Cases where some unfortunate young woman was left holding the baby, condemned thereafter either to a life of obscurity in the country or even to seclusion in a convent abroad, were indeed depressingly frequent: in 1676 Sarah Jennings, a maid of honour to the Duchess of York, only narrowly escaped being dragged home by her mother on the grounds that 'two of the maids of honour had had great bellies at court and she would not leave her child there to have the third'.[43] As Sarah kept her virginity until her marriage to John Churchill and was besides one of the most formidable characters ever to inhabit the English court she was doubtless quite capable of looking after herself; nevertheless parental fears that their pregnant daughters would end up as the flotsam and jetsam of a society outpaced by its own immorality were all too understandable.

Those single girls who hoped that a career at court would be a stepping-stone to a good marriage fundamentally misread the social situation. To the sophisticated rakes of Whitehall, sexual exploitation was one thing and marriage another, and the latter was only to be embarked upon with a partner of suitable wealth and standing. Miss Hobart, a lady-in-waiting to the Duchess of York, summed up the position when she complained that the gentlemen of her day looked 'upon maids of honour only as amusements, placed expressly at court for their entertainment' and she added that 'unless money or caprice make up the match there is little hope of being married'. Grammont's explanation for Miss Hobart's strictures was that she was a lesbian with a vested interest in preaching disenchantment with the opposite sex, but her assessment does not seem to have been particularly inaccurate. To take one example, both Sir John Reresby and the Duke of Richmond decided against marrying the beautiful Elizabeth Hamilton on the grounds that she was insufficiently wealthy, and certainly the King himself shared Miss Hobart's view that the majority of his courtiers were a mercenary lot, for in a letter to his sister he remarked: 'I find that the passion love is very much out of fashion in this country and that a handsome face without money has but few gallants upon the score of marriage.'[44]

It would of course be wrong to imply that the Restoration court was peopled exclusively by nymphomaniacs and roués who came to bad ends. Not all the maids of honour were affected by the moral climate, for John Evelyn, himself a man of the most rigid principles, described the Duchess of York's maid Dorothy Howard as 'a most virtuous and excellent creature and worthy to have been the wife to the best of men', while the worthy Margaret Godolphin, successively a maid of honour to the Duchess of York and the Queen, excelled even her in righteousness. Her conduct was governed by a series of self-imposed precepts which included rising early to have more time for prayer, eating sparsely and resolving 'not to talk foolishly to men; more especially the King'. These however were the exceptions: Evelyn was so sceptical that any maid of honour at the Restoration court was capable of preserving her virtue that it took seven years to convince him that Margaret Blagge was flawless, and in general there seems little reason to dissent from Pepys's verdict that there was 'nothing almost but bawdry at court from top to bottom'.[45]

At a time when the court behaved in a remarkably ungodly fashion it was perhaps ironical that the greatest domestic crisis of the reign should have been sparked off by fears that religious zealots posed a threat to the realm's stability. Fear of popery was a wound in the body politic that had never been drained of its poison, and in the summer of 1678 its condition was to become inflamed as never before. In August 1678 the King was informed that he was in imminent danger of assassination by popish extremists and that his death would be the signal for an uprising of Catholics co-ordinated by the Jesuits. In fact this so-called 'Popish Plot' was purely imaginary, supported only by the fabrications of a few unscrupulous tricksters, but although Charles himself remained sceptical, the allegations commanded widespread credence and in the ensuing panic numerous priests and six Catholic peers were arrested on charges of high treason. By the autumn the House of Commons saw conspiracy everywhere and demanded that all the Queen's Catholic servants should be replaced with Protestants; it was only with difficulty that the House of Lords persuaded them that the Queen should be permitted to retain in her household nine Catholic ladies 'for . . . it could not reasonably be supposed that they were persons from whom any assassination might proceed'.[46]

By then, however, the public was capable of believing anything, and Titus Oates, the charlatan and rogue on whose evidence the case against the Catholics primarily rested was so emboldened by his success that he became confident that he could net one of the biggest Catholic fish of all. On 24 November he informed the King that Queen Catherine was involved in the plot to murder him, an accusation which he repeated before the House of Commons four days later. That

Parliament was capable of seriously entertaining so fantastic a notion illustrates the mood of collective hysteria that prevailed at the time, but the King at least remained calm: ignoring demands from the Commons that he remove Catherine and her household from court, he summoned her back from Somerset House (where her establishment had been based since the death of Charles's mother) and installed her again in Whitehall. 'They think I have a mind to a new wife,' he commented, 'but for all that I will not see an innocent woman abused.'

Catherine responded by rewarding her husband in the way that he would most appreciate. With the outbreak of the popish terror the Duchess of Portsmouth, never a popular figure and now more than ever vilified as a foreigner and a Catholic, became so alarmed for her safety that she contemplated flight abroad. The Queen, however, had decided that as Charles had stuck by her so loyally when she was in peril, 'out of civility' she could 'do no less' than invite the Duchess of Portsmouth to be one of the nine Catholic ladies-in-waiting allowed her,[47] and Louise was persuaded that as a lady of the Bedchamber she would be afforded a sufficient measure of protection to enable her to remain in England. Even so she had some uncomfortable moments: in June 1680 the leaders of the Protestant party tried to indict her as a common whore before the grand jury of Middlesex and were only foiled when the presiding judge swiftly adjourned the proceedings, and in general the unpopularity of the Duchess was such that any appearance in public was unwise. On one occasion an angry mob surrounded Nell Gwynn's coach under the impression that the Duchess of Portsmouth was inside and a tense situation was only defused when Nell stuck her head out of the window with the immortal remark, 'Be quiet, good people, for I am the Protestant whore.' But if Louise had no natural store of wit to fall back upon in these difficult times she was quite wily enough to adapt to new circumstances. She went against the King's wishes by aligning herself with those who demanded the execution of Lord Stafford, one of the six Catholic lords accused of treason, and at his trial she stood in the court distributing sweetmeats to the witnesses for the prosecution. The Earl was duly pronounced guilty and went to the scaffold, another of Oates's innocent victims, but Louise could at least congratulate herself that her stance had earned her a novel popularity: by late 1680 she was to be seen riding around in her coach in the company of several eminent Protestant matrons, able 'to go where she will now she is a favourite of the House of Commons', in the words of one sarcastic observer.[48]

Louise did not remain the crowd's darling for very long; nevertheless by espousing the cause of 'the factious party' (as the Duke of York indignantly termed it) she had wriggled out of an awkward situation.

Apart from entailing a sacrifice of her personal feelings the Queen's retention of Louise in her household involved her in real inconvenience, for of the nine Catholic ladies permitted, only three were to be ladies of the Bedchamber and the remainder were to be maids of honour or dressers. Louise of course was not on the duty roster, but the two other Catholic ladies of the Bedchamber were expected to accompany the Queen to mass, and as Catherine's devotions took up a major part of her day the result was that they were now 'almost always on duty, which before they were but now and then upon, and but for a day at a time, so in effect they must be drudges'.[49]

Apart from Louise, the Queen's quota of Catholic ladies was selected by lot. Some of the unlucky ones who found themselves made unexpectedly redundant fled abroad for fear of persecution, obliged to start a new life when they had not unreasonably counted on years of secure employment. Lady Scroope, a widow who had been one of the Queen's dressers since her arrival in England, fled in late 1678 to France, which she found not at all to her taste, forlornly proclaiming to other English residents in Paris that she was 'little satisfied . . . having yet found nothing here that pleases her'. Jane Crane, another of the Queen's former dressers, and Frances Sheldon, who had lost her position as maid of honour in the purge of Catholics, also obtained leave 'to pass into parts beyond the seas'. Several other papist ladies, such as the Countess of Southesk (she who in happier days was said to have given the Duke of York the pox) and the Countess of Kinnoull, did likewise, with the result that Paris came to boast quite a large community of exiled Anglo-Catholics, disparagingly referred to as 'our English martyrs'.[50]

Not all the Queen's discharged Catholic ladies chose exile, however, and one of them nearly brought herself to grief when she decided to stay behind and fight her Protestant persecutors on their own ground. The Countess of Powis, whom Bishop Burnet once described as 'a zealous managing papist', had been a lady of the Queen's Bedchamber since January 1677, but in October 1678 her husband had been one of the six Catholic peers wrongfully arrested on treason charges, and a month later this had been followed by the act limiting the number of Catholics in the Queen's household. Although the Queen had offered to retain her as her servant, the Countess felt that 'in her circumstances' she would not be able to cope with the onerous workload of a lady of the Bedchamber, and had therefore handed in her resignation.[51]

This was perhaps as well, for Lady Powis was soon involved in intrigues which would have left her little time in which to serve the Queen. In 1679 she teamed up with Elizabeth Cellier, a somewhat shady popish midwife whom she employed to distribute charity among the Catholics awaiting trial in Newgate prison. There Mrs Cellier made the acquaintance of Thomas Dangerfield, a slippery operator who was imprisoned because of his debts. Realizing that he had talents she could make use of, Mrs Cellier procured his release and introduced him to the Countess, and the three of them now set out to discredit the Protestants, using the same weapons that had formerly been used against the English Catholics. Lady Powis used her contacts to secure Dangerfield an introduction to the Duke of York and the King, and he warned them that there was a party of extreme Protestants who were on the verge of revolt. When the lodgings of one of the alleged leaders of the uprising were searched incriminating documents were discovered, but they were soon exposed as forgeries and Dangerfield was obliged to admit that he had planted them there. He claimed that he had been acting on the Countess of Powis's instructions, and though she tried to disown him she was arrested and charged with treason on 4 November 1679. Whether the Countess had simply been duped by Dangerfield into believing there was a genuine danger of a Protestant *coup*, or whether she had employed him to disseminate a story that she herself had concocted remains obscure, but certainly she was fortunate that the case against her rested on the word of Dangerfield, who was so thorough a villain that even a seventeenth-century jury found difficulty in believing him. In February 1680 she was released from the Tower on bail; three months later the grand jury of Middlesex returned a verdict of ignoramus on the charges of treason preferred against her, and though her husband was not released from prison until four years later the pair of them could account themselves lucky to have escaped with their lives.

The Queen too had emerged from the crisis unscathed. Charles had supported her steadfastly throughout, consistently treating her with such kindness that the acid-tongued Lady Sunderland could report, 'The Queen . . . is now a mistress, the passion her spouse has for her is so great.' If so, however, she remained one of several, for though with the onset of middle age the King's sexual appetite had become less voracious, he was set in a routine of comfortable infidelity which he had no intention of abandoning. In his declining years he became, if anything, more devoted than ever to the Duchess of Portsmouth, but she still had to share his favours with Nell Gwynn and he also remained on friendly terms even with those ladies with whom he was no longer physically intimate. On 1 February 1685 John Evelyn saw the King at Whitehall 'sitting and toying with his concubines, Portsmouth, Cleveland and Mazarin' while in the background a party of courtiers sat round a table playing basset for high stakes. To Evelyn it was a scene redolent of 'inexpressible luxury and profaneness . . . and . . . as it were total forgetfulness of God' but nowadays it seems rather touching that the King should have been so constant in his affections. Charles had attained the mature contentment of a man whose problems, personal and political, had been ordered to his satisfaction and despite the opinion of the French ambassador that there was no other country 'in which women are so prone to backbite each other as in England' his wife and mistresses had also learned to live in amiable co-existence.[52]

Alas, this serenity was not to last for long: the day after the party which had so shocked Evelyn, the King was struck down by what proved to be his final illness, dying on 6 February 1685. Louise was to perform one final service for him, telling the French ambassador that he should alert the Duke of York to the King's wish to die a Catholic, with the result that Charles was secretly received into the faith on his deathbed. The King was sincerely mourned, not only by his mistresses and grieving widow (who returned to Portugal in 1692 and outlived her husband by twenty years) but by rich and poor alike, for whatever his failings, Charles was greatly loved. The same could not be said of his brother, on whose head the crown now rested.

The Later Stuart Court

'The Very Ladies Are Split Asunder'

The transition from the reign of Charles to James was achieved peaceably enough, but it was to be James's peculiar distinction that although opposition to him was virtually non-existent when he ascended the throne, a mere three years later he was to lose his crown without a shot being fired in his defence. With remarkable speed he had justified the fears of those who had dreaded the accession of a popish monarch, for his pursuit of militantly Catholic policies, carried out with a bland disregard of the laws and liberties of his kingdom, had convinced many of his subjects that he aimed at nothing less than the establishment of a Catholic and absolutist state modelled on Louis XIV's France. This the English would not tolerate.

His policies, however, had earned the firm support of his wife, who was twenty-six when her husband became King and a very different creature from the vivacious teenager who was seen gaily pelting her husband with snowballs soon after her arrival in England. Although still beautiful, Mary Beatrice had been saddened by her husband's repeated infidelities and by the deaths of all the children she had borne him, and had found consolation in her religion. She had indeed only agreed to marry her husband in the first place because the Pope, anxious that the recently converted James should be provided with a Catholic bride, had persuaded her to abandon her original intention of taking the veil. She had therefore come to England with a real sense of mission, and with James's accession it seemed that her opportunity to do good for her faith had come at last. As Duchess of York she had been a well-liked figure at court, but once Queen her popularity declined, partly because her 'outward affability much changed to stateliness' and she became more haughty and remote, but also because she was suspected of being 'a very great bigot in her way' who encouraged her husband in his misguided enterprises.[1]

At first, admittedly, all had gone well for the new King. The devoutly Anglican John Evelyn sourly noted that with James's encouragement 'The papists now swarmed at court' and Mary Beatrice's household, which had been purged of all English Catholics at the time of the popish plot, was now enlarged to accommodate Catholics such as the Duchess of Norfolk and Lady Tyrconnel. Thus far Mary Beatrice can have had few complaints, and it was an additional happiness that the King began his reign full of good resolutions, and 'spoke openly against lewdness and expressed a detestation of drunkenness'. Fired with pious zeal, he expelled from her lodgings in Whitehall his mistress of long standing, Catherine Sedley, and having compensated her with a pension of £4,000 he assured the Queen that he would never see her more. Alas, the habits of a lifetime died hard. Within months the French ambassador had discovered that Catherine was regularly smuggled into the Palace for assignations with the King and that Lord Rochester, brother of James's deceased first wife, encouraged the affair in hopes that a Protestant mistress might counterbalance the influence of the Catholic Queen. In January 1686 Mary Beatrice 'took very grievously' the news that James had agreed to create his mistress Countess of Dorchester, but she refused to concede victory to her rival. On answering a summons to his wife's apartments, James was surprised to be confronted by a bevy of priests who upbraided him for leading an ill life. Thoroughly nonplussed, James agreed to send the new Countess into exile, and after a period of haggling Catherine consented to depart for Ireland. But the Queen had not seen the last of her: within months she was back at court, having apparently 'gathered a fresh stock of impudence in Ireland' and as James found her as irresistible as ever 'that ill commerce was still continued'.[2] To her chagrin Mary Beatrice was obliged to endure what even the priests had proved powerless to prevent.

Unfortunately, in all other respects James received his priests' advice with unquestioning obedience. His subjects watched in horror as he set about dismantling the defences against popery that had been so laboriously erected in the past, but they could at least console themselves that the damage would be temporary, for James lacked a male heir and his two daughters by his first marriage were both staunch Protestants. The eldest, Mary, was married to the Dutch Prince of Orange and had defied all her father's attempts to convert her, and though James would no doubt willingly have bequeathed his crown to her younger sister Anne had she agreed to embrace his faith, she too was resolute on that point. Protestant Englishmen could relax on the assumption that after the King's death his policies would be reversed, but in late 1687 their complacency was shattered by the announcement that the Queen, who had been presumed incapable of bearing any more children, was once again pregnant.

James's incredulous subjects were aghast and some of them simply refused to accept that such appalling news could be true. Among these was Princess Anne, who in March 1688 confided to her sister in Holland her suspicions that the Queen was padding out her stomach and that her supposed pregnancy was nothing more than a gigantic deception that would enable the King and her to pass off a supposititious child as their rightful heir. She cited as proof the Queen's reluctance to undress before her ladies and her refusal to permit them to fondle her belly, and if this seems rather flimsy evidence to support so fantastic a charge, the Princess certainly had no wish to be convinced to the contrary. As the Queen's confinement drew near Anne withdrew to Bath, evidently reluctant to be present at the birth of a baby she denied had ever been in the womb.

In consequence she was absent when on 10 June 1688 the Queen gave birth to a son at St James's Palace, but according to custom the labour was witnessed by numerous gentlemen of the court and no fewer than twenty ladies. It would have been impossible to have perpetuated a fraud before so many onlookers; nevertheless Princess Anne and many others elected to believe that the new Prince of Wales was in fact a tiny impostor who had been smuggled into the Palace, possibly in a warming-pan. To Mary in Holland Anne wrote asserting that only Lady Sunderland, the wife of James's chief minister, and Charles II's old mistress, the Duchess of Mazarin, claimed to have felt the Queen's stomach during pregnancy, and they were 'people that nobody will give credit to'. Mary responded by sending her sister a detailed questionnaire on the exact circumstances surrounding the delivery, and though Anne's subsequent interrogation of one of the Bedchamber women who had attended the Queen throughout failed to unearth any evidence that might support her theory, she darkly pointed out to her sister that 'the servants, from the highest to the lowest are all papists' who she evidently considered would stick at nothing to achieve their ends.[3]

Whatever the doubts about the baby's birth, he stood to inherit the throne in due course, a prospect that by the summer of 1688 seemed so intolerable that on 30 June a committee of seven leading Englishmen invited William of Orange to bring an army to England and rescue it from the arbitrary rule of his father-in-law. By late September it was apparent to everyone that invasion was imminent and in a belated attempt to combat the slurs of Protestant propagandists, James convened an extraordinary meeting of the council in hopes of resolving for ever the doubts concerning his son's legitimacy. On 22 October 1688 all those who had witnessed the birth were required to give details to the assembled peers and dignitaries, which occasioned 'a long discourse of bawdry . . . that put all the ladies to blush'. The twenty ladies who had been present at the delivery gave explicit evidence that left little room for doubts concerning the child's identity. Lady Wentworth, a Protestant who had little reason to be untruthful, deposed not only that she 'did once feel the child stir in the Queen's belly' but also that she had seen the umbilical cord being cut. Isabella Waldegrave, another Protestant woman of the Bedchamber, declared that she had taken 'the afterburthen and put it into a basin of water and carried it into the Queen's closet'.[4] For all the good it did they could have saved their breath: the myth of the warming-pan baby was too convenient a fiction to be discarded simply because it happened not to be true.

On 5 November 1688 William landed at Torbay and was soon joined by the majority of James's army. This, combined with the decision of Princess Anne to flee London and declare herself for William, persuaded the King that his only recourse lay in flight. On the night of 9 December 1688 the Queen slipped out of Whitehall with her son and made her way to Gravesend, where a small group of trusted servants were waiting with a boat. From there they sailed to France, where they were joined on Christmas Day by James. They were received hospitably by the French King, who assigned them the Palace of St Germain, and there they presided over a sad little court composed of those nobles and their wives who were prepared to follow their King into exile and share the melancholy existence common to all emigrés, a compound of disillusionment and penury, false hopes and nostalgia.

On 12 February 1689 Mary of Orange joined her husband in England, where it had already been established that the two of them were to rule as joint sovereigns. She returned reluctantly, for though as a fifteen-year-old she had 'wept all afternoon and all the following day' when informed that she was to marry William and live with him in Holland, in the twelve years that had intervened she had come to love not only her dour and asthmatic bridegroom but his country too. By leaving it, she was deprived of the companionship of the women to whom she had been closest throughout her adult life, for though William had brought several of his countrymen with him, on the whole their wives declined to follow them to England, which they considered to be 'a devil of a country, so dirty and so wicked'. Making the best of a bad job, Mary sought to preserve at least some link with Holland by appointing as her Mistress of the Robes the Countess of Derby, who was Dutch in origin and spoke Flemish fluently, but as the Queen knew nothing of the English aristocracy, her selection of the other ladies who were to serve in her household was inevitably in the nature of a lucky dip. Sometimes her choice proved fortunate, as in the case of Lady Dorset, who was appointed a lady of the Bedchamber at the beginning of the reign and went on to become a great favourite with the Queen. Unfortunately, when better acquainted with some of Lady Dorset's colleagues the Queen came to hold a very low opinion of them, and there was one in particular whom she so disliked that when the lady fell ill she found herself wishing that she might die and so make room in the Bedchamber for the Countess of Nottingham, the wife of William's Secretary of War, whom Mary had discovered too late to be an infinitely more congenial companion. In the event, however, the lady recovered and it was Lady Dorset's sudden death that created the desired vacancy, an affliction which the penitent Mary interpreted as a manifestation of divine displeasure at her presumption.[5]

Accustomed to a somewhat cloistered existence at the Dutch court, Mary was shocked by the ingrained frivolity of the English aristocracy. In her diary she primly registered her horror at seeing 'so little devotion in a people so lately in such eminent danger' and if it was not to be expected that society's habits would be changed overnight she determined at least to instil a sense of higher values in her immediate circle. Under her auspices the court underwent a moral regeneration: as Bishop Burnet remarked in his memoirs 'the female part of the court had been in the former reigns subject to much censure . . . but she freed her court so entirely from all suspicion that there was not so much as a colour for discourses of that sort'. At her instigation needlework became all the rage which 'took ladies off from that idleness which not only wasted their time but exposed them to many temptations', and it was typical to find the Queen and her attendants at work on their embroidery while one of their number read aloud from some improving work,[6] a domesticated scene that would have held little appeal for the sophisticated ladies of Charles II's day.

Inevitably there were complaints that the court had become too subdued. William was the reverse of gregarious, and his health obliged him to spend as much time as possible away from central London, either at Hampton Court, or later in the reign at Kensington Palace. In consequence the social life of the court was gravely disrupted, which 'gave an early and general disgust'[7] and though Mary did her best to compensate for her husband's inhospitable nature she herself was a far from accomplished hostess. With the Revolution, the court had become not only more respectable but also more dull.

Unfortunately Mary's difficulties in adjusting to her new life in England were not lightened by the pleasures of renewed sisterly intercourse with the Princess Anne. As a child Mary had been very close to her sister, whom she 'was really extreme glad to see' on her return from Holland,[8] but the joys of reunion proved short-lived. Within months the sisters had fallen out over the accommodation arrangements for Anne's servants in the Palace of Whitehall, and matters became worse when Anne declined to let William assume charge of her finances and instead successfully applied to Parliament for an independent income of her own. Mary was enraged to find that Anne was no longer the placid and affectionate companion of her youth, but she had little doubt about who to blame for the transformation, convinced that it was Anne's best friend and confidante Sarah Churchill who was behind her truculent behaviour.

Anne's friendship with Sarah had its origins in her nursery where she had played with the then Sarah Jennings, a maid of honour to her stepmother, but the pair did not become really close till about 1682–3, by which time Sarah had already married for love a rising young army officer named John Churchill. Beautiful, strong-willed and amusing, Sarah was a dazzling adornment to the court, and though always hot-tempered and outspoken, initially this just seemed a part of the vitality and sparkle of youth and enhanced her attractiveness. She was the complete antithesis of the diffident and plodding Princess Anne, who found herself irresistibly drawn to this quicksilver creature, and by the time that the Princess's engagement to Prince George of Denmark was announced in May 1683, her affection for Sarah had ripened into passionate attachment.

To Anne's delight her father permitted her to appoint Sarah as one of her ladies of the Bedchamber, and though her marriage to her amiable but unremarkable princeling was a complete success, it in no way interfered with her feelings for her friend, which filled her life with an emotional intensity that the stolid George was not capable of inspiring. As Sarah later recalled, Anne accounted every moment that she was separated from her as 'a sort of tedious lifeless state', considering the letters that daily passed between them when apart to be no substitute for Sarah's presence. Anne was a woman with a remarkable capacity for devotion but as her frequent pregnancies ended either in miscarriage or in the loss of her children when young, she lavished on Sarah the affection that might otherwise have been focused on her offspring. Not only did Sarah bring into Anne's life a gaiety that made her forget her misfortunes as a mother, but the Princess knew also that she could expect from her disinterested advice of a sort not commonly available to one in her position. As Sarah put it in her memoirs, 'I laid it down for a maxim that flattery was falsehood to my trust and ingratitude to my greatest friend; and that I did not deserve much favour if I could not venture the loss of it by speaking the truth', and though she would carry this principle too far when Anne was Queen, at this stage of their acquaintance her forthrightness enabled the two women to have a freedom of intercourse which at the time was almost unthinkable between two persons of widely differing rank.[9]

In later years Sarah was to claim that in this remarkable relationship, the affection had all been on Anne's side and that it had been very disagreeable for one of her own 'sprightliness and cheerfulness of nature . . . to be perpetually chained as it were to a person whose other accomplishments had not cured the sullenness of her temper nor wholly freed her conversation from an insipid heaviness', but the relationship must have meant more to her than she later cared to imply, for when it subsequently disintegrated Sarah's reaction was too violent to be explicable solely in terms of injured pride. On Sarah's instructions Anne destroyed almost all the letters she received from her, but years afterwards Anne claimed that Sarah 'wrote to me as [I] used to do to her'. Anne's letters were full of fervent protestations of devotion and oft-expressed hopes 'that next to Lord Churchill I may claim ye first place in your heart', and if those she received from Sarah in return were even vaguely similar in tone, one must conclude that Sarah was not as dispassionate towards Anne as she wished to be supposed.[10]

Queen Mary had always had her reservations about Sarah and now she believed it was Sarah alone who was responsible for her difficulties with her sister. The Queen considered it pointless even to discuss with Anne the reasons for their estrangement as 'I saw plainly she was so absolutely governed by Lady Marlborough* that it was to no purpose,'[11] but she felt convinced that once she had succeeded in separating Anne and Sarah, the Princess would quickly come to heel. In this the Queen underestimated her sister: like many others after her (including Sarah herself), Mary mistakenly assumed that Anne lacked a will of her own but in reality the latter's mild exterior concealed a stubborn heart. As Mary would find out to her cost, once Anne had resolved upon a course of action, she was not easily deterred.

It was to be Mary's misfortune that she would try to strike at Sarah just at the time when her friendship with Anne had reached new heights. By late 1691 Anne had inaugurated the system specifically designed to enable her and Sarah 'to converse as equals made so by affection and friendship', whereby in her letters she adopted the pen name of Mrs Morley and addressed Sarah as Mrs Freeman. Furthermore in June of that year 'as an earnest of my goodwill' Anne had settled a pension of £1,000 a year on Sarah, in addition to the salary of £400 which she already enjoyed as her first lady of the Bedchamber.[12] Her commitment to Sarah was now such that it proved impossible for her to remain even on civil terms with her sister when the latter tried to come between the Princess and her servant.

On 20 January 1692 Sarah's husband was dismissed by the King from all his offices, and though William had reasons of his own for the move, both he and the Queen expected that it would also have the desirable side-effect of ridding them of Sarah, assuming that as the wife of a disgraced man she would automatically resign from royal service. Sarah, however, was never one to take a hint. Two weeks after her husband's dismissal she accompanied Princess Anne to a reception held by the Queen at Kensington Palace. The Queen was stupefied by such boldness, and the following day, 5 February, she dispatched to Anne a letter which not only made her feelings on the subject of the Countess of Marlborough very plain but rebuked the Princess for encouraging her defiance.

> It is very unfit Lady Marlborough should stay with you, since that gives her husband so just a pretence of being where he ought not . . . I have all the reason imaginable to look upon your bringing her as the strangest thing that ever was done . . . I must tell you it was very unkind in a sister, would have been very uncivil in an equal and I need not say I have more to claim . . . I know what is due to me and expect to have it from you.

* Sarah's husband had been made Earl of Marlborough in April 1689

For Anne this letter came as a clarion call to battle: to Sarah she wrote that she found the Queen's peremptory tone so offensive that even 'if I had any inclination to part with dear Mrs Freeman it would make me keep her in spite of their teeth', and in her reply to her sister she flatly refused to let Lady Marlborough go.[13] Mary's only response was to command her sister to vacate her lodgings at Whitehall and the Princess hastened to comply, leasing Syon House off the Duke and Duchess of Somerset and withdrawing to it with her household.

Thus began a war of attrition within the royal family that was to drag on for almost three years. Throughout the spring of 1692, Sarah repeatedly offered to make things easier for her mistress by resigning, but doubtless to her relief the Princess would not hear of it, greeting the very suggestion with 'the greatest passion of tenderness and weeping that is possible to imagine' and informing Sarah that, 'if you should ever do so cruel a thing as to leave me from that moment I shall never enjoy one quiet hour. And should you do it without asking my consent (which if I ever give you may I never see the face of heaven) I will shut myself up and never see the world more.' She insisted that never would she 'truckle to that monster . . . the Dutch abortive', electing instead to wait patiently for the 'sunshine day' when she and Mrs Freeman could once again live together in peace.[14]

Unfortunately the King and Queen proved equally inflexible. On 17 April 1692 Anne gave birth to a child which died almost immediately, and before she had even recovered from her confinement the Queen paid her a visit, not to offer her sympathy but to reiterate her demand that the Countess of Marlborough be dismissed. Anne still refused, whereupon the Queen swept from the sickroom, never to see her sister more. At the end of the month it was announced that anyone who called on the Princess would not be received at court, with the result that only 'some few generous spirited ladies' thought it worth their while to visit her. In May matters became even worse when the mendacious evidence of an informer landed Marlborough in the Tower on suspicion of high treason, but Anne stood by her friends, writing solicitously to Sarah and urging her to keep her spirits up by taking regular doses of ass's milk. The following month Marlborough was released on an appeal to Habeas Corpus but Anne's situation vis-à-vis her sister and brother remained the same. For two and a half years deadlock prevailed: for company and advice the Princess could depend only upon her immediate household (and she even suspected that some of them were spies in the pay of the King and Queen) but she would not abandon the Marlboroughs.[15] The dispute would indeed have dragged on much longer had not Queen Mary's unexpected death from smallpox on 28 December 1694 suddenly altered the situation.

Aware that the Jacobites could exploit for their own ends continued divisions between himself and the Princess, William decided that Mary's death made it imperative that he reconcile with his sister-in-law. The demand that the Countess of Marlborough be dismissed was quietly dropped and Anne was readmitted to court, and for the next eight years she acted as William's hostess at official functions and receptions. Yet though outward appearances were thus maintained there was little cordiality between Anne and William, for as Bishop Burnet remarked, their reconciliation 'went not much farther than what civility and decency required'.[16] In consequence William's death, on 8 March 1702, can have afforded Anne little sorrow.

For Sarah, as well as Anne, it must have seemed that 'a sunshine day' had dawned, for against all the odds she had emerged from the previous reign with her mistress's favour intact. She failed to realize, however, that Anne had taken on William and Mary not only out of friendship for her, but also because she wished to establish the principle that she had an inalienable right to choose for herself the members of her surrogate 'family' – as the Queen's household was significantly termed. When Sarah herself sought to restrict her mistress's freedom of choice in such matters, Anne would fight her as she had fought her own sister and brother-in-law, only this time she was Queen and the odds were stacked in her favour.

On Anne's accession, however, there was no sign of the coming rift. Finally able to reward her dear Mr and Mrs Freeman, the Queen showered them with favour. In the closing months of William's reign war with France had become inevitable, and among other honours Marlborough was made Commander-in-Chief of all English forces on the Continent, an appointment which he was soon to justify with a series of military victories that would make his name immortal. For her part Sarah was made Groom of the Stole, Mistress of the Robes and Keeper of the Privy Purse (the officer in charge of the money the Queen spent on charity, gambling, rewards for servants and numerous other everyday expenses). These offices carried with them salaries which totalled £5,600 a year (in addition to Marlborough's own income, which at the height of his power was estimated at £60,000) and Sarah was also made Ranger of Windsor Great Park and as such entitled to the lifetime tenure of a house within its grounds. Her two elder daughters (to whom Anne had already given wedding presents of £5,000 apiece) were made ladies of the Bedchamber at salaries of £1,000 a year. Finally, in October 1702 the Queen created Marlborough a Duke, endowing him with a pension of a further £5,000 a year, and when Parliament declined to grant this sum in perpetuity to his heirs the Queen sought to compensate with the offer of a further £2,000 a year from the Privy Purse funds. At that time Sarah would 'by no means take it' thinking that 'I had enough and my salaries were a great deal',[17] but there would come a day when she felt very differently.

Undoubtedly Sarah was well rewarded for her services but she took her responsibilities seriously, perhaps too much so. As Mistress of the Robes she was in charge of the royal wardrobe and as such expected to dictate the Queen's choice of clothing for every occasion. Unfortunately her taste was too plain for some people's liking and on occasion there were complaints that the Queen was not attired as richly as befitted her status. Sarah would have none of it, maintaining that 'it would have been ridiculous with her person and of her age to have been otherwise dressed',[18] while if the Queen herself ventured to protest Sarah put an end to all further discussion with an imperious 'Lord, Madam! It must be so'. The Duchess of Marlborough refused to accept that Anne's elevation in status had inevitably wrought a change in their relationship, and her failure to modify her behaviour accordingly was bound to give rise to friction.

Others too found Sarah's autocratic temper somewhat trying. The Duchess was clearly not an easy woman to work with, quick to take offence and intolerant of her subordinates. For example, she took full advantage of her right to any item of clothing that the Queen discarded, considering it quite praiseworthy that she left for the dressers a few overskirts and petticoats that she had no wish for herself, and finding it inexplicable when her colleagues complained that she could have been more generous. Early in her reign the Queen naturally took Sarah's side in any arguments, and on at least two occasions offered to dismiss ladies who had incurred the Duchess's displeasure;[19] nevertheless at times she must have been sorely tried by the way that her Mistress of the Robes augmented her cares as Head of State with these petty household disputes.

Even Sarah's laudable desire to enrich the Crown by cutting out corruption and waste within her department had its drawbacks. In return for prompt settlement of bills tendered by tradesmen who supplied the Queen with items for her wardrobe, Sarah demanded a reduction in their prices and by such methods she estimated that she saved almost £10,000 a year, which in her nine years as Mistress of the Robes represented an economy of 'near £90,000'. But as Sarah admitted, there were those who felt that her bargaining techniques were 'too hard upon the tradesmen I dealt with' (although she was adamant that all were treated fairly) and there were murmurs at the way that the Duchess discouraged her mistress from giving her ladies gifts of jewellery and fans as Queen Mary had been wont to do before her.[20] The Queen herself was concerned to stamp out the venality rife at court, and forbade the practice, grown common since the Restoration, whereby office holders sold their positions at court to the highest bidder, insisting instead that departmental heads make appointments on merit alone. Nevertheless the fact remained that it was a sensitive task to instil a sense of public accountability in courtiers accustomed to the freer ways of days gone by and one to which Sarah's abrasive manner was not ideally suited.

In the matter of household organization and economy the Queen was at least in sympathy with Sarah's aims, if not always with her methods, but when the Duchess turned her attention to State affairs their views were to diverge fatally. It was the Queen's misfortune to rule at a time when English politics were dominated as never before by internecine party strife. Of the two parties, the Tories were the more traditionalist, combining a devotion to the House of Stuart with a veneration for the established Church, while their rivals, the Whigs, were comparatively radical, seeing themselves as the enemies of despotism and the champions of liberty. At Anne's accession English society was virtually bisected on party lines, and the fashionable ladies of her day made no effort to remain politically neutral, declaring their allegiance for one or other of the parties in rather the same way that their forbears had tossed their gloves to favoured contenders in tournaments. 'The very ladies are split asunder into High Church and Low', the writer and clergyman Jonathan Swift noted in amusement in 1703, and feeling among women on political issues continued to run high for the remainder of the reign. Even the all-male political dining clubs of the day made some acknowledgement to the support they received from the opposite sex, for though women were barred from their meetings it was customary for the assembled gentlemen to drink the health of ladies who combined good looks with acceptable political sentiments. Thus Sarah's beautiful but diminutive daughter, Lady Sunderland, earned herself the sobriquet of 'The Little Whig' and became the toast of the Kit Kat Club, while at rival establishments like Jonathan Swift's Tory Band of Brothers, they raised their glasses to ladies such as Jane Hyde, 'a mighty pretty girl', who in July 1711 was 'just growing a top toast' in Tory circles.[21]

As a good churchwoman, the Queen herself inclined to the Tory Party, and at the beginning of the reign she was supported in this not only by Marlborough but also by his best friend and adviser, Sydney Godolphin, who was appointed Lord Treasurer in May 1702. Unhappily, Sarah was already an emphatic opponent of the Tories, considering 'the principles professed by those called Whigs seemed to be rational, entirely tending to the preservation of the liberties of the subject and no way to the prejudice of the Church as by law established', and her suspicion of the Tories was reinforced by her conviction that only the Whigs, with their hatred of absolutism, would be wholehearted in their support of the war against despotic France. Politics to Sarah was no mere modish diversion to be fitted in between visits to the milliner and dressmaker, but a cut-throat struggle in which one gave one's opponents no quarter, and she was determined to deploy her position as a trusted intimate of the Queen to maximum political advantage. If Anne favoured the Tories, Anne must be made to see reason, and when the Queen's first Government proved to be definitely Tory in complexion Sarah set to work with a will to remedy this state of affairs, and in her own ominous words 'did . . . speak very freely and very frequently to her Majesty upon the subject of Whig and Tory'.[22]

The Queen did not prove a docile pupil and it was not long before their exchanges took on an acrimonious tinge, and as early as 24 October 1702 there was a portent of future trouble when Anne wrote sharply to Sarah, 'I cannot help being extremely concerned you are so partial to the Whigs . . . Upon my word dear Mrs Freeman you are mightily mistaken in your notion of a true Whig; for the character you give of them does not in the least belong to them but to the Church' – by which the Queen meant the Tory party.[23] United in their outlook in the past, Anne and Sarah now found themselves on opposite sides of the political spectrum and it was Sarah's tragedy that she could not understand that the Queen's convictions were as sincere and deeply held as her own.

On 20 February 1703 the Marlboroughs suffered a grievous blow with the death from smallpox of their eldest and only surviving son. This misfortune coincided with the advent of Sarah's menopause, which she initially mistook for the first signs of pregnancy; when her mistake became evident she found it all the more difficult to accept the loss of a son who, as was now apparent, could never be replaced. Sarah locked herself away at her country house, refusing to let Anne visit her there; and indeed this period of mourning was to encourage in Sarah a taste for solitude which ensured that in future she went to court much less often. But though her personal contact with the Queen in consequence diminished, she was confident that even from afar she could exert her old magnetism over her former devotee and she continued to bombard Anne with letters crammed with political advice which the Queen found increasingly unpalatable, and all the more so because Sarah's tone, unbalanced as she was by her twin misfortunes, grew ever more strident.

For a time the Queen's ties of friendship with the Duchess transcended their political disagreements. In May 1703 the Queen was still fervently assuring the Marlboroughs of her devotion, and the following month Anne even wrote to Sarah encouraging her to express herself freely on political topics, assuring her that she could never 'be displeased at anything that comes from you'. Unfortunately Sarah took her at her word and her subsequent relentless attacks both on individual Tories and on the policy of the Tory party as a whole ensured that by the autumn of 1703 a note of coolness had crept into the Morley-Freeman correspondence. In particular, Sarah was enraged at the Tories' efforts to introduce a Bill for Occasional Conformity, aimed at tightening the existing restrictions on the employment of dissenters, but Anne refused to condemn the measure, affirming stoutly in December, 'I see nothing like persecution in this bill.'[24] With the Queen Sarah had failed, but she had better luck in other quarters, for throughout the summer and autumn of 1703 she had also inundated her husband and Lord Treasurer Godolphin with anti-Tory propaganda and this had contributed to a gradual shift in their allegiance from the Tories to the Whigs, with the result that Anne was soon to find that the two leading members of her Government no longer shared her Tory sympathies.

Curiously enough, in April 1704 the Tories themselves played into Sarah's hands when their leaders confronted the Queen with a series of unreasonable demands which prompted her to dismiss two of her more extreme Tory ministers and accept the resignation of another. The Queen had written playfully to Sarah that she hoped these developments would 'not be disagreeable to Mrs Freeman' but unhappily Sarah proved incapable of simply resting on her laurels. In

her opinion the Tories still had too much power, and as the year progressed her relationship with the Queen steadily deteriorated under the
incessant strain of her invectives against those who remained in
Government. Even Marlborough's magnificent victory over the French
at Blenheim in August 1704 could not repair the damage, so that by the
beginning of September Lord Treasurer Godolphin was writing
anxiously to the Duchess, 'I am very sorry to find Mrs Morley and Mrs
Freeman cannot yet bring things quite right. I am sure they will do it at
last, and when this case happens betwixt people that love one another
so well, it is not impossible but that both may be a little in the wrong.'[25]

Sarah, however, was in no mood to take the hint that she might be at
fault. Remorselessly she continued her campaign on the Whigs' behalf,
pushing her already creaking relationship with the Queen to breaking
point. It achieved nothing. On 17 November 1704 the exasperated but
defiant Queen reaffirmed her position: 'I have the same opinion of
Whig and Tory that ever I had' she informed Sarah crushingly, 'I know
both their principles very well and when I know myself to be in the right
nothing can make me alter mine.' The Duchess could not accept this.
Three days later she penned her mistress a letter of extraordinary
insolence in which she complained that Anne had 'sucked in with her
milk' so great a prejudice against the Whigs that it seemed she equated
them with the Roundheads who had executed her grandfather. If the
Queen so desired, the Duchess sarcastically went on, she was prepared
to own that the Roundheads had 'had cloven feet or what you please'
but she could not resist adding that in her opinion 'the extreme
weakness of that unfortunate King contributed as much to his misfortune as all the malice of those ill men; nay, I will venture to say more,
that it had not been possible for them to have hurt him if he had not
been governed by almost as bad people'. Finally Sarah had gone too
far: the Queen was outraged by the insult to her grandfather's memory
and by Sarah's implication that her situation was parallel to his half a
century before. On 21 November she told Sarah she saw no point in
answering her diatribe 'since everything I say is imputed either to par-
tiality or being imposed upon by fools and knaves' and when the Duchess responded with a threat to break off all further communication the
Queen did not try to change her mind. To Godolphin the Queen
expressed her doubts that Sarah would 'ever be easy with me again' and
for the next eight months her contact with the Duchess was to be
minimal.[26]

In August 1705, however, Sarah succeeded in patching up her connection with her mistress and in November it seemed that the seal had

been set on their *rapprochement* when the Tories infuriated the Queen by pressing ahead with a measure to which they knew she was virulently opposed. To Sarah, Anne wrote bitterly that she was now 'thoroughly convinced of the malice and insolency of them that you have been always speaking against', and expressed the hope that from now on 'Dear Mrs Freeman and I shall not disagree as we have formerly done.' Alas, it was not to be. Despite her disenchantment with the Tories, Anne could not yet bring herself to strengthen the Government by giving office to a leading Whig, although both Marlborough and Godolphin were imploring her to make the Duke's son-in-law, the Earl of Sunderland, one of her ministers. Sunderland was a particularly unfortunate choice, being so Whiggish as to be almost republican, and for months the Queen steadfastly resisted their entreaties. Sarah of course was incensed and in August 1706, convinced as ever of her unfailing rectitude, she entered the fray on her son-in-law's behalf. She wrote berating the Queen for her unaccountable aversion to the Whigs, declaring that she hoped that Anne would see her 'errors as to this notion before it is too late'. Anne misread 'notion' for 'nation' and was seriously offended, and it was only with great difficulty that Godolphin managed to soothe her.[27]

When Anne's mistake was pointed out to her she was nevertheless very ashamed at having jumped to hasty conclusions, and sought to make amends by sending the Duchess a kindly letter suggesting that she visit court so they could make up their quarrel in person, but the Duchess refused to relent until she had gained her point. Yet more letters poured in from her on the subject of Sunderland, with the result that she and the Queen were soon on worse terms than ever. The quarrel raged on seemingly interminably, and in October the Duchess reopened old wounds when she enquired of her mistress 'whether you have never heard that the greatest misfortunes that ever has happened to any of your family has not been occasioned by having ill advice and an obstinacy in their tempers . . . that is very unaccountable?' To this the Queen returned the freezing rejoinder that 'What you say you may be assured will not alter my mind.'[28]

Nevertheless, the Queen could not hold out for ever. On 18 November 1706 Marlborough returned from the Continent for the winter break in campaigning and though a somewhat more tactful advocate than his wife, he continued to press on the Queen Sunderland's claim to office. Faced with his insistence Anne relented on 3 December, and Sarah no doubt felt it to be her victory. But it had been the personal appeal of Marlborough, combined with the Queen's fear that Godolphin might resign if his wishes were not respected; that had carried the day for Sunderland; if anything, indeed, his mother-in-law had harmed his cause. By her jibes and importunities Sarah had destroyed the possibility that the crisis could be settled by rational discussion, and her intervention had removed the issue from the dry world of politics and set it against a background of personal conflict and mutual recrimination. Godolphin had had his manifold difficulties compounded by the Duchess's 'womanish quarrels' with her mistress and though eventually the Queen's resistance had been worn down, she regarded the appointment of Sunderland not as a statesmanlike concession but as a humiliating defeat for which she never fully forgave Sarah.

As Anne had feared, the appointment of Sunderland did nothing to solve her political difficulties, for the following year Marlborough and Godolphin urged her to make still further concessions to the Whigs, which the Queen, convinced that she had already gone too far, resolutely refused to grant. It was against this troubled background that Sarah made the discovery that was to shatter the last brittle remnants of her friendship with her mistress, for in mid-1707 she learnt that her cousin Abigail was on a better footing with the Queen than she herself.

The character of Abigail Hill remains, today, something of an enigma. Sarah's portrayal of her as a monster of ingratitude, possessed of a serpentine cunning, nowadays seems as overstated as a demon king in a pantomime. Independent contemporary evaluations of her are rare and, where they do exist, contradictory. Thus the Earl of Dartmouth described her as 'exceeding mean and vulgar in her manners, of a very unequal temper, childishly exceptious and passionate', but Jonathan Swift provided the case for the defence when he wrote that she 'was a person of plain sound understanding, of great truth and sincerity without the least mixture of falsehood or disguise; of an honest boldness and courage superior to her sex, firm and disinterested in her friendship and full of love, duty and veneration for the Queen her mistress', although on another occasion even he admitted that Abigail was too prone to 'give . . . a loose to her passion'.[29] When all is said and done indeed we know little more of Abigail's personality than that she was a fiery little woman with a talent for the harpsichord; her surviving letters are not sufficiently illuminating to enable us to make an impartial assessment of her character, and so when examining her role in history we are obliged for the most part to fall back upon Sarah's version of events, which, if not necessarily reliable, is certainly vivid.

Abigail Hill's mother was one of Sarah's father's many sisters, but he had lost contact with her after her marriage to a city merchant named Hill. In consequence Sarah had not even realized that these relatives existed until the closing years of the seventeenth century, when Mr Hill lost all his money in commercial speculation and a mutual friend had informed Sarah of the family's plight. It was a situation that brought out all that was good in Sarah's character: with brisk benevolence she provided immediate financial assistance, and when Mr and Mrs Hill died soon afterwards she took responsibility for their children. In 1697 Anne had at Sarah's request taken the eldest daughter, Abigail, as one of her women of the Bedchamber, and Abigail's younger sister Alice was also provided with a livelihood at court. On Anne's accession Abigail had retained her position, an arrangement that initially had suited Sarah well, for it seems that during her absences from court Abigail often deputized for her as Keeper of the Privy Purse, and by the time that the Duchess came to suspect that her cousin was anything other than a trusty and loyal subordinate it was too late to unseat her.

At exactly what stage Abigail made the transition from personal servant to royal companion remains obscure, although with hindsight Sarah was to date her rise in favour from as early as 1703. But it was only in May 1707 that Sarah, who for some time had been concerned that the Queen's Tory leanings were receiving secret encouragement from an unspecified source, focused her suspicions on Abigail, and wrote to warn her husband that Abigail 'does speak of business to the Queen'. Marlborough as yet was unconcerned, suggesting casually that Sarah 'might speak to her with some caution, which might do good, for she certainly is grateful and will mind what you say',[30] but in the coming weeks Sarah's enquiries not only confirmed her in the view that Abigail had set herself up as spokeswoman for the Tories, but suggested that she had become dangerously intimate with the Queen. Accordingly the Duchess wrote to Anne, accusing her of having turned against her, and although the Queen assured her that she was mistaken, Sarah demanded a private audience with her at which she could state her case in person.

On 17 July 1707 they had a painful meeting at Windsor, at which Sarah not only expatiated on her favourite theme of the Queen's disloyalty to Marlborough and Godolphin, but also for the first time made a passing reference to the malign influence of Abigail Hill. As the Queen reacted in a curiously jumpy fashion, the Duchess felt impelled to explore the subject further, and the following day she wrote elaborating on her mistrust of Abigail, suggesting that 'without knowing it or intending it' her cousin was guilty 'of feeding Mrs Morley's passion for Tories by taking all occasions to speak well of some of them and by giving you a prejudice to those that are truly in your interest'. This the Queen would by no means admit, returning sharply 'Your cousin Hill ... is very far from being an occasion of feeding Mrs Morley in her passion, as you are pleased to call it, she never meddling with anything', and insisting that Abigail's contacts with the Tories went no further than the purely social.[31]

At this Sarah abandoned all pretence of moderation: convinced that her cousin was deliberately perverting the royal will, she fired back that Abigail only consorted with 'Jacobites open or in disguise, misled Tories that are ... opposers of you in whatever lies in their way', but Anne was not to be cowed by such abuse. On 9 August, she signalled her defiance by informing Sarah that she had decided to promote Abigail's sister Alice to the position of Bedchamber woman, and Sarah could do nothing but acquiesce in this further infiltration by the Hills into her own domain. Nevertheless, in her letter acknowledging the Queen's decision, for the first time she insinuated that Anne's connection with Abigail could have an adverse effect on her reputation: 'I believe the secret begins to be discovered', she cautioned her mistress, ' ... My greatest concern now is to think of the prejudice it must do Mrs Morley ... which will make her character so very different from that which has always been given by her faithful Freeman.'[32] In the months to come the Duchess was to amplify on this muted hint and directly accuse the Queen of having a lesbian relationship with her waiting woman.

So far the Queen had consistently denied that her relationship with Abigail was anything more than that of mistress and servant, and as yet Sarah had no concrete proof that this was not so. Now, however, she made a fresh discovery which she took as confirmation that Abigail and Anne were in league against her. In September 1707 the Duchess learnt that at some time in the past months, Abigail had privately married a courtier named Samuel Masham. As patroness and saviour of the Hill family, Sarah felt that she should have been consulted beforehand but initially she was disposed to overlook the slight, prepared to attribute it simply to Abigail's 'bashfulness and want of breeding'. On visiting her cousin to congratulate her, Sarah graciously offered to break the news to the Queen, but to her surprise

Abigail replied that Anne had already learnt of her marriage from the gossip of the Bedchamber women. If so, Sarah wanted to know why Anne had kept the knowledge to herself, but when she hurried round to remonstrate with the Queen an even greater shock lay in store for her. Cornered by the angry Duchess, Anne blurted out 'I have a hundred times bid Masham tell it you, and she would not', a slip of the tongue that conjured up to Sarah a horrific vision of the Queen and Abigail in regular conference with one another, conspiring together against her interests.[33]

Convinced now that Abigail had betrayed her, Sarah determined to tax her cousin with her treachery and after an inconclusive exchange of letters, they met for a final showdown. The Duchess attacked at once, accusing her cousin of being responsible for the Queen's change of attitude towards her, but Abigail was nothing if not composed. As Sarah later recalled, she answered sweetly that 'she was sure the Queen, who had loved me extremely, would always be very kind to me', and the Duchess was so dumbfounded 'to see a woman whom I had raised out of the dust put on such a superior air' that she was still spluttering protests when Abigail calmly took her leave.[34] Thenceforth there was to be no direct communication between the cousins.

Abigail had won a round but the Duchess still had plenty of fight in her, not least because she enjoyed the full support of her husband and Godolphin, who had revised their initial opinion that Abigail posed a negligible threat to their power when it appeared that her political mentor was their own enemy, the adroit and supple Secretary of State Robert Harley. A moderate Tory, Harley had initially been one of the mainstays of the Marlborough-Godolphin political partnership but as they had drifted towards the Whigs, so he had turned against them and looked round for new allies. He found one in Abigail, who by coincidence was also his cousin as well as Sarah's, and whom he had groomed in the role of Tory apologist, training her to keep the Queen informed of his own point of view in the same way that Sarah acted as mouthpiece for her husband.

By the autumn of 1707 Marlborough and Godolphin had realized that Abigail and Harley were acting in concert to stiffen the Queen's dislike of the Whigs and they became as anxious as Sarah that Abigail's influence should be nullified. However, when they raised the subject with the Queen, Anne refused to admit that they had any cause for concern, and the Duchess of Marlborough's aggressive endorsement of her husband's complaints was hardly calculated to make the Queen more co-operative. Throughout the autumn of 1707 Sarah sorely tried the Queen's patience with her unceasing reproaches about Abigail, and by December the Queen's relations with the Duchess were at such a low ebb that she could hardly bear to speak to her. When Sarah paid her a Christmas visit Anne confined herself to giving her 'a very cold embrace and then without one kind word' dismissed her.[35]

By early 1708 the mutual distrust between the Queen on one hand and the Marlboroughs and Godolphin on the other had reached such a peak that it was clear that crisis could not long be averted. The first sign of impending trouble came when Sarah went to see Anne at Kensington and told her that as it was unlikely that Marlborough would remain in the Queen's service much longer, she wished to resign all her court offices and arrange for her daughters to take over her duties. Whatever the Duchess's faults, at that stage Anne was still loth to lose one who at one time had meant more to her than any other mortal and insisted that they 'must never part'. Eventually Sarah agreed to stay in office for the time being, but nevertheless she managed to extract from the Queen a promise that in the event of her resignation her positions at court would be distributed amongst her daughters.

Anne's difficulties, however, were far from over. Despite the Queen's denials, Marlborough and Godolphin were convinced that with her encouragement Harley was working secretly to form an alternative Government, but they were not prepared to give him time to mature his plans. On 8 February 1708 they informed the Queen that unless she dismissed Harley they could no longer remain in office. Determined to stand by Harley, the Queen refused their request, but when they carried out their threat of resignation it immediately became apparent that Harley was not capable of carrying out the business of Government without Marlborough's support. The Queen was obliged to dismiss Harley after all, and accept back Marlborough and Godolphin in the humiliating knowledge that her bid for independence had miserably failed and that in future her freedom of action would be severely curtailed.

Sensibly Anne tried to accept defeat gracefully and did her best to renew friendly relations with Sarah, but the Duchess showed no disposition to be conciliatory. In her opinion the Queen had behaved disgracefully towards Marlborough and Godolphin and moreover, although Harley had been dismissed, his ally Abigail remained in royal service and in Sarah's eyes constituted as great a threat as ever.

In an astonishing letter to the Queen she made the grandiose declaration that 'Your Majesty's favour to the Duchess of Marlborough was always looked upon as a peculiar happiness to your people because it naturally led you to put your chief confidence in the two ablest men of your kingdom . . . ' and demanded imperiously, 'Must she at last be disgraced for the sake of one raised by herself from nothing, one without a character, almost without a name?' Such fulminations did nothing to ease the strained relations between Queen and Duchess, and the crisis came when Sarah discovered that Abigail had abrogated some of her rooms at Kensington Palace. Sarah herself never utilized these, preferring to remain at St James's when in London, but she was not going to permit anyone else to benefit from them, and the Queen's feeble insistence that Abigail had never laid claim to them only goaded her further. On 31 March 1708 she wrote to the Queen to inform her that on account of her 'very hard and uncommon usage' she had resolved to withdraw into the country indefinitely.[36]

Sarah's appalled relatives and supporters begged her to reconsider, convinced that without the Duchess to keep her in check, Anne would hanker more than ever after a Tory ministry. Surprisingly, the Queen herself endorsed these pleas for the Duchess's return, for though the days had long gone by when she found unremitting joy in Sarah's company, she felt the spectacle of two middle-aged women squabbling interminably to be an undignified one which ill became them both. As she not unreasonably observed to Godolphin, the Duchess affected to believe that her absence from court would excite no comment but it was inevitable that some of the Queen's ladies would begin to talk of their estrangement and then 'the tattling voice will . . . in a little time make us the jest of the town'. Miserably the Queen concluded 'Some people will blame her, others me and a great many both', and advocated immediate cessation of hostilities.[37]

Sarah, however, was beyond the call of logic: in her view the vexed question of the Kensington lodgings obstructed the possibility of a lasting truce between herself and her mistress, and furthermore she had now come under the unsettling influence of Sir Arthur Maynwaring, a Whig playwright and a polemicist who encouraged her to behave ever more outrageously. In April 1708 he had remarked of the Queen's affection for Abigail, 'An inclination that is shameful . . . grows so uneasy by degrees that it wears itself away . . . A good ridicule has often gone a good way in doing a business; and this I am sure is of such a kind that it needs only to be mentioned to make it ridiculous.'[38] Sarah was to follow this advice with disastrous effect, and with Maynwaring as a collaborator she would in the months to come attain a level of folly which even she had hitherto eschewed.

The irony of it all was that though the Marlboroughs' fears of Abigail had reached massive dimensions, her power was not nearly so great as they imagined. Every time the Queen opposed policies advocated by Marlborough and Godolphin, they presumed she did it at the instigation of Abigail, but in reality the Queen was determined to be governed by nobody, and that included Abigail. Abigail was certainly ambitious for power and took every opportunity to promote the interests of her Tory friends, but her efforts bore little fruit. Her letters to Harley were full of complaints that the Queen seemed completely unreceptive to her advice: on one occasion she moaned that 'while she is hearing it she is very melancholy but says little to the matter',[39] and evidently Anne scrupulously avoided making disloyal reflections on her ministers. Although Abigail passed on to her advice and encouragement from Harley, the Queen refrained from replying and it is clear that both Mrs Masham and Harley were thoroughly disgusted by the Queen's reluctance to participate in secret intrigues.

Unfortunately none of this was apparent to Sarah. Although withdrawn from the court, she continued to conduct from a distance her anti-Abigail crusade, and in early July 1708 she sent the Queen yet another letter vilifying Abigail for encouraging Anne to undermine her General's war effort. Anne reacted with a sharp letter of 6 July, denying that Marlborough had any cause for complaint and demanding that in future Sarah, who after all had been responsible for Abigail's appointment in the first place, should refrain from criticizing her cousin. Sarah did not take this lying down. The following day she fired off another salvo, admitting that it was she who originally had brought Abigail to the Queen's notice but desiring her to 'remember that my commendations went no further than being a handy and faithful servant ... I never thought her education was such as to make her fit company for a great Queen. Many people have liked the humour of their chamber maids and have been very kind to them but 'tis very uncommon to hold a private correspondence with them and put them upon the foot of a friend.'[40] It is difficult to imagine a more insolent letter from a subject to a sovereign.

Unbelievably, however, worse was to come. In the summer of

1708 there had appeared a scurrilous ballad, probably penned by Maynwaring, which made open allusion to the Queen's supposed lesbian relationship with Abigail. Two of the verses ran thus:

> When as Queen Anne of great renown
> Great Britain's sceptre swayed,
> Besides the Church she dearly loved
> A dirty chamber maid . . .
>
> Her secretary she was not
> Because she could not write
> But had the conduct and the care
> Of some dark deeds at night.

Sarah was delighted with this unsavoury ditty, going so far as to sing it aloud in the drawing rooms of fashionable Whig ladies.[41] This, however, was not enough for her. Towards the end of July she decided to end her self-imposed exile from court and visited the Queen specifically in order to show her this ballad and another one similar in tone. Anne was naturally aghast that such coarse libels were in circulation and muttered something about her reputation. Delighted with the effect of her broadside, Sarah for the moment withdrew, but only in order to renew the attack in writing. In a letter of 27 July she remarked that she had been surprised that the Queen should even dare mention her reputation 'after having discovered so great a passion for such a woman, for sure there can be no reputation in a thing so strange and unaccountable to say no more of it. Nor can I think that having no inclination for any but of one's own sex is enough to maintain a character I wish may still be yours.'[42] Finally Sarah's hazy innuendoes about the ill effect that the Queen's relationship with Mrs Masham could have upon her name had crystallized into an open accusation that she was lesbian.

The charge that Abigail and Anne were lovers is so startling that it merits further discussion. Sarah evidently believed it to be the case, and as her knowledge of the Queen stretched back so many years this in itself might seem proof enough. Undeniably, in their youth Anne had been 'in love' with Sarah, and it could be argued that her natural lesbian tendencies had simply found full expression in her relationship with Abigail. But it must be stressed that there is nothing to suggest that Anne's feelings for Abigail ever remotely approached those she had once experienced for Sarah. Fond of Abigail though she undoubtedly was, she was clearly well aware of her faults, and furthermore was acutely conscious of the social barriers between them and made no effort to break them down as she had in the case of Sarah. Having tired of the Duchess, nothing seems more understandable than that the Queen should turn for companionship to a woman who had already established her worth as an indispensable and obliging servant, but Sarah was psychologically incapable of accepting that she was in any way to blame for her loss of favour, and preferred a more sensational interpretation of events. The Queen could never bring herself to answer any of Sarah's allegations, which the Duchess took as proof that they were true, but this is not necessarily so. In the seventeenth and eighteenth centuries people in England were still exceptionally prudish about homosexuality in women. In his *Memoirs of the Court of Charles II*, the French Count Grammont remarked in some amusement that the English, so sophisticated in some respects, were 'yet so uncivilized as never to have heard of that refinement in love of early Greece'[43] and it is hardly surprising that the shy and inarticulate Anne was unwilling to discuss a subject that even the Restoration rakes considered taboo. Sarah's allegations clearly afforded the Queen the profoundest mortification, but her failure to refute them is not necessarily indicative that she was ashamed of an illicit passion which she could not control, but simply that she was reluctant to demean herself by descending to Sarah's level.

The Queen did not deign to reply to Sarah's outburst but three weeks after the incident they were again thrown together when the Duchess came up to London to wait on her mistress at the public thanksgiving that was to be held at St Paul's in celebration of Marlborough's latest victory. As their coach neared the Cathedral, the Duchess noticed that Anne was not wearing the jewels that she had laid out for the occasion and a violent argument ensued. They were still wrangling as they mounted the Cathedral steps, whereupon the Duchess took it upon herself to tell the Queen to be quiet. Nevertheless, having returned home in a huff, Sarah again took up her pen and resumed the controversy, suggesting to Anne that it was Mrs Masham who had persuaded her to spurn her choice of jewels. The Queen, however, had had enough of Sarah's polemics and her reply was chilling and to the point, for she loftily informed the Duchess that 'after the commands you gave me in the Church of not answering you' she considered further communication between them to be undesirable.[44]

Unnerved by her tone, Sarah made some attempt to apologize and after a time the Queen relented so far as to agree to see her again, but the incident had marked a new low point in the ever-descending curve of their friendship. Furthermore, the Duchess was not sincerely contrite and it soon emerged that the differences between her and her mistress remained as great as ever. In September she and the Queen had two more painful meetings at which the Duchess behaved so aggressively that Anne was reduced to tears, and the Queen must have felt nothing but relief when Sarah finally retreated haughtily to her country house to nurse her grievances in private.

In late October, however, Sarah heard that the Queen's husband was on the verge of death and she thereupon notified her mistress that though at their last meeting, 'your usage of me was such as was scarce possible for me to imagine or for anybody else to believe', she considered it her duty to be present at such a juncture. Accordingly the Duchess was at Kensington Palace when the Prince died there on 28 October 1708, and she at once assumed command of the situation. The Queen, distraught with grief, wished to keep vigil over the body but Sarah told her it would be morbid if she remained at Kensington longer than was necessary, attributing Anne's understandable reluctance to bid farewell to her partner of over twenty-five years to her fear of separation from Mrs Masham. At length Anne submitted but asked that while preparations were made for her departure, Sarah should retire and send for Abigail to comfort her. Finding this 'shocking', the Duchess neglected to carry out this order but Abigail nevertheless contrived to be present as the Queen was setting out for St James's. Anne was hobbling toward her carriage leaning on Sarah's arm but as the latter indignantly recorded 'at the sight of that charming lady [Abigail] . . . I found she had strength to bend down towards Mrs Masham like a sail, and in passing by, went some steps nearer than was necessary to be nearer her'.[45]

To Sarah, too preoccupied with her own wrongs to be touched by an old friend's sorrow, this was 'a cruel touch' on the part of the Queen, but in reality it is she who emerges from the episode with the utmost discredit. Contemporary sources are unanimous that Anne was shattered by the death of a husband to whom she was devoted, but as this did not accord with Sarah's claim that the Queen and Abigail were in the throes of a lesbian love affair, she simply denied that her grief was genuine. In the circumstances it is hardly surprising that the Queen turned for comfort to the sympathetic Abigail, but Sarah chose to cite this as proof that her suspicions were justified. In the weeks to come, the Queen's every effort to mourn her husband would be twisted by the Duchess to fit her theory: when for example

Anne took to shutting herself up in the little rooms where George had transacted his business, Sarah asserted that it was because she wished to use them for meetings with Abigail. Only when Sarah again left court at the beginning of December was the Queen enabled to indulge her sorrow without fear of reproach.

All trace of affection between the two women was by now extinguished and henceforward they communicated only on matters relating to Sarah's court offices. Even here, however, trouble lay ahead. As Groom of the Stole, Sarah was accustomed to appoint whomsoever she pleased to the various minor posts that came under her jurisdiction as titular head of the Bedchamber, and she was entitled to do so by an ordinance passed in the reign of William III, which stated 'That our Groom of the Stool shall . . . dispose of the places of . . . our laundress and sempster . . . and all other inferior offices that . . . belong to our Bedchamber'. The same document nevertheless made it clear that the Sovereign had the power to override the wishes of the Groom of the Stole in such matters, and now that Anne and Sarah had fallen out, the Queen wished to assert her independence within the Bedchamber, the very arena in which Sarah had hitherto ruled supreme. This became clear in the summer of 1709, when the Queen required a new woman of the Bedchamber, and although Sarah put forward a candidate of her own for the post, she was overlooked in favour of Bella Danvers, the daughter of another of Anne's dressers who had served the Queen since childhood. Sarah was enraged: earlier in the year the Queen had neglected to consult her before raising the salary of the royal laundress, Elizabeth Abrahal, by five pounds a year; now she defied her wishes in the matter of Bedchamber appointments. In short, the Queen was treating her like a nonentity, and the Duchess, who detected Abigail's influence in all this, was determined not to stand for it. When she visited Windsor on 31 July she had a violent argument with Anne, but this only had the effect of eliciting from the Queen a letter announcing that thenceforth she would treat Sarah not as a friend but simply as 'Groom of [the] Stole and the Duke of Marlborough's wife'.[46]

It was in these very capacities, however, that Sarah was determined to make a nuisance of herself. On 6 August, she wrote to the Queen to tell her that her husband fully supported her, and railed at her mistress for failing to treat her with the same consideration that was shown to the other principal officers at court. 'I beg leave to explain that matter to you,' she fumed, 'when a place is vacant under any of your other officers, those Your Majesty does not allow them immediately to fill in, yet some regard is had to them and their recommendations . . . Is it not plain now from this that I am not used like others of the same rank?'[47] To this shrill interrogative the Queen returned no answer.

The quarrel festered on throughout the early autumn of 1709. At the end of September, Marlborough wrote to the Queen upbraiding her for her treatment of his wife, and the following month Sarah herself hurled another poison dart, expressing her surprise in a letter of 16 October that 'there can be any pleasure in company that one is ashamed to own'. It was nearing the end of the month before the Queen could bring herself to answer either of these missives, but on 25 October she wrote to Marlborough in the following acid terms: 'You seem to be dissatisfied with my behaviour to the Duchess of Marlborough. I do not love complaining but . . . I believe nobody was ever used by a friend as I have been by her ever since my coming to the Crown. I desire nothing but that she would leave off teasing and tormenting me and behave with the decency she ought both to her friend and Queen.' To Sarah she wrote equally bluntly the following day, complaining of her 'inveteracy . . . against poor Masham' and reaffirming her decision to have no dealings with her except in her official capacity.[48]

This however was by no means the end of the argument. The Queen's chilly letter to Sarah crossed with one from the Duchess to her, in which Sarah once again tried to assert her rights as Groom of the Stole and Mistress of the Robes. She had heard that the royal sempstress, Mrs Rainsford, was mortally ill, and she now wrote demanding that she should appoint her successor. The Queen responded with a caustic note indicative of her new sense of resolution. 'You need not have been in such haste,' she sarcastically informed the Duchess, 'for Rainsford is pretty well again and I hope will live a great while.' She added however that 'if this poor creature should die . . . I shall then hearken to nobody's recommendation but my own', and once and for all she established that it was she who held the ultimate authority over the royal household when she stated firmly 'there is no office whatsoever that has the entire disposal of anything under them but I may put in any one I please when I have a mind to it'.[49]

Sarah's response was hardly that of a sane woman. For three days she sat scribbling at her desk, transcribing copies of the Queen's early letters to her and recapitulating on the services she had rendered her in the past. She furthermore demanded that the Queen abstain from taking Communion until she had atoned for her maltreatment of her, backing this up with lengthy quotations from a current devotional work. In conclusion she promised that though she could 'not comprehend that one can be properly said to have malice or inveteracy for a viper because one endeavours to hinder it from doing mischief', she would refrain in future from attacking Abigail on condition that the Queen indicated that she had read and digested this extraordinary document.[50]

Not unnaturally the Queen was overwhelmed by this effusion, and a week later she returned only a short note saying she had not yet had time to read all the material. For her pains she received yet another stream of consciousness from the Duchess in which she once again concentrated her fire on the Queen's supposed lesbian connection with Mrs Masham and warned her that the relationship was becoming common knowledge.[51] This Anne simply ignored and upon that note the correspondence mercifully came to an end.

It was not long, however, before another crisis had brewed up. On 10 November Marlborough had returned from the Continent for his winter holidays, to be confronted by a demand from the Queen that he promote Abigail's younger brother, Captain Jack Hill, to the rank of colonel. This the Duke considered to be a ploy to humiliate him, and he decided that matters had reached such a stage that the Queen must now choose between Abigail and himself. In January 1710 he wrote to the Queen lamenting 'that after all I have done it has not been able to protect me against the malice of a Bedchamber woman' and telling her that he saw no alternative but to offer his resignation. Simultaneously a group of extreme Whigs in the House of Commons began to move for a parliamentary address demanding the dismissal of Abigail, an attempt to interfere in the internal arrangements of the royal household that constituted a gross insult to the Queen. The Queen reacted swiftly to counter this threat, instructing her Vice-Chamberlain 'to tell all her friends in the House of Commons . . . that any such address would be very disagreeable to her', and in the face of her determined opposition all support for the measure evaporated and it was quietly dropped.[52] To placate Marlborough, the Queen gave way about the appointment of Jack Hill but although it appeared that the incident could be forgotten when her General retracted his resignation, lasting damage had in fact been done. Marlborough had assured Anne that neither he nor his wife had had anything to do with the parliamentary address proposal but she remained convinced that they had been involved, and found this difficult to forgive.

The Duchess had spent much of the early part of 1710 away from court, attending the Queen only on important public occasions, but as it gradually dawned on her that Anne now regarded her with fixed dislike, Sarah became alarmed. Pondering the reason for her loss of favour, the Duchess decided it must be because others were feeding the Queen lies about her, and at the beginning of April she requested a private audience with her mistress at which she could vindicate herself. Having had enough of such encounters, the Queen tried to stall her but Sarah insisted on having a hearing, rashly promising that Anne need make no comment on what she had to say. On 6 April 1710 she finally had her way, having stationed herself outside the Queen's door at Kensington until she gained admittance.

It proved a barren victory. Even as Sarah began her defence, the Queen interrupted to tell her that she could put what she had to say in writing. The Duchess nevertheless doggedly rehearsed her piece, explaining that she believed that Anne had been misinformed about her behaviour, which drew from the Queen only the laconic comment that 'without doubt there were many lies told'. In growing desperation Sarah pressed on, but to no avail, for whenever she paused for breath Anne merely reiterated the same single grim sentence: 'You desired no answer and you shall have none.' This was the formula in which the Queen took refuge, the dry dust to which a once-thriving friendship had been reduced, and all Sarah's tears and pleas could elicit no other answer. Stung by her obduracy, Sarah voiced the bitter hope that the Queen 'would suffer for such an instance of inhumanity' but Anne could not be drawn. 'That will be to myself', was her tight-lipped return, and the interview was at an end.[53] The sobbing Duchess withdrew; she and the Queen were never to meet again.

On a personal level the Queen had broken with Sarah but while the Whig-orientated Government remained in power, Anne felt that she was still shackled to the Duchess. As the Queen well knew, Lord Treasurer Godolphin was devoted to the Duchess, and she was fearful that through him Sarah would still be able to bring indirect political pressure to bear on her. Had Godolphin agreed to cut his ties with Sarah, the Queen might have been prepared to retain him as head of her administration, but when the matter was mentioned to him he made it clear that he would stick by his old friend come what may.[54] That being so, the Queen wished to be rid of him, and this was where Mrs Masham came into her own. For two years she had fruitlessly peddled to the Queen her anti-Whig propaganda but now Anne wished to make use of the lifeline she could provide with the fallen

Robert Harley, for she had not only become disenchanted with her existing ministers but was convinced that they were no longer strong enough to prevent her from forming an alternative Government. Through Abigail she secretly renewed contact with Harley in about March 1710, and with him as her adviser she set about dismantling the ministry bit by bit. Having weakened the Government by selective dismissals, the Queen felt confident enough to remove Godolphin himself on 8 August 1710 and two days later Harley was appointed Chancellor of the Exchequer.

One problem nevertheless remained before Anne could feel herself fully emancipated from Sarah. Technically, the Duchess remained in possession of all her court offices and though the Queen longed to strip her of them, Sarah made it clear that she would not go without a fight. She refused to resign unless the Queen fulfilled her earlier promise and distributed her offices amongst her daughters and she warned Sir David Hamilton, whom the Queen had put in charge of these negotiations, that if she was dismissed without adequate recompense she would publish the letters Anne had sent her early in their relationship. The Queen was naturally appalled, remarking to Sir David that 'When people are fond of one another, they say many things, however indifferent, they would not desire the world to know,' but she insisted that the Duchess's outrageous behaviour had absolved her from observing her promise. Hamilton reported to her that when informed of this Sarah merely commented ominously 'that she wondered, when Your Majesty was so much in her power, that you should treat her so'. For months deadlock prevailed, with the Queen not daring to dismiss Sarah but refusing to succumb to blackmail and appoint her daughters, of whom she witheringly remarked, 'the one is cunning and dangerous . . . the other silly and imprudent' while the third, worst of all, 'was just like her mother'.[55] By January 1711, however, the Queen had determined to brave the consequences of removing Sarah whatever the risks, and having made up her mind she acted with a stubbornness worthy of her father.

As it became evident that the Queen was nerving herself to strike against Sarah, Marlborough prevailed upon his wife to write to Anne a letter of humble apology for her behaviour, but when he presented this to the Queen on 18 January he found that he had come too late. Despite his remonstrances, Anne insisted she must have from Sarah the gold key of the Bedchamber that was the insignia of her office. Even when Marlborough went down on his knees and pleaded that his wife might at least have ten days grace she did not relent, specifying that she must repossess the key within three. Marlborough had to return home and report the outcome to his wife, who promptly flew into one of her famous tantrums, flinging the gold key into the middle of the room and insisting that Marlborough return it there and then, even though it was late in the evening and he had undressed for the night.[56] The stark fact remained, however, that she had been ignominiously ejected from office. Too late Sarah had learnt what common sense should have told her before, namely that force of personality counted for nothing when confronted with the might of the monarch. It was a sad ending to a friendship between a Queen and her subject unique in English history.

However, Sarah did not leave court empty-handed. On her dismissal she submitted to the Queen her accounts as Keeper of the Privy Purse, but in her memoirs she admitted that before she did so she deducted from its funds £18,000, or nine years' arrears of the pension of £2,000 that she had initially rejected in 1702. A recent authority has suggested that a rather larger sum was involved. Sarah's surviving account books show that over the years she had withdrawn from the Privy Purse a total of £32,800 for her own use, much of it officially on loan from the Crown. The final volume of her account books is missing, so it is impossible to know whether she repaid these debts, but it seems likely that she did not, particularly in view of the fact that she complained that after she left office Harley refused to countersign her accounts, claiming that she owed the Crown a large sum of money.[57] Even if one accepts that Sarah was entitled to £18,000 of backdated pension, she would have made a profit of £14,800 on top of her official salaries by failing to refund the amounts she had borrowed, and although Sarah herself evidently considered that she deserved a share of the money she had saved the Crown during her years in the Queen's service this today seems somewhat dubious reasoning. The Queen herself apparently had some reservations about Sarah's financial dealings for she only approved the Privy Purse accounts after they had been submitted to her for a fortnight and it seems a plausible conjecture that she only decided to let them pass at all because she hoped that if she overlooked any discrepancies in the figures Sarah would refrain from publishing her letters.

If this was what the Queen had counted on, the threat was only narrowly averted. By the end of 1711 Sarah had produced the first draft of her autobiographical account of her life at court, which included extracts from several of Anne's early letters to her, and it was only with great difficulty that her friends dissuaded her from publishing it. As it was, she continued to work on her memoirs for the remainder of her long life, polishing and embellishing them to her satisfaction until they were finally published in 1742, two years before her death at the age of eighty-two. Naturally they created an enormous sensation, but the reaction was by no means entirely favourable and if Sarah had hoped that her account of events would vindicate her in the eyes of posterity she was sadly mistaken.

Had the Queen ever imagined that with the departure of Sarah her court would become a haven insulated from the unpleasantness of party strife, she was swiftly disillusioned. If anything, the divisions between the two parties became even more bitter towards the end of the reign, for the Whigs were enraged by the new Tory Government's peace initiatives towards France and saw no reason why they should conceal their feelings for the sake of the Queen's sensibilities. By the end of 1711 progress towards peace had been such that Anne felt able to dispense with Marlborough's services and accordingly on 31 December she dismissed her General. Two of his daughters, the Countess of Sunderland and Lady Rialton, had remained as ladies of the Bedchamber even after Sarah had been dismissed, but when their father was removed as well they promptly resigned their offices. Furthermore, the majority of Whig families thenceforth boycotted court functions altogether, and though the Queen was not deterred from giving a birthday party in February 1712 it must have been saddening for her to have presided over an assembly which so starkly reflected the bitter divisions within English society.

Worse still, the Queen found that like the Whigs before them, her new Tory ministers considered that household appointments were a political matter which could not be dictated solely by her personal preference. This first emerged when the Queen decided that Sarah's successor as Groom of the Stole and Mistress of the Robes should be the Duchess of Somerset, a woman whose life had been dogged at every step by misfortune and controversy. Having inherited an enormous fortune as a child, she had lost her first husband when only thirteen, whereupon her hand was claimed by Thomas Thynne, an ageing but wealthy rake. Finding him repulsive, she fled to the Continent immediately after the wedding, and in her absence her husband was murdered by another of her suitors, Count Charles Königsmark. Although there was no reason to suppose that she had had any knowledge of Königsmark's intentions, some people thereafter harboured an unjust suspicion that she was implicated in the murder, and her luck did not improve when in 1682 she took as her third husband the Duke of Somerset, an arrogant and pompous fool who lived off his wife's money and yet 'treated her with little gratitude or affection'.

Others, however, were more appreciative of her worth, among them the Queen, and on her accession to the throne she had made the Duchess one of her ladies of the Bedchamber. Since then the Duchess's dignity and forbearance had ensured that she rose steadily in the Queen's esteem, a development which Sarah had viewed with consternation. Gradually she had become convinced that the Duchess harboured secret ambitions of replacing her as Groom of the Stole and Mistress of the Robes, 'which design', she noted in a memorial dwelling at length on the Duchess's perfidy, 'I resolved to disappoint'. But in fact once she had lost her battle to force Anne to appoint her daughters as her successors, there was nothing she could do to prevent the Duchess being installed in her place.[58]

Despite Sarah's outrage, the Queen herself considered her appointment of the Duchess of Somerset to be a complete success. Quietly spoken and unmeddlesome, the Duchess was in almost every way a contrast to her tempestuous predecessor, and the Queen considered her a particularly suitable companion because she was nobly born and hence fitted by rank to be the foremost of her servants. In this of course she had an advantage over Abigail, and it was not long before a rivalry sprang up between the two women.

Abigail was not alone in her dissatisfaction with the Queen's affection for the Duchess. Although in most respects completely different from Sarah, the Tory ministry were fearful that the Duchess's political outlook was all too similar, for by January 1711 the Duke of Somerset had gone into Opposition to Harley's government and the Tories were convinced that his wife would lose no opportunity to lure the Queen into the Whiggish camp. In consequence Harley had tried to block the Duchess's appointment, but Anne would have none of it, pointing out 'that if she might not have the liberty to choose her own servants she could not see what advantage she had got from the change in her ministry'. Harley had had to submit, but to him and his colleagues the Duchess remained a sinister figure whom they imagined labouring constantly to erode the Queen's Tory loyalties. The slightest sign that the Queen was wavering in her commitment to the Tories had them squawking in alarm about the Duchess's pernicious influence. 'This is all your d----d Duchess of Somerset's doings', wailed the Tory Jonathan Swift in December 1711 when it seemed that the Queen was having second thoughts about endorsing the Government's peace plans, and a few days later he declared despondently, 'We must certainly fall if the Duchess of Somerset be not turned out.'[59]

But as earlier in the reign the Marlboroughs had overrated Abigail's powers, so now the Tories magnified out of all proportion the extent to which the Duchess of Somerset could influence events. Ironically her very strength with the Queen lay in the way that she refrained from pestering her on political topics: the Queen's physician, Sir David Hamilton, noted, 'She never pressed the Queen hard; nothing makes the Queen more uneasy than that',[60] and though the Duchess may have put in the occasional tactful word on behalf of the Whigs, compared to Sarah she was moderation itself.

Certainly one member of the Tory party would have cause to regret his hostility to the Duchess of Somerset. As a firm friend of all the leading Tories, Jonathan Swift had put his writing talents at the disposal of Harley's ministry and in December 1711 he thought to help them when he penned *The Windsor Prophecy*, a satirical poem in which he attacked the Duchess of Somerset and insinuated that she had been involved in Königsmark's murder of her husband thirty years before:

'Their cunnings mark [Konigsmark] thou for I have been told
They assassin when young and poison when old
O root out these carrots*, O thou whose name
Is Backwards and forwards always the same [i.e. Anna]
And keep close to thee always that name
Which backwards and forwards is almost the same. [Masham]

Proudly Swift showed these verses to Abigail, but to his surprise she warned him that 'she knew the Queen and she knew the Duchess of Somerset and she was convinced he would injure himself and his party by publication'. Alarmed by her advice he agreed to suppress them, but he acted too late, as numerous copies had already been printed and were soon in private circulation. Before long the Queen herself had come to hear of the lampoon and as Abigail predicted, she was incensed. Grimly she said 'that would have no influence on her to turn her respect from the Duchess'[61] and the poem's only achievement was to blight its author's hopes of ecclesiastical promotion, for thenceforward the Queen steadfastly refused to confer preferment on the man responsible for so scurrilous a rhyme.

---

* The Duchess had red hair.

Though determined not to part with the Duchess of Somerset, by the end of 1711 the Queen had come to accept that the Duke of Somerset's continued opposition to the Government meant that he could not remain indefinitely as Master of the Horse, a post that he had held since the beginning of the reign. For a time his dismissal was delayed by Anne's fears that he would remove his wife from court if he lost his job, but on 17 January 1712 Somerset was finally discharged. The Tories were jubilant, expressing fervent hopes that 'The Duchess will follow or he will take her away in spite', but in fact Anne had already initiated negotiations aimed at dissuading the Duke from taking this step. After some haggling Somerset had relented, and the Queen was delighted by his decision to let his wife stay with her, which she took to vindicate her lifelong claim that the Bedchamber was above politics. The Duchess of Somerset remained in service, 'in all respects a credit and ornament to the court', comporting herself with such discretion and amiability that 'she was by much the greatest favourite when the Queen died'.[62]

The Tories could at least console themselves that they had their own secret weapon in the Bedchamber in the shape of Abigail Masham, although the influence she wielded would fall far short of their expectations. On Sarah's dismissal she had inherited the least prestigious of her posts and become the Keeper of the Privy Purse, but she was prevented from being constantly at court by her regular pregnancies and the demands of motherhood, much to the fury of the Tories who were beside themselves at the reprehensible way that Abigail neglected her political duties in favour of her maternal ones. 'Lady Masham's eldest boy is very ill, I doubt he will not live; she stays at Kensington to nurse him which vexes us all,' the Reverend Jonathan Swift reported irritably in April 1713, 'She is so excessively fond it makes me mad; she should never leave the Queen but leave everything to stick to what is in the interest of the public as well as her own. This I tell her but talk to the winds.'[63]

He might have been more charitable had he realized that even when Abigail was with the Queen, her advice frequently made no impression on her. Abigail had been one of the most ardent advocates of the Duchess of Somerset's dismissal but the Queen's response was merely to 'condemn her for too much party zeal', and it is clear that Queen had no intention of allowing Abigail to acquire too great a sense of her own importance. To secure the passage through Parliament of the peace treaty with France it proved necessary to create a batch of new peers and Harley thought to please the Queen by including on the list the name of Samuel Masham. The Queen however proved distinctly unenthusiastic about the prospect of Abigail being raised to the aristocracy, protesting 'she never had any design to make a great lady of her and she should lose a useful servant about her person, for it would give great offence to have a peeress lie on the floor [i.e. when she slept in the Queen's room as her night nurse] and do several other inferior offices'. She was only brought to consent to the proposal 'upon condition she remained a dresser and did as she used to do' and she ensured that Abigail's elevation was achieved with the minimum of fuss, ordering her 'to live very privately that she may not get the envy of the people like the Duchess of Marlborough'.[64] The Queen had not rid herself of one tormentor simply in order to raise up another.

To a certain extent Harley himself was partly responsible for Abigail's lack of political importance. Once he had gained power he enjoyed unlimited access to the Queen and as he no longer required her services as an intermediary, he deemed it unnecessary to take Abigail into his confidence as much as he had done before. Naturally enough Abigail soon came to feel resentful of his neglect and gradually she began to turn towards Henry St John, Viscount Bolingbroke, Harley's young rival for the leadership of the Tory party. He in his turn cultivated her favour assiduously, and Harley's relatives even maintained that he went so far as to secure for her a share of the profits arising from the commercial treaty negotiated with Spain at the end of the war. As early as March 1712 it was noted that Harley and Lady Masham 'begin to be jealous of one another' and over the next eighteen months their relations continued to deteriorate steadily.

This did not matter while Harley retained the Queen's favour, but as time went by her faith in him had begun to waver and he came to regret that he had so thoughtlessly antagonized Abigail. By May 1714 he felt his political position to be so weak that he made a concerted effort to reconcile with his erstwhile ally, telling her that only the Whigs would benefit from their estrangement. But Abigail was not to be recaptured, and in July she told Harley bluntly: 'You never did the Queen any service nor are capable of doing her any.' Desperately Harley tried to retrieve his position by forging an alliance with the Duchess of Somerset but she proved equally unresponsive and on 27 July 1714 he was obliged to resign.[65]

It is doubtful that even if Harley could have effected a *rapprochement* with either Lady Masham or the Duchess of Somerset he could have clung to power. Fundamentally the Queen no longer considered him to be fit to lead the Government, and one of Swift's correspondents summed up the situation when he observed that Harley's fall did 'not altogether proceed from his old friend [Abigail] but from the great person [Anne] whom I perceive to be highly offended'. To the Cabinet the Queen justified Harley's enforced departure on the grounds that he was too often under the influence of drink, which made him ill-mannered and incoherent, and she was swift to knock on the head any suggestion that Abigail had been responsible for his undoing. When it was put to Anne that she had demanded his resignation 'because he had hindered her Majesty from giving grants to Lady Masham' she responded sharply that if Harley 'said so he was very ungrateful to Lady Masham'. To Abigail, Harley had once remarked 'You cannot set any one up, you can pull anyone down', but it seems that even with this somewhat negative assessment of her powers he rated them too highly.[66]

On 30 July the Queen entered on what proved to be a mortal illness and two days later she died. Abigail's friend Swift was fearful that she would be reduced to beggary by her mistress's demise and in his letter of condolence he urged her to bear her afflictions patiently, for 'although you have not been rewarded suitable to your merits I doubt not but God will make it up to you in another life'. He need not have concerned himself, for Abigail had no intention of waiting for celestial recognition of her services. Even while the Queen lay in a coma it was said – possibly untruthfully – that Abigail temporarily left Kensington 'to go and ransack for things at St James' and once Anne was dead both Abigail and her sister Alice attracted censure, for 'though they roared and cried enough whilst there was life . . . as soon as there was none they took care of themselves'.[67] These precautions, combined with the savings that Abigail and her husband had managed to amass during their years at court, enabled the Mashams to withdraw into comfortable retirement near Windsor until Abigail's death in 1734.

The reign of Queen Anne has often been seen as the golden age of the lady-in-waiting, a time when ministries rose and fell, wars were won or lost at the whim of petticoat dictators who ruled the kingdom from the Bedchamber. Few have questioned Bishop Burnet's remark apropos of the Duchess of Marlborough 'that there never was a more absolute favourite in a court', but whether her reputation was justified is open to doubt, for in a moment of unusual modesty even Sarah admitted that her attempts 'to get honest men into the service . . . never or very rarely succeeded . . . till the ministers came into it at last'. As for Abigail, who Sarah claimed 'could make the Queen stand on her head if she chose', she showed herself aware of her own limitations when she remarked plaintively to Harley in 1710, 'because I am still with the Queen people think me able to persuade her to anything I have a mind to have her do, but they will be convinced to the contrary one time or other'. Anne herself showed her true mettle when on one occasion it was put to her that she was being led astray by those who surrounded her and she exclaimed irritably, 'O fye! . . . Do they think I'm a child, and to be imposed upon, and that I have only integrity?' Though not a forceful personality, the Queen knew her own mind, and those who shared the view allegedly expressed by Sarah, that Anne was no more than 'a praying Godly idiot'[68], did so at their peril.

The Early Hanoverian Court

'So Uncommon a Seraglio'

On 20 September 1714 George Louis, Elector of Hanover and King of Great Britain, entered London in state. A distant cousin of Queen Anne, he had travelled from his German patrimony in order to claim the throne that was his by virtue of the fact that his new subjects deemed it preferable to have as a sovereign a Protestant foreigner rather than a Catholic Stuart. Having never visited England since his youth, George was inevitably something of an enigma to all people there save for a handful of diplomats and politicians, but doubtless many were already aware of one episode in his life that explained why he brought no queen with him from Hanover.

In 1682 George had been married to his cousin, Sophia Dorothea of Celle, and though she had borne him two children, in every other respect the union had been a failure. George had not been faithful but when after ten years of marriage Sophia Dorothea had taken as her lover a Swedish adventurer named Count Philipp von Konigsmark, George's family had intervened. On 1 July 1694 George himself had been absent when Konigsmark suddenly disappeared, having almost certainly been murdered on his way to an assignation with Sophia Dorothea. On George's return Sophia Dorothea consented to a divorce, possibly without realising that its terms would expressly prohibit her from taking another husband, and thenceforth she was denied access to her children and kept confined in her father's castle at Ahlden. There she remained when George inherited his new kingdom and it was only in 1726 that death finally ended her long captivity.

The story was a grim one but when George arrived in England the ladies there could at least console themselves that he brought with him abundant evidence that he was no misogynist. In his train was Melusine von der Schulenberg, a scrawny woman of forty-seven who was accompanied by the three daughters (officially designated her nieces) that she had borne George in the twenty three years she had been his mistress. They were soon joined in England by Sophia Charlotte von Kielmansegg, the corpulent and red-faced wife of George's Hanoverian Master of the Horse, and the King's affectionate reception of her soon gave rise to a widespread belief that she too was his mistress. In fact the evidence suggests that she was really George's half-sister, for his father had for many years conducted an affair with her mother, but as many Englishmen were unaware that these ties existed the confusion was understandable. The mob, 'highly diverted at the importation of so uncommon a seraglio', irreverently dubbed the pair 'the maypole and the elephant'[1] while even in more educated circles the fact that they both cordially hated one another naturally reinforced the impression that they were rivals in love.

Despite the misunderstanding the English were at least correct in thinking that both 'La Schulenberg' and 'La Kielmansegg' were worth cultivating, and it soon emerged that neither lady was averse to accepting an occasional bribe from courtiers anxious to secure their goodwill. The King himself also provided for them financially (though in this respect Melusine was to fare much better than Sophia Charlotte) and after a few years in England they were further rewarded when they were raised to the peerage in their own right. In 1719 Melusine was created Duchess of Kendal (having made it plain that she was not satisfied with the Irish title of Duchess of Munster that had been conferred on her in 1716) and three years later Sophia Charlotte was also awarded the English title of Countess of Darlington.

There were some at court who believed that the King had had a secret morganatic marriage with the Duchess of Kendal, but if this was so her position remained strictly unofficial and for years the position of England's first lady was filled by his daughter-in-law Caroline, Princess of Wales. She was married to the King's eldest son, George August, a choleric and strutting little man who worshipped his plump spouse but whose terror of being thought unfashionably uxorious led him to indulge as often as possible in conspicuous infidelity. No one was deceived by this behaviour however, for it was common knowledge that his adultery was occasioned more by bravado than desire, and that in all important matters he was guided by his wife.

It was in the household of this amiable but shrewd Princess that the English court ladies now sought employment. For some, the accession of the house of Hanover had dashed hopes of preferment that would not have seemed extravagant had Queen Anne survived a few years longer. Mary Granville, niece of the late Queen's Treasurer of the Household, Lord Lansdowne, 'had been brought up with the expectation of being maid of honour' but as her family were suspected of harbouring Jacobite sympathies they found themselves out of favour with the regime, and Mary had to dismiss all hopes of a court career and retire with them to their country house.[2] Yet such was the competition, and so limited the opportunities, that even those with impeccable political credentials frequently found that success eluded them in the scrum of place-hunters. The Countess of Bristol's husband had been a consistent supporter of the Hanoverian cause in England but though he had been rewarded with an earldom on George's arrival, his wife had failed to secure the coveted post of lady of the Bedchamber. A rival contender for the honour noted wryly in her diary that though she herself made no secret of her desire to be appointed, Lady Bristol 'had still a greater mind to be a lady of the Bedchamber than I had', but though she pursued her ambition with a grim determination of which few who were acquainted with her volatile and histrionic temperament would have thought her capable, her aspirations were doomed. She assiduously cultivated Mesdames Schulenberg and Kielmansegg in the evident belief that they could influence the Princess in her choice, but to no avail; nor did the most flattering attentions to the Countess Buckenburgh, the only German lady-in-waiting to have accompanied the Princess to England, produce results. In desperation the Countess then sought to displace those who had been more fortunate in the quest for office, threatening to have raised in the House of Commons the question of why the Italian-born Duchess of Shrewsbury had been appointed a lady of the Bedchamber when foreigners were prohibited by law from holding public office in England. Fortunately she soon dropped the idea but the Princess of Wales was nevertheless highly displeased that the Countess of Bristol should even have contemplated so presumptuous a proceeding and as a result Lady Bristol found that the glittering prospect of employment in the Bedchamber had become even more remote.[3]

The fortunate few who landed the plum positions in the Princess's household did not do so without a struggle. Four years before the King's accession Lady Cowper, the sourly observant wife of the new Lord Chancellor, had had the foresight to initiate a correspondence with the then Electoral Princess, and as this had been well received she was disappointed when, on the death of Queen Anne, her offer of her services elicited from Hanover only a non-committal reply. When the Princess arrived in England two of the ladies of the Bedchamber were named almost immediately but Lady Cowper was not approached and, assuming that her cause was hopeless, she steeled herself to endure this setback with a resignation that was normally alien to her nature. But all was not yet lost on the Bedchamber front, for she had made something of a conquest of Baron Bernstorff, an austere Hanoverian minister who had accompanied his master to England, and this helped tip the balance in her favour. At the end of October 1714 the Princess laughingly told Lady Cowper that she believed Baron Bernstorff, 'who never was in love in his life before', had evidently been smitten by her, and that evening the Baron himself was able to confirm that Lady Cowper had been appointed to the Princess's Bedchamber.[4]

Her pleasure at this was somewhat dissipated by the discovery that the Duchess of Shrewsbury had attained the same position. The Duchess was a notoriously flighty lady of Italian origin whom the Duke of Shrewsbury had reputedly taken for his mistress when travelling abroad, and whom he had only married because her brother had pursued him when he attempted to abandon her and forced him to redeem her honour. Arriving in England in 1707 she had been looked on askance by the ladies there, who considered that her talent to amuse in no way compensated for her lack of refinement. Nevertheless with what the English no doubt considered to be the typical effrontery of a parvenue, she swiftly conceived an ambition to be a lady of the Bedchamber thinking, in the sarcastic words of the Duchess of Marlborough, 'that it would wash off all stains and she was to make a great figure'. In the reign of Queen Anne she had never managed to attain her objective, but now she was to have better luck. As a fluent French-speaker she found it easy to entertain the new King, who did not in the least object that at times her conversation 'would exceed the bounds of decency' and whose favour to her was indeed so marked that it was whispered that 'she rivals Madam Killmansack'. At the Duchess's request he indicated to the Princess that 'it would be an obligation to him' if she would appoint the Duchess a lady of the Bedchamber, and though Caroline had heard enough about the Duchess's antecedents to have her reservations as to her suitability, when the King asked for the third time she had little choice but to agree.[5]

It was perhaps surprising that these pampered women should so ardently desire a post which was certainly no sinecure. The ladies of the Bedchamber were normally on duty for a week at a time, during which they were in constant attendance on their mistress. Should one of them fall ill during her period of waiting it was her responsibility to persuade a colleague to take her place on the understanding that the favour would later be returned in kind. For the delicate in health this could pose a real problem, for after several bouts of sickness one lady found that it took her so long to repay the friends who had stood in for her during her absence that she was unable to visit her husband in the country for over a month.[6]

Not only was the job time-consuming, the duties involved were also arduous. Unlike George I, who loathed the pompous rituals that were a traditional part of the Sovereign's existence, the Prince and Princess of Wales insisted on the punctilious observation of the ceremonious routines prescribed by etiquette, for, as one courtier observed, 'the trappings of royalty were as pleasing to the son as they were irksome to the father'. Inevitably this increased the demands placed on the ladies of the Bedchamber. In the Bedchamber itself their duties were admittedly minimal, consisting of little more than handing their mistress her shift in the morning and, if necessary, her fan. At the royal dining-table, however, more was required of them. The lady of the Bedchamber on duty had to take the covers off the dishes and carve portions for all members of the royal family who were present, before tasting her mistress's drink and then serving it to her on bended knee, a challenging task for the overweight or arthritic which one disgruntled attendant considered 'a very terrible fatigue to the lady-in-waiting'.[7]

Besides this the ladies had to endure the additional strains arising from their inability either to sit in the presence of royalty without a specific invitation, or to leave the room unless dismissed. After one particularly exhausting spell of duty Lady Cowper felt so 'ill from standing so long upon my feet' that on returning home she retired to bed for two whole days. Another lady had a still more unfortunate experience when, feeling that her bladder was about to burst but not daring to leave the royal drawing room without permission she resorted to the desperate expedient of urinating on the floor, which unfortunately produced a puddle as large as a dining-table for ten which threatened to engulf the shoes of the nearby Princess.[8]

All this was in return for a salary that was considerably less than that paid to Queen Anne's ladies of the Bedchamber. As Queen Regnant Anne had paid her ladies £1,000 a year, but Caroline's received only £500, apart from the Duchess of St Albans, who as

Groom of the Stole was awarded an additional £400. Money, however, was not everything, for the opportunities that household afforded for daily contact with the royal family were prized far more than its incidental financial rewards, an attitude illustrated by one courtier's remark that he considered 'a pension without an employment a poor thing, let it be never so great'. Those in the upper echelons of royal service so obviously enjoyed the esteem of the ruling house that even country neighbours who never came to court were impressed, a fact that the socially ambitious Lady Falmouth ingeniously tried to turn to her own advantage, pointing out that if she were appointed a lady of the Bedchamber her husband would automatically be able to exert more influence in local politics, which would be of benefit to the court. 'If he could be happy enough to go into the country with this mark of favour', she wrote coaxingly, 'it would be such a countenance to his interest at the next elections that I may without vanity say that there is not one subject in England that can do half the service.'[9] It was a good try, if an unsuccessful one, but Lady Falmouth was right in thinking that those who served the great thereby became greater themselves.

Once she had secured her own position, it was understood to be the duty of a lady of the Bedchamber to use her not inconsiderable influence to gain as many appointments and advantages as possible for her family and friends. Jonathan Swift, himself embittered by his failure to find an influential patroness who could have transformed his prospects in the Church, complained fretfully that in his experience of courts, 'the best lady there had some cousin, or near dependent, whom she would be glad to recommend for an employment, and would therefore hardly think of strangers' but for those with better connections the system worked well, resulting in a sort of eighteenth-century old girls' network which enabled the ladies of the Bedchamber to find nieces and cousins posts as maids of honour and dressers. But this was not all, for the influence of the Bedchamber ladies in matters of patronage extended beyond the royal household itself, so that Lady Cowper succeeded in obtaining for her brother-in-law the administrative position of Treasurer of the Stamp Duties, and for her uncle a place in the Lord Chancellor's department which earned him £1,000 a year. Even so her relatives were not satisfied, considering that she could have done better if she had exerted herself, and the mortified Lady Cowper, who had anticipated a different reaction, discovered to her chagrin that 'My Aunt expected I should have got her a place about the Princess and my Uncle another in the salt office.'[10]

As the Crown held the ultimate prerogative of mercy, a lady of the

Bedchamber could occasionally ask the authorities to reconsider the fate of an individual who in her opinion merited clemency. The Duchess of Shrewsbury admittedly went rather too far when, with the proverbial good heartedness of those of her former profession, she pleaded 'hard for a pardon for all the twenty-four' prisoners who had been sentenced to death after the Jacobite uprising of 1715. Lady Cowper fared rather better when she presented the Princess with a letter in which the convicted Jacobite Lord Carnwath begged that his life might be spared. Moved to tears by the appeal, the Princess promised that she would 'give him my honour to save him' provided that he made a full confession, and when Carnwath complied he was duly reprieved. In March 1728 Frances, Lady Hertford did a similar good deed when she procured a pardon for the poet Richard Savage by representing to her mistress that he should not hang for a murder that could not have been premeditated.[11] Clearly it could still prove to be a matter of life or death to have a 'friend at court' in the shape of a lady of the Bedchamber.

The women of the Bedchamber were really little more than glorified abigails, attending on the Princess when she rose, changed her clothes or went to bed, but though the position was much lower in the court hierarchy than that of lady of the Bedchamber it was still hotly sought after by untitled women of good birth. This was not necessarily the case on the Continent, for on a visit to the Imperial court in Vienna Lady Mary Wortley Montagu noted in surprise that 'the dressers are not at all in the figure they pretend to in England, being looked upon no otherwise than as downright chambermaids'[12] but at home it was evidently considered that the chance of associating with royalty compensated for the menial nature of the job. The concept of service to the Crown was still such that whatever the nature of the duties involved they were in no way held to diminish those who performed them, and the women of the Bedchamber could at least pride themselves on having attained a position of some standing at court which brought with it a salary of £300 a year.

Certainly Henrietta Howard had reason enough to be grateful for the security afforded her by her post as dresser to the Princess. At an early age she had married Charles Howard, the impoverished younger son of the Earl of Suffolk, but she and her husband had found life such a struggle at the court of Queen Anne that they had packed their bags and left for Hanover in hopes of commending themselves to the royal family there. In 1713 the couple returned to England, trusting that their prospects were assured in the coming reign, but for the moment they had little to live on but hope, for their marriage had not turned out well and they were in consequence neither happy nor prosperous. At last Queen Anne died and their foresight was rewarded, for Mr Howard was given a post about the King and his wife was appointed a woman of the Bedchamber to the Princess.

It was not long before Henrietta Howard took on duties of a rather more unorthodox nature. His Royal Highness, George August, considered an attractive mistress to be an essential accoutrement for a Prince of the Enlightenment and man of fashion and had initially hoped that he could persuade Mary Bellenden, one of his wife's maids of honour, to accept the part. Mary had given him no encouragement and the Prince had perforce to turn to her friend and confidante Mrs Howard, who, at thirty-three, was not blessed with Mary's youth or vivacity but at least was elegant and well-preserved and had none of the younger girl's inconveniently high ideals concerning matters of the heart. Soon the Prince's evening visits to Mrs Howard's apartments had become an inviolate part of his daily routine, but such was the discretion and self-effacement of the lady that even in that cynical age there were those who questioned whether the relationship was ever consummated. The more worldly, however, could not accept that George passed the hours he spent with her absorbed in conversation, for as Horace Walpole pointed out, Mrs Howard was hard of hearing and the Prince's 'passions were too indelicate to have been confined to platonic love for a woman who was deaf'.[13]

In return for her services Mrs Howard received a pension of £2,000 as well as 'several little dabs of money' which her lover gave her at sporadic intervals throughout their affair, and which enabled her to build herself an unpretentious villa at Twickenham. At times, however, she must have asked herself whether these modest returns justified the effort involved in earning them. Romance can hardly have entered into her calculations for her lover made it abundantly clear that his wife still held the primary place in his affections, and it is besides unlikely that a woman of Mrs Howard's cultivation and charm can ever have been in love with someone so thoroughly second rate as the Prince of Wales. The Princess, for her part, was well aware that her husband's affair with Mrs Howard in no way diminished his feelings for herself, and she was too sensible to be more than a trifle piqued by the situation. She regarded Mrs Howard with the supercilious contempt that a great actress might feel for an untalented understudy and her only revenge was to inflict petty indignities on her rival while she was about her work. The Princess always asked Henrietta to dress her hair in the mornings and in general reserved the more degrading duties for her to deal with, although making a point of calling her 'My good Howard' throughout.[14]

The Princess would doubtless not have been so tolerant if there had been any indication that Mrs Howard was meddling in affairs of State, for as Lady Cowper remarked, Caroline 'had no jealousy but for her authority'. In fact, the Prince of Wales was just as concerned as his wife to keep Mrs Howard's influence in check, for he did not think it became a man to be governed by his mistress, and in consequence Mrs Howard's power remained negligible. Unfortunately, not many people at court assessed the position correctly, with the result that the wretched Mrs Howard was pestered on all sides with applications that she could not satisfy. In 1722 Mrs Ann Pitt even offered to give her £1,000 if she would obtain for her brother a post as lord of the Bedchamber, and though as always in such cases Mrs Howard loftily rejected the bribe, it was in the dispiriting knowledge that even had she felt inclined to accept it, she could have secured little in return for the donors.[15]

Caroline's patronising behaviour towards Mrs Howard was in marked contrast to her treatment of another of her dressers, Mrs Charlotte Clayton. At one time Mr Clayton had managed the Blenheim estate, and in return the Duchess of Marlborough had secured his wife her position at court, and it was not long before Mrs Clayton's sound judgement and unswerving loyalty had established her high in the favour of the Princess of Wales. Caroline consulted her on a wide variety of matters and paid particular attention to her recommendations about household appointments, with the result that Mrs Clayton was regularly besieged with letters from court ladies anxious to enter the Princess's service. A typical example was Lady Pembroke, who wrote to Mrs Clayton at the beginning of the reign that though she was disappointed that the Princess had turned down her offer to serve her as a Bedchamber lady, she still lived 'in hopes that some time or other I shall have the honour of being near her and often with you', and it was no doubt partly in consequence of these complimentary sentiments that Lady Pembroke was appointed a lady of the Bedchamber when the next vacancy occurred.[16]

The arrival in England of the Prince and Princess of Wales had considerably brightened up society. Queen Anne had been both painfully shy and a semi-invalid and had presided over rather a dreary court, but though George himself was also of a retiring disposition he felt he should not neglect his social obligations, and he therefore encouraged his son and daughter-in-law to entertain extensively on his behalf. Twice a week they deputised for him at evening receptions, known as 'Drawing Rooms', which anyone could attend so long as they were suitably dressed, and they also gave regular balls at St James's which were smaller and more select. In consequence London became much more lively while the court was in residence, as Lord Chesterfield testified in 1716. 'As for the gay part of the town, you would find it much more flourishing than you left it', he reported approvingly to a friend. 'Balls, assemblies and masquerades have taken the place of dull formal visiting days and the women are become much more agreeable trifles than they were designed ... Puns are extremely in vogue and the license very great'.[17]

At the centre of all this gaiety were the Princess's maids of honour, an exceptionally pretty and carefree sextet, of whom two in particular attracted the admiration of contemporaries. Mary Lepell was universally considered a credit to the court, her outstanding beauty inspiring several poems in her honour, including some suggestive verses by Lord Chesterfield and Mr Pulteney which caused her considerable embarrassment:

> ... Were I king of Great Britain
> To Choose a minister well
> And support the throne I sat on,
> I'd have under me Molly Lepell ...
>
> Heaven keep our good king from a rising
> But that rising who's fitter to quell
> Than some lady with beauty surprising
> And who should that be but Lepell?

Her colleague, Mary Bellenden, was even more extravagantly lauded. Of her Horace Walpole remarked, 'Her face and person were charming; lively she was almost to *étourderie* and so agreeable she was that I never heard her mentioned afterwards by one of her contemporaries who did not prefer her as the most perfect creature they ever knew.'[18] The Prince of Wales desired her for his mistress but she unceremoniously rejected him, reserving herself instead for marriage with an impoverished cousin of the Duke of Argyll's.

The maids affected to despise the pleasures of the court, but they seem to have entered into them enthusiastically enough. To their friend, the poet Alexander Pope, they complained that 'the life of a maid of honour was of all things the most miserable' and he in response playfully commiserated with them on their tedious existence, gravely agreeing that it must be far from pleasant to have to 'eat Westphalia ham in a morning, ride over hedges and ditches on borrowed hacks, come home in the heat of the day with a fever, and (what is worse a hundred times) with a red mark on the forehead from an uneasy hat . . . As soon as they can wipe off the sweat of the day, they must simper an hour and catch cold in the Princess's apartment: from thence, as Shakespeare has it, to dinner, with what appetite they may, and after that, till midnight, walk, work or think, which they please.' It would seem, however, that the maids' amusements were neither so restricted nor so innocent as this would suggest. Sir Walter Scott, writing a century later, remarked that his knowledge of the period obliged him to 'admit that our grandmothers, however portentous the length of their stays, did not after all lace them so tightly', while at the time Lady Mary Wortley Montagu, who considered herself no prude, registered her shock that 'the appellation of rake is as genteel in a woman as a man of quality' and lamented that ' 'tis no scandal to say Miss – the Maid of honour looks very well now she's up again'. With the exception of Miss Meadows, an austere young woman whose chastity came to be almost proverbial at court, the reputation of Caroline's maids of honour was clearly not all that it might have been, although it was perhaps excessively uncharitable when an anonymous versifier described them as 'these maidens six without one virgin'.[19]

On the whole the Princess of Wales seems to have been remarkably broad-minded about the antics of the young ladies in her service. In 1720, it is true, she felt she had to accept the resignation of her flighty maid of honour Sophia Howe, after the latter became pregnant and then made a spectacle of herself by attempting to elope with her lover, only to be deserted by him at the last moment. Wherever possible, however, Caroline was prepared to be understanding if one of her servants found herself in trouble. In 1718 for example her unmarried sempstress managed to conceal for a time the fact that she was pregnant but when Caroline guessed the truth she told the girl that 'she had such a real kindness and compassion for her she was willing to save her if possible from any further censure from the world; and that if she would honestly confess to her and say she was truly sensible of her bad conduct . . . she would not only give her an opportunity of retiring, but restore her again to her place and favour in time'. On this occasion her good intentions were frustrated, for the girl promptly flew into a rage, 'said it was a vile aspersion and defied what the world could say of her', whereupon the Princess, feeling that her trust had been misplaced, dismissed her after all. Nevertheless, the fact that Caroline even attempted to save the girl's name shows that in many respects she was ahead of her time.[20]

When settling the Crown on the Hanoverian royal family the English Parliament had taken the precaution of declaring that in future no foreigner was to be employed in public office, but Caroline was allowed to bring with her two of her most trusted personal attendants. The kindly, if somewhat insipid, Baroness Gemmingen was appointed governess to Caroline's daughters, and the Countess of Buckenburgh, fat and good-natured, also came to England and stayed as an extra lady-in-waiting. It was, in all fairness, a modest enough continental invasion, but it was perhaps inevitable that there was intermittent friction between the two nationalities at court.

Differences in English and German obstetrical practice particularly strained relations, for when the Princess became pregnant there were disagreements as to who should assist at the birth. The Countess of Buckenburgh was convinced that the English doctors were incompetent bunglers who endangered the lives of both the Princess and her babies by using instruments before the labour had started, thus inducing premature birth. The English ladies naturally thought otherwise. In October 1716 tension caused tempers to flare when the Princess elected to have a German midwife deliver the child she was expecting. It proved to be a difficult labour, whereupon the ladies of the Bedchamber demanded that an English physician should be summoned. At this the German midwife 'refused to touch the Princess unless she and the Prince would stand by her against the English fraus, who she said were high dames and had threatened to hang her if the Princess miscarried', which so enraged the Prince that he threatened to 'throw out of the window whoever said so or pretended to meddle'. His fury effectively silenced the home team, although it did little to help his unfortunate wife, whose agony was only relieved when she was delivered of a dead son after five days in labour.[21]

Such quarrels were, of their very nature, rare, and anyway only derived from the concern that both English and German ladies felt for their mistress's welfare. In general the two nationalities contrived to subsist together amicably enough. By 1717 indeed, the Countess of Buckenburgh had settled down so well in her new home that she referred to England as 'this happy island' and spoke with regret of the possibility of leaving it.[22]

It was indeed not Anglo-German rivalry that posed the greatest threat to the court's tranquillity, but the bitter divisions that existed within the royal family itself. The King's relations with his eldest son, never good at the best of times, had steadily deteriorated since his arrival in England and by the end of 1717 they had reached breaking point. Accordingly on 28 November the King seized upon a trivial incident at the christening of his latest grandchild to effect a complete estrangement between the two branches of the family. On 2 December the King expelled his son from St James's Palace, and the Princess elected to leave with him although her father-in-law retained custody of her children. Worse was to follow, for the King not only made it known that anyone who visited the Prince and Princess while they were in disgrace would not be received at court, but refined the punishment by declaring that if any man in his employ had a wife who served the Princess one or other of them must resign their position, for he would no longer permit them to retain both. In consequence the Princess, who had barely recovered from her recent confinement and who had been seriously upset by the separation from her children, found that she was also expected to face the effects of the King's displeasure deprived of the company of many of her greatest friends.

Neither the Duchess of Shrewsbury nor the Countess of Dorset was affected because both their husbands were out of office, but the ruling nevertheless wrought havoc within the Princess's household. The Duchesses of St Albans and Montagu promptly decided that their interests lay with the King and resigned their places in the Bedchamber with unbecoming speed. Not everyone mourned their passing, for the Countesses of Bristol and Pembroke had both been scheming for years to become ladies of the Bedchamber and were hence delighted when they were invited to fill the vacancies that had been so unexpectedly created, but the Princess never forgave the two Duchesses for their callous desertion of her in her hour of need. At least, however, several other members of her household proved touchingly loyal throughout the crisis, and if the King's decree left many of them with no alternative but to resign, the Princess could console herself that they went from necessity rather than choice.

The case of Mrs Howard was perhaps exceptional, for it was hardly concern for her mistress that kept her tenaciously by her side. The quarrel in the royal family had in fact left her in an awkward predicament, for her husband was a Groom of the Bedchamber to the King, and though he had evicted her from his apartments in St James's some time before, he chose this moment to try and reassert his conjugal rights. He demanded that she resign her place about the Princess and resumed normal relations with him but Mrs Howard had no intention of doing any such thing, shielding her desire to remain with the Prince behind a decorous wall of devotion to her mistress. In vain did Mr Howard invoke the King's name and claim that it was the royal pleasure that she return to his side; Mrs Howard merely urbanely insisted that her first duty was to the Princess. As a last resort he threatened to obtain a warrant from the Chief Justice obliging her to return, but the King, who no doubt realized that Mr Howard was motivated more by a desire to inconvenience his wife than by zeal to see the royal command obeyed, had by that time lost all interest in the matter and curtly informed him 'that he needed not come to that extremity for he should not lose his place by her not resigning'.[23]

For those couples who were still happily married the situation was more complicated. Lady Cowper found herself in a terrible dilemma, torn between her anguish at the thought of abandoning the Princess in her pitiful state and her fear of ruining her husband's career. To the Princess she declared hysterically that she would have rather received a bullet in the head than the order to leave her service, and in desperation she wrote to the Duchess of Munster, begging her to persuade the King to exempt her from the ruling. Melusine managed to persuade George that in view of the Princess's precarious state of health he should make an exception in Lady Cowper's case and leave 'tout en status quo', but it proved no more than a temporary reprieve, for as the Princess grew stronger so the King's animosity revived, and in the middle of December Lady Cowper was once again instructed 'not to attend her any longer, having had leave to do it only during her illness'. This setback so upset Lady Cowper that her health was feared for and the Princess had to calm down her distraught servant by assuring her that there would always be room in the Bedchamber for her.[24]

Ejected from her post though she was, Lady Cowper nevertheless proved a good friend in adversity. Officially she was meant to see no more of the Princess, but in the months to come she contrived to remain in contact with her, on one occasion even visiting Mrs Clayton's London house in disguise for a secret rendezvous with her mistress. When at her Hertfordshire house, Cole Green, she proved an assiduous correspondent, and she was delighted when in April 1718 her husband resigned his post of Lord Chancellor, leaving her free to rejoin the Princess. By the summer of 1718 it was he rather than his wife who was in rural seclusion at Cole Green and he found himself writing to her with wistful jocularity that he perfectly understood 'you should find something more satisfaction in a court than you can in a retired minister (who you know is always a peevish creature) and so solitary a place'.[25]

For Mrs Clayton, the Princess's indispensable adviser and dresser, the upheavals at court had also brought heartbreak, for though she had declared herself determined to stand by her mistress her husband could not afford to give up his job at the Exchequer, which earned him £1,500 a year; as a result at the end of December 1717 she had reluctantly handed in her resignation. It was an especially distressing loss for Caroline, for hitherto she had relied on Mrs Clayton to advise her and the Prince in their confrontations with the King. In the spring of 1716, for example, she had written to Mrs Clayton complaining that although the King would soon be leaving England for a visit to Hanover, the ministry apparently intended to exclude the Prince from the Regency that would be set up in the monarch's absence, and she asked her to suggest a way of frustrating these plans. The Princess wanted to know whether Mrs Clayton thought that Lord Cowper might assist their cause, or whether it would be best to have the matter raised in Parliament by their friends in the Opposition, frankly assuring her servant 'The Prince will do nothing in it without your advice.'[26] Exactly how Mrs Clayton responded to this appeal remains unclear but it is evident that Caroline depended on her counsel in even the most sensitive of situations, and the Princess must have been appalled at the prospect of being deprived of it during one of the major crises of her life.

Fortunately for the Princess Mrs Clayton proved as determined as Lady Cowper to remain secretly in touch. The wet-nurse of the baby Prince had once been in Mrs Clayton's employ and for a time she and Caroline were able to use her as a messenger, until the death of the infant in February 1718 effectively blocked this channel of communication. Nevertheless the Princess still contrived to smuggle letters to her, for as she told Mrs Clayton, she felt that she could rely on her alone; she therefore entrusted to her the task of finding influential supporters who would help the Prince and Princess in their feud with the King. When in 1718 the King attempted to deduct £19,000 from his son's income in order to defray the expenses of his granddaughters' education, the Princess instructed Mrs Clayton to consult the Master of the Rolls, Sir Joseph Jekyll, as to whether this was legal. Presumably Sir Joseph gave an encouraging reply, for when the case was taken to law it went against the King, but soon another crisis arose with the introduction of the Peerage Bill, which the Prince and

Princess were determined should never reach the Statute Book. The Princess asked Mrs Clayton to help co-ordinate opposition to the measure, suggesting that she should find out whether Bishop Neville and Lords Carteret and Malpas were in favour of it, and then report to her in person under cover of darkness. As the weeks went by support for the Bill dwindled, and Caroline wrote to Mrs Clayton to tell her that it was her friends who had helped to bring about this satisfactory state of affairs, adding fulsomely that she was not surprised that they were prepared to perform such wonders for '*la meilleur et la plus honnête femme en tout respect*'.[27]

Occasional victories such as this could nevertheless not disguise the fact that an accommodation with the King was in the interests of the Prince and Princess for in the contest between father and son, King George had held every advantage. The Prince had little to offer those who craved either power or prestige, and though he and his wife tried to establish a glittering court at their new residence, Leicester House, the threat of the King's displeasure kept away all but malcontents and failures. In the circumstances the Prince could not hold out for ever, and after three years he agreed to come to terms with his father, formally offering his submission to the King on 23 April 1720.

Not everyone was satisfied by these developments. During the estrangement Lord Cowper had urged his wife to encourage 'that good and serious disposition you found in ye Prince and Princess during your last waiting to submit to his Majesty and to live as becomes ye most dutiful children', but now both he and his wife considered the surrender to be a dishonourable one. The terms of reconciliation had been negotiated by Cowper's rivals Sir Robert Walpole and Lord Townshend, but they had failed to persuade the King to allow his grandchildren to go and live with their parents at Leicester House. Lady Cowper felt that the Prince and Princess should either have relied on her husband to have obtained a better deal for them, or stuck to their principles and rejected the settlement as inadequate. While the bargaining was still in progress Lady Cowper had implored her mistress 'to insist upon her children for her own credit . . . for if the Princess gives up she will never have a faithful friend again, nor be considered a good mother', but Caroline, convinced that their best interests lay in peace at any price, ignored her.[28]

Fresh developments soon occurred to irritate Lady Cowper even further. Having stood by her mistress so faithfully during the crisis the Countess had considered it to be no more than her due when the

24 Queen Anne in the House of Lords by Peter Tillemans. The Queen is seated at the far end of the room, surrounded by her ladies-in-waiting.

25 Charlotte Clayton, Lady Sundon, engraved after an unknown original by Edward Harding

26 Henrietta Howard, Countess of Suffolk, attributed to Charles Jervas. She was 'forced to live in the constant subjection of a wife, with all the reproach of a mistress'.

27 Augusta, Princess of Wales and members of her household and family, by Jean-Baptiste
Vanloo. Mrs Herbert, a Woman of the Bedchamber, and Lady Archibald Hamilton
(holding the infant Prince Edward) stand behind the Princess.

28 Fanny Burney, by E. F. Burney

29 *The Prospect Before Us*: a Rowlandson cartoon on the Regency Crisis, December 1788. Madame Schwellenberg, bearing the mace, is leading Queen Charlotte and William Pitt towards the House of Lords.

30 Frances, Countess of Jersey, after D. Gardiner

31 Charlotte, Lady Douglas, engraved by Widdlemist after a drawing by A. Buck

32 Countess Oldi, engraved by T. Wright after a sketch by A. Wivell, 1821

33 Lady Flora Hastings, engraving dated 1840

34 A miniature of Baroness Lehzen, by Koeplee

35 *A Curious Instance of Ministerial Resuscitation*: a cartoon by John Doyle on the Bedchamber Crisis of 1839. Queen Victoria, surrounded by her ladies, is trying to revive Lord Melbourne.

36 Jane, Marchioness of Ely, *c*. 1880

37 Lady Augusta Bruce in 1859. Four years later the Queen was much upset by her marriage.

38 *The Drawing Room of Queen Victoria – a Ceremony of Presentation*, engraved by H. Melville after the original by J. Gilbert

39 Queen Elizabeth II with her maids of honour and Mistress of the Robes after her Coronation in 1953

Princess had promised that in the general reorganization of her household that was to follow the reconciliation with the King she would be promoted to Groom of the Stole, a position left vacant by the defection of the Duchess of St Albans. Soon, however, Lady Cowper's expectations were ruffled by disquieting rumours. She heard that the King had requested his daughter-in-law to reinstate the Duchess, whose behaviour during the crisis he had regarded as entirely correct. Worse still, the Duchess herself confided to an outraged Lady Cowper that as she had never formally relinquished her key of office she considered that she was still *de facto* Groom of the Stole. 'Marvellous!' fumed Lady Cowper in her diary, 'What could provoke the Princess to offer it to me . . . if she had it not in her power to give it? . . . Sure she thought me a tame fool, who minded not her interest at all, who consequently could be easily imposed upon.'[29]

Presently, however, Lady Cowper was soothed by an encouraging report that while in conversation with the Archbishop of Canterbury the Princess had complained of the way that the Duchess of St Albans constantly pestered her by begging to be taken back as Groom of the Stole. Once again Lady Cowper gave full rein to her hopes, but unfortunately her optimism was precipitate. The Princess had no intention of rewarding the Duchess of St Albans for her perfidy but she had decided that her successor as Groom of the Stole was to be the dull but inoffensive Countess of Dorset, an uncontroversial choice which would not displease the King. Lady Cowper was left as a mere lady of the Bedchamber, a position that no longer afforded her any pleasure, and the change in her attitude was reflected in the pages of her diary, which now became filled with sarcastic sneers at the manifold shortcomings of the Prince and Princess. When first appointed Lady Cowper had gushed that she was so charmed by the Princess's 'good nature and good qualities that I shall never think I can do enough to please her', but now her tone was very different. The Princess's susceptibility to flattery; her thoughtlessness in forcing Lady Cowper to copy out a memorandum when she was afflicted with a headache; even her shallow taste in plays, all came in for criticism from Lady Cowper's acid pen.[30] Thoroughly disenchanted, she nevertheless remained at court until her death in 1724 put an end to her worldly ambitions forever.

The reconciliation between St James's Palace and Leicester House never went much beyond the surface formalities, and King George still denied his son any influence over affairs of State. The King was happy enough, however, to slip back into his old reclusive habits and permit his son and daughter-in-law to resume their position as leaders of society, an empty role with which the Prince and Princess had perforce to content themselves until the King's death on 11 June 1727 finally transferred them to central stage.

It was confidently expected that the Prince and Princess would not be the only people whose situation would be transformed by the King's demise. As mistress of the Prince of Wales, Mrs Howard might have occupied a comparatively lowly position within the court, but it was felt that as *maîtresse en titre* to the new King she could not fail to be of considerable significance. As Lord Chesterfield put it, 'the busy and speculative politicians of the antechambers, who know everything, but know everything wrong, naturally concluded that a lady with whom the King passed so many hours must necessarily have some interest with him and consequently applied to her'. More than ever before she found herself the object of unwelcome attentions from courtiers who were convinced she had it in her power to transfigure their career and offers of bribes still came her way, albeit in the guise of delicately phrased compliments. To her credit Mrs Howard would have nothing to do with such proposals, despite the fact that the money would undoubtedly have been very useful, for though on his accession the King had raised her pension to £3,200 a year, by the standards of some of her predecessors she was by no means rich. But if Mrs Howard could justly pride herself on being incorruptible, she was also ineffectual, for the King kept her influence as tightly reined as ever. He brusquely rejected the majority of her suits, and on one occasion he was overheard shouting at her in her bedchamber, 'That is none of your business, Madam, you have nothing to do with that.' To her mortification Mrs Howard discovered that despite her long years of service with both the King and his wife, she still could not be of much assistance to even her greatest friends, and she sadly informed her old acquaintance, the poet John Gay, 'Upon my word, I have not had one place to dispose of, or you should not be without one.' 'Forced to live in the constant subjection of a wife, with all the reproach of a mistress', her position at court remained unenviable.[31]

At least for the moment, however, she found the prospect of losing it even more dire, and Mrs Howard had a nasty fright when her husband made another attempt to reclaim her. Having demanded an interview with the Queen he threatened to remove his wife forcibly from court, but fortunately for Mrs Howard Caroline had no wish to see her abducted, fearful that in that event the King would simply take another mistress who might prove an infinitely more dangerous rival than her woman of the Bedchamber. Howard was discomfited when the Queen told him sternly that he would be very unwise to take his wife away from court against her will, but though he withdrew for the moment, Caroline had not heard the last of him. He next had the audacity to propose that the Queen should compensate him for the breakdown of his marriage by paying him a pension of £1,200 a year but understandably enough Caroline felt 'that it was a little too much not only to keep the King's . . . trulls under my roof, but to pay them too', and so she 'pleaded poverty . . . and said I would do anything to keep so good a servant as Mrs Howard about me but that for £1,200 I really could not afford it.' Nevertheless Howard was not to be shrugged off so lightly and to his chagrin the King himself was eventually obliged to pay off the angry cuckold.[32]

Possibly the neutralization of her husband made Mrs Howard overconfident, for shortly after this incident she made a disastrous attempt to assert herself in the Bedchamber. For years she had endured the Queen's subtly administered pinpricks but they had evidently rankled and now she decided to tolerate them no longer. Assisting at the Queen's toilette one day she suddenly declined to follow the accustomed routine of kneeling before her mistress with the bowl of water for her morning ablutions, fierily declaring 'that positively she would not do it'. Declining to take issue with her there and then the Queen told her ominously that they would discuss the matter later, and having been dismissed Mrs Howard hastened to consult those well-versed in courtly lore as to the merits of her case. Alas, it soon emerged that she had chosen the wrong battleground. The various stages in the Queen's dressing ceremony had never been set down in writing but they had been long sanctified by tradition, and when Mrs Howard applied to that doyenne of dressers, Abigail Masham, the latter had no difficulty in remembering the procedures that had been followed in Queen Anne's day. According to her,

> the bedchamber woman came in to waiting before the Queen's prayers, which was before her Majesty was dressed. The Queen often shifted in a morning: if her Majesty shifted at noon, the bedchamber lady being by, the bedchamber woman gave the shift to the lady without any ceremony, and the lady put it on. Sometimes, likewise, the bedchamber woman gave the fan to the lady in the same manner; and this was all that the bedchamber lady did about the Queen at her dressing.
> When the Queen washed her hands the page of the back stairs brought and set down upon a side table the basin and ewer; then the bedchamber

woman set it before the Queen, and knelt on the other side of the table over against the Queen, the bedchamber lady only looking on. The bedchamber woman poured the water out of the ewer upon the Queen's hands.

The bedchamber woman pulled on the Queen's gloves when she could not do it herself . . .

The bedchamber woman brought the chocolate and gave it without kneeling.

In general the bedchamber woman had no dependence on the lady of the Bedchamber.[33]

There was no questioning such an authority. Her pretensions crushed, Mrs Howard resumed her duties and made no further protest, but the Queen was not prepared to let the incident pass without comment. As she subsequently recounted to her Vice-Chamberlain, Lord Hervey, Caroline took Mrs Howard aside one morning to say that she was pleased that they were again on good terms, 'but could not help adding . . . that I owned of all my servants, I had least expected, as I had least deserved it, such treatment from her, when she knew I had held her up at a time when it was in my power . . . to let her drop through my fingers – thus'.[34] Put firmly in her place, the chastened Mrs Howard abandoned all idea of defiance.

In 1731 Charles Howard inherited the title of Earl of Suffolk, and the Queen was in consequence obliged to promote his wife, for she accepted that it was not fitting that a countess should perform the work of a Bedchamber woman. Accordingly the Countess of Suffolk was offered the choice of becoming either a lady of the Bedchamber or Groom of the Stole and Mistress of the Robes. Thankfully Lady Suffolk accepted the second option, and the Countess of Dorset was prevailed upon to resign in order to make way for her. As a result Lady Suffolk became titular head of the Bedchamber staff, but her duties were less arduous than those of the Bedchamber ladies, for she did not have to wait on the Queen at meals. Her rise in status enabled her to spend more time at her villa in Twickenham and compelled Caroline to treat her with greater consideration; furthermore Lady Suffolk was pleased to find that she was no longer expected to dress the Queen's hair, but only to hand her mistress her jewels in the morning. Delighted with her new position, she confided to a friend that 'everything as yet promises more happiness for the latter part of my life than I have yet had a prospect of'.[35]

All this, however, could not disguise the fact that in one important respect her position at court was deteriorating. Gradually it became apparent that the King's feelings for the Countess of Suffolk were not what they had been. In public he either ignored her or was openly rude, and by the autumn of 1734 Lady Suffolk felt that the situation had become intolerable. She went to the Queen and with astonishing frankness told her that the King's coldness to her was such that it left her no alternative but to resign from court. The humour of so absurd a situation was not lost on the Queen, but she was nevertheless concerned that her husband would now take a new and more exacting mistress, and though even now she could not bring herself to drop the patronizing tone that she always adopted toward her rival, she implored her to reconsider. To no avail, however, for Lady Suffolk remorselessly insisted that the time had come for her to take her leave.

The King was delighted: 'What the devil did you mean by trying to make an old, dull, deaf, peevish beast stay and plague me when I had so good an opportunity of getting rid of her?' he was reported to have demanded of his wife.[36] Nor did the Countess of Suffolk regret her decision. A year after she left court she married George Berkeley, with whom she lived happily till his death in 1747. She survived him for twenty years, living quietly at her villa in Twickenham, surrounded by affectionate neighbours.

Though the Countess of Suffolk had been cast aside after nearly twenty years as George's mistress, Mrs Clayton's friendship with the Queen proved more enduring. Since the King's accession her influence over household appointments had proved stronger than ever and her goodwill was therefore valued accordingly. There were some people, indeed, who maintained that Mrs Clayton took unfair advantage of her relationship with the Queen, and though Lord Hervey insisted 'that she frequently employed the interest she had at court in favour of people who would in no way repay her', it is clear that unlike the Countess of Suffolk, Mrs Clayton had a somewhat ambivalent attitude to bribery. Admittedly she always angrily rejected outright gifts of cash, and when Lady Falmouth wrote asking her if she could put her name forward as a lady of the Bedchamber Mrs Clayton primly endorsed the letter: 'She offered Mrs Clayton a handful of bank bills, for which reason she never spoke more for her.' Other gifts, however, she deemed acceptable, making no demur when Lord Pembroke sent her a marble table 'as a small testimony of the sincere respect he has for you', but though Mrs Clayton evidently considered her integrity to be untarnished by such transactions, others had more exacting standards. In particular the old Duchess of Marlborough considered that Mrs Clayton abused her position, and came to regret that she had helped her to obtain it in the first place. When Mrs Clayton visited

Sarah wearing a valuable pair of earrings that she was said to have received from the Countess of Pomfret as a reward for having obtained the Earl of Pomfret the position of Master of the Horse to the Queen, the Duchess could hardly contain her anger. Lady Mary Wortley Montagu was also present, and as soon as Mrs Clayton had taken her leave the Duchess burst out to her, 'How can that woman have the impudence to go about in that bribe?' 'Madam,' said Lady Mary, 'how would you have people know where wine is to be sold unless there is a sign hung out?'[37]

The Prime Minister, Sir Robert Walpole, hated Mrs Clayton, whose interest with the Queen aroused his jealousy. It is difficult to credit his story that she once suggested to him that they 'unite . . . and govern the kingdom together', only to be deflated by his retort that 'he thought nobody fit to govern the kingdom but the King and Queen,' but certainly he regarded her as a rival rather than as a possible collaborator. He liked to boast that, he had 'soon clipped the wing of her ambition' but for all that Mrs Clayton's influence over the Queen remained stronger than he might have wished, and he was persistently irritated by her ability to persuade Caroline to award key ecclesiastical positions to Low Church divines of whom he disapproved. Walpole was even concerned that one day Mrs Clayton would succeed in turning the Queen against him altogether, and the mere report that Mrs Clayton had been seen conferring with his main political rival, Lord Carteret, was enough to put the Prime Minister in a panic. As it happened his fears were unfounded, but with Mrs Clayton constantly by the Queen's side it was understandable that Walpole could never feel entirely secure from the threat of a backstairs intrigue.[38]

In 1735 Mr Clayton's elevation to the peerage as Baron Sundon set the seal on his wife's eminent position at court. That position, however, rested solely on her standing with the Queen, and with Caroline's sudden death in 1737 she was once again plunged into obscurity. Thenceforward she lived a retired existence with her husband and died four years after her mistress, having reportedly suffered from 'fits of madness ever since her ambition met such a check'.[39]

The departure of the Countess of Suffolk had completely rejuvenated the King, and he had wasted little time in finding her successor. For some months he had dallied with his daughters' flighty governess, Lady Deloraine, whose recent remarriage made her no less willing to encourage the King's approaches. This was little more than a diversion, but in 1735 he was fired with genuine passion. In May he had gone to Hanover for a visit and while there he had embarked upon an affair with Amelia Sophie von Walmoden, an attractive married woman who was twenty-one years his junior. In his egoistic way he assumed that his wife would wish to enter into all his pleasures, and when he wrote to Caroline in England, he dwelled in such detail on his mistress's perfections that 'had the Queen been a painter she might have drawn her rival's picture at six hundred miles distance'.[40] For the Queen it was scant consolation that her husband should show himself so uxorious even in his infidelity, for the King showed a marked reluctance to bid farewell to his new conquest, and though he finally wrenched himself away in October 1735 he arrived in England in appalling humour, taking little trouble to conceal his impatience to return to Hanover as soon as possible.

The following year he re-visited Germany and the affair was resumed, occasioning serious concern to the Queen, who had again remained in England. Worse still, his prolonged absences abroad made him highly unpopular at home, so much so that at the end of the year Sir Robert Walpole indicated to Caroline that she must sacrifice her feelings for the sake of the Crown and lure her husband back by suggesting he bring Madame von Walmoden to England with him. When the Queen not unnaturally showed little enthusiasm for the idea Walpole was incensed, angrily attributing her perversity to the malign influence of 'those bitches Lady Pomfret and Lady Sundon'. Sternly he told Caroline that this was no time for sentimental self-indulgence, and eventually she came round to his viewpoint, actually going further than he wished by proposing that like the Countess of Suffolk before her, Madame von Walmoden's position should be regularized with the offer of a post in her household. Even to Walpole this seemed excessive, for he pointed out that 'the King's making one of the Queen's servants his mistress, or his mistress one of the Queen's servants were two things which nobody would see in the same light' and accordingly Caroline abided by the original plan and merely suggested to her husband that Madame von Walmoden should accompany him to England.[41] The King appeared delighted, instructing his wife to make preparations for his mistress's arrival, but in the end Madame von Walmoden failed to materialize, presumably because this cosy triangular arrangement held little appeal for her. Nevertheless the King was highly gratified by his wife's regard for his sensibilities and when he finally arrived in England in January 1737 his mood was greatly improved. He behaved much better towards his wife and appeared to have forgotten Madame von Walmoden altogether, content for the moment to amuse himself by reviving his somewhat dilatory courtship of Lady Deloraine.

Amorous by nature himself, it might be assumed that the King would have been entertained by the peccadilloes of his eldest son, Frederick Prince of Wales, but unfortunately none of Frederick's exploits ever seemed in the slightest bit endearing to either of his parents. Left behind in Hanover when the rest of his family had accompanied George I to England, Frederick had been permitted to join them the year after his grandfather's death, but was received by his parents with inexplicable hostility. As a personable youth of twenty-one he was nevertheless popular enough elsewhere and soon gained himself a reputation as something of a man-about-town. By the end of 1731 he had acquired a mistress in the shape of the Honourable Anne Vane, a maid of honour to the Queen who was unkindly described by one contemporary as a 'fat and ill-shaped dwarf'. If so, her appearance certainly did not prevent her from having success of a sort, for prior to her liaison with the Prince she had had affairs with both Lord Harrington and Lord Hervey, either of whom, indeed, might have been the father of the child that the Prince claimed as his own. For by April 1732 Miss Vane was pregnant, and had to apply to her mistress for leave to retire for some months to her grandfather's house in the country. The Queen, 'who knew her familiarities with the Prince, sent her word that she might go for good and all', whereupon her son endowed his mistress with a pension of £3,000 a year and set her up in an elegant house in Soho Square.[42] There, on 5 June 1732, she gave birth to a son whom the Prince proudly acknowledged, naming him Cornwell Fitzfrederick.

For a time all went well between the Prince and his mistress but after some months Frederick evidently considered that her attractions had begun to wane, for by the middle of 1733 his name was linked with several other ladies, including Miss Vane's own chambermaid. Although the affair lingered on in a desultory sort of way it seemed to have little future and Miss Vane accordingly started to look for a new protector, finding one in her old flame, Lord Hervey.

This was the more surprising considering that at the end of their previous affair they had been on the worst possible terms. Before the Prince had taken up with Miss Vane he and Hervey had been the best of friends, but latterly their relations had cooled, and Hervey had angrily supposed that Miss Vane had discouraged Frederick from seeing him out of fear that the Prince would learn from him her past history. In a rage he had written upbraiding her for her duplicity and threatening that unless she made amends 'he would discover what he knew of her and use her as she deserved', but unfortunately for him Miss Vane had called his bluff and showed the letter to the Prince. The Prince was enraged that anyone should dare so to insult his mistress, and although Hervey subsequently made every attempt to redeem himself, Frederick never forgave him.[43]

With the passage of time, however, Miss Vane herself proved more understanding. After a separation of about two years she and Hervey met several times accidentally and were soon resolved to make up their differences, 'till from ogling they came to messages, from messages to letters', eventually attaining 'all the familiarity in which they had formerly lived'.[44] Throughout the following year Miss Vane contrived to conduct simultaneous affairs with both Hervey and the Prince, apparently without raising the latter's suspicions, but towards the end of 1735, the Prince determined to finish with her, not because he had learned of her double-dealing but because his own marriage was imminent.

Exactly how he chose to break the news to her remains, however, unclear. According to one authority he 'civilly dismissed' her, explaining that 'decency required that he quit correspondence with herself' but adding that he would pay her £1,500 a year until she found herself a husband, upon which she would receive a further £20,000. Lord Hervey's version of events was different: he claimed that the Prince's offer of a pension was conditional on Miss Vane removing herself and her son to the Continent and that Frederick told her that 'if she would not live abroad she might starve for him in England'. Whichever account was true, Miss Vane evidently considered herself ill-used, and it was to Hervey that she turned to take revenge on the Prince. The Vice-Chamberlain, still smarting from Frederick's repudiation of him, proved only too willing to help, composing a letter for her to send to the Prince which dwelt on her plight in the most pathetic terms and reproached Frederick for seeking to cut her adrift after she had 'sacrificed my time, my youth, my character, the world, my family and everything that a woman can sacrifice to a man she loves'. On receipt of this letter Frederick unwisely showed it to several of his friends and as Miss Vane also did her best to publicise it, its contents were soon widely known. In the hubbub that ensued the Prince attracted almost universal obloquy while Miss Vane became the heroine of the hour, with the result, according to Hervey, that Frederick was obliged to abandon his harsh stance and settle the pension on Miss Vane without any preconditions attached.[45]

The victorious Miss Vane retired to Bath but she did not live to enjoy her triumph long for in February 1736 her son died and she only survived him by a month. The Prince had been genuinely upset by the loss of his child but he cannot have mourned the mother, and Lord Hervey too seems to have been unaffected by her death, if one may judge from the flippant tone of the passages in his memoirs relating to these events. For him her main function had been to serve as a means to discredit the Prince, and once she had outlived her usefulness he had no further interest in her.

Meanwhile, preparations for the marriage of the Prince of Wales went on apace. In April 1736 Frederick was to marry the Princess Augusta of Saxe-Gotha and the forthcoming event had engendered intense competition amongst ladies of the court desirous of inclusion in her household. The Prince himself was anxious that Lady Archibald Hamilton should be appointed a lady of the Bedchamber but even on this comparatively minor issue he and his parents proved unable to agree. The problem was that despite the fact that Lady Archibald was 'not young, had never been very pretty, and had lost as least as much of that small share of beauty she once possessed as it is usual to do at five and thirty, after being the mother of ten children', it was rumoured that the Prince had taken her for his mistress, a state of affairs apparently connived at by her husband. It was even said that the Prince had cast off Miss Vane not out of consideration for the feelings of his future wife but out of desire to devote himself exclusively to his pursuit of Lady Archibald. In the circumstances the Queen deemed it imprudent to grant her son's request, explaining that 'whether she believed Lady Archibald innocent or not, the Prince's behaviour to her had been so particular . . . that it was impossible to put Lady Archibald about the Princess without incurring the censure of the whole world'. As a compromise she agreed that she would only appoint three out of the Princess's quota of four ladies of the Bedchamber, so that if Augusta herself had no objection, Lady Archibald could be added to the list later. To the Prince this seemed unreasonable, and he felt all the more aggrieved when the King rejected his application to make the wife of his friend William Townshend one of the Princess's women of the Bedchamber on the grounds that Townshend had contact with the Opposition in Parliament.[46]

The widowed Lady Irwin had better luck, for on 6 April she exultantly informed her father that she had been selected as a lady of the

Bedchamber. 'Others that pretend to this honour are every day at court, many labouring in vain, and none but my Lady Torrington and me sure of success', she wrote complacently, although she felt somewhat irked when the Countess of Effingham was added to the list and superseded her as first lady of the Bedchamber. She was much more concerned, however, when it emerged that she and her colleagues had 'come in without the consent of the Prince and consequently not with his inclination', although, still flushed with triumph from her recent appointment, she noted 'I don't despair of making myself in time agreeable to the Prince; already he treats me with more regard.'[47]

Sure enough, the Prince soon had no complaints about the composition of his wife's household. His marriage took place on 26 April 1736, two days after the bride's arrival in England, and though it turned out that the Princess could speak no English, she was docile and eager to please and was prepared to accept the Prince's story that there was nothing whatsoever in the gossip that linked his name with Lady Archibald's. Convinced that Lady Archibald had been shabbily treated, the Princess obtained the Queen's permission to appoint her lady of the Bedchamber, Keeper of the Privy Purse and Mistress of the Robes, and it was not long before Lady Archibald had established herself in a commanding position within Augusta's household.

The Queen considered it no concern of hers that her daughter-in-law should inflict on herself Lady Archibald's presence but the following year both she and the King were incensed when Frederick blithely disregarded his father's express prohibition and appointed Mrs Townshend as one of the Princess's dressers. For the moment the King and Queen forbore to take any action against their son, but the incident constituted yet another item in the squalid catalogue of grievances which brought about such bitter divisions within the royal family.

At length the Prince went altogether too far. By the summer of 1737 the Princess of Wales was pregnant and the King and Queen signified that they wished the birth to take place at Hampton Court under their supervision. Nevertheless, when Augusta's labour started on 31 July the Prince, out of sheer desire to flout his parents' authority, smuggled her out of the Palace and transported her to London, screaming in agony all the while. Incredibly she suffered no permanent damage from her ordeal and gave birth to a healthy baby girl soon after she reached St James's, but the King and Queen were not prepared to overlook their son's deliberate defiance. They refused to accept his explanations and in September history repeated itself when the King turned his son out of St James's Palace and declared that thenceforth anyone who visited the Prince and Princess would be *persona non grata* at court.

Unlike his father the King did not pressure any of the Princess's ladies to leave her service, unwilling that his daughter-in-law should suffer as his wife had suffered twenty years before. But as it happened the Princess's household was greatly depleted anyway, for all the court knew from experience that in quarrels between a king and his heir it was the monarch who invariably emerged victorious, and since they had no wish to antagonize the stronger contender's Lady Torrington and the Countess of Effingham both resigned voluntarily. Abandoned by half her ladies the Princess was left isolated and more than ever dependent on Lady Archibald Hamilton, who now tightened her stranglehold over Augusta's household, obtaining positions in it for so many of her relatives that when Sir William Stanhope visited the Prince's house one day he did not bother to enquire the name of anyone he met, finding it simpler to address them all as either Mr or Mrs Hamilton. Lady Irwin too remained, not so much because she was devoted to her mistress as because she had no wish to forfeit her salary, for she had recently married an impoverished army officer and he had persuaded her to stay on, 'being' as he put it, 'a little shy and delicate of obliging my Lady Irwin to give up, without absolute necessity, what my fortune could make her no recompense for'.[48]

The royal family was still in schism when Queen Caroline was taken ill at the end of 1737, and after more than a fortnight of appalling suffering she died on 20 November, leaving the King heartbroken. For more than a month he could not bring himself to see any of the late Queen's ladies and even then he was overcome when attempting a conversation with the Duchess of Dorset and had to rush from the room in tears. 'Some little time after, thinking himself recovered, he returned, and covering his concern as much as he could, he went up to the Duchess again, and in some confusion began to say something very civil – of his great regard for her – the rest of the ladies – excellent servants – much in the Queen's favour – when he again burst into tears and so went out of the room, leaving them all in the same condition.' His sorrow even transcended his habitual meanness, for he undertook to continue paying the salaries of all his late wife's attendants, saying that 'he would have nobody feel her loss but himself'.[49]

Prostrated with misery though he was, it was not to be expected that the King would remain faithful to his wife's memory for the remainder of his life. He had indeed made that clear at her deathbed: as he knelt by her side in paroxysms of grief the Queen had calmly remarked that once she was dead he should remarry as soon as possible. 'Non', gasped out the King in between sobs, 'J'aurai des maîtresses.' Sure enough, after a decent interval had elapsed, he revived his relationship with Madame von Walmoden, inviting her over to England in June 1738. The following year she was divorced from her husband and in March 1740 the King created her Countess Yarmouth in her own right. Intuitive and sensible, she was not of a meddlesome disposition and 'never employed her credit but to assist his ministers, or to convert some honours and favours to her own advantage'. Initially indeed, she had remained discreetly in the background, but as the King grew older and more refractory his ministers occasionally used her as a tactful intermediary who could persuade him to accept unpalatable changes. To the end of his life the King might delude himself that he had never permitted a woman to rule him but Lady Yarmouth had more influence than he would have cared to admit, for as Lord Chesterfield remarked, 'even the wisest man, like the chameleon, takes without knowing it more or less the hue of what he is often upon'.[50]

With the death of Queen Caroline court life in England began to wane. The King and his eldest son lived in a near-permanent state of feud until Frederick's sudden death in 1751, so that the Prince and Princess of Wales could never become leaders of society as George and Caroline had been in their youth. As for the King himself, he remained sprightly well into old age, for as late as 1758 one observer noted that when he had company he was always 'gracious and polite to all the ladies and remarkably cheerful and familiar with those who are handsome or with the few of his old acquaintances who were beauties in his younger days'.[51] Nevertheless as a widower he entertained less than before and though the birthday parties of the King and the Princess of Wales were still highlights of the social calendar, the London Season was already acquiring an impetus of its own. The day was fast approaching when society in England would no longer revolve around the court.

The Later Hanoverian Court

'Laborious Watchfulness and Attendance'

On 25 October 1760 the sudden death of George II left his grandson and namesake as King of Great Britain. At twenty-two the new monarch was still a bachelor but it was not to be expected that he would remain unwed for long. Only the year before he had fallen passionately in love with Lady Sarah Lennox, who was the fifteen-year-old daughter of the Duke of Richmond and 'as beautiful as a girl could be'. Being a thoroughly upright young man he never entertained 'any improper thought with regard to her' and instead consulted his middle-aged friend and mentor the Earl of Bute as to whether he could with propriety make her his wife. Bute pronounced against marriage with a commoner and though despondent George dutifully accepted his ruling, reflecting stoically, 'I am born for the happiness or misery of a great nation and consequently must often act contrary to my passions'.[1]

It was nevertheless apparent to Bute that it would soon be necessary to find a legitimate outlet for those passions by selecting a suitable bride for the young man and George agreed that once he had had time to master his feelings for Lady Sarah, some enquiry should be made into the relative merits 'of the various Princesses of Germany'. Now that he was King the search was on in earnest and on 20 May 1761 he was able to send Bute a description of Princess Charlotte of Mecklenburg-Strelitz, who seemed possessed of all qualifications necessary in a queen. 'I own,' the King commented gloomily, ''tis not in every particular as I could wish, but yet I am resolved to fix here',[2] and so at the beginning of June an emissary was sent to the tiny German state bearing a formal proposal of marriage, which, as expected, met with a favourable response.

If the announcement of the King's engagement came as something of a shock to Lady Sarah and her family, it was received with great excitement by all those who were interested in court appointments. In July Horace Walpole had his nieces to stay for five days, throughout which they incessantly 'discussed the claim or disappointment of every miss in the kingdom for maid of honour'. The Earl of Bute found himself bombarded with requests for posts in the Queen's household, and as he had no hope of satisfying more than a fraction of the applicants it was inevitable that some would be disappointed by the eventual disposal of places. On 23 July Walpole informed Sir Horace Mann 'The new Queen's family consists of ... the Duchess of Ancaster, Mistress of the Robes and first lady of the Bedchamber; the others are the Duchess of Hamilton, Lady Effingham, Lady Northumberland, Lady Weymouth and Lady Bolingbroke.' He was correct in all particulars, save for the fact that Lady Egremont should also have been on the list of Bedchamber ladies, and on the whole he considered the line-up to be a creditable one. Not everyone, however, felt likewise. The Countess of Dalkeith had angrily turned down the chance of a position in the Queen's Bedchamber when she had learnt that she was expected to work with the Duchess of Hamilton, who had been born plain Miss Gunning, and was therefore considered an insufficiently illustrious colleague by the haughty Countess, who herself was the daughter of a duke. The Duchess of Bedford was also affronted, for instead of being offered, as she expected, 'the first post in the Queen's family', she had been overlooked altogether. The husbands of both these ladies soon went into Opposition, a fact attributed by knowledgeable observers to their wives' annoyance at the way the Queen's establishment had been settled.[3] To the King, who disapproved of women meddling in State affairs, it must have been highly vexatious that these purely domestic arrangements should have brought about such unfortunate political repercussions.

In August 1761 the Duchesses of Ancaster and Hamilton travelled to Germany in order to escort the Princess to her new home and on 7 September Charlotte landed in England. Her wedding took place the following day, and though King George had initially had his doubts about his bride-to-be, he soon expressed himself delighted with his new wife, whose virtuous outlook and unshakeable sense of duty accorded so well with his own temperament. While the King remained in good health the marriage was to be an exceptionally happy one, cemented by the fact that over the years the Queen presented her husband with a total of fifteen children.

In contrast to those princesses who in centuries past had travelled to England for marriage with the King or his heir, Charlotte was accompanied by few attendants from her own country. She had hoped to bring a large German suite with her, but the King had sent word that in view of his 'country very wisely not admitting foreigners to hold employments' she would not be able to do so. 'The utmost she can bring,' he decreed, 'is one or two *femmes de chambre* whom I own I hope will be quiet people, for by my own experience I have seen these women meddle more than they ought to do.' In consequence Charlotte had travelled with only two German ladies, Johanna Louisa Haggerdorn and Juliana Elizabeth Schwellenberg, who had been installed at court as joint Keepers of the Robes. According to Mrs Papendiek, the daughter of the Queen's hairdresser, the King came to regret that he had made even this limited concession, for though Madame Haggerdorn was 'a placid amiable ladylike woman' who seems to have been as unassuming as even he could wish, Madame Schwellenberg was an altogether more formidable personage. Mrs Papendiek claimed that having 'been with the Queen since her infancy' Madame Schwellenberg had gained 'a powerful ascendancy' over her mind and that by 1765 the King was so irritated by her arrogance and intrusiveness that he was only dissuaded from sending her back to Germany by the combined entreaties of the Queen and Madame Schwellenberg herself, who promised that henceforth she would be more tractable. This story, which rests solely on the second-hand reminiscences of Mrs Papendiek, should be treated with caution. Difficult and overbearing as Madame Schwellenberg was, this side of her character was hidden from the royal family for, like all bullies, she was as obsequious to her superiors as she was beastly to her subordinates. The King became genuinely fond of her, displaying great eagerness to see her when he was ill in 1789, and as Madame Schwellenberg was a regular visitor to the royal nursery his children shared his sentiments. The King's eldest son, the Prince of Wales, had a particularly soft spot for 'dearest Swelly', to whom he wrote the year before her death in 1797, 'No circumstance of life has or ever will change the affection I have ever felt for you from the earliest period of my infancy.'[4]

It is doubtful whether any of Madame Schwellenberg's colleagues would ever have addressed her so warmly. As in a badly run school or regiment, the royal household was one of those institutions where a rigid hierarchy and strict rules enabled second-rate individuals, who would not have gone far in the outside world, to domineer over their subordinates. Madame Schwellenberg was typical of such petty tyrants. Removed from her home and family, with no prospect of marriage, the only reason for her existence lay in the position of trust conferred on her by the Queen, and consequently she clung to the dignity and privileges that office brought with it with the fanaticism of one who does not know that life has more to offer. Those who failed to accord her the respect she considered as her due, or committed the slightest infringement of etiquette, were visited with the severest censure, and she was especially impossible when, as frequently happened, her health was undermined by severe asthmatic attacks. Though she and Madame Haggerdorn were theoretically meant to be on an equal footing at court she treated her as an inferior and had no concern for her welfare, even insisting that, whatever the weather, the windows of the coach they shared should be kept open during journeys, despite the fact that the consequent icy draughts left her colleague's eyes dangerously inflamed. She was equally vile to Madame Haggerdorn's successor, the novelist Fanny Burney, while she terrorized the more menial household servants to such an extent that when Fanny told her housemaid that another German lady was coming to take up a situation at court the girl burst into tears, 'for Mrs Schwellenberg's severity . . . has made all Germans feared in the house'. The Queen had no notion that her Keeper of the Robes was so 'noxious and persecuting'; in her opinion she was simply 'a faithful and truly devoted old servant' on whose loyalty she could depend implicitly.[5]

It was perhaps a comfort to Madame Schwellenberg's oppressed underlings to know that she had a rather more sinister reputation with the public at large. The ridicule and abuse to which public figures in the late eighteenth century were subjected seems incredible to us today and in this respect Madame Schwellenberg was a victim of her times. With her corpulent build and outlandish accent (described as half German and half highland) she was a gift to cartoonists and the Press, who delighted in the fiction that she operated a network of corruption, selling places in the court and administration to the highest bidder. In 1772 Horace Walpole noted 'Attacks began to be made in the papers on Madame Schwellenberg . . . as a powerful favourite' and thenceforth her name regularly appeared in the more scurrilous publications of the day. In particular the pseudonymous rhymester Peter Pindar picked her out for his raillery, speaking of her as one

> Whose palate loves a dainty dish
> Whose teeth in combat shine with flesh and fish,
> Whose Strelitz stomach holds a butt of beer,

Who soon shall keep a saleshop for good places
For which so oft the people squabble,
And thus provide for great and little rabble.[6]

In 1786 *The Times* took up the refrain, claiming that the Prince of Wales need not worry if he was in financial difficulties as 'Madame Shewlinbellyburghenhausen' was planning to loan him £100,000 'being *part* of the money she has saved in the service of his parents'. 'How generous!' they commented sarcastically, remarking a few days later that she could easily afford to make the loan as she was 'the greatest monied woman in England'. Such innuendoes were manifestly unjust, for she was not a grasping woman, declining to take any increase herself when the Queen raised the salary of the Keepers of the Robes from £127 to £200 a year. As those in charge of the purse-strings at court well knew, far from seeking to enrich herself through her position, Madame Schwellenberg was 'always . . . anxious that his Majesty should not be put to unnecessary expense on her . . . account'.[7]

The King's brother, the Duke of Gloucester, once remarked that in the early days of his marriage George had been so excited to have a young girl entirely at his disposal that he had 'determined she should be wholly devoted to him alone and should have no other friend or society.' Towards the end of her life the Queen herself confirmed this, reminiscing that her husband 'always used to say that . . . on account of the politics of the country . . . there never could be kept up a society without party which was always dangerous for any woman to take part in, but particularly so for the royal family.' She claimed that she considered this to have been a sensible precaution, but when she first arrived in England it was felt to be rather hard on her that her circle should be so restricted. Naturally she made numerous acquaintances at the Drawing Rooms that were held at St James's twice a week, but her husband discouraged her from cultivating more intimate relationships, and for company she had to depend exclusively on the ladies of the Bedchamber. In order to improve Charlotte's English it was arranged that they should assemble on four mornings a week to make polite conversation with their mistress, but these courtly seminars seem to have been agony for all concerned. Lady Egremont dismissed this aspect of her duties as 'a very triste affair', complaining that she and her colleagues grew 'tired of each other's clothes by seeing them so often; that they got by heart everything they wore by sitting in a circle and having nothing else to look at'.[8] It was hardly an atmosphere conducive to the breaking down of social barriers, and if anything the formal gatherings retarded the moment when the Queen felt quite at ease with her ladies.

When she finally became better acquainted with them she did not always like what she found. Had she had any say in the matter her choice of attendants would not necessarily have been the same as that of the King and the Earl of Bute. The Countess of Northumberland, a vulgar woman who liked 'show and crowds and junketing' would have been unlikely to have featured on her list and the Queen was doubtless relieved when in 1770 she took the hint and tendered her resignation because 'I had no longer the degree of favour I had before enjoyed.' The Queen also fell out with the Duchess of Argyll (formerly the Duchess of Hamilton, but she had switched titles when her second husband succeeded his father as Duke of Argyll in 1770). The Queen disapproved of her disregard of etiquette, her unpunctuality and even, so it was said, suspected her of flirting with the King. The final straw came when the Duchess tried to persuade her mistress to receive her daughter at court, despite the fact that the latter's reputation had been ruined in 1778 when she had left her husband and run off with the Duke of Dorset. Angrily the Queen told her husband that if the Duchess brought her daughter to court she would not address a word to either of them, adding trenchantly, 'if she leaves my family I shall but get rid of an impertinent person who has always behaved disrespectful to me'. In 1784 she had her way when the Duchess finally left her service, ostensibly because of ill health, but it was commonly believed that it was really on account of the Queen's continued refusal to receive her daughter.[9]

Fortunately the Queen had other Bedchamber ladies whom she found more congenial. She had a happy partnership with the Duchess of Ancaster, an 'easy, obliging, unaffected and well-bred' woman, who continued as Mistress of the Robes till her death in 1793, and when in 1770 Lady Holderness replaced the Countess of Northumberland, she was soon observed 'to have grown a particular favourite of the Queen'. In 1784 the Countess of Harcourt also became a lady of the Bedchamber, an appointment that was viewed with some astonishment by those who remembered a time when the Earl of Harcourt had been an opponent of the court and his wife had habitually 'abused the royal family and everything belonging to them', but in 1783 he had a change of heart and he and the Countess had since become 'a proverb even to courtiers of the most servile attachment to their Majesties'. Lady Harcourt was to become one of the Queen's greatest friends, remaining in royal service till Charlotte's death in 1818, and she subsequently recalled that when on one occasion she had said to her mistress, 'I should like to tell *you* something, but pray promise never to let the *Queen* know it', Charlotte had laughed and said 'oh no, *she* can have no business with what passes between us in our private unreserved condition.'[10] The Countess of Harcourt was however an exception, for to the end of her life the Queen felt able to drop her reserve with only a very few people at court.

Though the Queen could occasionally be light-hearted with her friends, the court she presided over was anything but frivolous. With the King and his wife, duty took priority over delectation, and their staid court faithfully reflected their worthy but dull way of life. The Queen would only receive at court women whose reputations were untouched by scandal, and 'as the presentation to the Drawing Room was then most particularly considered as the sole introduction to high life she had a powerful weapon to wield . . . by at once proscribing from her society all females of bankrupt or even ambiguous character'.[11] Unfortunately it was not a policy designed to produce scintillating assemblies and certainly the Drawing Rooms, at which one queued for hours in hot and overcrowded conditions, were such extraordinarily tedious affairs that it is difficult to comprehend why the more racy ladies of the day minded being excluded from them.

The court was no longer, as in days gone by, the leader of fashion. In a commendable attempt to boost the fortunes of the Spitalfields weavers the Queen asked all the ladies of the court to wear gowns of English silk but this 'gave no small amount of dissatisfaction among a few who prided themselves upon their French costumes'. She also disliked the current fad for wearing head-dresses made of tall feathers and for a long time banned them at court but, as Horace Walpole wryly observed, 'fashion remained in opposition and not a plume less was worn anywhere else'.[12] All this combined to ensure that the court was stripped of much of its glamour. Instead of being at the epicentre of society it stood in lofty detachment from the fashionable world, whose leaders despised the values espoused by the King and Queen and ignored the example set by them.

It was the rigid observation of etiquette that contributed as much as anything to the leaden atmosphere of the royal household, for etiquette was the deity before whom all at court must bend. The King and Queen's daily existence was governed by a formal framework of rules and regulations which provided them with the means whereby they could distance themselves from those with whom they came into regular contact, and thus preserve the mystique of royalty. Unfortunately the established code of conduct took no account of convenience or practicality and only someone who was superhuman could have conformed exactly with its requirements.

In December 1785 Fanny Burney, a young novelist who had recently been introduced to the King and Queen, gave her stepmother the following lecture on how to behave when in the royal presence:

> In the first place you must not cough. If you find a cough tickling in your throat, you must arrest it from making any sound; if you find yourself choking with the forbearance, you must choke – but not cough.
>
> In the second place you must not sneeze. If you have a vehement cold you must take no notice of it; if your nose membranes feel a great irritation you must hold your breath; if a sneeze still insists upon making its way, you must oppose it, by keeping your teeth grinding together; if the violence of the repulse breaks some blood vessel, you must break the blood vessel – but not sneeze.
>
> In the third place, you must not, upon any account, stir either hand or foot. If, by chance, a black pin runs into your head, you must not take it out. If the pain is very great you must be sure to bear it without wincing; if it brings the tears into your eyes, you must not wipe them off; if they give you a tingling by running down your cheeks, you must look as if nothing was the matter . . . If however, the agony is very great, you may, privately, bite the inside of your cheek, or of your lips, for a little relief; taking care, meanwhile, to do it so cautiously as to make no apparent dent outwardly. And, with that precaution, if you even gnaw a piece out, it will not be minded, only be sure either to swallow it, or commit it to a corner of the inside of your mouth till they are gone – for you must not spit.[13]

Fanny's tone was flippant, but as she discovered when she entered royal service a few months later these were precepts which were not to be taken lightly.

This, however, was only a beginning, for her catalogue of the dos and don'ts of court life was by no means an exhaustive one. It did not take into account various fundamentals, such as the rule forbidding anyone to initiate a conversation with the King and Queen or to eat in their presence, except on the occasions when the Queen invited a lady of the Bedchamber to share her table. Ladies who visited the Queen could not leave her presence of their own accord, and when requested to do so they had to back smoothly out of the room, a manoeuvre which Fanny Burney found almost impossible to execute 'without tripping up my own heels, feeling my head giddy or treading my train out of the pleats – accidents very frequent among novices in that business'. There were some who never managed to perfect the technique but others, such as the Duke of Argyll's daughter Lady Mary Coke, were brilliant at effecting a graceful retreat and even as an octogenarian she impressed an observer when, 'kicking her train behind her' she 'backed out of the room in capital style'.[14]

It was of course unthinkable for anyone to sit in the Queen's presence unless specifically invited to do so and as she did not readily grant permission her attendants were required to spend hours on their feet. Soon after Fanny Burney had taken up her post at court the Duchess of Ancaster remarked that she probably found it exhausting, for being 'unused to this work' she did 'not know yet what it is to stand for five hours following as we do'; but even those accustomed to spending long periods erect occasionally failed these endurance tests. On one occasion the Countess of Harcourt came near to collapse when with the Queen at the theatre, for having recently had influenza she lacked the strength to stand behind the Queen's chair throughout the whole performance. It was fortunate for her that one of her colleagues happened to be in the audience and was able to take over after the first act for the Queen made no allowances for fits of faintness in her ladies. When she was asked at the christening of her grand-daughter if the heavily pregnant Marchioness of Townshend could be seated during the ceremony, the Queen replied, 'blowing the snuff from her fingers, "She may stand, she may stand"'.[15]

Arduous as it could be to serve as a lady of the Bedchamber to Queen Charlotte, they were by no means the most hard-working members of her staff. They were no longer expected to wait on the Queen at meals, or to assist at her daily toilette, and the latter duty now devolved on a more professional inner ring of ladies-in-waiting, who resided permanently at court. By this time indeed, the purpose of the ladies of the Bedchamber was essentially to serve as little more than passive adjuncts to the Queen. Whenever the Queen appeared in public a Bedchamber lady was in attendance, bearing the royal train at Drawing Rooms, and following in her mistress's wake during such engagements as visits to universities, or outings to concerts and the theatre. In theory one of the ladies of the Bedchamber had also to be present when the Queen was at her country homes at Windsor and Kew, but Charlotte did her best to minimize her demands on them by employing supplementary ladies-in-waiting whose salaries were paid out of her own Privy Purse. Thus in 1788 Lady Courtown was engaged 'to attend the Queen in all country excursions and during all residences at Windsor and Kew', and such measures enabled the Queen to be more accommodating to her official Bedchamber ladies. In 1787, for example, she wrote to the Countess of Pembroke, who had entered her service five years previously, that if she wished she could ignore a summons to wait on her as 'there is a difference in the ladies waiting at court and in their being invited to Windsor'.[16]

The Bedchamber women, too, had a less oppressive timetable than in times gone past. Numbering six in all, they were each on call for just two months of the year and during that time they waited on their mistress only when she donned formal dress for public appearances. It was their prerogative to assist her when she put on her coronation robes, and one of them always supervised the final stages of her toilette on Drawing Room days, fastening her necklace and giving her her fan and gloves, before carrying her train to the door of the dressing room and handing it to the lady of the Bedchamber in waiting. But the days had gone when they catered to the Queen's more intimate needs and the aged Countess of Suffolk, who in 1761 had been consulted about the role the Bedchamber women should play in preparing the Queen for the coronation, must have rejoiced to see that the job no longer entailed the subservient attentions of yesteryear.[17]

The burden of work that had hitherto been shouldered by the Bedchamber women was now divided between the two Keepers of the Robes and their pair of assistants, the wardrobe women. The utmost dedication was expected of these ladies, who were supposed to regard royal service as a form of vocation rather than as a mere career. They resided permanently at court, having apartments at Windsor, St James's and Kew, and as they were entitled to no holidays the only time they had off was when they had occasional sick leave or were granted brief respites on compassionate grounds. Though not physically taxing, their duties were laborious and time-consuming, with little variation and no room for initiative. The wardrobe woman's day began at dawn, when she helped arrange the Queen's hair and assisted her into her underclothes, and ended about midnight, when she saw her into bed. The hours kept by the Keepers of the Robes were almost equally long, and Fanny Burney clearly felt herself entitled to every sympathy when she described to a friend her routine at Windsor.

A typical day ran thus: she rose at six and was summoned to the Queen's dressing room about half past seven. There she found one of the wardrobe women, who had already completed the preliminary stages of the Queen's toilette and who now handed Fanny the various items of clothing which she put on her mistress. This operation took about an hour and a half and Fanny then returned to her room, breakfasted, attended to correspondence, and went for a brief walk. On her return she was again summoned to assist at 'the irksome and quick-returning labours of the toilette,' for about midday the Queen swapped the comparatively informal clothes she wore in the morning for a more elaborate dinner gown. Madame Schwellenberg assisted Fanny at this second dressing of the day but even so it was not over till three o'clock, when Fanny returned to her room for a couple of hours' reading. At five she dined with Madame Schwellenberg, who expected to be kept amused throughout the meal, and when it was over she had to accompany Madame to her apartment for coffee and further conversation. At eight they re-occupied the eating room, where they had tea with the equerries, and then Fanny had to stay with Madame Schwellenberg for the remainder of the evening, until she was finally released by the necessity to go and help the Queen undress.[18] It was not, perhaps, so exhausting a schedule as Fanny liked to make out, for on an average day she attended on her mistress rather less than five hours, but the dispiriting aspect of the job was that leisure hours were so strictly regimented that she had no time for genuine relaxation.

Worst of all, however, was the fact that all ladies resident at court had virtually no social life of their own. They had no time to meet their friends outside of court, and they could only rarely entertain in their apartments as the Queen was reluctant to let outsiders into the Palace. Fanny Burney had even to assure her mistress that she 'would form no connection ... but with her consent; nor even maintain those already made and formed but by her knowledge,' and the Queen took full advantage of her promise, forbidding her to make the acquaintance of a party of aristocratic French refugees, despite the fact that Fanny had heard 'nothing but commendation' of the persons concerned. For those accustomed to move freely in society, such restrictions were hard. Mary Hamilton, a young woman who in 1777 was engaged as a lady-in-waiting to the Queen's three eldest daughters, subsequently recalled that when at court: 'My health and spirits suffered very much from leading a life of constant restraint, I felt myself unequal to it and regretted my loss of liberty – the situation became irksome and I had few opportunities of enjoying the society of many most dear and valuable friends – for it was totally inconsistent with the place I was in, to ask permission to live so much as I wished with those persons I loved.'[19] In the circumstances it was not surprising that Queen Charlotte had some difficulty in finding suitable servants, for well-bred ladies who combined the virtues of diligence, loyalty and discretion, and who were prepared to put their lives entirely at the Queen's disposal, were treasures not easily unearthed.

In her bid to find such paragons the Queen was prepared to look outside the traditional court circle. Her 1786 appointment of Fanny Burney as Keeper of the Robes excited almost as much surprise as would the appointment of Iris Murdoch or Margaret Drabble to the present-day staff at Buckingham Palace, and was particularly curious considering that Fanny herself remarked that the Queen had 'a settled aversion to almost all novels and something very near it to almost all novel-writers'. Nevertheless, the Queen had read and enjoyed both Fanny's first novel, *Evelina*, which had appeared anonymously in 1778, and its successor, *Cecilia*, and was less prejudiced than she might have been against Miss Burney because she and the King knew her father, the historian of music Charles Burney. Any remaining misgivings were dispelled when the Queen was introduced to Miss Burney by Mrs Delany, a sweet old lady for whom the King had procured accommodation in Windsor and whose taste in friends he and his wife much respected. The Queen was amazed to find that a best-selling novelist could prove so diffident and self-effacing, and reflected that it would be pleasant to have at court someone who was capable of conducting a stimulating conversation but who neverthe-less would instinctively know her place. She felt too that if she employed Fanny it would to some extent atone for Dr Burney's recent disappointment at being overlooked for the post of Master of the Queen's Band and therefore as Madame Haggerdorn was returning to Germany on grounds of ill health she determined to offer her job to Fanny.[20]

It seems never to have occurred to the Queen that her offer would be looked on as anything other than a heaven-sent opportunity, but for Fanny it came more like a thunderbolt. Since the success of her novels she had been welcome in intellectual circles, and having associated regularly with the likes of Johnson, Sheridan and Burke she knew it would be difficult to adjust to life within the confines of a court. Nevertheless her father was 'in raptures' when informed of the Queen's proposal and, not wishing to disappoint him, Fanny dejectedly accepted it.

During the next few years she frequently had occasion to regret her filial piety. The Queen, whenever she saw her, was invariably 'all sweetness, encouragement and gracious goodness' but Fanny still felt desperately homesick throughout her stay at court. Deprived of the company of friends she loved, and forced to spend her off-duty hours with people whom she did not necessarily find congenial, she suffered all the miseries of loneliness without being able to enjoy the luxury of solitude. Her worst trial, however, was the necessity for constant contact with Madame Schwellenberg, who considered her as little more than a minion, to be bossed and bullied with impunity, and though Fanny did her best to be agreeable, her colleague's autocratic behaviour made her life a misery. Like Madame Haggerdorn before her, Fanny began to suffer from sore eyes because of Madame Schwellenberg's predilection for travelling about with the windows of her coach open to the elements, and if Fanny unwittingly offended Madame she behaved with petty vindictiveness, refusing to offer her any food at dinner one evening when she discovered that Miss Burney had obtained the following afternoon off. It was of course all unbelievably trivial, but in an enclosed community like the court such 'cabals and rules and timidities' could assume an unwarranted significance.[21]

After five years in royal service Fanny decided that she could endure it no longer, and having discussed the matter with her father she resolved to hand in her resignation. Madame Schwellenberg became quite tearful about Fanny's departure, for in her own way she had grown very fond of her colleague and had no idea that it was her own behaviour that had largely inspired the move. For the Queen, however, it was an even more disagreeable shock as she had presumed that Fanny was 'hers for life' and though Fanny maintained that her health would not withstand a further term at court, the Queen evidently felt that she ought to have soldiered on regardless. Eventually however she resigned herself to Fanny's loss and generously awarded her a lifelong pension of £100 a year. Fanny finally left royal service in July 1791, but thereafter she kept in touch with both her mistress and her former colleagues, and even became quite fond of Madame Schwellenberg, who could hold no terrors for her now. Nevertheless, never for a moment did she regret her decision to leave court where, as she recorded, 'I was lost to all private comfort, dead to all domestic endearment. I was worn with want of rest and fatigued with laborious watchfulness and attendance. My time was devoted to official duties and all that in life was dearest to me – my friends, my chosen society, my best affections – lived ... in my mind only.'[22] At least however her sufferings were not in vain, for the journal that she kept during her years at court affords us a unique glimpse into the lives of a King and Queen at home, and Miss Burney's reputation now rests as much on her skill as a diarist as on the novels which she wrote prior to her introduction to the royal family.

The Queen had some problem finding a suitable successor to Miss Burney. Deciding that 'it would be dangerous ... to build upon meeting in England with one who would be discreet in point of keeping off friends and acquaintances from frequenting the Palace', she reverted to her original policy of importing Keepers of the Robes from Germany, but it was not a successful move. Mademoiselle Jacobi, the daughter of a Hanoverian clergyman, replaced Fanny Burney in 1791, but though she initially made a good impression on the Queen she soon squabbled with Madame Schwellenberg and swept back to Germany, 'ill and dissatisfied with everything in England'. Her successor, Madame Buckner, stayed an almost equally short time, and such a swift turnover in staff weighed heavily on the Queen's purse as she felt obliged to continue paying former servants a proportion of their salaries even if they had not been with her for long.[23] Nevertheless, she only had herself to blame, for while conditions at court remained so disagreeable, these constant resignations were inevitable.

If it was not particularly enjoyable to work in the Queen's household, there were of course other compensations. At the higher end of the court hierarchy, the ladies of the Bedchamber were paid £500 a year while the Bedchamber women did almost as well, receiving £300 in salary and being entitled besides to any clothes which the Queen discarded, a perquisite that was valued at £200 a year. The maids of honour were also paid £300 a year and though in the course of the reign they lost their right to be fed and housed at court they were compensated with board wages of £470 to be divided amongst the six of them. Rather unfairly, the Keepers of the Robes, who did more work than any of the above, had a salary of only £200 a year but they also had free accommodation and a footman to look after them in all the palaces. Salaries indeed accounted for a large proportion of household expenditure, but though the King and Queen were always anxious to reduce their domestic budget the Queen would never permit savings to be made at the expense of her ladies. In 1812 the Government decided to reorganize the financial arrangements for the royal household but the Queen fought their proposals fiercely,

complaining of 'the principle of extreme economy that seems to per-
vade the entire plan', and condemning as 'shabby' their suggestion of
depriving the maids of honour of their board wages as they had had 'a
right of time immemorial to a table' and they therefore deserved to be
compensated for the loss of the privilege.[24] Queen Charlotte's detrac-
tors have always alleged that she was a mean woman but certainly she
took her financial responsibilities towards her employees very
seriously.

Hitherto, of course, the salaries enjoyed by court officials had been
only one of the reasons why people sought employment there, but as
the era of limited monarchy dawned the advantages of having a position in the royal household became less apparent. 'The court,
independent of politics, makes a strange figure', mused Horace
Walpole in 1764, and as the Crown's control over the Government
and administration steadily weakened, so it became more difficult for
the royal family to look after their servants as they had done in the
past. Admittedly it took some time for the full implications of such
changes to be understood and the notion persisted that it could be
beneficial to have 'a friend at court'. Fanny Burney accepted her post
in the household partly because it was represented to her that it would
put her in a good position to further her father's career, and when
Mary Hamilton became engaged in 1784 to an impoverished young
man a friend remarked that it was as well she left court some years
before, as now no one could suspect her fiancé of harbouring 'ambitious views of increasing his fortune' on account of her interest with
the Queen.[25] But it is doubtful that even when in office Mary would
have represented a catch for a fortune-hunter, for by then the
supposition that court ladies had at their finger-tips an inexhaustible
supply of pensions and places had little to substantiate it.

Admittedly ladies-in-waiting could still occasionally obtain a relative or friend a post in the royal household itself, but beyond that
their influence was very circumscribed. Contrary to Fanny Burney's
hopes, her family derived little advantage from her position at court
for her father's career in no way benefited from it, and when Fanny
exerted herself on behalf of her sailor brother James the results were
pitiful indeed. He had blithely assumed that Fanny had only to say a
word and the Queen would arrange for him to be put in command of a
fine ship but though in May 1791 Fanny plucked up her courage and
spoke to her mistress of his hopes for promotion, it did him little
good. James did obtain an interview with the First Lord of the
Admiralty but the latter merely told him that there were not enough

ships available to provide for every young naval officer, and, as Fanny ruefully admitted, that was all 'that my court residence obtained for my marine department of interest'. In truth the calculating or ambitious no longer had much to gain from household office: General Goldsworthy, the King's equerry-in-chief, sardonically remarked to Fanny Burney that those who found life at court hard could at least console themselves with the thought that 'It's honour! That's one comfort, it's all honour!' – and with that the average royal servant had to be satisfied.[26]

In the autumn of 1788 what Fanny Burney described as 'the wearying lifeless uniformity of life at court' was disrupted by a traumatic interlude. For much of October the King had been troubled by a variety of disquieting symptoms and had been more excitable than usual. Then, during dinner on 5 November, he 'had broken forth into a positive delirium' and it had become clear that he was afflicted by no commonplace malady. Nowadays it is widely accepted that the King was suffering from porphyria but contemporaries presumed he was insane and he was consigned to the care of two keepers considered expert in the treatment of mental illness.

For the ladies who were at court during this time it was a period of almost unbearable strain. In the initial weeks of the crisis the Queen could rely only on those ladies who happened to be at Windsor when her husband had been taken ill, for in a moment of lucidity the King had made her promise that she would admit no one else till he was better. Lady Courtown and Lady Elizabeth Waldegrave, a lady of the Bedchamber to the Princess Royal, were in residence at the time, as were the three governesses to the royal children and Fanny Burney. They alone had to keep the Queen from nervous collapse, sitting up with her through the long nights when she waited to hear of any improvement in the King. All were soon worn out with worry and lack of sleep and the stress was such that within a few days the sub-governess Miss Goldsworthy collapsed and had to retire to bed. She was replaced by Madame Schwellenberg, who had originally been absent because of ill health, but whose hasty return to Windsor came as 'an addition . . . to the gloom of all'.[27]

On 29 November matters became still worse when the Prince of Wales ordered that his father should be removed to his house at Kew. Kew was not designed for winter residence and the cold and discomfort endured by all who moved there intensified the general depression. As before no visitors were permitted for fear of upsetting the

King, and so the little group at Kew were left isolated, with nothing to distract them from their gloomy thoughts. Not surprisingly Lady Courtown's health soon gave way under the strain and on Christmas Eve the Countess of Harcourt struggled down snowy roads in order to relieve her at her post.

It was now that politics intruded to render the situation still more fraught. The Prince of Wales had displayed an unfilial eagerness at the thought of reigning as Regent in his father's stead, but the Tory Government, headed by William Pitt, were anxious to curb his powers, for they knew that he wished to remove them from office and install in their place their enemies the Whigs. From a constitutional point of view the situation was one of immense complexity and as tempers rose it proved impossible for the Queen and her ladies to remain aloof from the dispute.

If the King recovered there would of course be no need for a Regency at all and the exact state of his mental health therefore became a question of supreme importance. By the beginning of 1789 the King's principal custodians, Dr Francis Willis and his son, declared that they could detect signs of improvement, and not unnaturally the Queen was inclined to believe them. When Dr John Warren, a physician whom the Prince of Wales had brought on to the case, dissented with their opinion, the Queen attributed his scepticism to political bias. Matters came to a head on 2 January 1789 when Warren prepared a bulletin which the Willises refused to endorse, claiming it gave too gloomy an account of the King's health. Angry and upset, the Queen sent the Countess of Harcourt and Lady Charlotte Finch to demand to know why Warren was so pessimistic, but though he declined to give a satisfactory explanation he would not alter his opinion, and after a short altercation the two ladies withdrew empty-handed.[28]

This incident was subsequently magnified out of all proportion, for in the heightened state of tension that prevailed in the capital the most absurd ideas gained credence. Dr Warren told his friends in London of the pressure that had been applied on him at Kew, and this soon gave rise to a rumour that the Queen wanted to have the King declared sane because in his enfeebled state he would be unable to prevent her from ruling the country in conjunction with Pitt. Mrs Harcourt, the sister-in-law of the Countess, wrote from London to tell her that 'the party' – as she disdainfully called the Opposition – were circulating the most preposterous rumours, claiming 'that fine things had come out about the Queen's interference; that she had sent you and Lady Charlotte Finch down to dictate to the physicians and make them alter the bulletins'. The controversy was fuelled by the writings of the satirists: Fanny Burney was shown one broadsheet in which both Madame Schwellenberg and the Countess of Harcourt were singled out for abuse. 'How infinitely licentious!' she commented, shocked, but worse was to come, for the cartoonists had also been at work. One Rowlandson drawing depicted the Queen and Pitt sharing the crown, while in the background Madame Schwellenberg strutted towards the House of Lords bearing the Chancellor's mace.[29]

Such was the excitement that it was said that the Countess of Harcourt and Lady Charlotte Finch were to be questioned in the House of Lords by the committee appointed to set up the Regency. The Countess assured her sister-in-law that if it came to that she was confident of acquitting herself well, for 'I should feel the courage of a heroine when speaking the language of *truth* warm from my heart in defence of injured and oppressed innocence'. To her husband she wrote in an equally defiant strain, declaring that her love for the Queen would sustain her through any ordeal and adding proudly, 'when I witness her wretchedness I cannot think of myself'.[30]

Aglow with righteous zeal, the Countess of Harcourt watched with satisfaction as the Queen's attitude towards her eldest son hardened. When at the end of January the Prince and his brother the Duke of York paid an unexpected visit to Kew, the Countess assumed they wished to browbeat their mother into admitting that the King was as mad as ever, so, ignoring their every hint that they wished to see the Queen alone, she hovered protectively by her mistress throughout their stay. Within a few days the Countess heard that the brothers had been much annoyed by her behaviour but she remained undaunted: 'A complaint, and that a strong one, is already made of my remaining in the room the other day when certain persons wanted to see the Queen *alone* . . . but I care little about it', she exultantly told her husband.[31]

In the event neither Lady Charlotte nor the Countess of Harcourt was summoned before the Regency committee but whether the Countess would have emerged from the enquiry so triumphantly as she expected is a moot point. Certainly she would never have deliberately misled anyone as to the state of the King's health but as a fervent admirer of Pitt, who trusted 'that those who are now struggling for power will only be dressed in a little brief authority', she was predisposed to believe any claim that George was on the road to recovery. Not permitted to see the King herself, she relied solely on the reports of the Willises, who themselves were ardent partisans of the Government and inclined to be over-optimistic about the King's condition. It was indeed Lady Harcourt who had initially recommended that the King should be entrusted to the Willises' care, for they had been called in some years previously when Mrs Harcourt's mother had gone mad and had apparently succeeded in curing her. The unfortunate woman had subsequently suffered a relapse and leapt from a window to her death, but despite this untoward occurrence Lady Harcourt's faith in the Willises remained complete. At Kew she became their confidante and champion and reported proudly to her husband, 'I am the only person with whom the Willises feel safe.'[32]

Furthermore, from her own evidence it would seem that Lady Harcourt was guilty of inflaming the Queen against her eldest son. Throughout the Regency crisis her sister-in-law Mrs Harcourt kept her informed of developments in London, taking care to pass on any titbits which were to the discredit of the Prince of Wales and his party. The majority of these Lady Harcourt relayed to the Queen, having decided 'never to give her pain unnecessarily, but never to conceal anything that, upon consideration, I think she should be informed of'. By denying the Prince an opportunity to see his mother alone she prevented him from putting his viewpoint to the Queen, which might at least have helped clear up some of the misunderstandings that divided them at the time. All this adds weight to the contention of Lady Louisa Stuart, a well-informed young lady who was no blind partisan of the Prince of Wales, that he was unfairly dealt with by his mother's ladies. According to her, Lady Courtown, the Countess of Harcourt, Mrs Harcourt and Lady Charlotte Finch all had 'their irons in the fire' and she declared that 'half the serious ill blood between the Queen and her sons had sprung from the tittle tattle of these women and the pains they have taken to convey backwards and forwards every idle story'. She provided no evidence to support her statement but certainly in the Countess of Harcourt's case it would seem that her fanatical loyalty to the King and Queen at times obscured her judgement and led her into unworthy intrigues.[33]

Perhaps the Countess of Harcourt would not have been so eager to believe all the Willises' assurances that the King was on the mend if she had been able to see the patient himself, for in the later stages of his illness his madness had taken a disturbing new turn. Although hitherto a devoted husband, he suddenly turned against the Queen and declared himself passionately in love with Elizabeth, Countess of Pembroke, an eminently respectable middle-aged lady of the

Bedchamber who was highly embarrassed to find that she had unexpectedly become an object of desire to the King. To his startled attendants the King raved of Lady Pembroke's perfections, employing obscene language of a sort that normally never crossed his lips. When his wife visited him at the end of December he told her that he would not share her bed till 1793 and it was Queen Esther – as he called Lady Pembroke – who now occupied all his thoughts. When he played cards he would pretend that the queen of hearts represented Lady Pembroke, 'kissing it whenever he saw it', and at the end of January he prattled so wildly of his loved one that Dr Willis had to give him a severe lecture, instructing his son to gag the King when the latter tried to shout him down. Fortunately his mania for Lady Pembroke was to be one of the final manifestations of the King's bizarre disease, for although the Willises had been premature in declaring that their patient was better, in the long run their optimism proved justified. As late as 22 February the King was still making occasional roguish allusions to Lady Pembroke, but by that time such lapses were becoming increasingly rare. By the end of the month it was clear that he was once again his normal self, and on 28 March the Queen was able to celebrate her husband's recovery by holding a Drawing Room at which all the ladies wore bandeaux round their foreheads emblazoned with the words 'God Save the King'.[34]

One awkward matter nevertheless remained outstanding. Throughout the crisis the Countess of Pembroke had behaved as a true friend to her mistress, for though it was said that the Prince of Wales had hoped that if she became his father's mistress he would be able to 'govern the King through her, thus oversetting the Queen's influence', the Countess was not the sort of woman to take immoral advantage of a sick man's passion. The Archbishop of Canterbury 'spoke to her seriously on the subject' but she soon set his mind at rest, and she made it clear to the King after his recovery that she would never have contemplated becoming his mistress. For the Queen Lady Pembroke's name nevertheless held painful associations, but despite her understandable reluctance, she forced herself to ask Lady Pembroke to join the royal family on their 1789 summer holiday at Weymouth. Her self-denial was rewarded, for in the event the 'visit, which was much dreaded, proved most serviceable' as Lady Pembroke behaved throughout the visit with such exquisite tact that it was not long before her hosts felt completely at ease with her.[35]

This, however, was not the final episode of this curious romance. The King's tragic affliction was subsequently to recur at sporadic intervals and in February 1804 he suffered one such attack. By June he was over the worst but unfortunately he emerged from the sickroom with his desire for Lady Pembroke revived. Although still remarkably good-looking, the Countess by now was seventy years of age, and society was much amused by reports that the King was bombarding this elderly dowager with love-letters and improper proposals. The Queen was said to show open displeasure at the attentions which her husband showed her lady of the Bedchamber but in fact as before Lady Pembroke was careful to give him no encouragement and so the situation passed off without too much embarrassment. As the King gradually became calmer, his wife and children were able to show their gratitude for the way that Lady Pembroke had prevented the crisis from escalating. The Queen's third daughter, Princess Elizabeth, spoke for her mother when she sent Lady Pembroke an account of the King's health in the autumn of 1804 and remarked, 'You see I speak openly and as I feel to *a friend*. You can enter into all our anxiety and feel for us.' The Queen too remained a regular correspondent and for many years the Countess retained her position in the Bedchamber. When she finally resigned in February 1818 her mistress wrote her a warm letter saying she regretted her departure but was proud to think that she could still give her 'the *name of a friend*'.[36]

Their enduring affection was perhaps more remarkable considering that in 1810 the King's clouded mind had finally been completely overshadowed by madness and as before he had developed an obsessive longing for the Countess of Pembroke. By now completely blind, he was kept confined at Windsor for the last ten years of his life and one observer reported that he passed his time immersed in wholly imaginary projects, 'creating various orders, especially a female one of which Lady Pembroke is to be the head, and often running riot into great obscenities'.[37] When not thus engaged he occupied himself playing on the harpsichord and talking to non-existent people and one may hope that in this state it seemed to him that Queen Esther at last sat by his side as joint sovereign of the realm of fantasy.

Of the many afflictions which were visited on King George III in the course of his long life, his sorrow at the behaviour of his eldest son was by no means the least. Born in 1762, George, Prince of Wales was in every way a contrast to his father. Extravagant and pleasure-loving, by the age of eighteen he had embarked upon a career of dissipation which no amount of admonitions from the King could persuade him to abandon. His name had been linked with a number of women, many of whom were unfit companions for a Prince of Wales, but in 1785 he had committed the crowning folly of taking for his wife Maria Fitzherbert, a widowed lady of impeccable virtue but also unfortunately a commoner and a Catholic. The marriage had been performed in secret and was technically invalid as the Prince had not obtained, as required by law, his father's permission, but for nearly a decade he and Mrs Fitzherbert had lived together as man and wife. Then, however, he had embarked on an affair with the Countess of Jersey and her ascendancy over him was soon so complete that in June 1794 he sent Mrs Fitzherbert a letter telling her that he could never see her more.

Frances, Countess of Jersey was a woman for whom the epithet 'bitch' seems inappropriate only because it fails to convey the almost feline quality of her malice. The daughter of an Irish bishop, in 1794 she was already in her forties and a grandmother too, but despite her respectable background she was the worst sort of *femme fatale*, calculating, sly and devoid of compassion. One contemporary described her as 'a clever, unprincipled but beautiful and fascinating woman, though with scarcely any retrieving really good quality', while another remarked of her that she only knew true happiness when she had 'a rival to trouble and torment'. But despite her shrewish nature she was possessed of formidable powers of seduction which encompassed both sexes; she even charmed the Queen, who originally had been suspicious of Lady Jersey, only to fall under her spell once the Prince of Wales had prevailed upon her to receive the Countess.[38]

Having persuaded the Prince to rid himself of one wife Lady Jersey now helped to reconcile him to the thought of taking another, for paradoxically enough the Prince had cast off Mrs Fitzherbert not only because he wished to devote himself wholeheartedly to his mistress but also because he was contemplating marriage with a foreign princess. By 1794 his load of debts had become oppressive and he knew that the Government would be unwilling to provide him with further financial assistance unless he took a bride of whom both King and Parliament approved. That he was already deeply involved with another woman he considered no impediment to a marriage which would, after all, be one of pure convenience, and Lady Jersey too was in favour of the plan, confident that she would have no difficulty outshining some dowdy foreign princess. Having made up his mind the Prince did not bother to make even the most perfunctory enquiries about his future wife, presuming that the daughter of any Protestant princeling would suit his purpose equally well, and in August 1794 he accordingly informed his delighted father that he had decided to marry his first cousin, Princess Caroline of Brunswick.

At Brunswick the Prince's proposal was received with rapture and for the next few months preparations were made for the Princess's journey to England. There was some difficulty in finding any English ladies who were prepared to go to Germany to collect the Princess, for at the time much of Europe was engulfed in war with revolutionary France and continental travel had in consequence lost much of its appeal. Caroline's mother had reluctantly agreed to accompany her daughter for part of the way and the situation was only saved in early March 1795 when a plea for help was sent to Mrs Harcourt, who had accompanied her soldier husband when he went on campaign abroad. She was tracked down at Osnaburgh and told to join the Princess as soon as possible, and though she lamented that she was in feeble health 'and want myself all the attention I shall be expected to pay another', she responded magnificently. She caught up with the Princess at Hanover, having travelled for four or five days along snow-covered roads, but though determined 'to do my best to discharge my duty', she had already decided that once she had delivered her cargo to England she would not accept a permanent situation about the Princess.[39]

There were plenty of people in England eager to take her place for the Queen had already received several enquiries from ladies, only one of whom she had ever met, as to whether they or their daughters might be appointed. As the Prince of Wales had the final choice in the matter she merely passed them on to him, but she might have done better to have referred them to the Countess of Jersey, for one observer noted that when the time came for selecting the Princess's servants 'Lady Jersey . . . named them all'.[40] This would not have mattered if she had confined herself merely to recommending others to positions, for the decision to appoint the Marchioness of Townshend as Mistress of the Robes, with the Countesses of Carnarvon and Cholmondley as Bedchamber ladies was in no way controversial. Unfortunately, in the manner of Barbara Palmer with Charles II, Lady Jersey also prevailed upon the Prince to appoint her as one of his wife's ladies of the Bedchamber.

On 5 April 1795 the Princess arrived in England accompanied by Mrs Harcourt and Lord Malmesbury, a distinguished diplomat who had seen enough of Caroline on the journey to know that she was not the sort of woman likely to appeal to a sophisticate like the Prince. Her appearance had little enough to commend it, but her manner was infinitely worse, for though fundamentally good-natured she was gauche and excitable and had no conception of how to behave in polite society. The marriage between her and the Prince would have had little chance of success under any circumstances but with Lady Jersey hovering malignly in the background it was doomed from the outset, for the Princess was in no way equipped to deal with so insidious a foe, and once in England she would blunder like some clumsy bluebottle into the silken web that the Countess had stretched out for her.

Right from the start the Countess of Jersey set out to humiliate the Princess as much as possible. When Caroline and her suite arrived at Greenwich there was no one there to welcome them as the Countess had successfully delayed the departure from London of the official reception committee, of which she was a member. When finally the cavalcade of coaches drew up the Countess stepped out bearing an unbecoming white satin costume which she insisted the Princess put on in place of the more flattering dress of blue muslin that Mrs Harcourt had selected for the occasion. Then she caked Caroline's cheeks with rouge, despite the fact that the Princess had a naturally florid complexion, and having seen to it that the girl would look positively clownish for her first meeting with the Prince, she made further difficulties by declaring that on the journey back to London she could not comply with etiquette by sitting opposite Caroline in the coach as she was always sick if she travelled with her back to the horses. Fortunately Lord Malmesbury would have none of this: silkily he told her that as ladies of the Bedchamber invariably had to travel backwards when in coaches with their mistress it was unwise of her to have accepted the post in the first place, but 'if she *really* was likely to be sick' she could always go with him in the second coach. 'This', he noted grimly, 'of course settled the business' and the glowering Countess had perforce to take her place opposite the Princess for the journey back to London.[41]

From then on, however, all went according to Lady Jersey's plan. The Prince was appalled when introduced to his bride, and at dinner that night his adverse first impression was only confirmed, for Caroline made a spectacle of herself in front of the royal family. She subsequently claimed that as soon as she had seen the Prince and his lady together she had known 'how it all was' between them and so, to the embarrassment of everyone present, she had spent the meal making coarse allusions to Lady Jersey.[42]

The marriage went ahead regardless, but though the Princess was soon pregnant, in every other respect it was a disaster. The Prince made no effort to hide his distaste for his bride or to disguise his preference for the Countess of Jersey, taking away from Caroline the pearl bracelets he had given her as a wedding present so that the Countess might deck her arms with them instead. His bitterness at being chained to a woman he detested was all the greater because the Government had failed to make the generous financial provision that he had assumed would be his when he married. To his fury he was obliged to cut down his expenditure, and among other economies he determined to dismiss his wife's four maids of honour, who in his opinion constituted 'the most useless' part of her establishment. His sister Princess Elizabeth wrote anxiously questioning whether the resultant saving of £1,200 justified exciting the ill-feeling of the girls and their families but the King did not object and the Prince remained adamant that he was unable as yet 'to resume the appearance due to my birth and which I am deprived of *through the infamous deceit of Pitt*'.[43]

The Princess's position was in no way improved when she provided her husband with an heir, for though she gave birth to a daughter on 7 January 1796 the Prince continued to spend as much time as possible with the Countess of Jersey while his wife was left alone at his London residence, Carlton House. Eventually, however, she determined to tolerate the situation no longer and in mid-April the Prince was astonished to receive from his wife a letter in ungrammatical French, informing him that in future she would refuse to dine alone with the Countess, 'a person whom I can neither like nor esteem, and who is your mistress'. The Prince refused to admit that his wife had any cause for complaint, icily reminding her that even when the Countess of Jersey was in attendance on her she could always summon one or more of her other ladies to make up a more companionable party. Furthermore he absolutely rebutted her charge that the Countess was '*my mistress as you* indecorously term her', insisting that she was no more than 'a friend to whom I am attached by strong ties of habitude, esteem and respect'.[44]

Caroline was not satisfied and the correspondence continued, but the Prince still had hopes that the matter could be settled in a civilized way. Using the embarrassed Countess of Cholmondley as an intermediary, he told Caroline that henceforth they would never be man and wife in the physical sense, an arrangement which he flattered himself would enable them to live hereafter in 'tranquil and comfortable society' with one another. Caroline, however, made it clear that she would be content with nothing less than the Countess of Jersey's resignation and to the Prince's horror she asked King George to adjudicate on the situation. This nevertheless failed to intimidate the Countess of Jersey, who forced her husband to complain to the King about the unjust accusations that had been levelled against her, and the unfortunate Prince now found himself trapped between two embattled women while his father looked on as umpire. Desperately the Prince told his wife that he could not dismiss the Countess as 'her removal would confirm every slander which has been so industriously propagated relative to her conduct towards you as well as the nature of her intimacy with me', but Caroline remained inexorable, pointing out, not unreasonably, that 'a woman whom I have reason to regard as the cause of the disunity that unfortunately exists between us cannot but be personally disagreeable to me'. Faced with this the Prince decided that the situation was beyond remedy, and as a last resort begged his father to allow him and his wife to separate. This the King refused, leaving his son with less room for manoeuvre than ever.[45]

By now the royal family were coming round to the view that the Countess of Jersey must be sacrificed to avert scandal. Towards the end of May the Press had begun to make veiled allusions to the dissensions between the Prince and his wife, expressing every sympathy with the Princess, and fear of further adverse publicity led Princess Elizabeth to write to her brother on 3 June that 'friends and foes are all of opinion that a *resignation must* take place for the sake of the *country* and the whole royal family'. The Prince still struggled feebly, but soon he was reduced to haggling about the exact timing and conditions of the Countess of Jersey's departure rather than refusing to countenance the idea at all, and on 29 June 1796 she was finally prevailed upon to hand in her notice.[46]

It seemed that Caroline had gained the day, but though she may have hoped that the departure of the Countess would form the prelude to a complete reconciliation between herself and the Prince, it soon emerged that the Countess of Jersey's loss of office had not affected her standing in any way. She continued to see a great deal of the Prince, and at his request she and her husband moved into the next door house to Carlton House, a cosy arrangement that boded ill for Caroline. The Countess was still received at court and singled out for attention by the Queen, whom many people wrongly considered to be responsible for her appointment in the first place. Only in 1798 did the Prince finally tire of the Countess of Jersey, and though their relationship was then terminated, the separation came too late to avert the complete breakdown of his marriage.

Despite the fact that the King had continued to resist the idea that his son and daughter-in-law should formally separate, in August 1797 Caroline and her household had moved to a rented house in Blackheath. For the sake of appearances apartments were kept for her at Carlton House, but thenceforth she and her husband effectively lived apart. At Blackheath at least one lady and one woman of the Bedchamber were supposed always to stay in the house with the Princess and she could also depend on the company of Miss Hayman, 'a very lively entertaining woman' who had been employed as sub-governess to Caroline's daughter until the Princess had persuaded her husband to agree that she should become her Keeper of the Privy Purse.[47] Within a short time, however, Caroline had decided that such ladylike companionship was not enough to keep her amused and had started to look for other diversions.

Freed from the trammels that her husband had imposed upon her, Caroline became more and more abandoned, entertaining extensively at Blackheath and not being over-selective in her choice of guests. If Queen Charlotte's court was too hidebound by etiquette, Caroline's went too far in the other direction and her parties soon acquired the reputation of being not altogether respectable. Her own behaviour at them encouraged this impression, for either her conversation verged upon the improper or she flirted outrageously with the gentlemen present, conduct which in those days of rigid social conventions was open to the most unfavourable interpretation. Her antics caused great distress to her ladies-in-waiting, but they were unable to restrain her, for the Princess reacted sharply to any suggestion that she should modify her way of life. Towards the end of 1800 for example Miss Hayman, who by nature was 'rough in manner ... blunt in speech but ... kind, true and trustworthy', had remonstrated with Caroline after the latter had withdrawn from the majority of her guests at a dinner party and spent the remainder of the evening closeted with 'some young man' in a room downstairs, behaviour which her Keeper of the Privy Purse felt could not be allowed to pass without comment. The next morning she plucked up her courage and represented to Caroline that English 'manners and modes of society were so different from those of other countries that what did not strike H.R.H. as at all particular would be thought so here and give rise to unpleasant and unjust remarks which a little more attention to our prejudices would prevent'. Although Miss Hayman had done her best to be tactful the Princess was enraged by her criticism, telling her roundly 'She neither liked nor desired nor improved by advice; that she had her ladies for attendants not counsellors', and making it plain that in future Miss Hayman should keep her opinions to herself.[48] Now that the Princess was in control of her own destiny, it would take more than a few well-meaning hints from her ladies to persuade her to alter the disastrous course she had mapped out for herself.

As she found criticism irksome, Caroline began to wish she could escape her ladies' prying gaze. She therefore proved more than accommodating when the Prince of Wales, impecunious as ever, sent her a message that she must cut down her establishment in order to save him money. Eagerly she declared that she would dismiss all four of her Bedchamber women, abolish the place of Mistress of the Robes and discontinue the practice of having a lady of the Bedchamber stay in the house with her, which would enable her to reduce the ladies' salaries from £500 to £400 a year. As for Miss Hayman, the Princess declared that her presence could also be dispensed with, explaining that 'she had determined to lodge her only at those times when she had occasion for her attendance on business' which would enable her to cut down expenditure on food bills. Instead she would make do with just one *dame de compagnie* who would need an allowance of no more than £200 a year, and who she no doubt hoped would be less censorious than the members of her former household.[49]

The Duke of Kent, who was in charge of conducting these negotiations on the Prince's behalf, was surprised that the Princess should display so commendable a sense of thrift. In particular her eagerness to part with Miss Hayman aroused his curiosity and though he was unable 'to find out whether this decision had originated in any other cause' the Prince of Wales evidently agreed that it was somewhat suspicious for, anxious as he was to save money, the retrenchments that were ultimately effected in the Princess's household were by no means as sweeping as those which Caroline had envisaged. When the Countess of Cholmondley left the Princess's household in 1802 she was not replaced, and one of the Bedchamber women, Miss Coleman, was also dispensed with, but otherwise her establishment was left intact. Nevertheless as the Prince had accepted that the ladies of the Bedchamber should no longer be resident, and Miss Hayman was also out of the house, the reforms enabled the Princess to enjoy a greater measure of freedom than before, a development which many of those who knew her well considered highly regrettable.[50]

It was in the autumn of 1801 that the Princess first made the acquaintance of Charlotte, Lady Douglas, a 'showy bold woman' who was as ambitious as she was unscrupulous and who would nearly succeed in encompassing Caroline's downfall. Originally a Miss Hopkinson, she had married Sir John Douglas, an officer in the marines who had seen distinguished service in the war with France but whose fortunes were now at a low ebb. Like the Princess, they had rented a house on Blackheath but they were 'shunned by all the respectable part of the neighbourhood', possibly because Lady Douglas was rumoured to be having an affair with her husband's former commanding officer, Sir Sidney Smith, who frequently came to stay at their house.[51]

The Princess was warned against the couple but she was nevertheless intrigued by these exciting new neighbours, and having introduced herself to Lady Douglas she took her up in a big way. Delighted with her new discovery, she showed her affection in the most uninhibited manner, for as Lady Douglas primly recorded, when the Princess came to visit she would 'run upstairs into my bedchamber, kiss me, take me in her arms, and tell me I was beautiful, . . . and such high flown compliments that women are never used to pay one another'. Evidently, however, at the time Lady Douglas was not unduly alarmed by these attentions, for when Caroline proposed in March 1802 that she spend some time with her as a temporary lady-in-waiting she accepted with alacrity. Caroline had recently fallen out with Miss Garth, one of her women of the Bedchamber, and she wanted Lady Douglas to take her place for a fortnight, explaining that she would be expected to attend her when she went out for walks or drives and to deal with her correspondence and visitors.[52]

Being so much with the Princess, Lady Douglas soon became the repository of all her confidences, for Caroline was naturally talkative and would say the first thing that came into her head, without pausing to reflect on the consequences. She had not the slightest regard for the truth and delighted in shocking her hearer with the most outrageous remarks, and as Lady Douglas was a good listener she learnt much of interest in their chats. On one occasion Caroline suddenly announced 'that she got a bedfellow wherever she could; that nothing was more wholesome', but worse still was the fact that she repeatedly told Lady Douglas that she was pregnant, and that when the child arrived she would pretend it was a foundling she had adopted.[53] To Caroline this was simply a piece of harmless fun, an amusing way of ensuring that her companion's attention was focused on herself; little did she guess that behind Lady Douglas's encouraging smile her mind was whirring, storing away the ammunition with which the Princess was so thoughtlessly providing her.

In October 1802 Lady Douglas went away for a time, and on paying the Princess a farewell visit she noted that she had recently become very fat and concluded that she was 'very near her time'. Sure enough, when she returned in early 1803 she found the Princess looking after an infant to whom she claimed to have given birth two days after last seeing Lady Douglas. After that Lady Douglas again spent some time elsewhere and when she reappeared at Blackheath in October 1804 she found that she was no longer welcome at the Princess's house. When Lady Douglas demanded an explanation from the Princess she received no reply, but a few days later two unsigned drawings arrived, addressed to Sir John and depicting his wife and Sir Sidney Smith in the act of making love. An obscene message was scrawled along the top and Lady Douglas identified the handwriting as the Princess's.[54]

Lady Douglas's chance for revenge came in 1805 when Sir John entered the service of the Duke of Sussex, brother-in-law of the Princess of Wales. Sir John told his master what his wife had heard the Princess say and Sussex in turn passed the remarks on to the Prince of Wales, and as a result in the summer of 1806 a commission of enquiry was appointed to conduct what was known as the 'Delicate Investigation' into the Princess's behaviour.

When summoned before the committee Lady Douglas affirmed she considered it her 'sacred duty' to reveal to them all she knew. She rehearsed her evidence at length and emphasized that 'independently of the Princess's confessions' she could 'swear she was pregnant in 1802'[55] a charge which, if proven and pursued to its logical conclusion, would have resulted in the Princess being convicted of high treason and executed. This aspect of the affair seems not to have bothered Lady Douglas in the slightest.

A host of lesser witnesses were then summoned to see if Lady Douglas's accusations could be verified. On the whole they could not: the Princess's wardrobe woman, Charlotte Sander, declared for example, 'I am sure the Princess was not pregnant; being her dresser I must have seen if she was', and she insisted that her mistress had been in perfect health throughout the autumn of 1802. After sustained enquiries the commissioners concluded that the child Lady Douglas had seen with the Princess was the baby of a Deptford dock labourer and his wife, and that Caroline was merely his adoptive mother.

Nevertheless Caroline did not emerge from the investigation with her reputation untarnished. The evidence of the Honorable Hester Lisle, a sister of the Earl of Cholmondley, who had been a Bedchamber woman to the Princess ever since the latter's arrival in England, was in some respects particularly damning, for though she insisted that the Princess could not have been 'far advanced in pregnancy without my knowing it' her description of Caroline's conduct towards Captain Manby, a naval officer who had been a regular visitor to Blackheath, caused raised eyebrows on the commission. According to Mrs Lisle the Princess 'behaved to him only as any woman would who likes flirting. I should not have thought any married woman would have behaved properly, who should have behaved as Her Royal Highness did to Captain Manby.' It was evidence such as this that led the commissioners to declare that though the graver charges levelled against the Princess were groundless, on some occasions her conduct had been 'such as must, especially considered her exalted rank and station, necessarily give occasion to very unfavourable interpretations'.[56]

Because of this criticism, for the time being the King refused to receive his daughter-in-law at court, but Caroline now made a belated effort to retrieve the reputation that she had so thoughtlessly cast away. As soon as she was shown the evidence against her, she set out to overturn it, writing to the King in August 1806 to point out that Mrs Lisle could not consider her guilty of serious misbehaviour as she still remained as one of her Bedchamber women. She suggested that the commissioners had drawn unwarranted conclusions from Mrs Lisle's evidence, which had been given under duress and which Mrs Lisle herself had not intended to be particularly incriminating. Her most serious strictures, however, were reserved for Lady Douglas: 'Your Majesty', she observed, 'will have an excellent portraiture of the true female delicacy and purity of my Lady Douglas's mind and character, when you will observe that she seems insensible that . . . she degrades herself by her testimony against me.' The Princess observed that on her own admission Lady Douglas had not disowned her after she supposedly confessed to being an adulteress, 'but was contented to live in familiarity with a woman who, if Lady Douglas's evidence of me is true, was a most low, vulgar and profligate disgrace to her sex'. She went so far as to insist that Lady Douglas be prosecuted for perjury[57] but no action was in fact taken against her and the Princess had to content herself with the fact that in March 1807 the Government recommended that the King should again receive his daughter-in-law at court. The Princess was allotted apartments at Kensington Palace so that she could divide her time between London and Blackheath and it seemed that she would be able to start life afresh.

Unfortunately her experiences had done nothing to check her exhibitionist tendencies. Her behaviour continued eccentric, to say the least, and her harassed ladies lived in constant dread of further scandals. The offer of a post in the Princess's household came to be regarded as a dubious honour, and when in December 1807 Caroline invited Lady Glenbervie to become Mistress of the Robes in place of the Marchioness of Townshend (who had resigned on the death of her husband) Lord Glenbervie had the gravest reservations about the appointment. In his diary he noted, 'The salary we understand is £500 and the situation (in times less revolutionary) highly respectable', but he admitted that with the Princess as her mistress he considered it likely that his wife would be subjected to a good deal of embarrassment in the course of her duties.[58]

Those duties were moreover substantial. Since the Delicate Investigation the Princess had resumed the habit of always having a Bedchamber lady in residence, which automatically made the job more demanding, particularly since the Countess of Carnarvon refused to fit in with the new arrangements and the others had to do her stint for her. Lord Glenbervie recorded in precise detail the timetable that his wife was expected to follow:

> The present arrangement for the attendance on Her Royal Highness is Lady Glenbervie three months, viz from October 9 to November 9, from February 9 to March 9, and from June 9 to July 9. She is succeeded on November 9, March 9 and July 9 by her sister Lady Charlotte Lindsay, who is succeeded in like manner by Lady Charlotte Campbell and she by the honourable Mrs Lisle who though one of the Bedchamber Women only (it being a rule that the Ladies must be *titrées*), attends her three months in the place of Lady Carnarvon. They have an apartment both at Kensington and Blackheath and attend the Princess everywhere, at dinner and supper, public places, court, airing, etc. Strictly the Princess's full establishment consists of four Women of the Bedchamber as well as four Ladies. Each of them ought to reside in their turns for a month at a time, and the Ladies never, but only to attend her Royal Highness in public. But from reasons of economy, two of the places have been left vacant and as the Prince has insisted that she should always have one of the ladies with her in public and she goes almost every night to the play or the opera she has by degrees established that the ladies are to reside with her in the manner I have described. This makes the situation much more troublesome than the place of Lady of the Bedchamber to the Queen.[59]

The heavy work schedule imposed on Caroline's ladies was by no means the worst of their worries. The trouble was that the Princess still took a childish delight in shocking them, ignoring the fact that it was in her own best interests to conform to their standards of behaviour. Lady Charlotte Campbell, who entered the Princess's service in 1809, recorded how Caroline would often request one of her ladies to accompany her on a walk in Kensington Gardens, and then 'all of a sudden she will bolt out at one of the smaller gates and walk all over Bayswater . . . at the risk of being insulted or, if known, mobbed – enjoying all the while the terror of the unfortunate attendant who may be destined to walk after her'. Often the ladies found themselves in decidedly unsavoury company, for over the years the Princess had become still less discriminating in her choice of dinner guests and the conversation at her table was on occasion such as 'made Lady Glenbervie hang down her head and look grave'. Furthermore, despite the trouble she had brought on herself by her thoughtless prattle, the Princess still occasionally let fall some startling allusion designed to transfix all present. Lady Glenbervie was thrown into confusion one evening when the Princess, gazing at the adopted child whose origins had occasioned so much controversy during the Delicate Investigation, remarked dreamily that it was a long time since she had been brought to bed with him. Though 'prepared . . . for many strange things', Lady Glenbervie 'was astonished and confounded beyond measure', much to the amusement of the Princess, who was delighted that she could still create such an effect with her random remarks.[60]

Despite the arduous nature of the job, the rewards of entering the Princess's service were disproportionately small. Caroline was irregular in the payment of her ladies' salaries, grumbling incessantly about her own financial situation without concerning herself about their pecuniary difficulties. Furthermore she was not only an exacting mistress, she was also a disloyal one, who made spiteful comments about her servants the moment their backs were turned. For twelve years the Marchioness of Townshend served Caroline devotedly as Mistress of the Robes, and she had given her much support during the Delicate Investigation, writing her letters of encouragement and proclaiming her belief in her innocence, yet after she had resigned in 1807 the Princess repaid her by putting it about that the Marchioness was having an affair with her stepdaughter's husband.[61] Though she complained that she was herself the victim of malicious tongues, the Princess had few reservations about ruining the reputations of others.

In February 1811 the Prince of Wales had become Prince Regent and from that point onwards he was in a better position to act against his wife. Outraged by her behaviour, in early 1813 he decided to reopen the Delicate Investigation, hoping that this time the charges against the Princess could be made to stick. As before he pinned his hopes mainly on the evidence of Lady Douglas, considering that the commissioners' previous rejection of her testimony had in no way discredited her, and while the investigation was in progress it was noted that Sir John and his lady were 'constantly with the inhabitants of Carlton House'.[62] Nevertheless, to the disappointment of the Regent, nothing further could be proved against the Princess, who now retaliated against her husband by writing to the Speaker of the House of Commons demanding that the findings of the enquiry be made public. The resultant parliamentary debate was a triumph for Caroline and a disaster for Lady Douglas.

Almost to a man the House of Commons rose in defence of this royal damsel in distress. Lord Castlereagh referred to Sir John and his wife as 'profligate persons' while Mr Whitbread denounced 'the obscene and disgusting depositions of Lady Douglas' and demanded that she be prosecuted for perjury. The debate excited great interest in the public and a wave of sympathy for Caroline swept the nation. Scores of meetings were held up and down the country in support of the Princess and at one such gathering her supporter Alderman Wood described the deposition of Lady Douglas as 'the ravings of a disordered imagination, transferring its own impure suggestions to the bosom of innocence'. Sir John and Lady Douglas did their best to weather the storm, declaring bravely that they stood by their earlier statements, but it was fortunate for them that they had not given evidence against the Princess in a court of law and that therefore it was impracticable to try them for perjury. Nevertheless they did not escape unscathed. Sir John was suspended from his post in the Duke of Sussex's household and expelled from his masonic lodge and thenceforth, in the satisfied words of one of the Princess's supporters, he and his wife 'hid their diminished heads no one knew where'.[63]

As it happened, this was not entirely accurate. In March 1814 Sir John died, his health broken down by his years on campaign abroad, but the Prince of Wales did not forget his widow. As late as 1823 he was still awarding her an annual pension of £200 although, presumably because of fears of public outcry, it was paid in the name of Miss Jeffreys.[64] Evidently the Prince still felt grateful to Lady Douglas for her role in the Delicate Investigation and only regretted that her revelations had commanded little credence elsewhere.

Although Caroline had emerged from the enquiry of 1813 as the heroine of the hour she found that her situation had not materially improved, and as her position in England remained ambiguous she determined to go abroad. In August 1814 she embarked for the Continent taking in her train Lady Charlotte Lindsay and Lady Elizabeth Forbes, a new addition to her household who swiftly quarrelled with the Princess and returned to England. Before long Lady Charlotte also proved unequal to the strain of accompanying Caroline on her peregrinations and at the end of March 1815 she too went home, leaving her mistress 'considerably annoyed at being forsaken by all her English attendants'. Fortunately, however, Lady Charlotte Campbell happened to be holidaying at Nice with her family and in response to an urgent appeal from the Princess she gallantly set off to join her at Genoa. Yet even the faithful Lady Charlotte proved unable to endure for long the Princess's gipsy-like existence. Once free of England Caroline's dress, deportment and choice of associates had become ever more outlandish, and in general her lifestyle was not one to which a well brought-up Englishwoman could easily adapt. As Lady Charlotte lamented, the Princess found it impossible to keep a good class of person about her 'for she is unreasonable in her demands on their services and leads so desultory a life and oftentimes one so wholly unfitting her dignity as a woman (much more as Princess of Wales) that those most attached to her can least bear to witness her downfall'. After a few months Lady Charlotte herself buckled under the strain and handed in her resignation.

From then on the Princess had to scrabble among the dregs of society to provide herself with servants. In December 1815 one observer caught a glimpse of her at a small Italian village surrounded by 'a low set of people. Many of the women were dressed up like itinerant show players and altogether looked unfit to be her attendants.' The Princess, however, was delighted by her new associates. Her principal lady was the Countess Oldi, the sister of Bartolomeo Pergami, a former quartermaster in the Italian army who had become Caroline's courier and also possibly her lover. The Princess claimed that Countess Oldi was a noblewoman who had fallen on hard times and had had to look for work, but Lady Charlotte Campbell, who still kept an eye on her former mistress, was not impressed: 'The Oldi is nobody, even by marriage, and before that she was a servant's sister of the lowest order', she proclaimed in disgust.[65] At least Countess Oldi was both placid and amiable, if somewhat bemused that the wheel of fortune had spun her into the orbit of this eccentric royal personage, but undoubtedly both she and her brother were out to feather their nests at the Princess's expense.

Countess Oldi remained with Caroline as the latter embarked on the final phase of her tragicomic life. On 29 January 1820 poor mad King George, for so long detached from reality, finally lost his grip on life itself, and now that her husband was on the throne Caroline determined to return to England to stake her claim as Queen Consort. Countess Oldi was with the new Queen when she landed at Dover on 6 June but Caroline soon discovered that there were not many respectable English ladies who were prepared to rally to her cause. Lady Charlotte Lindsay, whom Caroline regarded as one of her greatest friends in England, fled to the country on hearing of the Queen's return, for she knew that she could not avoid visiting her former mistress if she remained in London, but as Caroline's conduct had been 'for some time . . . notoriously disgraceful in the eyes of all Europe', she feared that by doing so she would compromise her own reputation.[66]

Deserted by those that she had thought she could depend on, Caroline was grateful that she at least still had the support of Lady Anne Hamilton. The daughter of the Duke of Hamilton, Lady Anne was a lanky spinster who had been in Caroline's service for a couple of years prior to the Princess's departure abroad, but at that time her mistress had despised her. She was a woman who had the knack of being always in the way without ever being of use, and Caroline had complained that though Lady Anne undoubtedly had 'many good qualities', she also had 'a love of meddling, prying and managing and a want of tact' that nearly drove her mad. As Lady Anne was both romantically inclined and yet absurdly virginal Caroline had nick-named her Joan of Arc, and had been relieved to see the back of her when she set out for the Continent in 1814.[67] Six years later, however, Caroline was delighted that anyone comparatively respectable should be prepared to add even the tiniest dash of class to her bizarre travelling circus and when on her own initiative Lady Anne had joined her abroad and suggested that she should accompany her to England, Caroline had accepted the offer with pleasure.

Certainly Caroline needed all the support she could get, for her husband had been kept informed of her movements while abroad and believed he had enough evidence to obtain a divorce from her. Accordingly in July 1820 the Government introduced in the House of Lords a Bill of Pains and Penalties against the Queen which, if passed, would have resulted in the dissolution of her marriage and would have prevented her from again taking up residence within the British Isles. This Caroline determined to fight and in the circumstances she could not allow Lady Charlotte Lindsay to disown her completely. In August the horrified Lady Charlotte was informed by Caroline's solicitor that at the forthcoming hearing she would be called to give evidence in the Queen's favour. Lady Charlotte pleaded that her testimony 'could be of little consequence, I had been so short a time with the Queen upon the Continent and had quitted her so long ago', but the solicitor insisted that she must appear, 'If it were only to show that I knew nothing against her.' She was left with no choice but to 'submit to this most disagreeable exhibition', consoling herself with the thought that 'Thank Heaven!' I do not from my own personal knowledge know anything that might criminate the Queen.'[68]

On 5 October Lady Charlotte was called to the witness stand, and having testified in Caroline's favour was subjected to a merciless cross-examination by the Solicitor General, who questioned her 'in as harsh a manner as if he had been endeavouring to bring out the confession of a murderer at the Old Bailey'. Nevertheless Lady Charlotte acquitted herself well, and though at one moment she burst into tears she soon collected herself and thereafter 'did not . . . flinch or falter'. When Lady Charlotte stepped down after two days in the witness box she felt confident that her evidence had been received with 'universal satisfaction' but she was wrong, for the King reacted by writing furiously to the Duke of York, 'Though I have lived a good many years in this world, still I never thought that I should have lived to witness so much prevarication, so much lying and so much wilful and convenient forgetfulness as I am sorry to say . . . Lady Charlotte Lindsay . . . displayed.'[69] Lady Charlotte herself was merely relieved that her ordeal had ended before she committed some major gaffe, and without even waiting for the trial to finish she slipped off to Italy for a well-deserved holiday.

Even in the House of Lords support for the Bill of Pains and Penalties was so limited that in November the Government had perforce to abandon it, but though the decision was highly popular with the public it earned Caroline few well-born adherents. The Countess Oldi still lingered in England, squabbling with Lady Anne Hamilton, of whom she was jealous but for whose continued support Caroline felt deeply grateful. As the Queen sadly observed, 'Poor Joan of Arc has really proved herself true to the name I used to give her *pour me moquer d'elle*. She has stayed with me through it all, and God he knows that was no small trial. Poor Soul! I hope he will reward her for her courage.'[70]

As it turned out, Lady Anne did not have to remain at her post for much longer. On 30 July 1821 Caroline was taken ill with inflammation of the bowels and a week later she died. Lady Anne was with her to the last but she was almost alone in genuinely mourning her mistress. The King made no attempt to disguise his joy and thenceforth he sought to sweep from his life anything that reminded him of his detested spouse. No one who had worked for Caroline was found alternative employment within the households of surviving members of the royal family, nor were they awarded pensions, despite the fact that after the Queen's death her legal adviser had written to the Prime Minister requesting that her principal servants 'will not be deemed unworthy of the protection which has been accorded to persons similarly circumstanced on the death of her late Majesty's royal predecessors'.[71]

Caroline had been predeceased by her daughter, and as old Queen Charlotte died on 17 November 1818 for the next decade there were few employment opportunities for ladies at the English royal court. The only unofficial position available, that of *maîtresse en titre* to the King, was occupied by Elizabeth, Marchioness of Conyngham, a corpulent vulgarian whose affections the King retained by dint of a heavy outlay on jewellery and gifts. But though he continued to see her till his death, towards the end of his reign he became more and more of a recluse, shunning public appearances and electing to spend the majority of his time at Windsor in the company of a few select friends. The social life of the court suffered accordingly and it would take George's brother William, who succeeded him as King in June 1830, to restore a semblance of gaiety to its proceedings.

The new King was a bluff former sailor who loved entertaining, and under his auspices the court lost much of its formality, although fortunately his wife Adelaide was on hand to ensure that standards did not deteriorate too much. Though she was enlightened enough to employ the Catholic Lady Bedingfield as a woman of the Bedchamber, Adelaide was in other respects the most strait-laced of women, and was accordingly determined to preside over a decorous court. She refused to receive the Duchess of St Albans, who had formerly earned her living on the stage (although considering the fact that the court was thronged with William's illegitimate children by his liaison with the actress Dorothy Jordan it would have perhaps been more sensible to have overlooked the Duchess's antecedents) and banned ladies from coming *décolletée* to her parties, in marked contrast to George IV, who had made low necklines virtually compulsory whenever he entertained. There were of course those who still elected to believe that the court was a sink of iniquity, and Adelaide was annoyed by persistent rumours that suggested that the King had fathered a child on one of her maids of honour.[72] Considering the King's past record it was perhaps not surprising that such stories thrived, and it was understandable that it was not until his niece Victoria ascended the throne that the court became once again a byword for respectability.

The Court of Queen Victoria

'Duty and Affection for Me'

At six o'clock in the morning of 20 June 1837 the late King's niece, Victoria, was awoken to be informed that she was now Queen of England. Though only eighteen years old and diminutive in stature, the new Queen was already a character to be reckoned with, and she wasted no time in turning her back on a past which had not been happy. During her adolescence she had become estranged from her widowed mother, the Duchess of Kent, whose chief adviser was an arrogant Irish upstart named Sir John Conroy. Conroy had hoped that when Victoria became Queen he and the Duchess would rule England through her, but though they had bullied and browbeaten the Princess in an effort to keep her subject to their will they had not been successful, and now that Victoria was Queen she was in a position to resist them in earnest. For the sake of appearances Victoria agreed that her mother should continue to reside with her but Sir John was not offered a new post, and had to make do with his old position of Comptroller of the Duchess of Kent's household. The Queen also made it clear that he would not be welcome at court but unfortunately he continued to hover in the background, a malignant puppeteer who had lost control of the strings of power but who would now do his best to entangle them.

When struggling for her independence from the Duchess and Sir John, Princess Victoria's principal ally had been her German governess, Baroness Lehzen. The daughter of a Lutheran churchman in Hanover, Louise Lehzen had come to England in 1819 to act as governess to Victoria's half-sister, the Princess Feodore. In 1824, however, she had been promoted to become governess to the five-year-old Princess Victoria, precisely because the Duchess and Conroy considered her to be too much of a nonentity to represent a threat to their plans for Victoria's future. In this they seriously under-estimated her. Pale and spindly, with a touch of the absurd about her, Lehzen nevertheless had latent powers of self-assertion. She lived for Victoria and was fiercely protective towards her, and though the Duchess and Conroy soon realized that it was she who instilled in the Princess the spirit to resist their encroachments, she defeated their every effort to dislodge her from her post. Now her charge was Queen and Lehzen reaped her reward. She declined an official position in the royal household but the Queen noted fondly in her journal, 'My *dear* Lehzen will ALWAYS remain with me as my friend',[1] and in the next few years the Baroness was to act as Victoria's unofficial Private Secretary, interesting herself in matters of household management, assisting with the Queen's personal correspondence, and in general establishing herself as a personage of some importance at court.

Freed from the oppressive yoke of the Duchess and Sir John, the Queen threw herself with animation into her new life. She was enchanted with her Whig Prime Minister, the urbane and charming Lord Melbourne, and deferred to his advice about household appointments. Unhappily almost all the ladies that Melbourne selected for her attendants were either married or related to the Whig grandees who comprised his Government, and this arrangement put in jeopardy the understanding that the Sovereign should be an impartial Head of State who was above the pull of party politics. The Mistress of the Robes was the Duchess of Sutherland, a noted beauty whose ardent social conscience did not preclude her from being among the foremost hostesses of her day, but who was also the sister of Lord Morpeth, a Cabinet Minister. Similarly the Marchioness of Tavistock, a senior lady of the Bedchamber, was the niece by marriage of the Leader of the House of Commons and her colleague Lady Normanby was the wife of the current Lord-Lieutenant of Ireland. This imbalance in the Queen's household did not pass without com-ment. In the *Quarterly Review* of July 1837 the Tory columnist John Wilson inveighed sternly against it, declaring 'It is neither constitu-tional in principle nor convenient in practice that the sovereign should be *enclosed* within the *circumvallation* of any particular *set.*' To the Queen such criticism seemed absurd. When Lord Melbourne reported to her that there had been complaints about the Whig bias of her ladies she noted simply in her journal, 'This amused me much.'[2] At this stage of her life indeed, the Queen was frequently disposed to look upon the funny side of things.

There was, however, one cloud on her horizon. The Queen

remained on cool terms with her mother and the unwanted Duchess flitted forlornly about the Palace, powerless to express her resentment at being excluded from her daughter's confidence. Victoria's feeling of ill-will soon communicated itself to her attendants with the result that there was an undercurrent of friction in the relations between the Queen's own household and that of the Duchess of Kent. It was later said that Baroness Lehzen's hatred for the Duchess was 'no secret', and the Queen and her ladies also held the Duchess's lady of the Bedchamber, Lady Flora Hastings, in marked distrust. Lady Flora was a sharp-featured spinster who had entered the Duchess's service in 1834, when she was twenty-eight. At the time the Duchess had hoped that she would be a congenial companion for her daughter but Victoria had taken against her, not least because she regarded Lady Flora as a supporter of Sir John Conroy. Now the Queen suspected that Lady Flora was still secretly working against her on behalf of the Duchess and Sir John and she told Lord Melbourne as much, informing him that Lady Flora was 'an amazing *spy* who would repeat everything she heard and that he better take care of what he said before her'. Both she and her Prime Minister 'agreed it was a very disagreeable thing having her in the house'.[3]

Many of the Queen's ladies shared her antagonism to Lady Flora. Mary Davys, the Queen's resident woman of the Bedchamber, declared, 'Lady Flora is civil to us all but restrained and uncommunicative; there will be no *friendship* with her'. Hostility to Lady Flora was increased by the knowledge that she was still a crony of Conroy's, now the bogeyman of the court, and Mary Davys asserted that even had Lady Flora asked her to visit her in her private sitting room she would not have accepted as 'I should be afraid of meeting *Sir John* who is there a good deal'.[4] The Queen's ladies collectively endowed Lady Flora with the contemptuous nickname of 'Scotty', and though in later life all things associated with Scotland held pleasant connotations for the Queen, at the time this was far from the case.

In early 1839, the Queen's dislike of Lady Flora entered a new and far more dangerous phase. Lady Flora had spent the Christmas holidays in Scotland, but on 10 January 1839 she returned to court, having travelled south in a post-chaise shared with Sir John Conroy. For the past month she had not been feeling well and on the day of her return she had a consultation with the court doctor, Sir James Clark. The symptoms she complained of were a tendency to biliousness and a pain low on the left side and Clark noted also that her abdomen was considerably enlarged. To him it seemed possible that Lady Flora was pregnant but as yet he kept his suspicions to himself, prescribed 'some very simple remedies', and awaited developments.[5]

Two days after Lady Flora's return the Queen and Lehzen detected the strange alteration in her figure. At this stage they too passed no comment, but the wretched woman's distended belly did not go unnoticed elsewhere. By the end of the month all the female part of the court were aware of it, and when at the end of January the Marchioness of Tavistock came into waiting 'she found the ladies all in a hubbub' and demanding that she, as senior lady of the Bedchamber, 'take some steps to protect their purity from this contamination'. The Marchioness of Tavistock was esteemed by her husband as 'the most discreet of ladies' but on this occasion she failed to live up to her reputation. The most prudent course she could have adopted would have been to have taken the matter up with either Lady Flora or the Duchess of Kent, but she did neither. The Marchioness subsequently declared that she had wished to speak to Lady Flora about it 'but circumstances occurred which prevented my carrying this wish into effect', a mysterious statement on which she refused to enlarge. Furthermore, 'not being on good terms with the Duchess', the Queen did not wish her mother to be brought into the matter at this stage. Instead, after consultation with the Baroness, and 'with Lehzen's concurrence', on 2 February Lady Tavistock undertook the 'painful duty' of communicating the suspicions concerning Lady Flora to Lord Melbourne.[6]

Melbourne reacted somewhat laconically, for he only told Lady Tavistock that he 'desired the ladies of the court to be quiet' but he took the matter seriously enough to summon Clark and ask him his opinion of Lady Flora's condition. Clark replied that though on the whole he deprecated gossip he had to admit 'that the appearance of Lady Flora in some degree substantiated' it. For the moment, however, both he and Melbourne agreed that 'no step should be taken in the matter' and that was the line the Prime Minister adopted when he discussed the matter with the Queen later that day, urging her to 'remain quite quiet'. The Queen agreed, but she felt sure that she had already correctly identified Lady Flora's indisposition and she did not hesitate to fix the blame on Conroy. 'We have no doubt that she is – to use the plain words – *with child*!' she confided in outrage to her diary, '. . . the horrid cause of all this is that Monster and Demon incarnate whose name I forbear to mention' – although she left her readers in little doubt as to whom she referred to.[7]

As a sophisticated man of the world Melbourne should have fore-seen that it would not be easy to keep gossip at court under control. Indeed, when another of the Queen's Bedchamber ladies, Lady Portman, came into waiting in mid-February, she found the court still seething with rumours. Into this maelstrom of scandal Lady Portman plunged with zest. She discussed the matter with the Queen and with Sir James Clark, whose view of the case convinced her 'that it was necessary for the honour of the court and for the character of Lady Flora Hastings that all doubt should be removed on the subject'. Accordingly, on 16 February, Clark was told that he should confront Lady Flora in as tactful a manner as possible by enquiring whether she was secretly married.[8]

Clark had already made one attempt to clear up the mystery by asking Lady Flora if he could examine her 'with her stays removed' but she had refused, and now he felt the time had come to be more direct. When he put his suggestion to Lady Flora she vehemently denied it, upon which, according to her, Clark 'became violent and coarse and even attempted to browbeat me'. In justification Lady Flora told him that of late her swelling had subsided, but Clark brushed these assurances aside, bluntly informing her 'that nothing but a medical examination could satisfy the ladies of the palace, so deeply were their suspicions rooted'. Lady Flora asked for time to consider 'this most revolting proposal' but her apparent anxiety for delay only served to convince Clark that his suspicions were well founded.[9]

Thereupon Lady Flora was told that she would not be admitted to the Queen's presence until her name had been cleared. The Duchess of Kent was informed of this decision by Clark and Lady Portman and the latter, in Lady Flora's words, 'took the opportunity of distinctly expressing her conviction of my guilt'. Up till then, the Duchess had been ignorant of the aspersions against Lady Flora and she did not believe them now. She discharged on the spot Sir James Clark, who hitherto had been her physician as well as the Queen's, and said she would never receive Lady Portman again. Furthermore she declared that if Lady Flora was debarred from court she too would absent herself from it.

Against the advice of the Duchess Lady Flora decided the next day that she would, after all, submit to a medical examination. This was carried out by Sir James Clark and another doctor of her choice and was witnessed by Lady Portman and Lady Flora's maid, who later claimed that Lady Portman's behaviour on this occasion was 'unnecessarily abrupt, unfeeling and indelicate'. Nevertheless, it seemed that Lady Flora had emerged triumphant from her ordeal, for the officiating doctors subsequently issued her with a certificate to the effect that 'there are no grounds for suspicion that pregnancy does exist, or ever did exist'.[10]

An apology to Lady Flora was evidently in order. That evening Lady Portman conveyed to her the Queen's regret at what had passed and said that Victoria was anxious to see her as soon as possible. She also deprecated her own role in the affair, admitting that 'perhaps no one had been so inveterate' against Lady Flora as she herself. Lady Flora gave her her hand 'in token of forgiveness', and though her health was not up to a meeting with the Queen until 23 February, on that occasion the encounter passed off well enough. The Queen expressed her contrition and Lady Flora assured her that for the sake of the Duchess of Kent 'she would suppress every wounded feeling'.[11] It seemed that the episode had come to a satisfactory conclusion.

Unfortunately a variety of circumstances contrived to ensure that the issue remained open. In the first place the Queen proved reluctant to make more generous reparation to Lady Flora because she felt that a question-mark still hung over her reputation. Shortly after the examination of Lady Flora the two doctors involved informed Melbourne that they still entertained private doubts as to her condition. The womb was undeniably enlarged, and though it was also undeniable that Lady Flora was technically a virgin it was not unknown for women to become pregnant without full intercourse having taken place. Melbourne had passed the substance of this on to the Queen, who in consequence had reverted to the private belief that Lady Flora was guilty of misconduct.[12]

In the second place an unholy alliance of troublemakers now aligned themselves with Lady Flora. A few of the more extreme Tories scented here an opportunity to discredit Melbourne's Whig Government and did their best to ensure that the scandal did not die down. Sir John Conroy too hoped to make capital out of the incident, and according to one observer it was he who subsequently incited 'Lady Flora to *jeter feu et flamme*'.[13] Besides this, the Duchess of Kent still felt aggrieved, believing that her daughter had hoped to discredit her by casting a slur on Lady Flora's integrity. Finally, it soon emerged that Lady Flora herself was by no means disposed to be so conciliatory as had originally appeared.

On 19 February, four days before her interview with the Queen, Lady Flora had written an account of her troubles to her brother, the second Marquis of Hastings, an excitable individual whose brain at the time was more than ordinarily enfevered by an attack of influenza. The letter had reached him a day later, and despite his indisposition the Marquis had rushed up to London, thirsting for vengeance. He had obtained an interview with Lord Melbourne, who had disclaimed responsibility, blaming the gossip of the ladies for the scandal, but though he urged Hastings to take no further action for the sake of the Queen, the Marquis was not to be fobbed off so easily. On 26 February he wrote to Melbourne to warn him that despite the authorities' evident desire to hush up the incident, he would not rest until he had punished 'all concerned in it'. In particular he ascribed his sister's difficulties to 'that *baneful influence* which surrounds the throne', an oblique reference to the Baroness Lehzen, whom the Hastings family believed to be responsible for all Lady Flora's wrongs. In some alarm Melbourne arranged for the Marquis to have an audience with the Queen, who assured him that in future Lady Flora 'should be treated with honour and kindness' but as this left him as uncertain as ever as to who exactly had originated the rumours Hastings remained dissatisfied.[14]

Accordingly he tried a new tack. In March 1839 he wrote to Lord Portman and the Marquis of Tavistock, demanding that they find out from their wives the name of the person who had first slandered his sister and asking specifically whether Baroness Lehzen was the guilty individual. Yet again his enquiries drew a blank: the two gentlemen confined themselves to an assurance on behalf of their wives that the Baroness was not to blame, but declined to apportion guilt elsewhere.

At this stage Lady Flora's mother, the Dowager Marchioness of Hastings (whom the Queen, in an intemperate moment, once described as 'a violent and foolish old woman'), entered the fray. On 7 March 1839 she wrote to Victoria asking her 'not to suffer the inventor of such falsehoods to remain without discovery', backing this up with a plea that Sir James Clark be dismissed. For her pains she received a letter from Melbourne to the effect that he could barely bring himself even to acknowledge 'so unprecedented and objectionable' a demand, and making it plain that her request would be ignored.[15]

In the meantime Lady Flora herself had not been idle with her pen. Throughout early March she had busied herself sending her various relatives inflammatory accounts of the ill treatment she had suffered at the hands of the court. To her sister Selina she wrote that the 'horrible conspiracy' was 'evidently got up by Lehzen who has found willing tools in Ladies Tavistock and Portman' and on 8 March she sent a similar letter to her uncle by marriage, Hamilton Fitzgerald, remarking that her only consolation lay in the reflection that her name was now completely cleared.[16] However, upon further inquiry in London clubs and coffee-houses, Fitzgerald discovered that belief in Lady Flora's innocence was by no means as widespread as she had imagined, and accordingly on 28 March he sought to vindicate his niece once and for all by publishing her letter in the *Examiner*. The Queen was enraged by his presumption, and thenceforth she abandoned all pretence of sympathy for Lady Flora, having no further communication with her till the middle of June. This did nothing to appease the Hastings family and in April the Dowager Marchioness of Hastings defiantly arranged for the correspondence between her and Melbourne to be printed. In the Queen's eyes this put the Marchioness beyond hope of redemption, but by now the sympathy of the public was swinging round in favour of Lady Flora and her family.

Matters stood thus when a political crisis intervened and rendered the situation still more complicated. For some weeks parliamentary support for Lord Melbourne's administration had been dwindling, and on 7 May 1839 the Prime Minister informed the Queen that his Government must resign. Distressed enough already by the unpleasant ramifications of the Flora Hastings affair, the Queen was distraught at the prospect of losing her much loved 'Lord M'. Melbourne was uneasily aware that even more might be at stake than she realized, for in view of the Whiggish disposition of the Queen's entourage the incoming Tories might wish to embark on a wholesale purge of the household, from which not even the Queen's ladies would be exempt. As yet, however, he clung to the hope that the Opposition would take the view that the political affiliations of her ladies were of no importance and hence would not demand changes in the household that could cause unnecessary distress to the Queen. At his parting interview with Victoria, Melbourne told her, 'Your Majesty had better express your hope that none of your Majesty's household, except those who are engaged in politics, may be removed . . . I think you might ask for that.'[17] At the time, of course, no woman could be directly involved in politics and so this would have obviated the need for the Queen to part with any of her ladies. In high hopes that the Tories would prove amenable, Victoria promised to do as he suggested.

The following day, 8 May, the Queen had her first meeting with the Tory leader, Sir Robert Peel, to whom she took a violent dislike. Peel explained that as his party did not have an overall majority in Parliament he did not feel strong enough to form a Government unless the Queen was prepared to demonstrate that he had her support. Gingerly he suggested that the Queen could show her solidarity by effecting changes in the household but Victoria checked him at once, replying as Melbourne had told her to do. At this stage Sir Robert made no comment and the Queen felt confident that he would ultimately bow to her will.

That evening the Queen gave an account of what had passed to Melbourne, who warned her that if Peel was not prepared to make concessions over the retention of the ladies it would 'not do to . . . put off the negotiation upon it'. He nevertheless added that if Peel forced the issue 'you may observe that in doing so he is pressing Your Majesty more hardly than any minister ever pressed a sovereign before',[18] fighting words which convinced the Queen of the rectitude of her case and left her more reluctant than ever to yield passively to Sir Robert's proposals.

On 9 May the Queen saw Sir Robert again. The interview proceeded smoothly enough until Peel touched upon the question of the ladies, and at once the Queen was on the offensive. She described the resultant exchange in the following terms: 'I said I could *not* give up any of my ladies and never had imagined such a thing; he asked if I meant to retain *all*? *All*, I said. The Mistress of the Robes and the ladies of the Bedchamber? he asked. I replied, *all*.' The Queen assured him that she never discussed politics with her ladies and remarked that many of her Bedchamber women and maids of honour were related to Tories, but Peel replied that he was not concerned with them but rather with the Mistress of the Robes and the ladies of the Bedchamber. The Queen turned his argument neatly on its head, retorting that '*they* were of more consequence than the others and I could *not* consent and that it had never been done before'. Desperately Peel urged that it was the fact that she was Queen Regnant that made the difference but Victoria was unmoved: 'Not here, I said, and I maintained my right.'[19]

After consultation with a colleague Peel warned her that he could not assume office on such terms. The Queen was delighted, though contemptuous that he should forsake power on so flimsy an issue: 'The Ladies his only support! What an admission of weakness!' she crowed. She wasted no time before appealing to Melbourne to resume

275

office, and in the general hurry and confusion he received the impression from her that Peel had intended to deprive her of all her ladies, whereas in fact Sir Robert had contemplated the removal of no more than a few key individuals. Convinced that the Tories were being unreasonably imperious, Melbourne chivalrously responded to the Queen's appeal, summoning his colleagues to a meeting and urging them to support a new Whig Government. A few of the Whigs were hesitant at the prospect of regaining power in such exceptional circumstances, but they rallied to their leader when he read out a pathetic letter from the Queen, expressing her fears that if she consented to Peel's proposals 'she might be deprived of her friends one by one, even to her dressers, and be surrounded by spies'. It was an emotive appeal, inspired by the Queen's recollection of the pressures that she had been subjected to in her youth, and the Whigs did not fail to respond. Declaring that 'it was impossible to abandon such a Queen and such a woman' they advised her to reject Peel's ultimatum on the grounds that the removal of her ladies was 'contrary to usage and repugnant to her feelings'.[20]

By the time that Melbourne discovered, on 10 May, that Peel had not intended to replace all her Bedchamber ladies, but only a select few, it was too late to retract, especially as the Queen remained adamant that none of her ladies should go. As the excitement subsided the Whigs felt somewhat shamefaced at the way things had turned out, but the fact remained that they were back in office while the Tories were excluded from power. This curious turn of events utterly disgusted some observers: the diarist Charles Greville fulminated, 'It is a high trial of our institutions when the caprice of a girl of nineteen can overturn a great ministerial combination and when the most momentous matters of government and legislation are influenced by her pleasure about her Ladies of the Bedchamber!'[21] And indeed, on mature reflection, it became apparent to almost all protagonists in the affair that the Queen had not behaved as befitted a constitutional monarch. Her own ardent identification with Whig interests and the known loyalties of her ladies precluded her from claiming, as Queens Regnant had done in the past, that the appointment of the ladies was an apolitical matter which concerned her alone. Despite its Ruritanian overtones the Bedchamber Crisis of 1839 had serious consequences, resulting as it did in the retention in office of a minority Government that had ceased to command the respect of the House of Commons, and though the Queen's youth and inexperience should be taken into account when assessing her role in the affair, it cannot be denied that she was seriously at fault.

At the time the Queen was delighted by the outcome of the Bed-chamber Crisis and only wished that the Lady Flora Hastings affair could have been managed equally satisfactorily. Unfortunately this was not to be. Admittedly in June 1839 matters took a turn for the better when the arch-intriguer, Sir John Conroy, was prevailed upon to retire to the Continent, and his departure paved the way for a reconciliation between the Queen and her mother, but in every other respect the outlook was bleak. Throughout May and early June the Hastings family had done their best to keep the controversy alive and sympathy for Lady Flora had grown apace. In the first few months of the year Lady Flora's health had shown no improvement and the Queen's apparently callous attitude in the face of her sufferings excited great animosity, so much so, indeed, that when in June Victoria attended Ascot she was hissed by the crowd. In private the Queen still clung to the fiction that Lady Flora was about to give birth, a belief that Lord Melbourne did nothing to discourage, and it was only towards the end of the month that her scepticism finally crumbled. By that time Lady Flora was so enfeebled that not even the Queen could doubt that she was mortally ill, and on 26 June she cancelled a court ball as a token of respect and offered to come and see the dying woman. The visit took place the next day, and visual proof of Lady Flora's pitiful condition finally excited the Queen's natural compassion. In her journal she recorded, 'I found poor Lady Flora stretched on a couch looking as thin as anybody can be who is still alive; literally a skeleton, but the body *very* much swollen like a person who is with child . . . I said to her, I hoped to see her again when she was better, upon which she grasped my hand as if to say, "I shall not see you again."' This deathbed reconciliation was however to have little effect, for towards the other protagonists in this sorry affair the Hastings family remained as hostile as ever. As Lady Flora's end drew nearer a message of goodwill arrived for her from the Marquis of Tavistock, saying that his wife was suffering great distress on her account. This the Hastings family refused to deliver, Lady Flora's sister remarking tartly that if the Marchioness of Tavistock was truly in need of consolation she could do no better than to apply to the Bishop of London.[22]

On 5 July 1839 Lady Flora died. She was found to be suffering from a tumour on the liver, which had swollen to a degree that had produced abdominal protuberance. Death was inevitable, but the Marquis of Hastings did not not scruple to declare that her illness was 'much INCREASED by the anxiety of mind her wrongs produced, and which at last hurried her into an untimely grave'. Others shared his view, with the result that the scandal was not buried with Lady Flora. Throughout the summer the columns of the Press remained full of invective about her maltreatment, the Tory *Morning Post* in particular abusing the Queen 'with the most revolting virulence and indecency'. Both Lord Portman and the Marquis of Tavistock felt compelled to write to the papers complaining of the unmeasured attacks on their wives, and the unpopularity of the court reached such proportions that the citizens of Shrewsbury refused to drink a toast to their new Lord-Lieutenant, the Duke of Sutherland, because his wife was 'at the head of the Queen's female household'.[23]

Gradually, however, the tide of indignation ebbed. When, on 16 September, Hastings published yet more correspondence and documents pertaining to the affair, most people felt he had 'pushed matters too far'. Although her family still made every effort to keep Lady Flora's memory alive, interest in her waned inexorably. Lady Flora had been an amateur poetess and a year after her death her family published a collection of her verse; but significantly the anthology did not include one of her poems which contained the following lines:

> Peace to each heart that troubled
> My course of happy years
> Peace to each angry spirit
> That quenched my life in tears
> Let not the thought of vengeance
> Be mingled with regret
> Forgive my wrongs dear mother!
> Seek even to forget.[24]

These were words which the Hastings family would have done well to heed.

The Lady Flora Hastings affair was one of the most traumatic episodes in the Queen's life. At the end of June, Mary Davys reported to one Cabinet Minister that though depressed, the Queen 'bore up, with royal courage, against all the calumnies to which the Hastings affair had given rise', but the shock of Lady Flora's agonizing death, and her own consequent unpopularity, weighed on Victoria's spirits for some months. Years later any reference to Lady Flora still awakened painful memories. With the passage of time the Queen came to see the Bedchamber Crisis in a humorous perspective, cheerfully admitting in 1854 that its cause was 'entirely my own foolishness', but with the Lady Flora affair it was otherwise. In 1872 Ernest Stockmar published a biography of his father, Baron Stockmar, who had been one of the Prince Consort's chief advisers, and in it was included a brief summary of the events surrounding Lady Flora's death. The Queen was most upset: 'Why rake up that, thank God! long-buried, terrible story of Lady Flora Hastings? . . . Why rake this up?' she wrote in agitation to her eldest daughter[52]. The Hastings family would no doubt have been pleased had they known that, forty-three years after her death, Lady Flora's shade still on occasion returned to haunt the Queen.

One by-product of the Lady Flora affair was that it left the Queen with a pathological hatred of gossip. Thenceforth discretion was a quality prized above all others at court and any lady in royal service was expected to be a model of circumspection. It was forbidden to keep a diary while at court and ladies were meant to be guarded even in their correspondence, for as one maid of honour observed in 1859, 'It makes the Queen furious if she thinks anything is written about what goes on here.' On the whole these regulations were observed: when one gentleman remarked to a prospective maid of honour that in her position he would break the rules and keep a secret diary, she replied tartly, 'then whatever you were you would not be a maid of honour.' The paramount importance of reticence was urged upon new arrivals at court, one lady cautioning a niece who was about to enter royal service that it was 'really a *Christian* duty' not to gossip, 'because if once a prejudice gets into a royal head it can never be got out again to the end of time'. In 1841 Lady Ravensworth gave similar advice to her daughter, Georgiana Liddell, at the start of her court career: 'Whatever you see, hear or think must be kept to yourself', she told her. 'It is almost needless to add that in whatever concerns your royal mistress your lips should be sealed, but you must likewise repulse all vain enquiries and impertinent questions, not rudely but decidedly.'[26]

Inevitably, in some respects this exaggerated regard for secrecy was counter-productive. An utterly trivial item of news often assumed the dimensions of a State secret, and one maid of honour complained, 'The most annoying part of this life is that mere nothings are shrouded in deep mystery, and one never knows what is going to happen till a few minutes before it comes off.' Marie Mallet, who became a woman of the Bedchamber in 1895, complained bitterly of the 'deadly level of caution and dullness' that governed life at court and admitted she felt 'sorely tempted to say something outrageous in order to enjoy the consternation that would promptly ensue'.[27] Yet though at times this discouragement of idle chatter was carried too far, on the whole its effects were beneficial. As the youthful Queen had learnt to her cost, in the hot-house conditions of a court, gossip could take root and flourish with terrifying ease, maturing into a noxious growth that could threaten to overwhelm the tree of State itself. In future the plant was stifled at birth, and if in the process the most harmless information was ruthlessly suppressed, the policy was justified by the paramount importance of preserving the Queen's serenity of mind.

The aftermath of the Lady Flora affair had left the Queen irritable and low and it would take courtship and marriage to restore her to her former spirits. On 10 February 1840 she married her cousin, Prince Albert of Saxe-Coburg and settled down to a blissful domestic life with her Consort, marred occasionally by the sort of intermittent teething troubles that beset almost all marriages. At first Albert was almost completely excluded from State affairs but gradually he assumed more responsibility, and it was his judicious influence that ensured that when Lord Melbourne's Government finally fell in 1841 the transition from a Whig to a Tory administration was this time comparatively smooth.

By May 1841 it was clear that the Whigs could not cling to power much longer. Melbourne himself was anxious that this time the Queen could not be accused of shirking her constitutional responsibilities, telling her 'that she must carefully abstain from playing the part she did . . . for that nothing but the forbearance of the Tories had enabled himself and his colleagues to support Her Majesty at that time'.[28] He was worried, however, that on coming to power Peel might try to score political points by dismissing almost all the Queen's ladies, thus demonstrating that in the abortive negotiations of 1839 he had acted within his rights. This the Prince undertook to avert by dealing in advance with Peel, and accordingly, at a series of secret meetings between Sir Robert and the Prince's secretary, George Anson, a compromise was worked out worthy of the elastic traditions of the British constitution.

Peel agreed that so long as those ladies in the Queen's household who had particularly close links with the Whigs gave in their resignations, apparently spontaneously, and were then replaced by ladies who were acceptable to his party, he would not press for further changes. The ticklish question of whether it was the Queen or her ministers who had control over the appointment of her ladies thus would not arise. Sir Robert proved most accommodating, stressing that he had no wish to impose anyone objectionable upon the Queen and indicating that he would be content if the Duchess of Sutherland, the Duchess of Bedford (as the Marchioness of Tavistock had become on the death of her father-in-law in October 1839) and Lady Normanby left the household.

In May 1841 the Queen seemed in a 'calm and reasonable' frame of mind, apparently accepting that the fall of the Whigs was inevitable and that in that event some of her ladies must resign.[29] As the summer progressed, however, she came to regret that these concessions had been wrung from her and when a general election was held in July 1841, the Queen did not disguise her desire for a Whig victory which would save her the necessity of making these disagreeable sacrifices. It was a forlorn hope. The Tories were returned by a large majority and the Queen had perforce to accept with as good a grace as she could muster their conditions for taking office. The three ladies resigned and their places were filled by others of whom Peel could approve, although the Queen deliberately refrained from taking into service any ardently Tory ladies as that would have politicized her Bedchamber still further. As she explained to Peel, her policy now would be to 'choose moderate people who should not have . . . to resign in case another administration should come in, as changing was disagreeable to her'.[30] By eschewing in future controversial appointments the Queen re-established her household on an apolitical footing, although after 1841 the system evolved that whenever there was a change of Government the Queen demonstrated her confidence in her new ministers by replacing her current Mistress of the Robes with a nominee of their choice.

In 1841 the changes in the Queen's household were easier for her to bear because Peel selected as the Duchess of Sutherland's successor the Duchess of Buccleuch, whom the Queen later described as 'a dear old friend . . . whom I was always pleased to see'. Perhaps more important was the fact that there was an element of detachment in the Queen's relations with her ladies which enabled her to cope with losing them. Melbourne had commented on this in 1839, remarking that Victoria seemed to show 'no particular liking to any of the ladies', which he thought 'strange'. The Queen had replied, 'I dared not, though I was very fond of some but that I never saw a great deal of them, and never talked of anything that interested me much to them. Lady Portman, Lady Barham and Lady Normanby I was very fond of . . . Lady Tavistock I also liked . . . as she was very discreet.'[31] These were hardly very strong feelings. In 1839 the Queen's refusal to part with her ladies stemmed not so much from her devotion to them as individuals, as from her realization that by taking a stand on this issue she could retain her beloved Lord M. By 1841 Albert had weaned her of her emotional dependence on Melbourne and in consequence she took in her stride the downfall of the Whigs and the enforced changes in her household. Vexed though she was to part with some of her ladies, her irritation proved short-lived.

This was significant for though in future the Queen was on affectionate terms with many of her ladies she was always conscious of a distance between herself and them. In later life Victoria admitted to her eldest daughter that she could talk freely to 'very few' of her ladies and she expected her family to follow her example, for in 1859 the Queen's second daughter, Princess Alice, confided to a friend that she 'was not allowed to see many of Mama's ladies intimately'. Mary Bulteel, who became a maid of honour in 1853, asserted that 'the relation of the Queen and the Prince to their household always had an element of stiffness in it, and you felt that they were pretty nearly indifferent as to which maid of honour, lady-in-waiting or equerry did the work'. In her opinion indeed, the Queen was 'on more natural terms with the servants' who instinctively knew their place and would not seek to presume on her affection. When Jane, Marchioness of Ely died in June 1890, after nearly forty years in royal service, the Queen paid her the ultimate compliment of remarking 'We looked upon her as almost one of ourselves', but the 'almost' was significant.[32] In the Queen's opinion the barrier that divided royalty from lesser mortals could never be fully breached.

Thus it was that though at times the ruling that there must be a new Mistress of the Robes on each change of administration inconvenienced the Queen, on the whole it occasioned her no real distress. Ironically indeed it proved more of a problem for the politicians, who had fought for the right to have a say in the Mistress of the Robes' appointment, and in particular the Liberal* Prime Minister, Gladstone, came to regret that the matter was any concern of his. As she grew older the Queen developed a hatred of this pedantic genius and in her view one of his manifold failings was his inability to provide her with acceptable Mistresses of the Robes. During his first administration, which lasted from 1868 to 1874, there was trouble in 1870, when ill health forced the Duchess of Argyll to resign after two years as Mistress of the Robes, and the Queen rejected most of the candidates that

---

* In the course of the nineteenth century the Whig Party evolved into the Liberal Party.

Gladstone proposed should succeed her. The Duchess of Grafton was 'too delicate'; the Duchess of Cleveland 'odd and not pleasant'; while the Duchesses of Norfolk and Somerset were 'impossible'. Eventually the Queen grudgingly accepted the Duchess of Sutherland, the daughter-in-law of her first Mistress of the Robes, consoling herself that though the Duchess was 'not perhaps [a] very wise little woman' she was at least 'no stranger, which is a great thing'.[33]

This, however, was only a foretaste of what was to come. In February 1886 Gladstone formed a new Government which was committed to the policy of Home Rule for Ireland, a policy of which the Queen violently disapproved. Many members of the aristocracy shared her views and in consequence Gladstone was unable to find a suitable duchess willing to serve as Mistress of the Robes. The Duchesses of Roxburghe and St Albans both turned the post down and the Queen imperiously rejected any other suggestions that Gladstone put forward. She objected to the Duchess of Leinster because she was only an Irish duchess and therefore insufficiently grand, and anyway was 'in very bad health and has seizures'. When Gladstone then proposed to offer the job to a marchioness the Queen dismissed the idea as preposterous: 'This has never been done – in my time or Queen Adelaide's', she exploded to her son.[34]

In the end the post of Mistress of the Robes had to be left temporarily vacant. The Queen was torn between fury that she should be so ill-served and delight that no duchess could be found who was prepared to align herself with Gladstone. 'I *know* it is NOT meant out of *want of respect for me*,' she told the Prince of Wales, 'but out of a *sense* of *patriotism* . . . Still it is atrocious of Mr Gladstone . . . to expose *me* to having only half a household.'[35] The situation was only resolved to the Queen's satisfaction when in August Gladstone resigned and was replaced by the Tory Lord Salisbury.

Unfortunately the story was the same in 1892, when Gladstone formed his final administration. The Duchesses of Roxburghe and Bedford both refused to serve as Mistress of the Robes and yet again the situation was left vacant. By that time Gladstone himself was sick of the whole business, complaining that he would not have expected the Mistress of the Robes' husband to have supported all his policies and therefore he failed to understand why no one suitable was prepared to take the post.[36] When in 1841 the ministers wrested from the Queen the right to appoint the Mistress of the Robes on her own initiative they little realized that they were fashioning a rod to scourge the backs of the coming generation of politicians.

In some respects Gladstone was wrong in thinking that by the 1890s the political outlook of the Mistress of the Robes had ceased to be of relevance, for as the Queen grew older her ladies tended to have rather more to do with State affairs than had been the case earlier in the reign. When the Queen was young she scrupulously refrained from discussing administrative matters with her ladies and would have been angry if anyone had ever accused her of departing from this policy, but after Prince Albert's death the political convictions of her ladies occasionally had an insidious effect upon her own viewpoint. Admittedly it remained impossible for any lady to persuade the Queen to modify a strongly-held conviction: she was, for example, exasperated when her old friend the Duchess of Sutherland became a supporter of Gladstone, and delighted in giving sarcastic imitations of the Duchess extolling Gladstone's virtues. However, when her ladies held views which accorded with the Queen's own they were sometimes capable of subtly reinforcing her prejudices. By the mid-1870s the Queen was a fervent Tory, as were the majority of her household, a state of affairs deplored by the Queen's Private Secretary, Sir Henry Ponsonby, who was himself a Liberal. He told his wife in a letter from court in April 1873:

> There seems to be a general Tory atmospheric disturbance . . . Not a day passes without some crime being attributed to the government – some sneer uttered about them or some *denigréing* remark – most of which go to the Queen and set her against the ministers. Perhaps now it does not matter whether the Queen dislikes them or not, but I think Sir R. Peel was right in insisting that the Ladies of the Bedchamber should change with the Government. Incessant sneers or conversation against a policy always damages. I must say the Queen says as little as possible but one can't help seeing she is impressed by it.[37]

Another problem that became noticeable towards the end of the reign arose from the fact that as the Queen grew older she could do less for herself, and therefore tended to delegate to her ladies tasks which were not strictly within their province. In particular her fading eyesight made it difficult for her to read official documents and so she sometimes asked one of her ladies to do it for her, much to the horror of staid civil servants who were appalled that anyone unauthorized should have access to classified information. In 1898 Marie Mallet, who had become an extra woman of the Bedchamber three years before, reported to her husband that Sir Arthur Bigge, Assistant Private Secretary to the Queen, had been 'rather cross' with her, because the Queen had made me read some War Office box to her and he thinks it absurd that military messages should go through the ladies! But that is the natural result of having a sovereign of eighty! I am sure I wish she *would* see her gentlemen oftener. I frequently am invited to put my nose into other people's affairs and dislike it particularly, but I am sure the tendency now will be for me and my colleagues to do more and more.

Earlier that year Viscount Esher, Secretary to the Office of Works, had complained of the same thing. 'As the Queen ages she does not see her Secretaries sufficiently often', he noted in his journal, 'Her ladies read papers to her and bring down messages.' Because of the fabled discretion of the Queen's ladies, this casual arrangement did not have any serious consequences, but at the time, as Esher drily observed, it occasionally made for 'complications'.[38]

More serious was the fact that after Prince Albert's death the Queen occasionally used her favourite lady of the Bedchamber, Jane, Marchioness of Ely, as a sort of unofficial intermediary in political transactions. Admittedly, the widowed Marchioness, who had entered the Queen's service in 1851, was a most improbable *éminence grise*. Timid and overworked, she lived in terror of incurring the Queen's displeasure and was always fretting herself into 'imaginary fusses'. She was the sort of woman whom it is almost irresistible to bully and the Queen did not try to fight the temptation, denying Lady Ely permission to see her son while she was in waiting and expecting her to be on duty for long periods at a time. Nevertheless the Queen relied on her implicitly and appreciated the fact that the Marchioness was utterly devoted to her. When the Queen wished to give instructions to members of her household she rarely approached them directly, preferring to employ a third person, and it was Lady Ely who often acted as her personal messenger. The Marchioness invariably delivered these communications in a mysterious whisper, which left her listeners in some confusion as to exactly what she had intended to say,[39] but if there was reason to doubt her competence as an emissary, her trustworthiness was beyond question. It was this that led the Queen to make use of her in political dealings that verged upon intrigue.

In 1877 Russia and Turkey were at war and the Tory Government, much to the Queen's approval, adopted a pro-Turkish stance. The Liberal Opposition were enraged by this and knowing that her Private Secretary Henry Ponsonby was a Liberal sympathizer, the Queen took to bypassing him when communicating with the Tory leader Lord Beaconsfield. Instead she kept in touch with the Prime Minister via Lady Ely, who conducted a correspondence on the Queen's behalf with Monty Corry, Beaconsfield's Private Secretary. Ponsonby soon grew to be aware of this arrangement and tried to be philosophical about it, declaring that he would not have wanted to pass on the Queen's violently anti-Russian sentiments, but the Queen's habit of using this unofficial channel of communication did mean that Ponsonby was left in ignorance of various developments of which, as the Queen's Private Secretary, he should properly have been kept informed.[40]

Despite the Queen's support it was evident by the autumn of 1879 that Beaconsfield's Tory administration was tottering and the Queen was again faced with the dreaded spectre of a Liberal Government with Gladstone at its head. Determined to avert this, the Queen dispatched Jane Ely to Ponsonby, asking him to tell his Liberal friends that she would never again accept Gladstone as Prime Minister. These precautions availed her little, for Gladstone was returned to power by the general election of April 1880, but apparently undaunted the Queen again pressed Lady Ely into service, hoping that she could persuade Ponsonby to initiate on her behalf a secret correspondence with Beaconsfield. Knowing that it was quite improper for a sovereign to communicate with the Leader of the Opposition, Ponsonby indignantly refused, but the Queen nevertheless managed to make alternative arrangements which enabled her and Beaconsfield to keep in touch until the latter's death in 1881.[41]

In June 1885 the Liberals were succeeded by a Tory ministry but by the end of the year Gladstone's return to office seemed imminent and the Queen lived in dread that he would then introduce Home Rule for Ireland. In a bid to frustrate him she instructed the Marchioness of Ely to write to Liberal Members of Parliament who were known to have doubts about Home Rule, urging them to withdraw their support from Gladstone. On 22 December 1885 the Marchioness conveyed to Mr Forster Osborne the Queen's hopes that he would 'stand by the moderate, patriotic and loyal men who will not agree with the wild plans of Mr G.,' explaining that the Queen would consider it 'a real misfortune for the country and for the whole world' if Gladstone resumed power. Yet again these stratagems proved fruitless, for in February 1886 Gladstone became Prime Minister for the third time, but the Queen and her intrepid lady-in-waiting were not beaten yet, for via Lady Ely the Queen obtained advice from the Tory leader Lord Salisbury as to the best ways of combatting Gladstone's plans for Home Rule.[42]

The importance of these manoeuvres should not be exaggerated.

Although on occasion the Queen evidently hoped that through Lady Ely she could influence political developments, her tactics were rarely successful and had a minimal effect on the course of history. Nevertheless, the fact that she could even make the attempt, using Jane Ely as her willing tool, undoubtedly contravened the spirit of the constitution and was to the credit of neither Queen nor lady-in-waiting.

Prince Albert undoubtedly would not have approved of this *modus operandi* and had he survived it is unlikely that the Queen would have become involved in such underhand proceedings. Ironically enough, in the early years of his marriage Prince Albert himself had had problems with a meddlesome female at court, becoming drawn into a power struggle with his wife's old governess, Baroness Lehzen. Though the Duchess of Kent had presented no problem to the Prince, from Albert's point of view Lehzen had all the characteristics of the music-hall mother-in-law, for the Queen was always apt to think that the Baroness knew best and to defer to her judgement in preference to Albert's. Lehzen in turn was jealous of what influence the Prince did enjoy and so in the circumstances it was not surprising that the two were soon on the worst of terms. By the summer of 1841 the Prince was in a 'constant state of annoyance' at Lehzen's interference and he only refrained from insisting that the Baroness be dismissed because he knew that the Queen would never agree without 'an exciting scene'.[43]

The final showdown came in early 1842. By that time the Queen had had two children, a girl and a boy, and Albert suspected that Lehzen hoped to retain her influence over Victoria by controlling the royal nursery. In January 1842 the Queen and her husband had a violent disagreement about the upbringing of the children, which broadened into an argument about the Baroness's position at court. Harsh words were exchanged, which brought home to Victoria the depth of Albert's feelings on the subject, and once her own temper had cooled she came to see that her governess must be sacrificed for the sake of her husband. From that time Lehzen's days were numbered. Albert told her that she could not remain at court indefinitely, and realizing that she was beaten the Baroness effected a graceful retreat, slipping away from England in September 1842 to take up residence with her sister in the German town of Buckeburg. From then on she and the Queen corresponded regularly, but they never spoke to one another again, and though to the end of her life Victoria remained grateful for the way that the Baroness had stood by her in her youth, she came to resent the marital misunderstandings that had arisen on Lehzen's account. 'After I came to the throne she got to be rather trying,' the Queen wrote in 1870, 'and especially so after my marriage, but never from any evil intention, only from a mistaken view of duty and affection for me.'[44] As with many other people, the Queen's childhood ties had been loosened by her marriage, and by tugging at them too hard Lehzen had only succeeded in undoing them altogether.

Having rid himself of Lehzen, the Prince set about reorganizing the court to his own liking. Nowadays the word 'Victorian' has come to be synonymous with priggishness but, when young, Queen Victoria was much more easygoing than her husband. Albert was known to be 'extremely strait-laced and a great stickler for morality' whereas the Queen initially 'was rather the other way', taking a dislike to one lady because of the 'odour of sanctity' that surrounded her. That, however, was the aroma that the Prince desired should permeate the court and his will prevailed, for as an obedient wife the Queen soon joined forces with him to stamp out the old lax ways. On first ascending the throne the Queen had had some difficulty keeping her maids of honour in order but now they were subjected to strict discipline and at Windsor a 'horrid new set of rules' was instituted, forbidding them to leave the Castle before lunch, or to walk in the afternoons unchaperoned. Gentlemen callers, including even the girls' brothers, had to be entertained in a special waiting room downstairs rather than in the maids' private sitting rooms. The maids bemoaned 'the tyranny which is exercised over us' and complained that Windsor felt 'like a prison' but Prince Albert considered the new system to be a great improvement.[45]

Under his auspices, too, steps were taken to tighten up the procedures governing admissions to royal Drawing Rooms, and in future no lady could be presented to the Queen if there was any doubt as to her reputation. This rule was rigidly adhered to, as Lord Derby found in 1852, when he asked the Queen to reconsider the case of one seventy-year-old woman who in extreme youth had run off with a schoolboy lover. The couple had since married and lived blamelessly together for decades but the Queen insisted that 'it would not do to receive her now at court . . . It was a principle at court not to receive ladies whose characters are under a stigma.'[46]

Those who gained entry to the Drawing Rooms must often have wondered if it was worth it, for even the most charitably disposed observer once admitted that they were always 'rather a trial'. In 1874 *The Times* even published some anonymous letters complaining that ladies should not be subjected to the ordeal of standing for hours in stuffy and congested rooms in the often unfulfilled hope of catching a glimpse of the Queen. In one letter 'a mother' lamented that her two daughters had returned from a Drawing Room, 'Pale and exhausted, with their dresses torn and spoilt, and one of them has been laid up with a severe headache ever since.' The Queen, however, was not prepared to change the arrangements, brushing aside a suggestion that in future refreshments should be provided for the ladies with the crisp retort 'that it would cause delay and turn a Drawing Room into a party'.[47]

When Prince Albert had first introduced his high-minded ideas at court not everyone had been pleased. Lord Melbourne in particular was wont to grumble 'This damned morality would undo us all', and certainly it was nearly the undoing of Lord Palmerston, Foreign Secretary in successive Whig Governments. Palmerston, a notorious womanizer, had been Foreign Secretary when Victoria ascended the throne and at first the Queen had succumbed to his charm, pronouncing him 'very agreeable and amusing'. Soon afterwards, however, Palmerston had spoilt this initial good impression when during a stay at Windsor he had forced his way into the bedroom of Mrs Brand, a Bedchamber woman of the Queen, and attempted to seduce her. The attempt failed dismally as Mrs Brand was unsporting enough to raise the alarm, with the result that a report of the outrage soon reached the Queen's ears. She was horrified, and though at the time Melbourne managed to smooth the matter over, the incident was to have serious repercussions years later. After her marriage the Queen told her husband of Palmerston's misdemeanour, and he was shocked beyond measure, considering that anyone capable of such a 'fiendish scheme' was automatically unfitted for high offce. Even a decade after the event his objections to Palmerston on this score had not been overcome and the Queen and the Prince's ingrained hostility was such that when the Prime Minister dismissed Palmerston from the position of Foreign Secretary in 1851, they were delighted.[48]

The cloistered atmosphere of the court ensured that life there was far from exciting, much to the disgust of some of the younger members of the household. One maid of honour grumbled in 1849, 'the dullness of our evenings is a thing impossible to describe', while another put it rather more tactfully when she remarked 'Everything else changes, but the life here never does and is always exactly the same from day to day and year to year.' Nor were the duties of the ladies-in-waiting so challenging as to distract them from the monotony of their existence. When in waiting the ladies of the Bedchamber were expected to chaperone the maids of honour and to entertain any visitors who might be staying with the Queen. The maids of honour helped to look after guests, and as the Queen frequently had foreigners to stay fluency in both German and French was an essential qualification for a court career. In the afternoons the maids had to wait in to see if the Queen wished to be accompanied on her afternoon drive, and only if the Queen remembered to send word that she would not be requiring them that day were they free to amuse themselves as they pleased. On some evenings the Queen dined in private with her husband, but in general her ladies were invited to eat with her, and after dinner one of the maids either entertained the company with a song or played on the piano. For novices this could be something of a trial: when Georgiana Liddell first performed at court the Queen noticed that she had omitted a 'shake' or trill that normally came at the end of the song. Immediately she asked the girl's sister, 'Does not your sister shake, Lady Normanby?' only to be told, 'Oh yes, Ma'am, she is shaking all over.' As the girls gained confidence, however, these recitals seemed less of an ordeal and after a year at court Georgiana could declare 'I always like playing and singing with her Majesty.'[49]

Of the eight maids of honour, two were always on duty, each maid spending a total of three months every year at court. For this they received a salary of £400 a year, a respectable income in those days, although a large proportion of it was accounted for by the necessity of fitting themselves out in suitable clothes. In addition they were given as their badge of office a miniature of the Queen, surrounded by diamonds and mounted on a ribbon bow, and whenever they were on duty they wore this, pinned on the shoulder like an order.

As the reign progressed the Queen liked to vary her routine with regular trips abroad and a number of ladies always accompanied her on such occasions. Further diversity was introduced when in 1845 the Queen bought a property at Osborne on the Isle of Wight, an acquisition that was followed seven years later by the purchase of a Scottish estate, Balmoral. Thenceforth the Queen and her husband spent as much time as possible at these holiday homes, a development not altogether welcomed by many of the household, who found the new royal residences somewhat uncomfortable and remote. Balmoral was particularly dreaded as it was freezing cold, but the Queen herself seemed impervious to the chill, refusing to have fires lit in the house and expecting her attendants to participate in any outdoor activities that amused her. One wretched lady complained that Her Majesty thought nothing 'of sitting for hours on a pony going at a foot's pace and coming home frozen', while a young colleague described life at Balmoral as 'utterly dull', adding fretfully, 'We have *no* duties to perform to occupy our minds and the weather is horribly cold and wet . . . We just exist from meal to meal and do our best to kill time.'[50] Such indeed were the rigours of life at Balmoral that all at court did their best to avoid having to accompany the Queen when she left for her Scottish holidays.

Members of the household might complain of the boredom and discomfort they were expected to endure in the name of duty but before 1861 the atmosphere at court was on the whole a happy one. In that year, however, tragedy struck. The first blow came in March, when the Queen was greatly distressed by her mother's lingering death from cancer. She found some consolation in taking on as a resident woman of the Bedchamber her mother's former attendant, Lady Augusta Bruce, assuring her that 'the thought of having *you*, who dearest Mama loved as a child, near me in the future, is an indescribable comfort to my poor bleeding heart'.[51] In the coming months Lady Augusta made herself indispensable to the Queen and it was she who would help Victoria to cope when at the end of the year death made a much more terrible incursion into the royal family.

On 14 December 1861, after a short illness, the Prince Consort died of typhoid fever. The Queen was shattered. Numb with grief, she withdrew into her shell, refusing to see the majority of her household. For a time the sight of a happily married woman became anathema to the Queen and she hid herself away from even old friends such as Baroness Churchill, a lady of the Bedchamber since 1854, because she had 'never known grief' and therefore could not possibly assuage hers. Lady Augusta Bruce was one of the few people whose company the Queen could tolerate and Victoria later admitted that in this time of sadness Lady Augusta 'was everything' to her. The Queen's eldest daughter, the Crown Princess of Prussia, was rather irritated by Lady Augusta's ascendancy, commenting with acerbity that the Queen was only attached to her 'Because she said "Yes Ma'am" to everything and that if she said "No Ma'am" a few times the Q. would cease to think her the paragon of cleverness she now does', but more charitable observers realized that in the Queen's fragile state of nerves gentle handling was necessary. The Queen's eldest son, the Prince of Wales, appreciated this, telling Lady Augusta that he did not think his mother could have borne the loss of her husband if it had not been for her.[52]

For more than two years the Queen lived in seclusion, shunning all contact with her people. Gradually, however, she came to terms with Albert's death and resumed her responsibilities as ruler but the court was never the same again. While never exactly gay, in Albert's day it had at least been cheerful, but now an air of profound gloom hung over all.

The outward signs of this were manifest enough, as for the remainder of the reign the Queen's Bedchamber ladies were ordered to wear mourning whenever they were in waiting. Long periods of mourning had always been a feature of court life, for the household had had to don black if even a distant connection of the Queen's died, and to Victoria's disgruntled attendants it seemed that an exceptionally high rate of mortality prevailed amongst her relatives. In 1851 the Queen admitted to Lady Caroline Barrington that 'she had been nine months in mourning each year for the last three or four', and her ladies had had to spend an equally high proportion of their time shrouded in black. Understandably they found these gloomy observances somewhat trying, betraying not a little irritation when some obscure member of the Queen's family thoughtlessly died. 'There is a horrid Queen of Sardinia dead', one maid of honour wrote in disgust in 1855, '. . . too distressing with all my pretty coloured gowns'.[53]

After the Prince Consort's death, however, the situation became immeasurably worse. The Queen seemed to derive a macabre satisfaction from her weeds, retreating behind a barricade of crape and bombazine that shielded both herself and her ladies from the outside world. For a year after Albert's death no member of the household was permitted to appear in public out of mourning and though after that time the Queen relented so far as to let her maids of honour appear at court in the semi-mourning colours of white, mauve or grey, at the slightest excuse they were again plunged into unrelieved black. In October 1889 one maid of honour, Marie Adeane, had just invested in a new tweed suit to wear at Balmoral when the Queen decreed there should be six weeks of court mourning for the late King of Portugal – 'and he was only a first cousin once removed!' Poor Marie only possessed one warm black dress and dreaded the cold winter evenings that awaited her at Balmoral: 'It is a lesson *never, never* to buy anything but black', she concluded in depression.[54]

In her bereaved condition the Queen naturally found consolation in her religion but it was not in her nature to indulge in extravagant exhibitions of piety. She always reacted sharply to any attempt by her ladies to compromise her independence of mind in religious matters and in 1875 firmly rejected a plea from the Countess of Gains-borough, a lady of the Bedchamber for thirty-six years, to go and see a pair of American Evangelists who were touring Britain. She told her severely, 'Though I am sure they are very good and sincere people . . . this sensational style of excitement . . . is not the religion which *can last* and is not, I think, wholesome for the mind or heart.' Understatement in religion was indeed what appealed to the Queen and after Albert's death she became distinctly Low Church, taking communion according to the rites of the Scottish Church in 1873 and seeking to ensure that the Anglican hierarchy maintained a hostile front to Rome. Among those blamed for these developments was the Presbyterian Lady Erroll, a humourless fanatic who became a lady of the Bedchamber in 1873, but one may doubt whether she really had much influence over her mistress, for often her effusions left the Queen unmoved. In January 1896 the Queen was greatly distressed by the death of her son-in-law, Prince Henry of Battenberg, and Lady Erroll's attempts to cheer her up failed dismally. 'Oh Your Majesty', she had gushed, 'Think of when we shall see our dear ones in Heaven . . . We will all meet in Abraham's bosom.' 'I will NOT meet Abraham', the Queen had snapped, noting in her diary that night, 'Dear Leila, not at all consolatory in times of trouble.'[55]

As a widow the Queen evidently derived comfort from the thought of being surrounded by a grieving sisterhood, dedicated to the memory of dear departed ones, for many of her ladies had also lost their husbands. In 1865 it was with definite satisfaction that she reported to her daughter that the Duchess of Atholl, widowed the year before, was in waiting 'in her weeds . . . a great comfort to me'. Lady Caroline Barrington scored bonus points because she had not only lost her husband but he had died insane, and thus as one who had 'had much sorrow' the Queen could regard her as a real kindred spirit. It always upset the Queen when widows remarried, even in cases when the first husband had hardly been worthy of great devotion beyond the grave. When in 1875 the widowed Lady Clifden, who served occasionally as an extra lady-in-waiting, an-nounced her engagement the Queen lamented 'She is quite throwing herself away on an insignificant young officer six years younger than herself and not very recommendable', although she added caus-tically that she was not surprised as Lady Clifden had 'never shown much discrimination in her choice or she would not have married Lord Clifden'.[56]

It is perhaps not altogether surprising that the Queen found the remarriage of widows to be almost sacrilegious but it is less easy to condone her selfish attitude when single ladies in her household married. Disliking as she did changes in household personnel, the Queen had always felt somewhat aggrieved when her ladies had been claimed by husbands, and as early as 1842 Lord Melbourne had had to chide her for it, reminding her on the engagement of a maid of honour, 'Your Majesty having generally chosen handsome and attractive girls for the maids of honour, which is very right, must expect to lose them in this way.' While Albert was alive the Queen did her best to follow this advice and on the whole succeeded in stifling unworthy feelings of resentment, telling Georgiana Liddell on her engagement, 'We only hope you will be as happy through a long life as *we are*; I *cannot* wish you *more* than this.' Once Albert had gone, however, his grieving widow saw it as a real betrayal when her ladies abandoned her to start happier lives elsewhere. The worst shock of all came in November 1863 when Lady Augusta Bruce announced that she was to marry the Dean of Westminster, Dr Stanley. To her uncle the Queen wrote indignantly, 'You will be sorry to hear . . . that my dear Lady Augusta at *forty-one* . . . has, most unnecessarily, decided to marry (!!) . . . It has been my *greatest sorrow* and trial *since* my misfortune! *I* thought she would *never* leave *me*! . . . She will remain in my service and be often with me but it cannot be the same for her first duty is *now* to another.' Poor Lady Augusta was made to feel like a criminal and it was some time before the Queen could bring herself to be civil to the elderly fiancé. Eventually her better nature triumphed, and shortly after her marriage Lady Augusta was able to report to her husband that the Queen had been to visit and 'spoke very kindly of you dearest; not a word of reproach'.[57]

As the Queen grew older her dislike of change in the household grew still more pronounced and with the self-centredness of the elderly she made less attempt to hide her displeasure when her ladies married. When preliminary enquiries were made as to whether a young lady would make a suitable maid of honour the girl in question was always asked whether she was 'engaged or likely to be engaged' and an answer in the affirmative automatically disqualified her. When these precautions failed and a suitor appeared from nowhere to claim the girls the Queen was visibly ruffled. '*Most* unnecessary' was the usual comment with which she greeted forthcoming marriages. In 1891 Marie Adeane 'had rather a bother with the Queen' when she handed in her notice on her engagement to Bernard Mallet. The

Queen made it clear that she wished the marriage to be deferred as long as possible and grew quite refractory when it emerged that this did not fit in with Marie's plans, all of which was from Marie's point of view 'very flattering but somewhat inconvenient'. Firmly but politely Marie refused to budge, and seeing that further representations were useless the Queen gave way, but the maid of honour was left in no doubt that her forthcoming departure was 'still a sore point' with her mistress. Four years later all was forgiven, if not forgotten, for Marie returned to court as an extra woman of the Bedchamber and the Queen told her she was delighted to have her back, gaily reminding her 'How very angry I was when you married.'[58]

Towards those ladies of her household who were married the Queen did her best to be considerate, not always with success, for owing to her curious blend of naïvety and egoism it rarely struck her that her ladies might find it a hardship to be away from home for long periods. This had been evident even while Albert was alive: in 1854 the Prince had gone without her on a short visit to France and the Queen had complained that she found this 'prolonged absence' very trying. 'Four days absence!' commented the diarist Charles Greville, 'H.M. thinks nothing of taking her ladies from their husbands and families for a month together.' At times, admittedly, the Queen made special arrangements specifically designed to overcome this problem: both Lady Caroline Barrington and Marie Mallet were allowed to bring their children to court for short stays, and on several occasions the Queen secretly invited Bernard Mallet to Windsor, giving Marie the unexpected pleasure of spending the weekend with her husband. Nevertheless, however much her ladies might appreciate such thoughtful gestures, these intermittent treats could not make up for the regular separations from their families that they had to endure in the name of duty. In this respect their husbands suffered too, at times decidedly unwillingly, for some of them felt keen resentment at the way the demands of royal service had deprived them of their wives. On one occasion the Earl of Antrim, whose wife Louisa became a lady of the Bedchamber in 1890, was so incensed by her absence at court that with his bare hands he smashed into matchwood a small table belonging to his wife, growling all the while. 'Why should my wife have to wait on anyone? Like a damn servant!' he used to demand of his family in moments of stress.[59]

Even after Prince Albert's death occasional gleams of gaiety alleviated the gloom of the court. Periodically the household put on amateur dramatic productions, despite the disapproval of Lady

Erroll, who considered that anything connected with the theatre was 'the work of the devil', and who made it clear that she regarded all her colleagues to be 'backsliders and unregenerate'. Sometimes too after the Queen had gone to bed the household were able to let themselves go, Louisa Antrim reporting that one night 'Princess Beatrice played in the ballroom and we all danced a Russian mazurka – and kept it up wildly till one'. There were even some evenings when the Queen herself proved a fund of amusement, for though the atmosphere in the dining room was sepulchral when her mood was low, if in the right frame of mind she could still hold the table enthralled with her anecdotes and imitations. It was indeed the opportunity of being near so remarkable a personality as the Queen that atoned for the frustrations of life at court, for as Marie Mallet declared, 'I always feel fascinated when I am with her and forget all the inconveniences and worries connected with her service.'[60]

X

The Court Today

On 22 January 1901 Queen Victoria died and was succeeded by her eldest son Edward, by then already in his sixty-first year. Having waited so long to attain his inheritance the new King was determined to extract the maximum amount of enjoyment from it. Though on the throne for a much shorter time than his mother he, like her, would lend his name to an era, but with its hallmarks of gaiety, luxury and extravagance it was to be the very antithesis of that which had preceded it. As one court lady succinctly put it, 'The reaction from the austerity and rigid moral code of Queen Victoria's court caused the pendulum to swing in the opposite direction.'[1]

The change in atmosphere was apparent as soon as the statutory year and a half of court mourning had expired. The King then decreed that in place of the afternoon Drawing Rooms at which his mother had received ladies he would hold evening receptions at Buckingham Palace. These were altogether more enjoyable affairs than the old Queen's grim presentation parties, for now ladies were permitted to bring with them gentlemen escorts and supper and refreshments were provided. Furthermore, for the first time in more than fifty years, regular court balls were held at Windsor, graced by all the prettiest women in society.

Edward's wife Alexandra was a fitting adornment to these glamorous assemblages. Forty years before Queen Victoria had selected this Danish Princess as her son's bride because she combined an entrancing appearance with great sweetness of character and though Alexandra was now well into middle age her beauty remained undimmed. That, however, had not prevented her husband from developing a roving eye and their marital history had been punctuated by numerous infidelities on his part. Alexandra on the whole accepted the situation philosophically, and she was careful to remain on civil terms with her husband's principal mistress, Alice Keppel. King Edward in his turn took full advantage of her understanding attitude, and even at his coronation he did not neglect his lady friends. To enable them to have a good view of the proceedings he installed several of them in a box overhanging the chancel of Westminster Abbey, irreverently nicknamed 'the King's loose box'.[2]

In one respect however, the King was a more considerate husband than many of his forbears for he did not select his mistresses from among the ranks of his wife's ladies-in-waiting. This, admittedly, was not a great sacrifice, for Queen Alexandra tended to surround herself with elderly dames whose attractions were in no way comparable to hers. The Shah of Persia indeed misunderstood the situation when visiting Windsor and advised the King to remedy what he regarded as a very sad state of affairs. 'These are your wives?', he solicitously enquired of his host, on seeing the Queen's assembled ladies, 'They are old and ugly. Have them beheaded and take new and pretty ones.'[3] Fortunately the King was able to indulge his appetite without recourse to these sanguinary arrangements but, easily tempted though he was, he evidently considered that his wife's ladies-in-waiting had little to recommend them.

The doyenne of the ladies-in-waiting was the Mistress of the Robes, the Duchess of Buccleuch, who had already served three terms in that office under Queen Victoria. Described as 'something of a terror to novices and débutantes yet not devoid of kindly instincts', she was acknowledged to be 'a great figurehead to the court'.[4] Other veterans from Queen Victoria's day were the Countess of Antrim and the Dowager Countess Lytton, whom Queen Alexandra retained as ladies of the Bedchamber, and even two of the four maids of honour could in one sense be considered as relics of the late Queen's court, for both Sylvia Edwardes and Doris Vivian had originally been in her service. In almost all her household appointments indeed, Alexandra clung to the familiar, installing as one of her two extra ladies of the Bedchamber the Countess of Macclesfield, whom Queen Victoria had originally selected as the Princess's lady-in-waiting more than forty years before. At the time the appointment had been greeted with some derision by sophisticated members of society, Lord Stanley of Alderley declaring in disgust 'That precise little stick Lady Macclesfield is to be appointed. In short the Queen wishes the new court to be as dull and stupid as her own'. It was just as well, however, that some flighty socialite had not been given the job, as Lady Macclesfield had

had to take charge when in January 1864 Alexandra's first child had arrived two months prematurely, and had successfully delivered the baby herself. 'No one but Lady Macclesfield to do everything which the nurses do!' Queen Victoria had commented at the time, torn between shock and admiration, and the incident had naturally helped to cement the bond of affection between the Princess and her elderly lady-in-waiting. When in 1911 Lady Macclesfield died after spending almost fifty years in royal service Queen Alexandra noted sadly that she had always looked on her as a second mother.[5]

Of all her ladies-in-waiting, however, Alexandra was closest to her woman of the Bedchamber, Charlotte Knollys, a plain woman with a governessy manner who had entered her service in 1872. The sister of King Edward's Private Secretary, Francis Knollys, she devoted herself entirely to Alexandra, accompanying her when she went on trips abroad and rarely taking so much as a day's holiday. The majority of the royal family regarded her with somewhat grudging tolerance, mockingly referring to her as 'Miss Charlotte', but Alexandra herself was utterly dependent on her. Some people indeed found it somewhat disconcerting that the Queen was inclined to put Miss Knollys's interests before all other considerations, and the royal family expressed some ill-feeling when for months after Queen Victoria's death Alexandra refused to move into Buckingham Palace on the grounds that it did not contain suitable accommodation for her woman of the Bedchamber. Only when she was sure that Charlotte would be 'well lodged' did the Queen relent.[6]

At times the most considerate of mistresses, Alexandra could also be the very reverse, making no allowance for her servants' natural desire to lead private lives of their own. She had no qualms, for example, about repeatedly persuading one of her dressers to postpone her marriage to a woodman on the Sandringham estate, assuring her that it would be easy to set a more convenient date. 'Just this once, Bessie,' she would plead, 'I cannot do without you *this* time.'[7] Like many absent-minded people, the Queen took a certain pride in her vagueness, little thinking that at times her behaviour was both irresponsible and spoilt. In 1910 her maid of honour Blanche Lascelles became engaged to Lord Lloyd and the Queen promised to attend the wedding, but in May King Edward died and the court was plunged into mourning. As a special favour Alexandra entreated Blanche to delay her marriage until mourning was over, thus enabling her to attend the festivities as planned. Loyally the young couple agreed, putting off the service till November 1911. Finally the day came. The guests assembled, a seat was reserved for the Queen at the front of the church, and bride and bridegroom awaited her arrival. The Queen did not appear. Notoriously unpunctual, on this occasion she had forgotten about the engagement altogether, and after a considerable delay the ceremony had to proceed without her. The unfortunate Lloyds had delayed their marriage to no good purpose.

Queen Alexandra's successor as Queen Consort, Queen Mary, was in every way a contrast to her. Conscientious and reserved, she was of a much more reflective turn of mind than her dizzy mother-in-law, and her temperament accorded well with than of her husband, King George V, a stern disciplinarian who put duty before all else. Even as a young woman she had never identified with that 'smart set' with whom King Edward had felt so at home, confiding to her governess that she did not altogether approve of '*leurs* goings on'. King George held the values of the fashionable world in even greater contempt than did his wife and throughout their reign the emphasis at court was very much on traditionalism. By 1911 a fashion had come in for slightly shorter skirts which showed an inch or two of leg, but one maid of honour was disconcerted to find that 'in court circles ankle bones were not countenanced' and that all her dresses had to conform 'to the exact regulation court length'. As it happened this was not Queen Mary's fault, for she herself had excellent legs and secretly yearned to adopt the shorter hemline, but knowing her husband's antipathy to change she feared exciting his displeasure. She even asked her lady of the Bedchamber, Mabell, Countess of Airlie, if she would test the King's feelings by wearing one of the new short skirts when she was next at court. The stratagem proved unavailing: the King made no secret of his disapproval, Lady Airlie had hastily to let down her hemline and Queen Mary had to abandon all thought of donning one of the daring new outfits.[8]

Despite her conventional outlook Queen Mary was not entirely unadventurous in her choice of ladies-in-waiting, for one of her ladies of the Bedchamber was Lady Desborough, an unashamed hedonist whose flamboyant style seemed rather out of tune with the sober character of the court. When younger Lady Desborough had been a leading member of that group of wits and aesthetes who had been nicknamed 'The Souls' after one contemporary complained that they spent much of their time discussing the state of their souls, and since her marriage she had always been surrounded by admirers, not all of whom, it seems, remained on strictly platonic terms. Nevertheless, one of her friends subsequently insisted that though 'She might – like all other agreeable *femmes du monde* – give an impression of light metal . . . Etty Desborough was fundamentally sound and the truest friend that ever lived' and it was doubtless these stalwart qualities that appealed to Queen Mary. Even so several of Etty's associates were surprised that she was prepared to affiliate herself with so un-exciting a court, one lady remarking doubtfully, 'I hope you find it a good bedchamber to frolic in; Mary III [*sic*] seems to be such a dull woman, but I daresay her *surrounders* interest you.' Etty's son, Julian Grenfell, took an even dimmer view of her court appointment: 'It is really too disgusting for words and so ridiculous', he told her, 'One looks on all those things as dead and gone like "Chop off her head" or as only belonging to pantomime. But I suppose you have simply *got* to do it, which makes it all a very grim joke . . . Shan't you be able to resign it soon? It does make me angry.'[9]

Before the Great War young bloods such as Julian Grenfell might dismiss the monarchy as an irrelevance, but it was indeed that terrible cataclysm that gave the Queen a chance to show that she was more than a mere figurehead. Traditionalist though she was, her method of tackling the incidental problems that arose out of the war was essentially constructive and she was aided in her approach by the fact that several members of her household already had some experience of dealing with voluntary organizations. Even before the outbreak of war the Queen had discussed ways of improving the standard of nursing services for the armed forces with her lady of the Bedchamber Mabell, Countess of Airlie, whose years on the board of Queen Alexandra's Imperial Nursing Service made her well qualified to advise on such matters. Now that war was a reality she and the Countess of Airlie devoted much attention to organizations such as the Army Nursing Board, of which the Queen became president in 1926. Apart from this the Queen and her ladies were also actively involved in charitable work designed to assist the civilian population to cope with the disruptive effects of total war. In these ventures the expertise of Lady Bertha Dawkins, a woman of the Bedchamber who had already been of great assistance to the Queen in the conduct of her peacetime charitable activities, proved invaluable; even in the first weeks of the war Lady Bertha could declare to her daughter that she and the Queen were 'frightfully busy trying to get through a scheme for helping poor women who have no work owing to the war',[10] and their efforts continued throughout the next four years.

In a somewhat curious attempt to aid the war-effort, the King banned all alcoholic drink at court for the duration of the war, and Lady Desborough sent one of her friends 'a sad account of Windsor Castle "on the water-waggon"', assuring him that 'tempers were but little improved by temperance'. Possibly feeling that her husband sometimes lost all sense of proportion in his wartime demands for economy within the household, Queen Mary occasionally resorted to subterfuge to protect the interests of her employees. When the future Lady Curzon visited Windsor in 1915 the Queen invited her to come and see the room that she had just had redecorated for the maids of honour, adding conspiratorially, 'Don't say anything to the King about it because he thinks I ought not to have anything of this sort done in wartime. I really have to have it done, however, because my poor maids of honour had no sitting room of their own.'[11]

After the war had ended the Queen continued with her charitable activities, assisted by such able lieutenants as Lady Cynthia Colville, who had spent years working on behalf of a child welfare organization in Shoreditch and who had indeed turned down the opportunity of becoming a Liberal candidate for that borough, preferring instead to become a woman of the Bedchamber. Yet despite Queen Mary's untiring zeal in the name of good causes she never really caught her subjects' imagination, for she found it quite impossible to unbend in public and only a few privileged members of her household and family realized that a warm personality lay behind the formal manner. As Mabell, Countess of Airlie remarked in her memoirs, 'She had an eager enjoyment of life and a sense of fun, carefully controlled like all her emotions, but always rippling beneath the surface . . . She was not always the dignified Queen Consort known to the world.'[12]

On 20 January 1936 King George V died and there ensued the brief reign of Edward VIII, an uninspiring one-act tragedy that culminated in his abdication on 11 December. He was succeeded by his brother the Duke of York, who now became King George VI, and who with his wife Elizabeth rose magnificently to the challenge that had been thrust upon them by King Edward's departure. The Duchess of York had previously employed only two full-time ladies-in-waiting but though of necessity her household was now enlarged both Lady Helen Graham and the Honourable Mrs Geoffrey Bowlby remained with her, helping her to face up to the wider responsibilities of a Queen Consort. Lady Helen Graham, who had been in the Duchess's household since 1926, was particularly indispensable during this trying time and one of her colleagues was later to assert 'we could never have got through it without her'.[13] Her death in 1945 deprived the Queen of a much-trusted friend.

Hardly had the Queen accustomed herself to her new role than she and her husband had to face the still greater challenge presented by war with Nazi Germany. To this Queen Elizabeth responded with her now legendary aplomb. Determined that in the event of invasion she would not be taken hostage by the enemy, she and her ladies learnt how to use rifles and revolvers so that they could fend off would-be kidnappers. She remained in London during much of the Blitz, facing up to the very real threat of death with apparent insouciance, and her infectious good spirits communicated themselves to the ladies of her household despite the fact that, in addition to the normal wartime pressures, their workload had been increased by the absence of many of their male colleagues on active service abroad. As one lady-in-waiting put it,

> Not only did the Queen have all the courage in the world, she had the power to transfer it to you. When London was being heavily bombed and one had all sorts of problems to contend with at home I used to arrive feeling more or less battered at the Palace to go into waiting and then I would have to take over the current problems there. Altogether life was rather a strain, yet once I had seen the Queen I felt absolutely all right and ready to face anything.[14]

In the years since the war Queen Elizabeth has shown the same indomitable spirit, fulfilling her duties like a seasoned professional and infallibly leaving pleasure in her wake. As Queen Mother she has continued to carry out a heavy programme of engagements and she is supported in her work by a devoted staff, including two ladies of the Bedchamber and four women of the Bedchamber. Of these, three have been members of her household since the time when she was Queen, the Dowager Viscountess Hambleden, Lady Jean Rankin and the Honourable Mrs John Mulholland having been between them in royal service for a total of one hundred and fifteen years. Like the Queen Mother herself they have carried on working well past retirement age: when one lady-in-waiting recently suggested that she was too old for the job the Queen Mother merely enquired, 'What about me?' and there was no more talk of resignation. It is not, of course, duty alone that impels these ladies to stay at their posts but also a very real affection for their mistress. Years ago one member of her household remarked of her and her husband, 'They believed you could be staff and a very dear personal friend at the same time'.[15]

In the household of our present Queen, Elizabeth II, there are eleven officially accredited ladies-in-waiting, although some of these serve the Queen only on a part-time basis. Of the ladies-in-waiting, the most important is the Mistress of the Robes, who is normally, though not invariably, a Duchess. The Queen's first Mistress of the Robes was Mary, Duchess of Devonshire, who played an important part in the coronation ceremony of 1953. It was she who assisted the Lord Great Chamberlain to prepare the Queen for her anointing, removing her crimson robe and afterwards replacing it with the Robe Royal, or Pall of the Cloth of Gold. In 1967 the Duchess of Devonshire retired and the present Mistress of the Robes is the Duchess of Grafton, who previously served the Queen as a lady of the Bedchamber. The role of the Mistress of the Robes today is principally ceremonial: she waits on the Queen on occasions such as the Opening of Parliament and garden parties at Buckingham Palace and is in waiting when foreign dignitaries come to England on state visits, but the Duchess of Grafton also shares some of the duties of the ladies of the Bedchamber and frequently accompanies her mistress when she goes on tour abroad. The old arrangement whereby Queen Victoria had to change her Mistress of the Robes with each new government has long since been tacitly abandoned, and today the Mistress of the Robes is seen as a symbolic prop to the throne, rather than the power behind it.

At the moment the Queen has two ladies of the Bedchamber, the Marchioness of Abergavenny and the Countess of Airlie, and one extra lady of the Bedchamber, the Countess of Cromer, who is only very occasionally in attendance. Together with the Mistress of the Robes and a woman of the Bedchamber, a lady of the Bedchamber waits on the Queen at the opening of Parliament and one of the Ladies generally accompanies her on her more important engagements, such as a grand civic function. Their duties have decreased in the course of the twentieth century, for in Queen Alexandra's day a lady of the Bedchamber had always to be at court, and it was only under Queen Mary that the system evolved whereby the Bedchamber ladies merely 'attended the Queen for her bigger and more impressive engagements'. Even so, a lady of the Bedchamber remained in London whenever the Queen was at Buckingham Palace in order that her mistress could, if she so desired, summon her at very short notice. During the Second World War this practice was discontinued, for Queen Elizabeth sensibly remarked that it was absurd that her ladies of the Bedchamber should run the risk of being bombed when there was no real necessity for their presence,[16] and since that time they have been available only for specific engagements.

The duties of the women of the Bedchamber are both more demanding and more diverse than those of the ladies, for they assist the Queen on a much more regular basis. There are four women of the Bedchamber who are each on duty for a fortnight at a time, the three extra women of the Bedchamber standing in for them when they are on holiday or ill. There is a suite of rooms provided for their use at Buckingham Palace, but the majority of them have accommodation of their own in London and do not spend the night at the Palace unless they have to accompany the Queen to an early engagement the following morning. However, one woman of the Bedchamber always stays at Windsor, Sandringham or Balmoral when the court is officially in residence there, although they do not accompany the Queen when she merely goes to the country for the weekend.

One of the main tasks of the women of the Bedchamber is to deal with a proportion of the Queen's personal correspondence, and in particular to send individual replies to the hundreds of letters that the Queen receives every year from children. In the past it was this secretarial aspect of their duties that took up the majority of their time: at the beginning of the century Charlotte Knollys complained that she often had to answer as many as sixty letters a day, and Queen Mary's woman of the Bedchamber, Lady Cynthia Colville, frequently had to sit up till past one o'clock in the morning in order to dispose of all the mail that had accumulated.[17] Nowadays the situation has in some respects improved, for replies are usually typewritten and as the Queen is Queen Regnant rather than Queen Consort her Private Secretary's office handles much of the business that would otherwise have devolved on the women of the Bedchamber. They do not, for example, have to deal with appeals for charitable donations, or to suggest appropriate courses of action to people in trouble who have written to the Queen for advice, matters which would previously have fallen within their province. Nevertheless the quantity of mail with which they have to deal remains prodigious and events such as the Queen's Silver Jubilee, or the birth of Prince William of Wales always result in a big increase in the postbag and put further pressure on the women of the Bedchamber.

A lady-in-waiting always accompanies the Queen on her official engagements, the usual arrangement being that a lady of the Bedchamber is in attendance whenever the Queen and her husband undertake engagements together, while a woman of the Bedchamber is on duty on those days when the Queen appears in public without the Duke of Edinburgh. On such occasions the lady-in-waiting has to ease the pressure on her mistress in as many ways as she can. She can contribute to the success of each visit simply by being friendly, helping tongue-tied civic dignitaries to overcome the fright that so many people feel in the presence of the royal family, or chatting to a Lady Mayoress whose husband is looking after the Queen. When the Queen goes on a 'walkabout' the lady-in-waiting follows behind, ready to relieve her of the numerous gifts that well-wishers press upon her, so that by the end of the afternoon the lady-in-waiting often resembles an overloaded Christmas tree, weighed down by bouquets of flowers, bags of sweets and cuddly toys.

Shortly after a foreign ambassador arrives in England he is received at Buckingham Palace by the Queen and if he is a married man a woman of the Bedchamber is always at the Grand Entrance of the Palace to greet his wife, whom she looks after until the time that the ambassador has finished presenting his credentials and his wife is able to join him for an audience with the Queen. When the Queen has guests to lunch or dinner the lady-in-waiting on duty helps to put them at their ease, and such social skills are particularly valuable during the Queen's tours abroad, when she frequently entertains foreigners on board the royal yacht *Britannia*.

These foreign tours indeed entail a great deal of work for all involved, for like the Queen herself the ladies-in-waiting present have not only to cope with such unavoidable inconveniences as jet-lag and upset stomach but they have also to be impeccably dressed throughout and to treat everyone they encounter with grace and affability. They also have to conform without question to the customs and lifestyle of the country concerned: when the Queen visited Morocco in 1980 it was agreed that for the first time women would be allowed into the Palace at Rabat but the Duchess of Grafton and Mrs John Dugdale were suddenly ordered out of the room in which they and the Queen were awaiting the King of Morocco's arrival for lunch. Although reported to be 'rather ruffled', they complied, and it was only when the King changed his mind and decided not to eat with his visitors that they were able to rejoin their mistress.[18]

Apart from her attendance on the Queen at home and abroad, there is a whole range of miscellaneous duties which the lady-in-waiting on duty discharges on request. When the royal children were young it was a woman of the Bedchamber who normally made the arrangements for their parties or outings with friends, although time has naturally relieved the ladies-in-waiting of this particular responsibility. Other problems, however, remain equally pressing, such as the difficulties created by the Queen's inability to go out in public without attracting attention, which obliges her to delegate to her women of the Bedchamber tasks such as Christmas shopping or buying flowers for friends who are in hospital.

Queen Mary's woman of the Bedchamber, Lady Cynthia Colville, remarked in her memoirs that she was often amused by the common assumption that ladies-in-waiting like herself 'were responsible for the Queen's wardrobe and for lowly domestic jobs', for by the twentieth century such matters had become the concern of the Queen's dressers, described by one of Queen Mary's maids of honour as a pair of 'highly trained responsible women, as well they should be, to be in charge of so large a wardrobe [and] to have the handling of almost priceless jewels'. Today the Queen's principal dresser is Miss Margaret Macdonald, the daughter of a Scottish gardener, who became Princess Elizabeth's nurserymaid in 1926 and has remained with her ever since. Besides bringing the Queen her morning tea, she discusses with her what outfits will be worn on each engagement and supervises the packing of the royal luggage when the Queen goes on tour abroad. Out of a working partnership that has spanned more than fifty-five years there has sprung a very real friendship, and the Queen's relationship with Miss Macdonald (whom she calls Bobo) has been described as 'almost telepathic'.[19]

In his memoirs the Duke of Windsor described the royal establishment as 'a mixture of ancient and modern usage – a unique and more or less self-contained community in which an aeroplane and a garage full of the latest motor cars exist in congenial juxtaposition with Plantagenet ritual, Tudor costumes and Victorian etiquette',[20] but in those cases where ancient forms proved incompatible with the requirements of the modern world the structure of the royal household was modified accordingly. The position of maid of honour has been one such casualty of the march of time. By the beginning of the twentieth century they were already in decline, for whereas Queen Victoria had expected two maids of honour to be in residence at the court at all times, Queen Alexandra required their presence only when she was in London or when she and her husband entertained at Windsor during Ascot week. Four maids of honour were quite adequate for her needs (Queen Victoria had had eight) and even so they could all count on being free from July till November. They were still expected to have some musical ability and to have a grasp of at least two languages but it was already understood that their principal function was to be 'ornamental rather than useful'. Under Queen Mary their contribution was even more limited and after the First World War she did not bother to find replacements for maids of honour who left the household. The Honourable Jean Bruce was the last maid of honour to serve regularly at court and when in 1935 she was promoted to the rank of woman of the Bedchamber the position of maid of honour fell into abeyance.

It was not, however, altogether defunct. At the coronation of our present Queen, six maids of honour were in attendance, all unmarried, as tradition decreed, although Lady Rosemary Spencer-Churchill (who at twenty-three was the eldest maid) was already engaged and had specially to delay her wedding until the coronation was over. The maids had to carry the Queen's train as she processed up the aisle, and in preparation for this task the Duke of Norfolk drilled them 'like guardsmen'. As they had to remain standing throughout much of the two and a half hour ceremony, the maids were advised to tuck ampoules of smelling salts into the wrists of their long white gloves, and the Archbishop of Canterbury took the additional precaution of secreting a bottle of brandy behind the rood screen so that he could offer a reviving nip to any girl who felt faint. Fortunately, none of them collapsed and all six were lustily cheered when they appeared with the Queen on the Palace balcony once the ceremony was over.[21]

The Queen's ladies today receive a modest salary which is really little more than a clothes allowance for it is part of the job to have an extensive wardrobe stocked with hats and evening dresses which they might not in normal circumstances require. Though in the past the post of lady-in-waiting was a profitable one, the present level of pay is much lower and bears no comparison with, say, the earnings of Queen Anne's ladies of the Bedchamber who in 1702 received £1,000 a year, a sum of which the modern equivalent would be approximately £35,500. Far from representing a sizeable income the salary of a lady-in-waiting today barely covers the expense she incurs in the course of her duties. As Mabell, Countess of Airlie put it, 'Those who have the privilege of being appointed lady-in-waiting serve Her Majesty out of love and loyalty. The badge of office, which is chosen individually by each successive Queen, is its own reward.'[22] Today the emblem of the lady-in-waiting is a diamond brooch in the shape of the letter E, worn on special occasions such as state banquets, the state Opening of Parliament and Palace garden parties. The honours system affords the Queen another opportunity to show her appreciation of the work done by her ladies-in-waiting and many members of the household belong to the Royal Victorian Order, which lies in the personal gift of the monarch. The Duchess of Grafton, for example, is a Dame Grand Cross of the Royal Victorian Order, and the Marchioness of Abergavenny a Dame Commander, as are two of the women of the Bedchamber, Lady Abel Smith and the Honourable Mary Morrison. Their two colleagues, Lady Susan Hussey and Mrs John Dugdale, are both Commanders of the Royal Victorian Order, and so are the Countesses of Airlie and Cromer.

The tragic prevalence of terrorism today has added a hidden dimension to the role of lady-in-waiting which cannot be ignored. Terrorism is not of course a wholly novel phenomenon: in 1900 for example Edward and Alexandra, at that time Prince and Princess of Wales, were fired upon in Brussels by a young anarchist named Sapido, whose bullet fortunately missed them and harmlessly embedded itself in Charlotte Knollys's bun. Nevertheless, despite constant police surveillance, the danger today remains acute, as was graphically demonstrated in 1974 when an armed madman named Ian Ball tried to kidnap Princess Anne as she drove down the Mall. The Princess's lady-in-waiting, Miss Rowena Brassey, was with her at the time, and had to crouch by the car while Ball fired several rounds from his gun. Both the Princess and Miss Brassey escaped unharmed but four people, including two passers-by, were wounded in the incident. When in 1961 Harold Macmillan suggested that the Queen should cancel a forthcoming visit to Ghana, which he feared would be disrupted by terrorist attacks, she told him simply 'Danger is part of the job'.[23] Regrettably, the same thing applies today to the profession of lady-in-waiting.

Those who enter royal service tend to regard it as a lifelong commitment and the majority of the Queen's ladies have been with her for at least twenty years, although the Countesses of Airlie and Cromer, who became ladies of the Bedchamber in 1973 and 1969 respectively, are relative newcomers to the household. In the case of most of the ladies-in-waiting, however, their association with the Queen does not date back beyond the time when they first joined her staff, for as a rule she did not select her servants from among her immediate circle of friends. If a vacancy occurs in the royal household it is often up to an existing lady-in-waiting to suggest someone that she thinks would make a suitable colleague and who is not only available but is also loyal, efficient and discreet. The last quality is perhaps the most important of all, for in the face of seemingly insatiable curiosity about the royal family every lady-in-waiting must develop the knack of being evasive without seeming discourteous. Anne Beckwith-Smith, appointed a lady-in-waiting to the Princess of Wales in September 1981, mastered this technique with apparent ease: when questioned by the Press about her new job she referred all enquiries to Buckingham Palace, and on being pressed for a comment she would say no more than, 'I am thrilled, delighted and terribly honoured to be chosen. Will that do?'[24]

Having lost its position as the guiding force in British politics, the court today cannot even claim to be at the centre of society, which in the old-fashioned sense of the word has ceased to exist. The London Season has staggered on, but it does so without the official imprimatur of the Crown, for in 1958 the Queen discontinued the annual presentation parties at Buckingham Palace, at which scores of débutantes made their curtsey to her, a time-consuming charade which benefited only a privileged minority. By the second half of the twentieth century such functions no longer seemed relevant to the role of the monarch, who is not only the Head of State but also a symbol of national unity. In the thirty years since the Queen came to the throne she has fulfilled these dual responsibilities with undoubted virtuosity, but though her success as a ruler indisputably owes much to her own personality, the contribution of her devoted staff cannot be overlooked. The Queen herself would be the first to acknowledge the part played by her ladies-in-waiting, who assist her in the execution of her duties and provide her with companionship and support.

Royal service is a profession with a long and distinguished pedigree, even though it is true that in the past some ladies combined a career at court with pursuit of the oldest profession of all. On the whole, however, these were the exceptions, and it would be unjust to overlook those generations of ladies-in-waiting who for centuries oiled the wheels of monarchy by rendering ungrudging service to the Crown. It is their mantle which has fallen on the ladies-in-waiting of our present Queen, who follow in the very best traditions of royal servants over the ages. In 1947 King George VI was overheard remarking sadly that his eldest daughter would be 'lonely all her life', but since the Queen's accession her ladies-in-waiting have ensured that, far from having to discharge her responsibilities in solitary splendour, she can always rely on the support of a group of utterly dependable women, whose loyalty is beyond question, and who have dedicated their lives to her service.

Notes

Abbreviations Used in the Notes

Additional MS: Additional Manuscripts in the British Museum

CDSP: Calendar of State Papers, domestic series, 1547–1704. Longman & Co, 1856–1924

Cal. Span.: Calendar of Letters, Despatches & State Papers relating to the negotiations between England and Spain, Ed. Pascul de Gayangos. H.M.S.O, 13 Vols, 1862–1954. Eyre & Spottiswoode

Cal. Span., Elizabeth: Calendar of Letters and State Papers relating to English affairs preserved principally in the archives at Simancas (Elizabeth), Ed. M.A.S.Hume. 4 Vols, 1892–99. H.M.S.O, Eyre & Spottiswoode

Cal. Ven. and CPSV.: Calendar of State Papers and Venetian manuscripts relating to English affairs existing in the archives and collections of Venice

CSPF: Calendar of State Papers, Foreign Series, 1558–92, Longman 1863–1980

DNB: *Dictionary of National Biography*

HMC: Historical Manuscripts Commission

LC: Lord Chancellor's Records in the Public Record Office

L. & P.: *Letters and Papers, Foreign and Domestic of the Reign of Henry* VIII . . ., Ed. James Gairdner and R.H.Brodie. 21 Vols, 1862–1910. (Eyre & Spottiswoode)

LS: Lord Steward's Records in the Public Record Office

PRO: Public Record Office

RA: Royal Archives, Windsor

SP: State Papers in the Public Record Office

Strickland: Strickland, Agnes, *Lives of the Queens of England*

Introduction

1 Snyder, III, 1290

2 Bury, I, 1

3 Walpole, *Letters*, XV, 317 n.

4 *Household Ordinances*, vi

5 Strickland, I, 64; ibid., 205–6; H. Hall, iv

6 *Calendar of Patent Rolls 1247–58*, 613; ibid., 109, 474; *Calendar of Patent Rolls 1232–47*, 211, 286

7 Carmi Parsons, 29, 37, 84

8 Blackley & Hermansen, XIII–XIV; ibid., 173; Furnivall, 56

9 Myers, *Household of Edward IV*, 84; Furnivall, 162–3; Froissart, I, 246

10 M.Galway, *Alice Perrer's son John*, in Eng. Hist. Review lxvi 1951; George Holmes 69; Kay, 116

11 Froissart, III, 478; ibid., 465–6

12 Froissart, IV, 471; G.Mathew, 28; *Chronique de la traison et mort de Richard deux, 164*

13 Strickland III, 108–9; G.Mathew, 152; Myers, *Household of Edward IV*, 10; DNB, Henry VI; Hibbert, *Court at Windsor*, 27

14 George Smith, 16; Myers, *English Historical Documents*, 1169
15 Myers, *Household of Elizabeth Woodville*, 451–2
16 Leland, IV, 226; *Household Ordinances*, 127, 121; ibid., 125

Chapter I
1 L. & P., I, i, 41
2 Paul, 236; L. & P., VI, 278
3 L. & P., XV, 81; L. & P., XIV, ii, 5; Chapman, *Boleyn*, 173, quot. L. & P., VIII, 425
4 *Household Ordinances*, 164, 208; L. & P., I, i, 562; ibid., 493; ibid., XII, ii, 340
5 Martiennsen, 38
6 *Ellis, Original Letters*, First Series, I, 81; Cal. Span., II, 548
7 E.Hall, I, 40
8 E.Hall, I, 171
9 Cal. Span., supplement to vols I and II, 39
10 E.Hall, II, 49
11 Childe-Pemberton, *passim*; Cal. Ven., III, 455
12 L. & P., X, 181
13 Friedmann, II, 321
14 Paul, 126
15 Strickland, IV, 121; Mathew, 105
16 Cal. Span., IV, i, 818–9
17 Cal. Span., IV, ii, 154; L. & P., VI, 266
18 L. & P., XII, ii, 48, 341
19 L. & P., VI, 472
20 L. & P., VI, 584–7
21 L. & P., IX, 288, 290; Cal. Span., V, i, 570
22 L. & P., VI, 282; Cal. Span., IV, ii, 788
23 Cal. Span., V, i, 264
24 Cal. Span., V, i, 280
25 L. & P., VIII, 104
26 L. & P., X, 374
27 Cal. Span., V, ii, 84
28 ibid.
29 L. & P. X, 359, 397
30 N.H.Nicolas, *Excerpta Historica*,

261–2; L. & P., X, 378; Cal. Span., V, ii, 126
31 G. Cavendish, 452, 455, 454
32 Cal. Span., V, ii, 126; N.H.Nicolas, *Excerpta Historica*, 261–2
33 L. & P., X, 361–3
34 Cal. Span., V, ii, 127
35 L. & P., X, 451, 487, 500–501
36 L. & P., XII, ii, 114, 231, 253
37 L. & P., XII, 254–5, 328
38 L. & P., XII, ii, 348
39 *Ellis, Original Letters*, Second Series, II, 110–11
40 L. & P., XIII, ii, 296
41 L. & P., XVI, 436
42 L. & P., XIV, ii, 108; L. & P., XV, 9; L. & P., XV, 43
43 Strickland, IV, 339; L. & P., XV, 462; ibid., 366
44 *Ellis, Original Letters*, Second Series, II, 41; L. & P., XIV, ii, 263; ibid., XV, 81; Fox, V, 516
45 Strype, *Ecclesiastical Memorials*, I, ii, 462
46 L. & P., XVI, 616
47 L. & P., XIV, 201–3; ibid., XV, 9
48 Strickland, IV, 398–99; L. & P., XVI, 631; ibid., 617–8
49 Strickland, IV, 412
50 L. & P., XVI, 616
51 HMC, Bath, II, 9–10; L. & P., XVI, 608–9; 616; 622; ibid., 617–8
52 Strickland, IV, 421; L. & P., XVI, 616; HMC Bath, II, 9–10; L. & P., XVI, 618; L.B.Smith, 189, quoting P.R.O. S.P. 1/167/f160
53 L. & P., XVI, 618; ibid., 613, 652
54 L. & P., XVI, 618; L. & P., XVII, 13
55 L. & P., XVI, 613; L. & P., XVII, 13, 62
56 Cal. Span., VI, i, 473; L. & P., XVII, 51
57 L. & P., XXI, ii, 386
58 Foxe, V, 553–4
59 L. & P., XXI, i, 589; Foxe, V, 547–8
60 Foxe, V, 559–60

Chapter II
1 Strickland, V, 108

2 Vertot, II, 104
3 Prescott, 84
4 H.Clifford, 62–3
5 H.Clifford, 68–9
6 Cal. Span., XI, 189; ibid., 204; *Complete Peerage*, Northampton; Strickland, V, 429, 341
7 Cal. Span., XI, 215–16
8 Cal. Span., XI, 213
9 Cal. Span., XI, 252; Cal. Span., XII, 180
10 Cal. Span., XI, 289; ibid., 328
11 Cal. Span., XI, 344; Cal. Span., XII, 144; ibid., 316
12 Erikson, 335; Cal. Span., XI, 333; Vertot, II, 243
13 Cal. Span., XI, 359; Vertot, II, 258
14 Wood, III, 304–8
15 *Chronicle of Queen Jane*, 128; ibid., 49
16 Cal. Span., XII, 214
17 Hume, *Philip*, 156
18 Hume, *Philip*, 157–8; ibid., 171, 163; R.Smith, 30
19 Hume, *Philip*, 164, 170, 153
20 Vertot, IV, 342; Cal. Ven., VI, i, 140
21 HMC, Rutland MS. I, 310
22 Vertot, V, 362; Cal. Span., XI, 395
23 H.Clifford, 68–9; ibid., 70
24 H.Clifford, 72

Chapter III
1 *Sidney Papers*, I, 375
2 *Sidney Papers*, II, 45, Rowse, *Ralegh*, 104
3 Nichols, *Elizabeth*, III, 425–6
4 Nichols, *Elizabeth*, I, 269–70; ibid., II, 480
5 HMC, *Hatfield Papers*, II, 10; N.Williams, *Elizabeth*, 194; Harington, I, 235
6 Goff, 275; Rawson, *Rich*, 21; *Sidney Papers*, I, 271
7 V.A.Wilson, 44; Bradford, *Parry*, 14; Nichols, *Elizabeth*, II, 403
8 Dunlop, 116
9 Ellis, Second Series, II, 273, 310
10 *Sidney Papers*, I, 361, 381; ibid., II, 66

11 Bradford, *Parry*, 23; Nicolas, *Hatton*, 255–6; Strype, *Life of Matthew Parker* (Oxford 1821), I, 572
12 Bradford, *Parry*, 10; Birch, *Elizabeth*, I, 136
13 HMC, *Rutland MSS.*, I, 232; *Sidney Papers*, I, 381; ibid., II, 87
14 Ellis, Second Series, III, 192; *Sidney Papers*, II, 123; Stone, *Crisis*, 100
15 Strickland, VI, 412; *Sidney Papers*, II, 97
16 *Sidney Papers*, II, 132, 159
17 Rawson, *Rich*, 226; Chamberlain, 65; Rawson, *Rich*, 21
18 Klarwill, 114
19 Cal. Span., *Elizabeth*, I, 95–6; Klarwill, 123–5
20 Cal. Span., *Elizabeth*, I, 112–13; Klarwill, 153–4
21 Klarwill, 113–14
22 *La Mothe Fénélon*, III, 468
23 Camden, 268
24 Cal. Span., *Elizabeth*, I, 220–21; CSPF, 1562, 12–15, 81, 463
25 Strickland, *Scottish Queens*, II, 438
26 Camden, 227
27 Carleton Williams, 114
28 Cal. Span., *Elizabeth*, I, 45; Wright, I, 8–9
29 CSPF, 1556–60, 1–2
30 Chapman, 2 *Tudor Portraits*, 186, 193, 197, quoting Harleian MS., 6286
31 CSPF, 1561–2, 277
32 Camden, 58–9
33 Ellis, Second Series, II, 279, 282; Cal. Span., *Elizabeth*, II, 4
34 Wright, I, 207
35 E.K.Chambers, *Lee*, 161; Harington, I, 359–60
36 Devereux, I, 156–7
37 HMC, Rutland MS., I, 321–22
38 HMC, Rutland MS., I, 107; HMC, *Bath*, IV, 158
39 Chamberlain, 151
40 *Leicester's Commonwealth* (1641 ed.), 32; Lodge, III, 17–18
41 Holles, 70; Jenkins, 187

42 Cal. Span., I, 472; *Notes & Queries*, vol. 167 (1934), 435; Cal. Span., Elizabeth, II, 511
43 Jenkins, 238; Camden, 232–3; G.F.Warner, XLV
44 Jenkins, 305
45 Nichols, *Elizabeth*, III, 455
46 Jenkins, 306; Birch, *Elizabeth*, II, 282
47 Birch, *Elizabeth*, II, 362; *Sidney Papers*, II, 92–3, 95
48 *Sidney Papers*, II, 174
49 Aubrey, 418
50 J.Winton, *Ralegh*, 113
51 Rowse, *Ralegh*, 164, 231
52 Rutland MS., I, 94; B.M.Ward, 61–2
53 Newdigate-Newdegate, 10–11, 12–13, 32
54 CDSP, Addenda, 1580–1628, 411; Newdigate-Newdegate, 42
55 Williams, *Queen's Men*, 252; Newdigate-Newdegate, 44; DNB Pembroke
56 *Sidney Papers*, II, 98; Harington, I, 234, 361, 232–3
57 Harington, I, 166
58 Camden, 659; HMC, *Hatfield Papers*, III, 438
59 Chamberlain, 140
60 Nichols, *Elizabeth*, III, 613

Chapter IV
1 Nichols, *James*, I, 124
2 Chambers, *The Elizabethan Stage*, 200; Clifford, 8; see CDSP, 1611–18, 595, 585
3 Lodge, III, 88
4 Birch, *James*, I, 449–50
5 Thoms, 345; Tillières, XXVII
6 PRO E101/438/7; E101/438/11; SP16/474/3; SP14/94/55; Carey, 76
7 CDSP, 1603–11, 208; McClure, II, 63; CDSP, 1603–11, 113; CDSP, 1611–18, 58; ibid., 446
8 CDSP, 1603–11, 602; Birch, *James*, I, 284; Nichols, *James*, II, 754

9 CDSP, 1611–18, 387, 456; Strickland, VII, 429
10 Birch, *James*, II, 194; CDSP, 1611–18, 184, 602
11 McClure, II, 436; Lodge, III, 157
12 Goodman I, 199; Birch, *James*, I, 71; ibid., 226
13 Harington, I, 350–1
14 Clifford, 16; ibid., 9
15 Hutchinson, 177; Weldon in *Secret Hist.*, I, 338; Clifford, 8; DNB, William Knollys
16 McClure, II, 247, 217; Birch, *James*, I, 278–9; *Divine Catastrophe of House of Stuart* in *Secret Hist.*, III, 396; PRO SP 14/12/6
17 Cornwallis, 46
18 Durant, *Arbella*, 117; ibid., 125; ibid., 109
19 Lodge, II, 97; Bradley, II, 197
20 Bradley, II, 238
21 Bradley, II, 248; ibid., 251
22 Goodman, I, 168; Winwood, II, 155; Cornwallis, 41; Weldon in *Secret Hist.*, II, 5; Bradley, II, 190; A.Wilson 685
23 Strickland, VII, 469
24 Nichols, *James*, I, 314; Strong & Orgel, I, 11; Winwood, II, 43–4; Nichols, *James*, II, 354
25 Strong & Orgel, I, 46, 43; Winwood, III, 239
26 Goodman, I, 168; Weldon in *Secret Hist.*, I, 375–6
27 Nichols, *James*, II, 414
28 Amos, 82
29 *State Trials*, II, 818; ibid., 807; Weldon in *Secret Hist.*, I, 389; *State Trials*, II, 807
30 Wilson, 693
31 *State Trials*, II, 932; Gibbs, 311; *State Trials*, II, 936
32 Birch, *James*, I, 407
33 Gibbs, 361; Birch, *James*, I, 407; Gibbs, 365
34 Weldon in *Secret Hist.*, I, 427
35 Wilson, 699
36 CDSP, 1619–23, 9; ibid., 93; quot. Mathew, *Jacobean Age*, 329

37 McClure, II, 206
38 McClure, II, 216
39 Birch, *James*, I, 438; ibid., 417; McClure, II, 141
40 Weldon in *Secret Hist.*, I, 442
41 CDSP, 1623–5, 105–6; Wilson, 727
42 Lockyer, 70, 68
43 Wilson, 728; Goodman, II, 183
44 Weldon in *Secret Hist.*, I, 442; Birch, *James*, II, 217; Weldon in *Secret Hist.*, I, 443–4; CDSP, 1619–23, 49
45 Cornwallis, 125
46 Birch, *Charles*, I, 35; Tillières, 89; Ludlow, III, 306; Tillières, 92
47 Richelieu, V, 144–5
48 Ludlow, III, 306; HMC, Eleventh Report, 25; Ellis, First Series, III, 212–3; HMC, Eleventh Report, 38
49 Ellis, First Series, III, 210–11; Tillières, 127
50 Ludlow, III, 308; Tillières, 135; Ellis, First Series, III, 237–9
51 Ellis, First Series, III, 239; ibid., 240–45; CDSP, 1625–6, 399; Birch, *Charles*, I, 140
52 Denbigh, 50; HMC, Eleventh Report, 83, 85
53 Birch, *Charles*, I, 388
54 PRO SP16/275/23; Suckling, *Works*, ed. Hazlitt (1874), I, 29; PRO, 31/3/53 fo. 52; CDSP, 1628–9, 81; ibid., 310
55 CPSV, XXII, 264, 281
56 *Household Ordinances*, 341, 347; Hutchinson, 127
57 Strong & Orgel, I, 384; HMC, Rutland MSS., I, 477–8
58 *Histrio-Mastix*, 214
59 CDSP, 1634–5, 595, 96
60 Huxley, 202–3; Birch, *Charles*, II, 230
61 Knowler, II, 165; Albion, 209
62 Albion, 162; Knowler, II, 120
63 Henrietta Maria, 32
64 Clarendon, *Rebellion*, IV, 149 n.
65 de Motteville, I, 206

Chapter V
1 Clarendon, *Life*, I, 377
2 Pepys, I, 265; Clarendon, *Life*, I, 384
3 Grammont, 192–93; Clarendon, *Life*, I, 387
4 Burnet, I, 303; Pepys, I, 320; Clarendon, *Life*, I, 392, 394
5 CDSP, 1663–64, 255; Evelyn, *Diary*, III, 360–61
6 CDSP, 1663–64, 264; PRO LS, 13/35, fo. 8; PRO LS, 13/32/fo. 8
7 PRO LS, 13/34/fo. 30; PRO LS, 13/36/fo. 59; Treasury Books, IV, 520; Treasury Books, III, 660; CDSP, 1668–9, 308; Evelyn, Godolphin, 53
8 PRO LS, 13/35/fo. 31; PRO LS, 13/32; fo. 17; PRO LS, 13/34/fo. 30; PRO LS, 13/32/fo. 26; PRO LS, 13/35
9 CDSP, 1662, 391–92
10 Pepys, VII, 336–7; E. Hamilton, *Illustrious Lady*, 23–4
11 Pepys, II, 229
12 Strickland, VIII, 288; Pepys, III, 68
13 Clarendon, *Life*, II, 167; Grammont, 115; Evelyn, *Diary*, III, 320–21
14 HMC, Beaufort MS., 53; CPSV, XXXIII, 154; P. Stanhope, LXXXIV; Pepys, III, 117
15 HMC, Beaufort MS., 52–3; CPSV, XXXIII, 171
16 Clarendon, *Life*, II, 172
17 Strickland, VIII, 319
18 Clarendon, *Life*, II, 192; CPSV, XXXIII, 183
19 Clarendon, *Life*, II, 193–4
20 Sergeant, 81; Strickland, VIII, 330; Pepys, IV, 112; CDSP, 1663–4, 160
21 Clarendon, *Life*, II, 178; Burnet, II, 168–69 n.; Pepys, VII, 159
22 Jusserand, 93; Pepys, IV, 68; HMC, Verney Papers, 480
23 Pepys, IV, 174, 177; ibid., 232; ibid., 216
24 Hartmann, *Belle Stuart*, 11;

Andrews, 37; Grammont, 129; Pepys, IV, 371

25 Burnet, I, 484; Grammont, 257
26 PRO LC, 3/73/fo. 187; Pepys, IX, 23; HMC, Rutland MS, II, 22; Boswell, 137
27 Burnet, I, 484; *Manuscripts of St George's Chapel*, ed. Sir John Neale, (1957) 60–61; Dasent, *Nell Gwynn*, 37
28 E.Hamilton, *Illustrious Lady*, 136; Burnet, I, 483–4
29 Forneron, 93; Masters, 140
30 Cowper, 94; Reresby, 303
31 Grammont, 195; ibid., 203, 199; Pepys, IV, 1; Burnet, I, 416
32 Pepys, VII, 158, 297; Grammont, 228; Pepys, VIII, 6
33 Grammont, 329; Burnet, II, 16
34 Evelyn, *Diary*, IV, 13; Pepys, VII, 404
35 Forneron, 22, 24–5
36 Forneron, 66–7, 92
37 Hartmann, *Vagabond Duchess*, 187; ibid., 218–9
38 E.Hamilton, *Illustrious Lady*, 152
39 Forneron, 95
40 E.Hamilton, *Illustrious Lady*, 152; Masters, 143–48; J.H.Wilson, 127, 155–6
41 CDSP, 1663–4, 542; Treasury Book, IV, 143; Grammont, 258
42 Pepys, V, 275; Grammont, 255–6
43 HMC, Rutland MS., II, 49–50; ibid., 32
44 Grammont, 273–4; Hartmann, *Charles II and Madame*, 94
45 Evelyn, *Diary*, IV, 69; Evelyn, *Godolphin*, 14; Pepys, IV, 1
46 *Commons Journals*, IX, 548
47 HMC, Beaufort MS., 83
48 H.Sidney, II, 136
49 HMC, Beaufort MS., 83
50 *Savile Letters*, 76–7; CDSP, 1678, 616
51 HMC, Rutland MS, II, 36; HMC Beaufort MS., 83
52 H.Sidney, I, 86; Evelyn, *Diary*, IV, 413; Forneron, 191

Chapter VI

1 Evelyn, *Diary*, IV, 319; Dalrymple, II, i, 174
2 Evelyn, *Diary*, IV, 418; Burnet, III, 13; Campana de Cavelli, II, 90. Evelyn, *Diary*, IV, 497; Burnet, III, 121; Oman, 96
3 Dalrymple, II, i, 171, 175; Chapman, *Mary II*, 266
4 E.Hamilton, *William's Mary*, 193; *At the Council Chamber in Whitehall 22nd October 1688*, 15
5 Chapman, *Mary II*, 163; E.Hamilton, *William's Mary*, 224; Doebner, 42
6 Doebner, 11; Burnet, IV, 239–40
7 Burnet, IV, 3
8 Doebner, 10
9 D.Green, *Queen Anne*, 56; *Conduct*, 11
10 D.Green, *Queen Anne*, 56; D.Hamilton, *Diary*, 23; D.Green, *Sarah*, 47
11 Doebner, 24
12 *Conduct*, 13; Gregg, 82; *Conduct*, 36
13 *Conduct*, 44–5; Additional MS. 61418, fo. 166, printed Gregg, 87; *Conduct*, 55
14 *Conduct*, 73; ibid., 75–6; ibid., 85; Gregg, 89
15 Ailesbury, I, 308; Additional MS. 61414, fo. 169; Curtis Brown, 56–7
16 Burnet, V, 7
17 *Conduct*, 297; Rowse, *Early Churchills*, 252; Marlborough, *Letters from Madresfield Park*, 19
18 Additional MS. 61424, fo. 15b
19 Additional MS. 61417, fo. 185, printed Strickland, XII, 167–8; Additional MS. 61416, fo. 209–11
20 *Conduct*, 279; Burnet, III, 407 n.
21 Swift, *Correspondence*, I, 38–9; Swift, *Journal to Stella*, II, 475, ibid., I, 317
22 *Conduct*, 136–7
23 Curtis Brown, 98–9
24 Additional MS. 61416, fo. 85b,

printed Gregg, 173; Curtis Brown, 123

25 Curtis Brown, 144; Snyder, I, 366

26 Curtis Brown, 153; Additional MS. 61416 fo. 195–195b; Curtis Brown, 99–100; Gregg, 193

27 Conduct, 159; Coxe, Marlborough, II, 13

28 Coxe, Marlborough, II, 15; Private Correspondence, I, 52

29 Burnet, VI, 36–7 n.; Swift, Prose Works, VIII, 153; Swift, Correspondence, II, 67

30 Gregg, 112, Additional MS. 61422, fo. 197; Snyder, II, 790

31 Additional MS. 61417, fo. 67, printed Gregg, 244; Churchill, II, 284

32 Additional MS. 61417, fo. 83, printed Gregg, 245; Private Correspondence, I, 87

33 Conduct, 182; ibid., 183

34 Conduct, 206

35 Conduct, 208

36 Additional MS. 61417, fo. 125; Coxe, Marlborough, II, 204

37 Curtis Brown, 244; Gregg, 274

38 Private Correspondence, I, 113

39 HMC Portland MS., IV, fo. 96

40 Snyder, II, 1025; Additional MS. 61417, fo. 145b, printed Curtis Brown, 229; Additional MS. 61417, fo. 147–8, printed D.Green, Sarah, 314

41 Poems on Affairs of State, VII, 309, 306

42 Additional MS. 61417, fo. 153, printed D.Green, Sarah, 318

43 Grammont, 264

44 Churchill, II, 418

45 Churchill, II, 478; Private Correspondence, I, 414–15

46 Stowe MS., (British Museum) 563, fo. 7, 2–3; Additional MS. 61417, fo. 181; ibid., fo. 189

47 Additional MS. 61417, fo. 189

48 Additional MS. 61418, fo. 3; Churchill, II, 641; Conduct, 224–5

49 Curtis Brown, 286

50 Additional MS. 61418, fo. 50–53, printed A.T.Thomson, II, 509–13

51 Private Correspondence, I, 234–5

52 Conduct, 233; Wentworth Papers, 103

53 Conduct, 239–44

54 D.Hamilton, Diary, 9

55 D.Hamilton, Diary, 12–13; 23

56 Additional MS. 61422, fo. 120, 140

57 See Gregg, 329; Additional MS. 61420, fo. 104

58 Additional MS. 61422, fo. 69

59 Swift, Prose Works, VIII, 146; Swift, Journal to Stella, II, 435; ibid., 443

60 D.Hamilton, Diary, 46

61 Strickland, XII, 351; ibid., 349; D.Hamilton, Diary, 40

62 Swift, Journal to Stella, II, 467; Burnet, VI, 34–5 n.

63 Swift, Journal to Stella, II, 658.

64 Swift, Prose works, VIII, 168; Burnet, VI, 36–7 n.; Wentworth Papers, 285

65 Biddle, 258, 281; Wentworth Papers, 274; Swift, Correspondence, II, 67; Holmes, 216

66 Swift, Corrrespondence, II, 81–2; D.Hamilton, Diary, 67; Biddle, 273

67 Swift, Correspondence, II, 109; Wentworth Papers, 408, 418

68 Burnet, Supplement, 291–2; Private Correspondence, I, 246; ibid., II, 111; HMC Portland MS., IV, fo. 536; D.Hamilton, Diary, 44; Burnet V, 454 n.

Chapter VII

1 Walpole, Reminiscences, 30

2 Delany, First Series, I, 12

3 Cowper, 3; Halsband, Hervey, 22; Cowper, 14–15

4 Cowper, 6

5 Cowper, 8; Burnet, V, 452n.; Additional MS. 61422 fo. 133b; Cowper, 8–9; Wentworth Papers, 439

6 Bristol Letterbooks, II, 91

7 Hervey (1884 ed.), I, 88; Suffolk

Correspondence, I, 292; *Bristol Letterbooks*, III, 37

8 Cowper, 21; Hatton, 196
9 *Wentworth Papers*, 434; Thomson, *Sundon*, I, 318
10 *Suffolk Correspondence*, I, 249; Cowper, 24–5; ibid., 26–7; ibid., 31
11 Cowper, 113; ibid., 81, 85; DNB, Savage
12 Montagu, *Complete Letters*, I, 267
13 Walpole, *Reminiscences*, 65–6
14 Hervey (1931 ed.), II, 472–3; Walpole, *Reminiscences*, 68
15 Panshanger MS., D/EP F 205, fo. 64; Cowper, 123; Melville, *Suffolk*, 175–6
16 Thomson, *Sundon*, I, 235–6
17 *Chesterfield Letters*, II, 669
18 Melville, *Maids*, 180; Walpole, *Reminiscences*, 60
19 *Suffolk Correspondence*, I, 360–61 n.; Melville, *Suffolk*, 45–6; Montagu, *Complete Letters*, II, 32; Ilchester, 300
20 Delany, First Series, 68–9; Ilchester, 300
21 Cowper, 126–7
22 Panshanger MS. D/EP F203, fo. 12–14
23 HMC, Portland, V, 547
24 Panshanger MS. D/EP F201, fo. 172; ibid., F204, fo. 86; HMC, Portland, V, 548; Panshanger MS. D/EP F201, fo. 23
25 Panshanger MS. D/EP F203, fo. 34; ibid., F 193, fo. 56
26 HMC, Portland, V, 547, 550; RA, Additional, 28/36
27 RA, Additional, 28/38; ibid., 46; ibid., 47; ibid., 48; ibid., 50
28 Panshanger MS. D/EP F193, fo. 60; Cowper, 129
29 Cowper, 154–6; ibid., 163
30 Cowper, 166, 168, 167, 172
31 *Chesterfield Letters*, III, 1407–8; See, *Suffolk Correspondence*, I, 245–6; Hervey (1931 ed.), 472–3;

ibid., 380; Melville, *Suffolk*, 187; Hervey (1931 ed.), I, 43
32 Hervey (1931 ed.), II, 472–4
33 Hervey (1931 ed.), II, 474; *Suffolk Correspondence*, I, 292–3
34 Hervey (1931 ed.), 474
35 Thomson, *Sundon*, I, 242–3; ibid., 233; *Suffolk Correspondence*, II, 1–2
36 Hervey (1931 ed.), II, 601
37 Hervey (1931 ed.), 67; Thomson, *Sundon*, II, 316–17; ibid., 238; Walpole, *Letters*, I, 159
38 Walpole, *Letters*, I, 159; Hervey (1931 ed.), 66–7; ibid., II, 396; ibid., III, 753–4
39 Walpole, *Letters*, I, 159
40 Hervey (1931 ed.), II, 458
41 Hervey (1931 ed.), II, 491; ibid., 605, 602
42 HMC, Egmont, I, 235; ibid., 218; ibid., 225
43 HMC, Egmont, I, 390; ibid., 265–6; HMC, Carlisle, VI, 96
44 Hervey (1884 ed.), II, 192
45 HMC, Egmont, II, 198; Hervey (1931 ed.), II, 480; 482
46 Hervey (1931 ed.), II, 475; ibid., 554
47 HMC, Carlisle, VI, 165; ibid., 171
48 Hervey (1931 ed.), III, 838; ibid., 849–50; HMC, Carlisle, VI, 187
49 HMC, Carlisle, VI, 191; *Wentworth Papers*, 533
50 Hervey (1931 ed.), III, 896; Walpole, *Reminiscences*, 58; Additional MS. 38880, fo. 99
51 Chevenix Trench, 270

Chapter VIII
1 Lennox, I, 26; Bute, 39
2 Bute, 39, 55
3 Walpole, *Letters*, V, 94, ibid., 89, 74; HMC, *Various Collections*, VIII, 179; Walpole, *George III*, I, 206; Lennox, I, 60
4 Bute, 58; Papendiek, I, 16; ibid., 141, 36; ibid., 17; Aspinall, *Prince of Wales*, III, 255

5 Papendiek, I, 16; D'Arblay, III, 338; ibid., IV, 487; ibid., III, 10
6 Northumberland, 63, n.; Walpole, *Last Journals*, I, 542; Pindar, *Works*, I, 494
7 *The Times*, 10 July 1786, 2c; ibid., 12 July 1786, 2d; Additional MSS. 17870 & 17871 fo. 2b
8 *Harcourt Diary*, 43–5; *Harcourt Papers*, VI, 99–100; Coke, III, 65
9 Walpole, *George III*, I, 334; Northumberland, 97; Walpole, *Last Journals*, I, 17; Coke, I, 142; Walpole, *Last Journals*, II, 202–3; Aspinall, *George III*, V, 654; Bleakley, 193
10 D'Arblay, II, 421; Walpole, *Last Journals*, I, 125; Glenbervie, I, 214; *Harcourt Papers*, III, 170; ibid., IV, 79
11 *George III, his Court and Family*, 131
12 Papendiek, I, 33; Walpole, *Letters*, XII, 46
13 D'Arblay, II, 352–3
14 D'Arblay, II, 440; ibid., 469; ibid., 473–4; Bury, I, 3
15 D'Arblay, II, 469; ibid., IV, 78, Bury, II, 7
16 D'Arblay, IV, 100; *Pembroke Papers*, 359
17 D'Arblay, II, 405; Suffolk, II, 262
18 D'Arblay, II, 396-401
19 D'Arblay, III, 181; ibid., IV, 351; Mary Hamilton, 127
20 D'Arblay, III, 33; Delany, Second Series, III, 360–61 n.
21 D'Arblay, III, 10; ibid., III, 339–40; ibid., 343–4, 360
22 D'Arblay, IV, 434; ibid., 392
23 D'Arblay, IV, 452; ibid., V, 363; Papendiek, II, 267; D'Arblay, V, 363
24 *Royal Kalendar*; Papendiek, II, 17; Aspinall, *Prince of Wales*, VIII, 333; D'Arblay, II, 363–4; Aspinall, *Prince of Wales*, VIII, 333
25 Walpole, *Letters*, VI, 115;

26 D'Arblay, II, 363–4; Mary Hamilton, 205
26 D'Arblay, IV, 376; ibid., IV, 399–400; ibid., IV, 429; ibid., III, 64–5
27 *Harcourt Papers*, IV, 31; D'Arblay, IV, 157
28 *Harcourt Papers*, IV, 125; ibid., 129–30
29 *Harcourt Papers*, IV, 153; D'Arblay, IV, 253; Greenwood, II, 225
30 *Harcourt Papers*, IV, 175, 158
31 *Harcourt Papers*, IV, 241
32 *Harcourt Papers*, IV, 141; Fulke Greville, 126, 147; *Harcourt Papers*, IV, 132
33 *Harcourt Papers*, IV, 141; Louisa Stuart, II, 146
34 Fulke Greville, 139–40, 142, 165, 199; Frampton, 22–3 n.
35 *Harcourt Diary*, 41–2; ibid., 28
36 Granville Leveson Gower, I, 462; ibid., II, 25; Pembroke MS., Personal 23, Princess Elisabeth-Lady Pembroke, 24 Nov 1804; ibid., Queen-Lady Pembroke, 27 Feb 1818
37 Aspinall, *Prince of Wales*, VII, 292
38 Frampton, 84; Granville Leveson Gower, I, 359; *Farington Diary*, I, 71; Malmesbury, III, 166
39 *Harcourt Papers*, V, 625, 630
40 Glenbervie, II, 88
41 Malmesbury, III, 217; Mary Frampton, 84 n.; Malmesbury, III, 217–18
42 Bury, I, 14; Malmesbury, III, 219
43 Bury, I, 23; Aspinall, *Prince of Wales*, III, 73; ibid., 70
44 Aspinall, *Prince of Wales*, III, 168–70
45 Aspinall, *Prince of Wales*, III, 177-9; ibid., 184–5; ibid., 187 and n.; ibid., 188–9; ibid., 190–94
46 Aspinall, *Prince of Wales*, III, 201; ibid., 246 and n.
47 Aspinall, Prince of Wales, III, 374–5; Glenbervie, II, 88; Aspinall, *Prince of Wales*, III, 375

48 Bury, I, 400; Glenbervie, I, 260
49 Aspinall, *Prince of Wales*, IV, 235–7; ibid., 241; ibid., 237
50 Aspinall, *Prince of Wales*, IV, 241; Glenbervie, I, 281
51 *Farington Diary*, III, 292; Louisa Stuart, III, 187
52 Huish, I, 131; ibid., 133–4
53 Huish, I, 197; ibid., 140; ibid., 150
54 Huish, I, 152; ibid., 165
55 Huish, I, 197
56 Huish, I, 211; *The Book*, 33–4; Aspinall, *Prince of Wales*, V, 404
57 Huish, I, 311, 328, 331, 333, 424
58 Glenbervie, II, 1
59 Glenbervie, II, 87–8
60 Bury, I, 16; Glenbervie, II, 79; ibid., 18–19
61 Bury, I, 106; Glenbervie, II, 21
62 Knight, I, 221
63 Huish, I, 473, 491 ; *Vindication of Lady Douglas*, 16; Aspinall, *George IV*, I, 181 n.; Huish, I, 545
64 Aspinall, *George IV*, I, 181, n.; ibid.,III, 499
65 Bury, II, 53; ibid., 29; ibid., 129
66 Aspinall, *George IV*, II, 281 n; Berry, III, 239
67 Bury, I, 111–12
68 Berry, III, 247–8
69 Berry, III, 256; Aspinall, *George IV*, II, 371
70 Bury, II, 310
71 Aspinall, *George IV*, II, 497; n.
72 Frampton, 371; *Jerningham Letters*, II, 371–2

Chapter IX
1 *Girlhood*, I, 198
2 *Quarterly Review*, July 1837, 247; *Girlhood*, I, 243
3 *Statement of . . . Lady Flora Hastings*, 57; Woodham-Smith, 162, quot. RA *Journal*, 23 April 1838
4 Dormer Creston, 307
5 *The Late Lady Flora Hastings*, 27
6 Greville, IV, 145–6; *Statement of . . . Lady Flora Hastings*, 18; ibid., 26;

Longford, *Victoria*, 96, quot. RA *Journal*, 21 Feb 1839; *Statement of . . . Lady Flora Hastings*, 26
7 *Statement of . . . Lady Flora Hastings*, 7; *The Late Lady Flora Hastings*, 27; Woodham-Smith, 165, 164. quot. RA *Journal*, 2 Feb 1839
8 *Statement of . . . Lady Flora Hastings*, 6, 31; *Late Lady Flora Hastings*, 28
9 *Late Lady Flora Hastings*, 27–8; *Statement of . . . Lady Flora Hastings*, 47; ibid., 5; Jerrold, 289; *Late Lady Flora Hastings*, 28
10 *Statement of . . . Lady Flora Hastings*, 58; ibid., 45; *Late Lady Flora Hastings*, 29
11 *Statement of . . . Lady Flora Hastings*, 45; ibid., 46–7; Woodham-Smith, 167–8 quot. RA *Journal*, 23 Feb 1839
12 Longford, *Victoria*, 99, quot. RA *Journal*, 19 Sept 1839, and RA Z486, *The Case of Lady Flora Hastings*
13 Greville, IV, 153
14 *Statement of . . . Lady Flora Hastings*, 9; ibid., 12
15 Woodham-Smith, 175 quot. RA *Journal*, 16 April 1839; *Statement of . . . Lady Flora Hastings*, 38; ibid., 42
16 Jerrold, 261; *Statement of . . . Lady Flora Hastings*, 61
17 *Girlhood*, II, 16
18 Victoria, *Letters*, First Series, I, 202, 204
19 *Girlhood*, II, 171
20 Broughton, V, 192–3, *Girlhood*, II, 178
21 Greville, IV, 167
22 Woodham-Smith, 179, quot. RA *Journal*, 25–7 June 1839; Jerrold, 274–5
23 *Statement of . . . Lady Flora Hastings*, 44; Greville, IV, 188; ibid., 208
24 Greville, IV, 212; Jerrold, 285

25 Greville, VII, 10; Fulford, *Darling Child*, 53
26 M.Ponsonby, 40; Mallet, XVII; E. Stanley, 23–4; Bloomfield, I, 22–3
27 Mallet, 13; Mallet, 178
28 Victoria, *Letters*, First Series, I, 337
29 Victoria, *Letters*, First Series, I, 338
30 Victoria, *Letters*, First Series, I, 390
31 *Girlhood*, II, 103–4
32 Longford, *Victoria*, 571; A.L.Kennedy, 63; M.Ponsonby, 6; Victoria, *Letters*, Third Series, I, 614
33 Fulford, *Your Dear Letter*, 254
34 Victoria, *Letters*, Third Series, I, 57–8
35 ibid.
36 Victoria, *Letters*, Third Series, III, 150, 153
37 A.L.Kennedy, 83, 67; A.Ponsonby, 154
38 Mallet, 147; Esher, I, 214
39 A.L.Kennedy, 224; A.Ponsonby, 58, 57
40 A.Ponsonby, 166–7
41 Victoria, *Letters*, Second Series, II, 47–8; Longford, *Victoria*, 436
42 Victoria, *Letters*, Second Series, III, 174; Longford, *Victoria*, 490
43 Victoria, *Letters*, First Series, I, 381
44 Victoria, *Letters*, Second Series, II, 64
45 E.Stanley, 120; Bloomfield, I, 34
46 Victoria, *Letters*, First Series, II, 455
47 V.Watson, 230–31
48 Greville, VI, 441; Woodham-Smith, 304
49 E.Stanley, 176; Bloomfield, I, 108; Lyttelton, 282; Mallet, 4; Bloomfield, I, 19–20, 96
50 A.Stanley, 232; Mallet, 37
51 A.Stanley, *Later Letters*, 25 n.
52 A.L.Kennedy, 186, 189; A. Stanley, *Later Letters*, 27
53 E.Stanley, 205, 287
54 Mallet, 32
55 Victoria, *Letters*, Second Series, 386; Longford, 402; Princess Marie Louise, 144–5

56 Fulford, *Your Dear Letter*, 26; Victoria, *Letters*, Second Series, II, 386; Fulford, *Darling Child*, 195
57 Victoria, *Letters*, First Series, I, 496; Bloomfield, I, 134; Victoria, *Letters*, Second Series, I, 113–14; A.Stanley, *Later Letters*, 27
58 Mallet, 4; ibid., 32; ibid., 44; 54; 61
59 Greville, VII, 58–9; Creevey, II, 327; Mallet, 72–3; Longford, *Antrim*, 15, 79
60 Mallet, 78, 91; Longford, *Antrim*, 17; Mallet, 165

Chapter X
1 Airlie, 106
2 Longford, *Antrim*, 97
3 Madol, 151
4 Escott, 32–3; Ormathwaite, 139
5 Fulford, *Dearest Mama*, 289 n; Battiscombe, 280
6 Pope-Hennessy, 356
7 Battiscombe, 203
8 Pope-Hennessy, 314; K.Villiers, 7; Airlie, 129
9 Asquith, 132; Mosley, 200, 193
10 Airlie, 129–30; Pope-Hennessy, 491
11 Mosley, 244; Curzon, 111
12 Airlie, 146–7
13 Laird, *Queen Mother*, 145
14 ibid., 216
15 Donaldson, 105; Laird, *Queen Mother*, 83
16 Colville, 108; Laird, *Queen Mother*, 225
17 Tisdall, *Unpredictable Queen*, 105; Colville, 123
18 *Daily Telegraph*, 29 October 1980
19 Colville, 109; K. Villiers, 195; Laird, *How the Queen Reigns*, 54
20 Windsor, 289
21 Stott, 'Where have you gone to my pretty maids', *passim*
22 Airlie, 127
23 Duncan, 16
24 *Daily Mail*, 26 September 1981

Bibliography

Ailesbury, Thomas, *Memoirs of Thomas Earl of Ailesbury*, 2 Vols, Roxburghe Club, 1890

Airlie, Mabell Countess of, *Thatched with Gold*, Ed. Jennifer Ellis, Hutchinson, 1962

Akrigg, G.P.V., *Jacobean Pageant*, Hamish Hamilton, 1962

Albion, Gordon, *Charles I and the Court of Rome*, Burn Oates & Washbourne, 1935

Amos, Andrew, *The Great Oyer of Poisoning: Trial of the Earl of Somerset*, Richard Bentley, 1846

Andrews, Allen, *The Royal Whore*, Hutchinson, 1971

Anglo, Sydney, *Spectacle, Pageantry and Early Tudor Policy*, Oxford University Press, 1969

Arkell, R.L., *Caroline of Ansbach*, Oxford University Press, 1939

Ashdown, Dulcie M., *Ladies-in-Waiting*, Arthur Barker, 1976

Aspinall, Arthur (Ed.), *George III = Later Correspondence of George III*, 5 Vols, Cambridge, 1962–70
  Prince of Wales = Correspondence of George Prince of Wales, 1770–1812, Cassell, 8 Vols, 1963
  George IV = Letters of George IV, 3 Vols, Cambridge, 1938

Asquith, Margot, *The Autobiography of Margot Asquith*, Ed. Mark Bonham-Carter, Eyre & Spottiswoode, 1962

At the Council Chamber in Whitehall, 22nd October, 1685

Aubrey, John, *Brief Lives*, Ed. Oliver Lawson Dick, Penguin edition, 1978

'Aulicus coquinariae' in *Secret History of James I* (Edinburgh 1811) Vol II

Aylmer, G.E., *The King's Servants*, Routledge & Kegan Paul, 1974

Bagley, J.J., *Margaret of Anjou, Queen of England*, Herbert Jenkins, 1948

Battiscombe, Georgina, *Queen Alexandra*, Constable, 1969

Beattie, J.M., *The English Court in the Reign of George I*, Cambridge University Press, 1967

Berry, Mary, *Extracts of the Journals and Correspondence of Miss Berry*, Ed. Lady Theresa Lewis, 3 Vols, Longman Green & Co, 1865

Bevan, Bryan, *Nell Gwynn*, Robert Hale, 1969
  Charles II's French Mistress, Robert Hale, 1972

Biddle, Sheila, *Bolingbroke and Harley*, George Allen & Unwin, 1975

Bingham, Caroline, *James I of England*, Weidenfeld & Nicolson, 1981

Birch, Thomas, *Elizabeth = Memoirs of the Reign of Queen Elizabeth*, 2 Vols, A. Millar, 1754
  James = The Court and Times of James I, 2 Vols, Henry Colburn, 1849
  Charles = The Court and Times of Charles I, 2 Vols, Henry Colburn, 1849

Blackley, F.D., and Hermansen, G. (Eds), *The Household Book of Queen Isabella of England*, University of Alberta Press, Alberta, Canada, 1971

Bleakley, Horace, *The Story of a Beautiful Duchess; being an account of the life & times of Elizabeth Gunning, Duchess of Hamilton & Argyll*, Constable, 1908
Bloomfield, Georgiana Baroness, *Reminiscences of Court and Diplomatic Life*, 2 Vols, Kegan Paul Trench & Co, 1883
*The Book. Being the whole of the depositions on the investigation of the conduct of the Princess of Wales . . . by C.V.*Williams, Sherwood Neely & Jones, 1813
Boswell, Elenore, *The Restoration Court Stage*, Harvard University Press, Cambridge, Massachussetts, 1932
Bradford, C.A., *Parry = Blanche Parry*, 1925
   Helena Marchioness of Northampton, George Allen & Unwin, 1936
Bradley, E.T. *Arbella Stuart*, 2 Vols, Richard Bentley, 1889
Bristol Letterbooks. The Letterbooks of John Hervey, 1st Earl of Bristol, 3 Vols, Suffolk Green books, No. I, 1894
Broughton, John Cam Hobhouse, Baron, *Recollections of a Long Life*, Ed. by his daughter Lady Dorchester, Vols 5 & 6, John Murray, 1911
Brownlow, Emma, Lady, *Eve of Victorianism*, John Murray, 1940
Burnet, Gilbert, *History of his own Times*, Ed. the Earls of Dartmouth and Hardwick, 6 Vols, 1833
Bury, Lady Charlotte, *Diary of a Lady-in-Waiting*, 2 Vols, John Lane, the Bodley Head, 1908
Bute, Lord, *Letters from George III to Lord Bute*, Ed. Romney Sedgwick, Macmillan, 1939
Byrne, Muriel St Clare, *The Lisle Letters*, 6 Vols, University of Chicago Press, 1981
Camden, William, *History of Elizabeth*, 1675
Campana de Cavelli, Marquise de, *Les derniers Stuarts à St Germain en Laye*, 2 Vols, Paris 1871
Carey, Robert, *Memoirs of Robert Carey, Earl of Monmouth*, Ed. F.H.Mares, Oxford, 1972
Carleton, Dudley, *Dudley Carleton and John Chamberlain*, Ed. M.Lee, Rutgers University Press, New Brunswick, New Jersey, 1972
Carleton Williams, Ethel, *Bess of Hardwick*, Longmans, 1959
   Anne of Denmark, Longmans, 1970
Carlisle, Nicholas, *An Enquiry into the Place and Quality of His Majesty's Most Honourable Privy Chamber*, Payne & Foss, 1829
Carmi-Parsons, John, *The Court and Household of Eleanor of Castile in 1290*, Pontifical institute of mediaeval studies, Toronto, 1977
Cathcart, Helen, Article on ladies-in-waiting in *Woman's Weekly*, 9 June 1973
   Her Majesty, W.H.Allen, 1962
Cavendish, Lady Frederick, *Diary of Lady Frederick Cavendish*, Ed. John Bailey, 2 Vols, John Murray, 1927
Cavendish, George, *Life of Cardinal Wolsey*, Harding & Lepard, 1827
Chamberlain, John, *Letters written by John Chamberlain in the Reign of Queen Elizabeth*, Camden Society, 79, 1861
Chamberlayne, Edward, *Angliae Notitia, or the Present State of England*, 1669–1707
Chamberlayne, John, *Magna Britannia Notitia, or Present State of Great Britain*, 1710–1755
Chambers, E.K. *Lee = Sir Henry Lee*, Oxford, 1936
   The Elizabethan Stage, Vol. I, Oxford, 1923

BIBLIOGRAPHY

Chapman, Hester, *Anne Boleyn*, Jonathan Cape, 1974
    Lady Jane Grey, Jonathan Cape, 1962
    Two Tudor Portraits, Jonathan Cape, 1962
    Mary II, Jonathan Cape, 1953
Chesterfield Letters. Letters of Philip Dormer Stanhope Earl of Chesterfield, Ed.
    John Bradshaw, 3 Vols, Swan Sonnenschein & Co, 1892
Chevenix Trench, Charles, *George II*, Allen Lane, 1973
Childe-Pemberton, W.S., *Elizabeth Blount and Henry VIII*, Eveleigh Nash, 1913
Chronicque de la traison et mort de Richart deux, Ed. Benjamin Williams, English
    History Society, 1846
Chronicle of Queen Jane and two years of Queen Mary, Ed. J.G.Nichols, Camden
    Society, 1850
Churchill, Randolph, S., *They Serve the Queen*, Hutchinson, 1953
Churchill, Winston, S., *Marlborough, His life and times*, 2 Vols, George Harrap,
    1947
Clarendon, Edward, *Life = Life of Edward Earl of Clarendon*, Vols I & II, Oxford
    1759
    History of the Rebellion and Civil Wars in England, Ed. W.Owen Maisey,
        6 Vols, Oxford, 1888
Clifford, Anne, *Diary of Lady Anne Clifford*, Ed. Vita Sackville-West, Heinemann,
    1923
Clifford, Henry, *Life of Jane Dormer, Duchess of Feria*, Burns & Oates, 1887
Clitherow Letters, *Glimpses of King William IV & Queen Adelaide in letters of the
    late Miss Clitherow*, Ed. G.Cecil White, R.Brimley Johnson, 1902
Coke, Lady Mary, *Letters and Journals of Lady Mary Coke*, 4 Vols, Kingsmead
    reprints, 1970
Colville, Lady Cynthia, *Crowded Life*, Evans Bros, 1963
Complete Peerage, by G.E.Cokayne, Ed. H.A.Doubleday & Lord Howard de
    Walden, Revised by Vicary Gibbs, 12 Vols, St Catherine Press, 1929
Conduct: *An account of the conduct of the Dowager Duchess of Marlborough from
    her first coming to court until the year 1710*, by Nathaniel Hooke, 1742
Cornwallis, Jane, Lady *Private Correspondence*, S.J.Bentley, 1842
Court and City Kalendar, 1756–69
Court and City Register, 1726–69
Cowper, Mary, Countess, *Diary 1714–20*, John Murray, 1864
Coxe, William, *Marlborough = Memoirs of the Duke of Marlborough*, 3 Vols,
    Henry F.Bonn, 1847
Creevey, Thomas, *Creevey Papers*, Ed. Herbert Maxwell, 2 Vols, John Murray, 1903
Creston, Dormer, *The Youthful Queen Victoria*, Macmillan, 1952
Curtis, Gila, *Life and Times of Queen Anne*, Weidenfeld & Nicolson, 1973
Curtis Brown, Beatrice, *Letters and Diplomatic instructions of Queen Anne*,
    Cassell, 1935
Curzon, Marchioness of, *Reminiscences*, Hutchinson, 1955
Cust, Lionel, *King Edward VII and his Court*, John Murray, 1930
Dalrymple, Sir John, *Memoirs of Great Britain and Ireland*, 3 Vols, 1790
D'Arblay, Fanny, *Diary and Letters of Madame d'Arblay*, Ed. by her niece Charlotte
    Barrett with preface and notes by Austin Dobson, 6 Vols, Macmillan, 1904
Dasent, A.I., *Nell Gwynn*, Macmillan, 1924
    Private Life of Charles II, Cassell, 1927

BIBLIOGRAPHY

Davidson, L.C., *Catherine of Braganza*, John Murray, 1908
Delany, Mary, *Autobiography and Correspondence of Mary Granville, Mrs Delany*,
  Ed. Lady Llandover, 1st Series, 3 Vols, Richard Bentley, 1861; 2nd Series, 3 Vols,
  Richard Bentley, 1862
Denbigh, Cecilia Countess of, *Royalist Father and Roundhead Son*, Methuen, 1915
Devereux, Walter B., *Lives and letters of the Devereux*, 2 vols, John Murray, 1853
Dictionary of National Biography
'Divine Catastrophe of House of Stuart', In *Secret History of James I*, Vol. II,
  Edinburgh, 1821
Doebner, R., *Memoirs of Mary Queen of England*, David Nutt, 1886
Donaldson, Frances, *King George VI and Queen Elizabeth*, Weidenfeld & Nicholson,
  1977
Duff, David, *Alexandra, Princess and Queen*, Collins, 1980
Duncan, Andrew, *The Reality of Monarchy*, Heinemann, 1970
Dunlop, I., *The Palaces and Progresses of Elizabeth I*, Jonathan Cape, 1962
Durant, David, *Bess of Hardwick*, Weidenfeld & Nicolson, 1977
  Arbella Stuart, Weidenfeld & Nicolson, 1978
Dutton, R., *English court Life*, Batsford, 1963
Ellis, Henry, *Ellis' Original Letters*. 1st Series, 3 Vols, 1824
  2nd Series, 4 Vols, 1827
  3rd Series, 4 Vols, 1846
Erikson, Carolly, *Bloody Mary*, J.M.Dent, 1978
Escott, T.H.S., *King Edward and his court*, T.Fisher Unwin, 1903
Esher, Reginald, *Journals and Letters of Reginald Viscount Esher*, Ed.
  Maurice V.Brett, Vol. I, Ivor Nicholson & Watson, 1934
Evelyn, John, *Diary*, Ed. E.S.deBeer, 6 Vols, Oxford 1955
  Godolphin = *Life of Mrs Godolphin*, Ed. Harriet Sampson, Oxford, 1939
Farington Diary, Joseph Farington, *Farington Diary*, Ed. James Greig, 8 Vols,
  Hutchinson, 1922–8
Fea, Allen, *James II and his Wives*, Methuen, 1908
Fénelon, La Mothe, *Recueil des dépêches, rapports, instructions et mémoires des
  ambassades*, Volume III, Paris et Londres, 1840
Finch Diary, *Diary of Lady Charlotte Finch*, Mss in Leicester County Record Office,
  Finch Mss, DG7, D7
Forneron, H., *Louise de Kerouaille, Duchess of Portsmouth*, 1887
Fox Davies, Arthur Charles, *Their Majesties' Court*, Caxton Pub Co., 1907
Foxe, John, *Acts and Monuments*, Vol V, Religious Tract Society, 1877
Frampton, Mary, *Journal of Mary Frampton*, Ed. H.G.Mundy, Sampson, Low,
  Marston Searle & Rivington, 1885
Fraser, Antonia, *Charles II*, Weidenfeld & Nicolson, 1979
Friedmann, Paul, *Anne Boleyn*, 2 Vols, Macmillan, 1834
Froissart, *Sir John Froissart's Chronicles of England, France and the Surrounding
  Countries*, Trans. Thomas Jonnes, 5 Vols, Hafod Press, 1803
Fulford, Roger, Ed., *Dearest Child*, Evans Bros, 1977
  Dearest Mama, Evans Bros, 1968
  Your Dear Letter, Evans Bros, 1971
  Darling Child, Evans Bros, 1976
Fulke Greville, Robert, *Diaries of Colonel the Hon. Robert Fulke Greville*, Ed.
  F.Mckno Bladon, John Lane, 1930

BIBLIOGRAPHY

Furnivall, F.J., *Life Records of Chaucer*, Kegan Paul Trench Trubner & Co, 1900
George III, his court & family, R.Bentley, 1820
Gibbs, Philip, *King's Favourite: The Love Story of Robert Carr, and Lady Essex*, Hutchinson, 1909
Girlhood of Queen Victoria, The, Ed. Viscount Esher, 2 Vols, John Murray, 1912
Glenbervie, Sylvester, *Diaries of Sylvester Douglas, Lord Glenbervie*, Ed. Francis Bickley, 2 Vols, Constable, 1928
Goff, Cecilie, *A Woman of the Tudor Age*, John Murray, 1930
Goodman, Godfrey, *The Court of King James I*, Ed. J.S.Brewer, 2 Vols, Richard Bentley, 1839
Grammont, Count, *Memoirs of*, by Anthony Hamilton, Ed. Walter Scott, Routledge, 1905
Granville Leveson Gower, *Granville Leveson Gower, 1st Earl Granville, Private Correspondence*, Ed. Castalia Countess Cranville, 2 Vols, John Murray, 1916
Green, David, *Queen Anne*, Collins, 1970
Sarah, Duchess of Marlborough, Collins, 1967
Greenwood, Alice Drayton, *Lives of the Hanoverian Queens of England*, 2 Vols, G.Bell, 1911
Gregg, Edward, *Queen Anne*, Routledge & Kegan Paul, 1980
Greville, Charles, *The Greville Memoirs*, Ed. Lytton Strachey and Roger Fulford, 8 Vols, Macmillan 1938
Grew, Marion S. and Edwin S., *The Court of William III*, Mills & Boon, 1910
The English Court in Exile, Mills & Boon, 1911
Hall, Edward, *Henry VIII*, Ed. Charles Whibley, 2 Vols. L.C. & E.Jack, 1904
Hall, Hubert, *Court Life under the Plantaganets*, Swan Sonnenschein & Co, 1890
Halsband, Robert, *Lord Hervey*, Oxford 1973
Hamilton, David, *Diary of Sir David Hamilton*, Ed. Philip Roberts, Oxford 1975
Hamilton, Elizabeth, *Henrietta Maria*, Hamish Hamilton, 1976
The Illustrious Lady, Hamish Hamilton, 1980
William's Mary, Hamish Hamilton, 1972
The Backstairs Dragon, Hamish Hamilton, 1969
Hamilton, Mary, *Mary Hamilton, Afterwards Mrs John Dickenson, at Court and at Home, from Letters and Diaries, 1756–1816*, Ed. Elizabeth & Florence Anson, John Murray, 1925
Handover, P.M., *Arbella Stuart*, Eyre & Spottiswoode, 1957
Harcourt Diary, 'Mrs Harcourt's diary of the court of King George III', in *Miscellanies of Philobiblon Society*, XIII, 1871–2
Harcourt Papers, Ed. Edward William Harcourt, 14 Vols, Privately Printed, Oxford, 1880–1905
Hardy, Alan, *The King's Mistresses*, Evans Bros, 1980
Hardy, B.C., *Philippa of Hainault and Her Times*, John Long, 1910
Harington, John, *Nugae Antiquae*, Ed. Thomas Park, 2 Vols, 1804
Hartmann, C.H., *La Belle Stuart*, Routledge, 1924
The Vagabond Duchess, Routledge, 1926
Charles II and Madame, Heinemann, 1934
Harvey, Nancy Lee, *Elizabeth of York*, Arthur Barker, 1973
Hatton, Ragnhild, *George I, Elector and King*, Thames & Hudson, 1978
Hatton Correspondence, *Correspondence of the Family of Hatton*, 2 Vols, Camden Society, 1878

BIBLIOGRAPHY

Hedley, Olwen, *Queen Charlotte,* John Murray, 1975

Henrietta Maria, *Life and Death of that Matchless Mirror of Magnaminity and Heroic Virtues, Henrietta Maria de Bourbon,* 1669

Herbert, Lord, Ed., *Henry Elizabeth and George; Letters and Diaries of Henry 10th Earl of Pembroke and his Circle,* Jonathan Cape, 1939

Hertford Pomfret Correspondence, *Correspondence between Frances Countess of Hertford, and Henrietta Louisa, Countess of Pomfret, 1738–1741,* 3 Vols, Richard Philips, 1805

Hervey (1931) John, Lord Hervey: *Some materials towards the reign of King George II,* Ed. Romney Sedgwick, 3 Vols, Eyre & Spottiswoode, 1931

Hervey, John, Lord, *Memoirs of Reign of George II,* Ed. J.W.Croker, 2 Vols, John Murray, 1848

Hibbert, Christopher, *The Court at Windsor,* Longmans, 1964

   The Court of St James, Weidenfeld & Nicolson, 1969

   George IV, Vol. I, Longmans, 1972

Historical Manuscript Commission (HMC): Rutland Papers, Vols I, II, 12th Report, Appendix, parts IV & V

   Beaufort Mss, 12th Report, Appendix IX

   Verney Papers, 7th Report, part I

   Portland Mss, Vols IV & V, 15th Report, Appendix, part IV

   Egmont Mss, 3 Vols, 1920–3

   Carlisle Mss, 15th Report, Appendix, part VI

Hogrefe, Pearl, *Tudor Women,* Iowa, 1975

Holles, Gervase, *Memorials of the Holles Family,* Camden Society, 3rd Series, Vol 55, 1937

Holme, Thea, *Caroline: A Biography of Caroline of Brunswick,* Hamish Hamilton, 1979

Holmes, Geoffrey, *British Politics in the Age of Anne,* Macmillan, 1967

Holmes, George, *The Good Parliament,* Oxford University Press, 1975

Hopkirk, Mary, *Queen Over the Water,* John Murray, 1953

Household Ordinances, *A Collection of Ordinances and Regulations for the Government of the Royal Household . . . from King Edward III to King William and Queen Mary,* Society of Antiquaries, 1790

Huish, Robert, *Memoirs of her Late Majesty, Caroline Queen of Great Britain,* 2 Vols, T.Kelly, 1825

Hume, Martin, *The wives of Henry VIII,* E.Nash & Grayson, 1927

   Spanish Chronicle = Chronicle of King Henry VIII of England, Trans. M.A.S. Hume, 1889

   Philip = The Coming of Philip the Prudent, In The Year After the Armada, T.Fisher Unwin, 1896

Hutchinson, Lucy, *Memoirs of Colonel Hutchinson,* 2 Vols, Longman, Hurst Rees Orme & Brown, 1922

Huxley, Gervase, *Endymion Porter,* Chatto & Windus, 1959

Ilchester, Lord, Ed., *Lord Hervey and his Friends,* John Murray, 1950

Ives, E.W., 'Faction at the Court of Henry VIII: the Fall of Anne Boleyn', in *History,* 57, June 1972

Jameson, Anna, *Beauties of the court of Charles II,* London, 1833

Jenkins, Elizabeth, *Elizabeth and Leicester,* Victor Gollancz, 1961

Jerningham Letters, Ed. Egerton Castle, 2 Vols, Richard Bentley, 1896

BIBLIOGRAPHY

Jerrold, Clare, *Fair Ladies of Hampton Court*, John Long, 1911
   The Early Court of Queen Victoria, Eveleigh Nash, 1912
Jesse, J.H., *Memoirs of the Court of England during the Reign of the Stuarts*. 3 Vols, Richard Bentley, 1855
   Memoirs of the Court of England from the Revolution in 1688 to the Death of George II, 3 Vols, 1843
Johnstone, Grace, *Leading Women of the Restoration*, Digby Long & Co, 1891
Johnstone, Hylda, 'The Queen's Household', in T.F.Tout, *Chapters in the Administrative History of Mediaeval England*, Vol v, (1930) pp. 231-289
Jusserand, J.J., *A French Ambassador at the Court of Charles II*, T.Fisher Unwin, 1892
Kay, F.George, *Lady of the Sun*, Frederick Muller, 1966
Kelly, Amy, *Eleanor of Aquitaine and the Four Kings*, Cassell, 1952
Kennedy, A.L., Ed., *My Dear Duchess: Social and Political Letters to the Duchess of Manchester 1858-1869*, John Murray, 1956
Klarwill, Victor Von, *Queen Elizabeth and some Foreigners*, John Lane, Bodley Head, 1928
Knight, Cornelia, *Autobiography of Miss E. Cornelia Knight*, Ed. J.W.Kaye, 2 Vols, W.H.Allen, 1861
Knowler, William, *Letters and Despatches of the Earl of Strafford*, 2 Vols, W.Bowyer, 1739
Lacey, Robert, *An Elizabethan Icarus: Robert Earl of Essex*, Weidenfeld & Nicolson, 1971
   Majesty, Hutchinson, 1977
Laird, Dorothy, *How the Queen Reigns*, Hodder & Stoughton, 1959
   Queen Elizabeth the Queen Mother, Hodder & Stoughton, 1966
The Late Lady Flora Hastings, *Statement of the Marquis of Hastings etc.*, 1839
Le Comte, Edward, *The Notorious Lady Essex*. Robert Hale & Co, 1970
Leland, John, *De Rebus Britannicis Collectanea*, Volume IV, 1770
Lennox, Lady Sarah, *Life and letters of Lady Sarah Lennox*, Ed. Countess of Ilchester and Lord Stavordale, 2 Vols, John Murray, 1901
Lindsay, William Alexander, *The Royal Household*, Kegan Paul Trench Trubner, 1898
Lockyer, Roger, *Buckingham*, Longmans, 1981
Lodge, Edmund, *Illustrations of British History*, 3 Vols, John Chidley, 1838
Longford, Elizabeth, *Victoria = VictoriaR.I.*, Weidenfeld & Nicolson, 1964
   Antrim = Louisa Lady in Waiting, Jonathan Cape, 1979
   The Queen Mother, Weidenfeld & Nicolson, 1981
Ludlow, Edmund, *Memoirs of Edmund Ludlow*, Vol. III, Vevray, 1699
Lyttelton, Sarah, Baroness, *Correspondence of Sarah Spencer Lady Lyttelton, 1787-1870*, Ed. Mrs Hugh Wyndham, John Murray, 1912
Lytton, Edith, Lady, *Lady Lytton's Court Diary 1895-1899*, Ed. Mary Luytens, Rupert Hart Davis, 1961
McClure,N.E., Ed., *Letters of John Chamberlain*, 2 Vols, Philadelphia, 1939
Macgibbon, David, *Elizabeth Woodville*, Arthur Barker, 1938
Madol, Hans Roger, *Private life of Queen Alexandra*, Hutchinson, 1940
'Maids of Honour to the Queen', in *The Girls' Realm*, November 1904
Mallet, Victor, Ed., *Life with Queen Victoria*, John Murray, 1968
Malmesbury, James, Earl of, *Diaries and Correspondence of James Harris, 1st Earl of Malmesbury*, Ed. 3rd Earl of Malmesbury, Vol. III, Richard Bentley, 1844

Marie Louise, Princess, *My Memories of Six Reigns*, Evans Bros., 1956

Marlborough, Sarah, Duchess of, *Letters from Madresfield Court*, John Murray, 1875

Martiennsen, Anthony, *Katherine Parr*, Secker & Warburg, 1973

Masters, Bryan, *The Mistresses of Charles II*, Blond & Briggs, 1979

Mathew, David, *The Courtiers of Henry VIII*, Eyre & Spottiswoode, 1970

 The Jacobean Age, Longman Green & Co, 1938

Mathew, Gervase, *The Court of Richard II*, John Murray, 1968

Matthew, Tobie, *A Collection of Letters made by Sir Tobie Matthew with a Character of Lucy Countess of Carlisle*, 1660

Mattingly, Garrett, *Catherine of Aragon*, Jonathan Cape, 1942

Mavor, Elizabeth, *The Virgin mistress: the Life of the Duchess of Kingston*, Chatto & Windus, 1964

Melville, Lewis, *Maids = Maids of Honour*, Hutchinson, 1927

 Suffolk = Lady Suffolk and her Circle, Hutchinson, 1924

Montagu, Lady Mary Wortley, *The Complete letters of Lady Mary Wortley Montagu*, Ed. Robert Halsband, 2 Vols, Oxford, 1966

Morrah, Dermot, *The Work of the Queen*, William Kimber, 1958

Mosley, Nicholas, *Julian Grenfell*, Weidenfeld & Nicolson, 1976

Motteville, Madame de, *Mémoires sur Anne d'Autriche et sa Cour*, Vol. I, Paris 1886

Murray, Amelia, *Recollections 1803–37*, Longman Green & Co., 1868

Myers, A.r., *The Household of Edward IV*, Manchester University Press, 1959 'The Captivity of a Royal Witch', *Bulletin of John Ryland's Library*, 24, 1940

 'The Household of Queen Margaret of Anjou', *Bulletin*, 50. 1957–8

 'The Household of Queen Elizabeth Woodville 1466–7', *Bulletin*, 50, 1967, 1968

Narratives of the Reformation, Ed. J.G.Nichols, Camden Society, 1859

Newdigate-Newdegate, A., *Gossip from a Muniment Room*, David Nutt, 1898

Nichols, John, *Elizabeth = Progresses and public processions of Queen Elizabeth*, 3 Vols, 1823

 James = Progresses, Processions & Magnificent Festivities of King James I, 4 Vols, 1828

Nicolas, Harris, *The Life and Times of Sir Christopher Hatton*, Richard Bentley, 1847

 Privy Purse Expenses of Elizabeth of York, William Pickering, 1830

Norsworthy, Laura, *Lady of Bleeding Heart Yard*, John Murray, 1935

Northumberland, Duchess of, *Diaries of a Duchess: Extracts from the Diaries of the First Duchess of Northumberland*, Ed. James Greig, Hodder & Stoughton, 1926

Notes & Queries, 'Lettice Countess of Leicester', Vol. 167, 1934, pp. 435–8

 'Notes on the Countess of Buckingham' by S.R.Gardiner, 4th Series Vol. 7, (1871) pp. 469–71

Oman, Carol, *Mary of Modena*, Hodder & Stoughton, 1962

Ormathwaite, Lord, *When I was at Court*, Hutchinson, 1937

Pansanger Mss, in the Hertford County Record Office

Papendiek, Charlotte, *Court and Private life in the time of Queen Charlotte*, Ed. Mrs Vernon Delves Broughton, 2 Vols, Richard Bentley, 1887

Paul, John, E., *Catherine of Aragon and her Friends*, Burn & Oates, 1966

Pegge, Samuel, *Curialia: an Historical Account of Some Branches of the Royal Household*, 2 Vols, 1791

Pembroke Papers, Ed. Lord Herbert, Jonathan Cape, 1950

Pepys, Samuel, *Diary of Samuel Pepys*, Ed. Robert Latham and William Mathews, II Vols, Bell & Hyman, 1970–1983

Pindar, Peter, *Works of Peter Pindar*, 4 Vols, 1816

Plowden, Alison, *Tudor Women*, Weidenfeld & Nicolson, 1979

Poems on Affairs of State, Ed. George de F.Lord, 7 Vols, Yale University Press, 1963–1975

Pollock, John, *The Popish Plot*, Duckworth, 1903

Ponsonby, Arthur, *Henry Ponsonby, Queen Victoria's Private Secretary: His Life from Letters*, Macmillan, 1942

Ponsonby, Frederick, *Recollections of Three Reigns*, Eyre & Spottiswoode, 1951

Ponsonby, Mary, *A Memoir, Some Letters and a Journal*, Ed. Magdalen Ponsonby, John Murray, 1927

Pope-Hennessy, James, *Queen Mary*, George Allen & Unwin, 1959

Prescott, H.F.M., *Mary Tudor*, Eyre & Spottiswoode, 1953

Private Correspondence of Sarah, Duchess of Marlborough, 2 Vols, Henry Colburn, 1837

Prynne, William, *Historio Mastix*, 1633

Pullar, Philippa, *Gilded Butterflies*, Hamish Hamilton, 1978

'Queen Alexandra's Maids of Honour', in *Girls' Realm*, December 1904

Rawson, Maud, S. *Penelope Rich and her Circle*, Hutchinson, 1911

Read, Evelyn P., *Catherine Duchess of Suffolk*, Jonathan Cape, 1962

Reid, Stuart J., *John and Sarah, Duke and Duchess of Marlborough*, John Murray, 1914

Reresby, Sir John, *Memoirs, 1634–89*, Ed. J.A.Cartwright, 2 Vols, Longman Green & Co. 1875

Richardson, Aubrey, *Famous Ladies of the English Court*, Hutchinson, 1899

Richardson, Joanna, *The Disastrous Marriage: a Study of George IV and Caroline of Brunswick*, Jonathan Cape, 1960

Richelieu, Cardinal, *Memoires*, Vols V and VI, Paris, 1821

Rival Duchess, *The Rival Duchess or Court Incendiary, in a Dialogue Between Madame de Maintenon and Madame M.*, 1708

Rowse, A.L., *Ralegh = Ralegh and the Throckmortons*, Macmillan, 1962
  The Elizabethan Renaissance: the Life of a Society, Macmillan, 1971
  The Early Churchills, Penguin, 1972

Royal Kalendar, 1768–1720

St Clare Byrne, Muriel, *The Lisle Letters*, 6 Vols, University of Chicago Press, 1981

Savile Letters, Ed. W.D.Cooper, Camden Society, 71, 1858

Secret History of the Court of James I, (= *Secret Hist.*) 2 Vols, Edinburgh, John Ballantyne and Longman Hurst Rees Orme & Brown, London, 1811

Sergeant, Philip, *My Lady Castlemaine*, Hutchinson, 1912

Seymour, William, *Ordeal by ambition*, Sidgwick & Jackson, 1972

Sidney Papers, Ed. A.Collins, 2 Vols, T.Osborne, 1746

Sidney, Henry, *Diary of Times of Charles II*, Ed. R.W.Blencowe, 2 Vols, 1843

Smith, George, *The Coronation of Elizabeth Woodville*, Ellis, 1953

Smith, Lacey Baldwin, *A Tudor Tragedy: The Story of Catherine Howard*, Jonathan Cape, 1961

Smith, Richard, 'Life of Lady Magdalen Dacre', in A.C.Southern, *Life in an Elizabethan Recusant House*, Sands, 1954

Snyder, Henry L., *The Marlborough–Godolphin correspondence*, 3 Vols, Oxford, 1975

Stanhope, Philip, *Philip Stanhope, 2nd Earl of Chesterfield, his Correspondence with Various Ladies*, Fanfrolio, 1930

Stanley, Augusta, *Letters of Lady Augusta Stanley, 1849–1863*, Ed. Albert Baillie and Hector Bolitho, Gerald Howe, 1927
    Later letters = The Later letters of Lady Augusta Stanley, Ed. A.Baillie and Hector Bolitho, Jonathan Cape, 1929

Stanley, Eleanor, *Twenty Years at Court.*, Ed. Mrs Steuart Erskine, Nisbet, 1916

State Trials, Ed. William Cobbett, Vol. II, R.Bagshaw, 1809

Statement of . . . Lady Flora Hastings, *Statement of the case of the late Lady Flora Hastings, including documents and the whole correspondence with Viscount Melbourne, the Marquis of Tavistock and Lord Portman. By the Marquis of Hastings*, London, Henry Wright, 1839

Steinman, G.S., *Memoirs of Barbara Duchess of Cleveland*, 1871
    Althorp Memoirs, 1869
    Some particulars contributed towards a memoir of Mrs Middleton, 1864

Stone, Lawrence, *The Crisis of the Aristocracy*, Oxford, 1963
    The Family, Sex and Marriage, Weidenfeld & Nicolson, 1977

Stopes, Charlotte Carmichael, *Henry, Third Earl of Southampton*, Cambridge, 1922

Stott, Catherine, 'Where have you gone to my pretty maids?', article in *Sunday Times* colour magazine, 27 May, 1973

Strachey, Lytton, *Elizabeth and Essex*, Chatto & Windus, 1928

Strickland, Agnes, *Lives of the Queens of England*, 12 Vols, Henry Colburn, 1840–1848
    Lives of the Queens of Scotland, Vol. II, William Blackwood 1851
    Lives of the Tudor Princesses, Longman, 1868

Strong, Roy and Orgel, Stephen, *Inigo Jones and the Theatre of the Stuart Court*, 2 Vols, Sotheby Parke Bernet, University of California Press, 1973

Stuart, Lady Louisa, *Gleanings from an Old Portfolio*, Ed. Mrs Godfrey Clark, 3 Vols, privately printed, Edinburgh, 1895

Suffolk Correspondence, *Letters to and from Henrietta Countess of Suffolk and her Second Husband, the Honourable George Berkeley*, 2 Vols, John Murray, 1824

Swift, Jonathan, *Journal to Stella*, Ed. Harold Williams, 2 Vols, Oxford, 1948 *Prose Works*, Ed. Herbert Davis and Iran Ehrenpreis, Oxford, 1953, Vol. VIII: *Memoirs relating to that change which happened in the Queen's Ministry in 1710: An enquiry into the behaviour of the Queen's last Ministry*
    Correspondence, Ed. Harold Williams, Vols I & II, Oxford, 1963

Thoms, W.J., *The Book of the Court*, Henry G. John, 1844

Thomson, A.T., *Memoirs of Sarah Duchess of Marlborough*, 2 Vols, Henry Colburn 1839
    Memoirs of Viscountess Sundon, 2 Vols, Henry Colburn, 1847

Tillières, Comte Leveneur de, *Mémoires*. Ed. M.C.Hippeau, Paris, 1863

Tisdall, E.E.P., *Queen Victoria's Private Life*, Jarrolds, 1961
    Unpredictable Queen, Stanley Paul & Co., 1953

Vertot, René, *Ambassades de Messieurs de Noailles en Angleterre*, 5 Vols, Leyde, 1763

Victoria, *Letters: Letters of Queen Victoria*, 1st series, Ed. A.C.Benson and Viscount Esher, 3 Vols, John Murray, 1907; 2nd Series, Ed. George Earle Buckle, 3 Vols, John Murray, 1926–8; 3rd Series, Ed. George Earle Buckle, 3 Vols, John Murray, 1930–2

Villiers, Katherine, *Memoirs of a Maid of Honour*, Ivor Nicholson & Watson, 1931

Vindication of . . . Lady Douglas: *A Vindication of the Conduct of Lady Douglas During her Intercourse with the Princess of Wales*, London, 1814

Walpole, Horace, *Reminiscences* = *Reminiscences Written by Horace Walpole in 1788 for the Amusement of Miss Mary and Miss Agnes Berry*, Ed. Paget Toynbee, Oxford, 1924

    Letters = *Letters of Horace Walpole*, Ed. Paget Toynbee, 16 Vols, Oxford, 1903–25

    George III = *Memoirs of the Reign of George III*, Ed. G.F.Russell Barker and Sir Denis le Marchant, 4 Vols, Lawrence & Bullam, 1894 *Last Journals* = *The Last Journals of Horace Walpole, during the reign of George III, from 1771–83*, with notes by Dr Doran, Ed. A.Francis Steuart, 2 Vols, John Lane, Bodley Head, 1910

Ward, B.M., *The seventeenth Earl of Oxford*, John Murray, 1928

Warner, G.F., *Voyage of Robert Dudley to the West Indies*, Hakluyt Society, 1899

Watson, Vera, *A Queen at Home*, W.H.Allen, 1952

Wedgwood, C.V., *Thomas Wentworth, Earl of Strafford*, Jonathan Cape, 1961

Weldon, Anthony, 'The Court and Character of King James', in *Secret History of the Court of James I*, Edinburgh John Ballantyne and Longman Hurst Rees Orme & Brown, London, 1811

Wellington Correspondence, *A Selection from the Private Correspondence of the First Duke of Wellington*, Ed. the Duke of Wellington, Roxburghe Club, 1952

Welsford, Enid, *The Court Masque*, Cambridge, 1927

Wentworth Papers, Ed. J.J.Cartwright, Wyman & Sons, 1883

White, Beatrice, *Cast of Ravens*, John Murray, 1965

Wilkins, W.H., *Caroline the Illustrious*, 2 Vols, Longmans Green & Co., 1901

Williams, Neville, *Henry VIII and his Court*, Weidenfeld & Nicolson, 1971

    Elizabeth Queen of England, Weidenfeld & Nicolson, 1967

    All the Queen's Men, Weidenfeld & Nicolson, 1972

Wilson, Arthur, 'The Life and Reign of James I', in *The Complete History of England*, Volume II, London, 1719

Wilson, Derek, *A Tudor Tapestry*, Heinemann, 1972

Wilson, J.H., *Nell Gwynn*, Fred Miller, 1952. (Ed.)

    The Rochester-Savile Letters, Columbus Ohio State University Press, 1941

Wilson, Violet A., *Queen Elizabeth's Maids of Honour*, John Lane, Bodley Head, 1922

Windsor, Duke of, *A King's Story*, Cassell, 1951

Winwood, Ralph, *Memorials of Affairs of State*, 3 Vols, T.Ward, 1725

Wood, Mary Anne Everett, *Letters of Royal and Illustrious Ladies*, Vols. 2 & 3, Henry Colburn, 1846

Woodham-Smith, Cecil, *Queen Victoria, Her Life and Times*, Vol. I, Hamish Hamilton, 1972

Wright, Thomas, *Queen Elizabeth and Her Times*, 2 Vols, Henry Colburn, 1838

Zagorin, Perez, *The Court and Country*, Routledge & Kegan Paul, 1969.

Index

Abbott, George, Archbishop of Canterbury, 111
Abel Smith, Henrietta Alice, Lady, 309
Abergavenny, Patricia, Marchioness of, 304, 309
Abrahal, Elizabeth, 186
Act of Six Articles (1539), 43
Adeane, Marie *see* Mallet, Marie
Adelaide, Queen of William IV, 265–6
Airlie, Mabell, Countess of, 300–2, 308
Airlie, Virginia, Countess of, 304, 309
Alba, Duchess of, 56
Albert, Prince Consort, 280, 282, 284, 287–9, 291–2, 295
Alençon, Duke of, 72–3
Alexandra, Queen of Edward VII, 297–300, 304, 307, 309
Alice Maud Mary, Princess, 282
Ancaster, Mary, Duchess of, 229, 233, 236
Anjou, Henry, Duke of, 71–2
Anne, Queen, 1: Protestantism, 162; flees London, 163; relations with sister, 165; marriage, 165–6; and Duchess of Marlborough, 165–76, 179–93, 197; accession, 169; and politics, 171–6, 179–80, 182, 189–90, 192–7; childlessness, 173; and Abigail Hill, 176–90, 194–6, 198; lesbianism questioned, 183–4; death of husband, 185–6; and Duchess of Marlborough's financial accounts, 191; and Duchess of Somerset, 192–5; death, 197, 206; character, 198, 207
Anne of Bohemia, Queen of Richard II, 7
Anne Boleyn, 2nd Queen of Henry VIII, 13–14; marriage, 19–27; coronation, 23; downfall, 28–9; beheaded, 30–1
Anne of Cleves, 4th Queen of Henry VIII, 13, 35–8
Anne of Denmark, Queen of James I, 94–8, 100–1, 106–8
Anne, Princess, 309
Anson, George, 280
Antrim, Louisa, Countess of, 295–6, 298
Antrim, William, 6th Earl of, 295
Argyll, Elizabeth, Duchess of (wife of 5th Duke), 229, 233
Argyll, Elizabeth Georgiana, Duchess of (wife of 8th Duke), 282
Arlington, Henry, 1st Earl of, 146, 150
Arlington, Isabella, Countess of, 146
Army Nursing Board, 301
Arthur (eldest son of Henry VII), 22

Arundel, Alathea, Countess of, 127
Arundel, Countess of (sister of Catherine Howard), 39, 53
Ashley, Sir Anthony, 117
Ashley, Kat, 61, 70–1
Askew, Anne, 44–6
Atholl, Anne, Duchess of, 293
Aubrey, John, 88
Augusta, Princess of Wales, 224–5, 227

Bacon, Anthony, 66
Bacon, Francis, Lord, 68
Baker, Dame Frances, 135
Balfour, Sir William, 128
Ball, Ian, 309
Balmoral, 290–1
Barham, Frances, Lady *see* Gainsborough, Frances, Countess of
Barrington, Lady Caroline, 292–3, 295
Barton, Elizabeth ('Nun of Kent'), 25, 35
Basset, Anne, 13, 32–3, 35–6, 42
Basset, Katherine, 32, 35–6
Basset, Sir John, 32
Bassompierre, Maréchal de, 122
Battenberg, Prince Henry of, 293
Baynton, Edward, 25
Baynton, Isabel, Lady, 39
Beaconsfield, Benjamin Disraeli, Earl of, 285–6
Beatrice, Princess, 296
Beckwith-Smith, Anne, 310
Bedchamber: ladies of the, 10, 61–2, 96, 135, 203–5, 218, 241, 305; women of the, 10, 135, 205, 217–8, 237, 305
Bedford, Duchess of (*formerly* Marchioness of Tavistock), 268, 270, 274, 277, 281
Bedford, Adeline Marie, Duchess of, 283
Bedford, Gertrude, Duchess of, 229
Bedford, Isabel, Countess of, 5
Bedford, Lucy, Countess of, 94–5, 98–9, 106–7, 118
Bedford, Margaret, Countess of, 63
Bedingfield, Charlotte, Lady, 265
Bellasyse, Susan, Lady, 148
Bellenden, Mary, 206, 208
Berkeley, Sir Charles, 132–3
Berkeley, George, 215
Bernstorff, Baron, 202
Berry, Mary, 2
Bigge, Sir Arthur, 284
Bill of Pains and Penalties (1820), 264
Biset, Emma *and* Margaret, 4
Blount, Sir Christopher, 87

Blount, Elizabeth (*later* Tailboys), 18
Boleyn, Elizabeth, Lady (*née* Howard), 13, 19, 30
Boleyn, Mary (*later* Carey), 18–19, 61
Boleyn, Sir Thomas, 13, 18
Bolingbroke, Diana, Countess of, 229
Bolingbroke, Henry St John, Viscount, 196
Borrow, Lady, 61
Borth, François, 69
Bowlby, Hon. Mrs Geoffrey, 302
Boynton, Catherine (*later* Talbot), 134
Brand, Susan Sophia, 289
Brassey, Rowena, 309
Bray, John, Lord, 50
Brereton, William, 29
Brett, Anne (*later* Cranfield), 118
Breumer, Baron, 69
Bridges, Katherine, 97
Bridgewater, Katherine, Lady, 42
Bristol, Elizabeth, Countess of, 201, 211
Brown, Mary, 49
Browne, Alys, Lady, 35
Bruce, Lady Augusta (*later* Stanley), 291, 294
Bruce, Hon. Jean, 308
Brydges, Elizabeth, 92
Buccleuch, Charlotte Anne, Duchess of, 281
Buccleuch, Louisa Jane, Duchess of, 298
Buckenburgh, Johanne Sophie, Countess, 201, 210
Buckingham, Edward, 3rd Duke of, 17
Buckingham, George Villiers, 1st Duke of, 99, 112, 115–20, 122–3
Buckingham, Katherine, Duchess of (*née* Manners), 117, 120, 123
Buckingham, Mary, Countess of (*née* Beaumont; *then* Compton), 115–7, 121, 123
Buckner, Madame, 241
Bulmer, Joan, 39, 43
Bulteel, Mary, 282
Burghley, William, 1st Baron, 64, 78, 80
Burke, Edmund, 239
Burnet, Gilbert, Bishop of Salisbury, 145, 157, 164, 169, 197
Burney, Charles, 239, 242
Burney, Fanny (Mme d'Arblay), 231, 235–43, 245
Burney, James, 242
Bute, John, 3rd Earl of, 228–9, 233

Caceres, Francesca de, 15
Calisto (masque), 145
Campbell, Lady Charlotte, 259–60, 262
Carew, Sir George, 67
Carew, Lady, 64
Carew, George, Baron, 116
Carew, Sir Nicholas, 27
Carey, Elizabeth, Lady, 97
Carey, Katherine *and* Philadelphia, 61
Carey, Mary, 35
Carey, Sir Robert, 94, 97
Carey, William, 19
Carleton, Sir Dudley, 107
Carlisle, James, 1st Earl of, 122–3

Carlisle, Lucy, Countess of, 120, 122–4, 128–9
Carnarvon, Elizabeth, Countess of, 250, 259
Carnwath, Alexander, 7th Earl, 205
Caroline, Queen of George II: marriage, 200; and husband's infidelities, 200, 206–7, 217, 219, 221; household, 200–1; and ceremonial, 203; as social leader, 207–10, 212–3, 216; pregnancies, 210; and George I's animosity, 211–2; and Peerage Bill, 213–4; and Lady Cowper, 214–5; reconciled with George I, 215; and Countess of Suffolk, 216–9; and Charlotte Clayton, 219–20; death, 220, 226–7; and son, 224–5
Caroline of Brunswick, Queen of George IV, 2; marriage, 250–4; character and behaviour, 251, 254–5, 258, 260, 262; and Lady Jersey, 251–3; separation from George, 254; suite, 255–6, 259–60; and Lady Douglas, 256–7; 'Delicate Investigation', 257–61; relations with George III, 258–9; travels abroad, 262–3; George proceeds against, 264; death, 265
Carr, Robert *see* Somerset, Robert, Earl of
Carteret, John, Baron (*later* Earl Granville), 214, 220
Cary, Simona, 134
Castlemaine, Barbara, Countess of *see* Cleveland, Barbara, Duchess of
Castlemaine, Roger, 1st Earl of, 136–8
Castlereagh, Roger, Viscount, 261
Catherine of Aragon, 1st Queen of Henry VIII, 12, 14–18; marriage annulled, 20–6; death, 27
Catherine of Braganza, Queen of Charles II: marriage, 131, 133, 137–8, 156; Portuguese suite, 136–8; and Countess of Castlemaine, 139–42; and Frances Stuart, 142–3; and Duchess of Portsmouth, 146, 156; and Catholicism, 155–8; windowhood in Portugal, 159
Catherine Howard, 5th Queen of Henry VIII, 37–41; executed, 42
Catherine de Medici, 72
Catherine Parr, 6th Queen of Henry VIII, 43–7
Cavendish, Charles, 103
Cavendish, Elizabeth (*later* Stuart), 102
Cavendish, William, 99
Cecil, Anne (*later* Countess of Oxford), 89–90
Cecil, Sir Robert (*later* 1st Earl of Salisbury), 101
Cecil, Elizabeth, Lady, 95
Cellier, Elizabeth, 158
chamberers, 10
Chamberlain, John, 99, 113
Chandos, Lady, 88
Chapuys, Eustace, 24–5, 27–8, 31, 34, 42–3
Charles I, King: court masques, 108; and Buckingham, 118–9; accession and court, 118–9; marriage, 118–21, 124; court standards, 124–5; offends Puritans, 125;

monopolies and patents, 125–6; and Strafford, 128–9; and Civil War, 129–30; Sarah Churchill insults, 174
Charles II, King: marriage, 131, 133, 137–8, 141–2; Restoration, 131, 134; court, 134–7; mistresses, 136–45, 149–52, 158–9; and French, 149–52; rewards mistresses, 152–3; and Catholicism, 155–9
Charles V, Emperor, 51, 55–6
Charles, Archduke of Austria, 69–70
Chaundos, Elizabeth, 5
Charlotte, Queen of George III: marriage, 228–9; suite, 230–5, 239, 241; isolation, 232–3; and etiquette, 234–9; and Fanny Burney, 239–41; finances, 241–2; and husband's illness, 243–5, 247; and regency, 245–6; and Lady Jersey, 249, 253; death, 265
Chesterfield, Philip, 2nd Earl of, 136–7, 147
Chesterfield, Philip, 3rd Earl of, 208, 216, 227
Cholmondley, Georgiana, Countess of, 250, 255
Christina (attendant on Matilda of Scotland), 3
Churchill, Arabella (later Godfrey), 148
Churchill, Jane, Baroness, 291
Churchill, Sarah see Marlborough, Sarah, Duchess of
Clanricard, 4th Earl, 83
Clarencieux, Susan, 49–52, 57–8
Clarendon, Edward, 1st Earl of, 131, 136, 138–40, 151–2
Clark, Sir James, 269–71, 273
Clayton, Charlotte see Sundon, Charlotte, Lady
Cleveland, Barbara, Duchess of (née Villiers; then Countess of Castlemaine), 136–45, 149, 151–2, 159
Cleveland, Catherine, Duchess of, 283
Clifden, Eliza, Lady (later Stirling), 293
Clifford, Lady Anne, 100
Clifford, Mabel, 14
Clinton, Elizabeth, Lady, 71
Cobham, Frances, Lady, 62, 71–2
Cobham, Henry, 8th Baron, 68, 103
Cobham, Nan, 29
Coke, Sir Edward, 113, 117
Coke, Frances, 117
Coke, Lady Mary, 236
Coleman, Miss, 255
Colville, Lady Cynthia, 302, 305, 307
Compton, Sir William, 17
Con, Father George, 127–8
Conroy, Sir John, 267–72, 277
Conway, Edward, 1st Viscount, 121
Conyngham, Elizabeth, Marchioness of, 265
Cordoba, Donna Francisca de, 56
Cornbury, Henry, Viscount, 138
Cornwallis, Sir Frederick, 102
Cornwallis, Henrietta Maria, 144
Cornwallis, Jane, Lady (née Mewtas), 98, 106
Cornwallis, Sir William, 98
Corry, Montague (later Lord Rowton), 286

Cosyns, Mrs, 30
Coucy, Lady Mary de, 8
Courtenay, Henry, 50–1, 53–4
Courtown, Countess of, 236, 243–4, 246
Cowper, Mary, Lady, 201–5, 207, 212–5
Cowper, William, Baron (later 1st Earl), 212–4
Crane, Jane, 157
Cranfield, Lionel, Earl of Middlesex, 117
Cranmer, Thomas, Archbishop of Canterbury, 21, 40
Cromer, Esmé, Countess of, 304, 309
Cromwell, Thomas (later Earl of Essex), 21, 24, 28–31, 33–6, 38, 49
Cromwell, Thomas, 4th Baron, 123
Culpeper, Thomas, 40–2
Cumberland, Margaret, Countess of, 93
Curzon of Kedleston, Grace, Marchioness of, 302

Dacre, Magdalen, 56
Dangerfield, Thomas, 158
Dalkeith, Caroline, Countess of (later Townshend), 229
Daniel, Samuel, 107
Danvers, Bella, 186
Darlington, Sophia Charlotte (von Kielmansegg), Countess of, 200–1
Darnley, Henry, Earl of, 73–4
Dartmouth, William, 1st Earl of, 176
Davys, Mary, 269, 278
Davis, Moll, 145
Daubeney, Henry, Lord, 32
Dawkins, Lady Bertha, 301
Delany, Mary, 239
de Lisle, Philippa, 5
Deloraine, Mary, Lady, 220–1
Denbigh, Susan, Countess of, 120–3, 126, 129–30
Denbigh, William, 1st Earl of, 117
Denham, Lady Margaret, 147–9
Denny, Joan, Lady, 39, 45
Derby, Anne, Countess of, 12
Derby, Dorothea, Countess of, 164
Derby, Edward, 14th Earl of, 288
Derby, Elizabeth, Countess of, 95, 101
Dereham, Francis, 38–40
Desborough, Ethel (Etty), Lady, 300–1
Devereux, Lady Dorothy (later Perrot), 82
de Vere, Lady Susan, 95
Devonshire, Mary, Duchess of, 304
Diana, Princess of Wales, 310
Dorchester, Catherine, Countess of, 148, 161
Dormer, Jane (later Duchess of Feria), 49–50, 56, 58
Dorset, Edward, 4th Earl of, 123
Dorset, Elizabeth, Countess (later Duchess) of, 211, 215, 218, 226
Dorset, John, 3rd Duke of, 233
Dorset, Mary, Countess of, 164
Douglas, Charlotte, Lady, 256–7, 261
Douglas, Sir John, 256–8, 261
Douglas, Lady Margaret, 35, 39
Dover, Treaty of (1670), 152

Drummond, Jane (*later* Roxburgh), 96–8, 101, 104
Dryden, John: *Indian Emperor*, 144
Dudley, Lady Amy, 71
Dudley, Ambrose *see* Warwick, Ambrose, Earl of
Dugdale, Mrs John, 306, 309

Edgcumbe, Catherine, Lady, 35, 37
Edward I, King, 4
Edward II, King, 5
Edward III, King, 5–7
Edward IV, King, 8, 10–11, 33, 137
Edward V, King, 10
Edward VI, King, 33, 46, 48–9, 71
Edward VII, King, 291, 297, 309
Edward VIII (Duke of Windsor), 302, 307
Edwardes, Sylvia, 298
Effingham, Annie, Countess of, 225–6
Effingham, Elizabeth, Countess of, 229
Egremont, Alicia Maria, Countess of, 229, 232
Eleanor of Aquitaine, Queen of Henry II, 3
Eleanor of Castile, Queen of Edward I, 4–5
Eleanor of Provence, Queen of Henry III, 4
Elizabeth I, Queen, 10; birth, 24, 26; accession, 47; and Mary Tudor, 58–9, 71; and religion, 59, 65–6, 92, 100; court, 60–5, 92, 100; temperament and character, 62–3; marriage suitors, 69–73; succession question, 73, 76–80, 93; and Lady Lennox, 73–5; and Grey sisters, 78–81, 102–3; displeasure at marriage of ladies, 81–9; and Leicester, 84–8; and Raleghs, 88–9; and Essex, 91–2; decline and death, 93; thrift, 97
Elizabeth II, Queen, 304, 307, 309–10
Elizabeth, Queen of George VI, 302–4
Elizabeth, Princess (daughter of George III), 248, 252–3
Elizabeth Woodville, Queen of Edward IV, 9, 11
Elizabeth of York, Queen of Henry VII, 11
Ely, Jane, Marchioness of, 282, 285–7
Emma (attendant on Matilda of Scotland), 3
Erroll, Eliza Amelia, Countess of, 293, 296
Esher, William B., 1st Viscount, 285
Essex, Frances, Countess of (*later* of Somerset), 91, 101, 109–13
Essex, Robert, 2nd Earl of, 67–8, 87–8, 91–3
Essex, Robert, 3rd Earl of, 109–10, 112
Essex, Walter, 1st Earl of, 85
Evelyn, John, 154–5, 159, 161
Examiner (journal), 274
Exeter family, 33–4
Exeter, Gertude, Marchioness of, 13, 24–5, 27, 31, 34–5, 50, 53–4
Exeter, Henry, 1st Marquis of, 24, 27, 34

Falkland, Elizabeth, Viscountess, 126
Falmouth, Charlotte, Lady, 204, 219
Falmouth, Mary, Lady, 144
Feilding, Lady Elizabeth, 122
Feodore, Princess, 267

Feria, Duke of, 50, 56
Finch, Lady Charlotte, 244–6
Finch, Mary, 49
Fines, Miss, 111
Fisher, John, 21
Fitton, Mary, 90–1
Fitzfrederick, Cornwell, 222, 224
Fitzgerald, Hamilton, 274
Fitzherbert, Mistress, 36
Fitzherbert, Maria, 249
Fitzjames, 148
Fitzwater, Elizabeth, Lady, 12, 17
Fitzwater, Walter, 6
Fitzwilliam, Jane, Lady, 45
Forbes, Lady Elizabeth, 262
Forman, Dr Simon, 110, 112–3
Foxe, John, 50
Francis II, King of France, 17
Franklin, James, 112
Fraser, Alexander, 153
Frederick, Prince of Wales, 222–7
Froissart, Jean, 7

Gainsborough, Frances, Countess of (*formerly* Barham), 281, 293
Gardiner, Stephen, Bishop of Winchester, 38, 43–5
Garter, Order of the, 5
Garth, Frances, 256
Gay, John, 216
Gemmingen, Baroness, 210
Gentlemen Soapboilers, 126
George I, King, 199–200, 211, 214, 216
George II, King: marriage, 200; mistresses, 200, 206–7, 216–22, 227; and ceremonial, 203; as society leader, 207–8, 216; expelled by father, 211; reconciled with father, 214–5; accession, 216; and Howard, 217; expels son, 226; and wife's death, 226; death, 228
George III, King: accession, 228; marriage, 228–9; and politics, 229; character of court, 234–6; malady, 243–8; and Countess of Pembroke, 246–8; and Prince of Wales, 248–9, 253; ostracises Caroline, 258; death, 263
George IV, King: and Mme Schwellenberg, 230; regency, 244–6, 261; character, 248–9; and Mrs Fitzherbert, 249; and Lady Jersey, 249, 251–3; marriage, 249–54; Caroline separates from, 254; and investigation of Caroline, 261–2; accession, 263; proceedings against Caroline, 263; death, 265
George V, King, 300–2
George VI, King, 302, 310
George, Prince of Denmark, 165, 185–6
Gerard, Jane, Lady, 141
Gertrude (Anne of Cleves' companion), 36
Gery, Anne, 135
Gladstone, William Ewart, 282–4, 286
Glenbervie, Catherine, Lady, 259–60
Glenbervie, Sylvester, 1st Baron, 259
Gloucester, Thomas of Woodstock, Duke of, 7

Gloucester, William Henry, Duke of, 232
Godfrey, Col. Charles, 148
Godolphin, Margaret, 155
Godolphin, Sydney, 172–7, 179–80, 182, 189–90
Goldsworthy, Martha Caroline, 243
Goldsworthy, Gen. Philip, 243
Goodman, Godfrey, Bishop of Gloucester, 99, 108
Grafton, Fortune, Duchess of, 304, 306, 309
Grafton, Marie Anne Louise, Duchess of, 283
Graham, Lady Helen, 302–3
Grammont, Count, 142, 153, 154, 184
Granville, Mary, 201
great ladies, 9–10, 13
Grenfell, Julian, 301
Greville, Charles, 276, 295
Grey, Lady Jane, 48
Grey, Lord John, 65, 79–80
Grey, Lady Katherine (later Countess of Hertford), 48, 65, 76–80, 102
Grey, Lady Mary (later Keyes), 48, 65, 80–1
Grey of Ruthin, Elizabeth, Lady, 96
Groom of the Stool (Stole), 96–7, 135, 186
Guise, Duchess of, 152
Gunilda (attendant on Matilda of Scotland), 3
Gwynn, Nell, 145–6, 152, 156, 159

Haggerdorn, Johanna Louisa, 230–1, 239–40
Hales, John, 79
Hambleden, Patricia, Dowager Viscountess of, 303
Hamilton, Lady Anne, 263–5
Hamilton, Lady Archibald, 224–6
Hamilton, Sir David, 190
Hamilton, Elizabeth, 154
Hamilton, Margaret, Marchioness of, 119–20, 122, 127
Hamilton, Mary, 238, 242
Hamilton, Duchess of see Argyll, Elizabeth, Duchess of
Harcourt, Elizabeth, Countess of, 233–4, 236, 244–6
Harcourt, Mary, 244, 250–1
Harding, Mary, 82
Harington, Sir John, 64, 92, 100
Harington, Mary, Lady, 95
Harley, Robert (later 1st Earl of Oxford), 179–80, 182, 190–1, 193, 195–8
Harrington, William, 1st Baron (later 1st Earl), 222
Harryse, John, 14
Hassan II, King of Morocco, 306
Hastings, 2nd Marquis of, 273, 277–8
Hastings, Anne, Lady (née Stafford), 12, 17–18
Hastings, Elizabeth, Lady, 95
Hastings, Lady Flora, 269–74, 277–9
Hastings, Flora, Dowager Marchioness of (mother of above), 273–4
Hastings, Sir George, 17
Hastings, Lady Selina, 273, 277
Hatton, Elizabeth, Lady, 95, 115

Haustede, Margerie, 4
Hawkins, Lady, 91
Hawtrey, Sir Richard, 81
Hayman, Miss, 254–5
Heneage, Anne, Lady, 61
Henrietta Maria, Queen of Charles I, 96; marriage, 118–21, 124; French retinue, 118, 120–2; court, 119–20, 122, 124; Catholicism, 119–20, 126–8; and Lady Carlisle, 123–4; and court masques, 124–5; leaves England in Civil War, 129–30; returns to England, 130; and Anne (Hyde), 133; death, 156
Henriette Anne, Duchess of Orleans, 142, 146
Henry I, King, 3
Henry II, King, 3
Henry III, King, 4
Henry IV, King, 8
Henry V, King, 8
Henry VI, King, 8
Henry VII, King, 10–11
Henry VIII: court, 11–12, 46; accession, 12; jousting and festivities, 16–17; affairs and mistresses, 17–19, 26–7; and Anne Boleyn, 19–21, 25–8, 31; 1st marriage annulled, 20–5; and Jane Seymour, 27–9, 31; purges Exeters, 34; and Anne of Cleves, 35, 37; and Catherine Howard, 37–40, 42; and Catherine Parr, 43–6; death, 46; succession, 47
Henry, Prince (James I's son), 108–9
Herbert, Anne, Lady, 45
Hertford, Anne, Countess of see Somerset, Anne, Duchess of
Hertford, Edward, Earl of, 76–9, 102
Hertford, Frances, Countess of, 83–4, 95
Hertford, Frances, Lady, 205
Hertford, Katherine, Countess of see Grey, Lady Katherine
Hervey of Ickworth, John, Baron, 219, 222–4
Hill, Alice, 177–8, 197
Hill, Abigail see Masham, Abigail, Lady
Hill, Captain Jack, 188
Hobart, Miss, 154
Hoby, Mary, Lady, 61
Holbein, Hans, 35
Holderness, Mary, Countess of, 233
Holland, Elizabeth, 23
Holland, Henry, 1st Earl of, 123
Home Rule for Ireland, 283, 286
Horsman, Margery, 32
Howard, Charles see Suffolk, Charles, Earl of
Howard, Dorothy, 155
Howard, Frances see Hertford, Frances, Countess of
Howard, Henrietta see Suffolk, Henrietta, Countess of
Howard, Lady Mary, 92
Howard, Sir Robert, 151
Howard, Lady Thomas, 61
Howard, Lady William, 39, 42
Howe, Sophie, 209
Huntingdon, Catherine, Countess of, 67
Huntingdon, Henry, 3rd Earl of, 75

Hussey, John, 32–3
Hussey, Lady Susan, 309
Hutchinson, Lucy, 101
Hyde, Anne see York, Anne, Duchess of
Hyde, Jane, 172

Irwin, Anne, Lady, 224, 226
Isabella of France, Queen of Edward II, 5
Isabella of France, 2nd Queen of Richard II, 7

Jackson, Martha, 135
Jacobi, Mlle, 241
James I, King: extravagances and court standards, 92, 99–101; accession, 93–4; favours, 98–9; and Arbella Stuart, 104–5; marriage, 106; sex life, 108–9; and Robert Carr, 109; and Buckingham, 112, 115–6
James II, King (formerly Duke of York): first marriage, 131–3, 147; mistresses, 147–9, 161; second marriage, 148; and Duchess of Portsmouth, 157; unpopularity, 159, 162–3; accession, 160; Catholicism, 160; exile, 163
Jane Seymour, 3rd Queen of Henry VIII, 13–14, 27–8, 31, 33, 46
Jekyll, Sir Joseph, 213
Jennings, Sarah see Marlborough, Sarah, Duchess of
Jermyn, Henry, 124
Jersey, Frances, Countess of, 249–53
Johnson, Samuel, 239
Jones, Inigo, 107
Jonson, Ben, 107
Jordan, Dorothy, 266

Katherine Parr, 6th Queen of Henry VIII, 15
Katherine (Anne of Cleves' companion), 36
Keepers of the Robes, 237, 241
Kendal, Melusine (Schulenberg), Duchess of, 199–201, 212
Kent, Edward Augustus, Duke of, 255
Kent, Victoria Mary Louisa, Duchess of, 267–72, 277, 291
Keppel, Alice, 298
Kerouaille, Louise de see Portsmouth, Louise, Duchess of
Keyes, Thomas, 80–1
Killigrew, Harry, 132
Kingston, Sir William, 30
Knollys, Charlotte, 299, 305, 309
Knollys, Francis, 299
Knollys, Lettice, Lady, 48, 61, 66
Knollys, Lettice see Leicester, Lettice, Countess of
Knollys, Sir William, 90–1
Knyvet, Thomas, 90
Königsmark, Count Charles, 192, 194
Königsmark, Count Philipp von, 199

ladies-in-waiting: position and duties, 2–5, 9–11, 13, 61–2, 95–6, 135, 203–5, 236, 290, 305–7, 309–10; allowances and rewards, 4, 9, 14, 62, 97–9, 134–5, 203–4, 232, 236–7, 241, 290, 308; as royal

mistresses, 5–6; titles, 9–10; living conditions, 14; provision and feeding of, 62, 97, 134–5; favours and influence, 66–8; as sources of information, 68–9; extravagances, 99–100; physical strain, 203, 236; behaviour and etiquette, 235–6; see also individual offices and titles
Lake, Sir Arthur, 101
Lake, Lettice, Lady, 101
Lane, Maud, Lady, 45
Lascelles, Blanche (later Lloyd), 299
Lassels, John, 40
Lassels, Mary, 40
Latimer, Hugh, Bishop of Worcester, 44
Launcreona, Agnes de, 7
Laundress of the Body, 96
Lee, Sir Henry, 90
Lehzen, Louise, Baroness, 267–70, 273, 287–8
Leicester, Lettice, Countess of (née Knollys; later Blount), 85–8
Leicester, Robert, 1st Earl of, 62, 66, 69, 71, 75, 78, 84–7
Leighton, Lady, 61
Leinster, Caroline, Duchess of, 283
Lely, Sir Peter, 134
Lennox, Frances, Duchess of, 99, 126, 129
Lennox, Margaret, Countess of, 73–6
Lennox, Matthew, 4th Earl of, 73
Lennox, Lady Sarah, 228–9
Lepell, Mary, 208
Liddell, Georgiana, 279, 290, 294
Lindsay, Lady Charlotte, 259, 262–4
Lisle, Hon. Hester, 257
Lisle, Joan, Lady, 13–14, 29, 32–3, 35–6, 44
Lloyd, George, 1st Baron, 299–300
Lorraine, Duke of, 37
Louis XIII, King of France, 119, 122
Louis XIV, King of France, 149, 152, 160
Lowe, Mother, 36
Lytton, Edith, Dowager Countess, 298

Macclesfield, Mary Frances, Countess of, 298–9
Macdonald, Margaret, 307
Macmillan, Harold, 309
maids of honour, 9–10, 13, 61–2, 241–2, 279, 290, 307–8
Mallet, Bernard, 294–5
Mallet, Marie, 279, 284, 292, 294–6
Malmesbury, James, 1st Baron (later Earl), 250–1
Malpas, George, Lord (later 2nd Earl Cholmondley), 214
Manby, Captain Thomas, 258
Mann, Sir Horace, 229
Manners, Lady Bridget, 82–3
Manners, Lady Katherine see Buckingham, Katherine, Duchess of
Manox, Henry, 38, 40
Margaret of Anjou, Queen of Henry VI, 9
Margaret of Austria, Queen, 19
Margaret Tudor, Queen of James IV of Scotland, 73

Marlborough, John, 1st Duke of, 1 : marriage, 154, 165; William III dismisses, 167; military successes, 169, 174; and politics, 172, 175–7, 179–80, 182; relations with Queen Anne, 190–1; dismissed, 192
Marlborough, Sarah, Duchess of, 1; preserves honour, 154; relations with Queen Anne, 165–76, 179–91, 193, 197; marriage, 154, 165; offices and rewards, 169–71, 186, 190; Whiggism, 172–5, 179–80; insults Charles I, 174; and Abigail Hill, 176–88; offers resignation, 180–1; ejected from office, 190–1; financial accounts, 191; autobiography, 191–2; on Duchess of Shrewsbury, 202; helps Charlotte Clayton, 207, 219–20
Mary of France (sister of Henry VIII), 16, 76
Mary I (Tudor), Queen, 17–18, 31; and Anne Boleyn, 24–7; accession and reign, 48–51; Catholicism, 48–9, 58–9; marriage to Philip of Spain, 51–8; and Wyatt rebellion, 54–5; false pregnancy, 57; decline and death, 58
Mary II, Queen of England, 161, 163–8, 169, 171
Mary, Queen of Scots, 69, 73–4, 76–7
Mary, Princess of Orange, 124, 131–3
Mary of Modena, Queen of James II, 148, 160–3
Mary, Queen of George V, 300–2, 307–8
Masham, Abigail, Lady (née Hill): relations with Queen Anne, 176–90, 194–8; marriage, 178–9; and Duchess of Somerset, 193–4; title, 196; retirement and death, 197; and bedchamber duties, 217
Masham, Samuel, 1st Baron, 178–9, 196
Masque of Beauty, 99
masques: under Henry VIII, 16, 19; Stuart, 98–101, 106–8, 124–5, 145
Mathew, Toby, Dean of Durham, 66
Matilda, Queen of William I, 3
Matilda of Scotland, 1st Queen of Henry I, 3
Maynwaring, Sir Arthur, 181, 183
Mazarin, Hortense, Duchess of, 150–1, 159, 162
Meadows, Mary, 209
Melbourne, William, 2nd Viscount: and Lady Flora Hastings, 268–74, 277; government fortunes, 274–6, 280; and Queen's suite, 275–6, 281–2, 294; and court etiquette, 289
Melville, Sir James, 74
Mendoza, Diego de, 52
Mendoza, Donna Maria de, 56
Mewtas, Jane see Cornwallis, Jane, Lady
Middlemore, Mary, 98
Mistress of the Robes, 96–7, 135
Mistress of the Sweet Coffers, 96–7
Mitchell, Sir John, 116
Monmouth, Anne, Duchess of, 144
Monmouth, James, Duke of, 144
monopolies, 98, 125–6
Montague, Sir Henry (later Earl of Manchester), 116

Montagu, Mary, Duchess of, 211
Montagu, Lady Mary Wortley, 205, 209, 220
Montagu, Walter, 125
Montpensier, Anne Marie Louise, 130
More, Sir Thomas, 21
Morning Post, 278
Morpeth, George, Viscount (later 7th Earl of Carlisle), 268
Morrison, Hon. Mary, 309
Morton, Margaret, 39–41
Mother of the Maids, 97
Mountjoy, Charles, 8th Baron (later Earl of Devonshire), 101
Mountjoy, William, 4th Baron, 18
Mulholland, Hon. Mrs John, 303
Munster, Duchess of see Kendal, Melusine, Duchess of

Naunton, Sir Robert, 116
Navarra, Donna Hieronima de, 56
Newport, Anne, Countess of, 127–8
Newport, Mountjoy, 1st Earl of, 128
Norfolk, Agnes, Dowager Duchess of (formerly Countess of Surrey), 12, 22
Norfolk, Augusta, Duchess of, 283
Norfolk, Bernard Marmaduke, 16th Duke of, 308
Norfolk, Elizabeth, Duchess of, 22–4, 38, 40, 42, 53
Norfolk, Mary, Duchess of, 161
Norfolk, Thomas, 3rd Duke of, 23–4, 28, 38
Norfolk, Thomas, 4th Duke of, 69
Normanby, Maria, Marchioness of, 268, 281, 290
Norris, Henry, 29–31
Northampton, William, 1st Marquis of, 50
Northumberland, Anne, Countess of, 164
Northumberland, Elizabeth, Countess (later Duchess) of, 229, 233
Northumberland, John, Duke of (formerly Warwick), 48, 50, 54
Nottingham, Katherine, Countess of, 93
Nottingham, Margaret, Countess of, 95, 97

Oates, Titus, 155–6
Occasional Conformity, Bill for, 173
Oldi, Angelina, Countess, 262–4
Orleans, Duchess of see Henriette Anne
Osborne, Forster, 286
Osborne (Isle of Wight), 290
Overbury, Sir Thomas, 110–4
Oxford, Elizabeth, Countess of, 11–13
Oxford, Robert, 9th Earl of, 7
Oxford, Edward, 17th Earl of, 89–90, 92

Palmerston, Henry John, 3rd Viscount, 289
Papendiek, Charlotte, 230
Parker, Matthew, Archbishop of Canterbury, 66
Parr, Anne, 14
Parry, Blanche, 61, 65–6, 82
Parry, Sir Thomas, 104
Peel, Sir Robert, 275–6, 280–1, 284
Peerage Bill (1718), 213–4

Pembroke, Barbara, Countess of, 207, 211
Pembroke, Elizabeth, Countess of, 237, 246–8
Pembroke, Thomas, 8th Earl of, 219
Pembroke, William, 1st Earl of, 50, 53, 55
Pembroke, William, 3rd Earl of, 91, 123
Penalva, Countess of, 140
Pennington, Margaret, 14
Pepys, Samuel, 132, 137, 140–1, 149, 155
Percy, Sir Henry (later Earl of Northumberland), 19
Pergami, Bartolomeo, 262
Perrers, Alice, 5–7
Perkins, Sir Christopher, 117
Perrot, Thomas, 82
Philip II, King of Spain, 51–2, 55–8
Philip, Prince, Duke of Edinburgh, 306
Philippa of Hainault, Queen of Edward III, 5
'Pindar, Peter', 231
Pitt, Ann, 207
Pitt, William, 244–5, 252
Pole family, 33–4
Pole, Sir Geoffrey, 34
Pole, Margaret, 12
Pole, Reginald, Cardinal, 34
Polewhele, Sir William, 91
Pomfret, Henrietta Louise, Countess of, 220–1
Pomfret, Thomas, 1st Earl of, 220
Ponsonby, Sir Henry, 284–6
Pope, Alexander, 208
'Popish Plot' (1678), 155
Porter, Mrs Endymion, 127
Portman, Edmund, 1st Viscount, 273, 278
Portman, Emma, Lady, 271–2, 274, 281
Portsmouth, Louise (de Keroualle), Duchess of, 141, 145–6, 150, 152, 156–7, 159
Powis, Elizabeth, Countess of, 157–8
Presence Chamber, ladies of the, 10, 61
Price, Goditha, 147
Privy Chamber, ladies of the, 9–10, 13, 61–2, 97
Prynne, William, 125
Pulteney, Sir William (Earl of Bath), 208
Puritans, 125, 127–8
Pym, John, 129

Quarterly Review, 268

Radcliffe, Mary, 66–7, 82
Rainsford, Anne, 187
Ralegh, Lady see Throckmorton, Bess
Ralegh, Sir Walter, 65, 88–9
Ranking, Lady Jean, 303
Ravensworth, Maria Susannah, Lady, 279
Renard, Simon, 50–2, 55–6
Reresby, Sir John, 154
Restwold, Alice, 39, 42
Rialton, Henrietta, Lady, 192
Rich, Penelope, Lady, 68, 93, 95, 101
Rich, Sir Richard, 45
Richard II, King, 7
Richard III, King, 10
Richmond, Charles, 3rd Duke of, 143, 154

Richmond, Frances, Duchess of, 137, 141–4
Richmond, Mary, Duchess of, 35, 39
Richmond and Somerset, Henry, 1st Duke of, 18
Rivers, Mary, Countess of, 11
Roberts, Jane, 144
Rochester, Lady, 53
Rochester, Robert, Viscount see Somerset, Robert, Earl of
Rochester, John, 2nd Earl of, 144, 161
Rochford, George, Viscount, 25, 29–30
Rochford, Jane, Lady, 26, 31, 35, 37, 39–42
Romeyn, John le, 4
Roos, Anne, Lady, 101
Rowlandson, Thomas, 245
Roxburghe, Anne Emily, Duchess of, 283
Roxburghe, Robert, 1st Earl of, 98
Royal Victorian Order, 309
Russell, Jane, 51–2
Russo-Turkish war (1877), 285
Rutland, Edward, 3rd Earl of, 67
Rutland, Eleanor, Countess of, 32, 35–6
Rutland, Elizabeth, Countess of, 82

St Albans, Abbot of, 6
St Albans, Diana, Duchess of, 203, 211, 215
St Albans, Grace, Duchess of, 283
St Albans, Harriot, Duchess of, 265–6
St Georges, Jeanne, 118–20
St John, Lady, 96
St Loe, Lady see Shrewsbury, Elizabeth, Countess of
Salinas, Maria de, 15
Salisbury, Katherine, Countess of, 101, 115
Salisbury, Margaret, Countess of, 24–5, 32–5
Salisbury, Robert, 3rd Marquis of, 283, 286
Sander, Charlotte, 257
Sanderson, Mrs (laundress), 126
Sandwich, Edward, 1st Earl of, 132
Sandys, Edwin, 51
Savage, Richard, 205
Schwellenberg, Juliana Elizabeth, 230–2, 238, 240–1, 243, 245
Scott, Sir Walter, 209
Scroope, Mary, Lady, 157
Scrope, Philadelphia, Lady, 68
Scrope, Sir Richard, 12
Scudamore, Sir James, 83
Scudamore, Mary, Lady, 65, 68, 83
Sedley, Catherine see Dorchester, Catherine, Countess of
Seymour, Edward, 1st Earl of Hertford see Somerset, Edward, 1st Duke of
Seymour, Edward (son of Earl of Hertford), 102
Seymour, Lady Jane, 77–8
Seymour of Sudeley, Thomas, Baron, 28, 47
Seymour, William, 104–5
Sheffield, Lady Douglas see Stafford, Lady
Sheldon, Frances, 157
Shelton, Madge, 27
Shelton, Mary see Scudamore, Mary, Lady
Sheridan, Richard Brinsley, 239
Shirley, Sir Thomas, 82

Shore, Jane, 137
Shrewsbury, Adelaide, Duchess of, 201–2, 205, 211
Shrewsbury, Elizabeth, Countess of (Bess of Hardwick; formerly Lady St Loe), 74–6, 78, 102, 105
Shrewsbury, George, 6th Earl of, 75–6
Shrewsbury, Gilbert, 7th Earl of, 84, 103
Sidney, Sir Henry, 63
Sidney, Lady Mary, 63, 69–70
Sidney, Sir Robert, 61, 65, 67–8, 88
Simier, Jean de, 86
Smeaton, Mark, 29–30
Smith, Sir Sidney, 256–7
Smith, Sir Thomas, 67, 80
Somerset, Anne, Duchess of (formerly Countess of Hertford), 35, 44–5, 47–8
Somerset, Charles, 6th Duke of, 192, 195
Somerset, Edward Seymour, 1st Earl of Hertford and Duke of, 28, 47–8, 76
Somerset, Elizabeth, Duchess of, 192–6
Somerset, Jane Georgiana, Duchess of, 283
Somerset, Robert, Earl of (formerly Viscount Rochester), 101, 109–14
Sophia Dorothea, wife of George I, 199
Southesk, Anne, Countess of, 147, 157
Southesk, Robert, 3rd Earl of, 147
Southwell, Elizabeth, 92
Southwell, Elizabeth, Lady, 95
Spencer-Churchill, Lady Rosemary, 308
Stafford, Anne see Hastings, Anne, Lady
Stafford, Lady (formerly Lady Douglas Sheffield), 61, 66, 84–6
Stafford, Sir Edward, 86
Stafford, Elizabeth see Fitzwater, Elizabeth, Lady
Standen, Anthony, 66
Stanhope, Sir William, 226
Stanley of Alderley, Henry Edward John, 3rd Baron, 298
Stanley, Arthur Penrhyn, Dean of Westminster, 294
Stockmar, Baron, 278
Stonor, Mrs, 15, 30
Strafford, Thomas Wentworth, Earl of, 128–9, 156
Stuart, Arbella (later Seymour), 76, 99, 102–6
Stuart, Lord Charles, 75–6, 102
Stuart, Frances see Richmond, Frances, Duchess of
Sturley, Frideswide, 51–2, 57
Suckling, Sir John, 123
Suffolk, Barbara, Countess of, 136–8
Suffolk, Catherine, Duchess of, 35, 39, 43, 45, 48, 63, 77
Suffolk, Charles, 9th Earl of, 205–6, 211–2, 216–8
Suffolk, Henrietta Howard, Countess of: as royal mistress, 205–7, 211–2, 216–7, 219–20; as Mistress of the Robes, 218; 2nd marriage (to Berkeley), 219; and duties, 217, 237
Suffolk, Henry, Duke of, and 3rd Marquis of Dorset, 48, 51

Suffolk, Katherine, Countess of, 95, 101, 109, 114–5
Suffolk, Thomas, 1st Earl of, 109, 114
Sunderland, Anne, Countess of (née Churchill; wife of 3rd Earl), 192
Sunderland, Anne, Countess of (née Digby; wife of 2nd Earl), 158, 162, 171
Sunderland, Charles, 4th Earl of, 175–6
Sundon, Charlotte, Lady, 207, 213–4, 219–21
Sundon, William, Baron, 220
Surlyard, Mr, 32
Surrey, Agnes, Countess of see Norfolk, Agnes, Dowager Duchess of
Sussex, Augustus Frederick, Duke of, 257
Sussex, Mary, Countess of, 32–3, 35, 39, 45
Sussex, Thomas, 3rd Earl of, 86
Sutherland, Anne, Duchess of, 283–4
Sutherland, George, 2nd Duke of, 278
Sutherland, Harriet, Duchess of, 268, 278, 281
Swift, Jonathan, 171–2, 176, 193–5, 197, 204

Tailboys, Gilbert, 18
Talbot, Gilbert see Shrewsbury, Gilbert, 7th Earl of
Talbot, Colonel Richard, 134
Tavistock, Francis, Marquis of (later 7th Duke of Bedford), 273, 278
Temple, Phyllis, 141
Thomas, W.J.: Book of the Court, 96
Throckmorton, Arthur, 61
Throckmorton, Bess (latter Ralegh), 61, 88–9
Thynne, Thomas, 154, 192
Times, The, 232, 288
Tonge, Thomas, 49
Tories: under Anne, 172–9, 192–3, 195; under Victoria, 274–6, 281, 284, 286
Torrington, Lady, 225–6
Townshend, Anne, Marchioness of, 236, 250, 259–60
Townshend, Charles, 2nd Viscount, 214
Townshend, Mr & Mrs William, 224–5
Trevor, Miss, 153
Turner, Anne, 110, 112–3
Tylney, Katherine, 39–42
Tyrconnel, Frances, Lady, 161
Tyrwhit, Elizabeth, Lady, 45

Vane, Hon. Anne, 222–4
Vasavour, Anne, 90, 92
Vasavour, Frances, 82
Vaughn, Rowland, 65
Venegas, Inez de, 15
Victoria, Queen: accession, 266, 267; and Lehzen, 267–70, 287–8; suite, 268–9, 274–6, 281–3, 307; and Lady Flora Hastings, 272–4, 277–9; and political affiliations of ladies, 274–8, 281–4, 304; caution over gossip, 279–80; marriage, 280, 287–8; relations with ladies, 281–2; and official affairs, 284–7; opposes Home Rule, 286; and court discipline, 288–91; widowhood, 291–4; religion, 293;

displeasure at marriage of ladies, 294–5;
death, 297; and Alexandra, 299
Victoria, Crown Princess of Prussia (later
Empress of Germany), 291
Villiers, Eleanor, 124
Villiers, Sir George, 115
Villiers, John, 117
Vivian, Doris, 298

Waldegrave, Lady Elizabeth, 243
Waldegrave, Isabella, 163
Wallingford, Elizabeth, Viscountess, 101,
114–5
Wallingford, William, Viscount (later Earl of
Banbury), 114–5
Walmoden, Amelie Sophie von see Yarmouth,
Amelie, Countess of
Walpole, Horace, 2, 206, 208, 229, 231, 234,
242
Walpole, Sir Robert, 214, 220–1
Walsingham, Audrey, Lady, 95–8, 101
Walsingham, Sir Francis, 67, 86
Warmestre, Miss (later Lady Taaffe), 153
Warren, Dr John, 244
Warwick, Ambrose Dudley, Earl of, 50
Warwick, Anne, Countess of, 65–7, 82, 93
Weaver, Elizabeth, 145
Wells, Winifred (later Wyndham), 144,
152–3
Wendover, Manor of, 6
Wentworth, Lady Isabella, 163
Weston, Richard, 112
Weston, Sir Thomas, 29–30

Weymouth, Elizabeth, Viscountess, 229
Whigs: under Anne, 172–9, 192–3, 196;
under Victoria, 274–6, 280–2
Whitbread, Samuel, 261
White, Rowland, 61, 65, 76–8, 88
Willelma, Lady (attendant on Eleanor of
Provence), 4
William I (the Conqueror), King, 3
William III, King (William of Orange), 161,
163–5, 167–9
William IV, King, 265–6
William, Prince of Orange, 131
William of Wales, Prince, 305
Williams, John, 116
Willis, Dr Francis (and son), 244, 246–7
Wilson, Arthur, 114, 116
Wilson, John, 268
Wiltshire, Elizabeth, Countess of, 22
Winwood, Sir Ralph, 112
Wolsey, Thomas, Cardinal, 16, 19–21
Wood, Alderman, 261
Worcester, Edward, 4th Earl of, 95
Worcester, Elizabeth, Countess of, 13, 29
Wotton, Edward, 67
Wotton, Margaret, Lady, 99
Wriothsley, Thomas, 1st Baron, 41, 45–6
Wyatt, Sir Thomas (the elder), 19, 48, 53–4

Yarmouth, Amelie Sophie (von Walmoden),
Countess of, 221, 227
York, Anne Hyde, Duchess of, 131–3, 147–9
York, Edmund de Langley, 1st Duke of, 7
York, Frederick Augustus, Duke of, 245, 264